COGNITIVE CONSTRAINTS ON COMMUNICATION

SYNTHESE LANGUAGE LIBRARY

TEXTS AND STUDIES IN
LINGUISTICS AND PHILOSOPHY

VOLUME 18

COGNITIVE CONSTRAINTS ON COMMUNICATION

Representations and Processes

Edited by

LUCIA VAINA

Center for Cognitive Science, M.I.T., and Computer Science Department, Boston University

and

JAAKKO HINTIKKA

Department of Philosophy, Florida State University

D. REIDEL PUBLISHING COMPANY

A MEMBER OF THE KLUWER ACADEMIC PUBLISHERS GROUP

DORDRECHT / BOSTON / LANCASTER

Library of Congress Cataloging in Publication Data

Main entry under title:

Cognitive constraints on communication.

(Synthese language library ; 18)
Includes index.
1. Interpersonal communication. 2. Cognition. 3. Human
information processing. 4. Semiotics. 5. Psycholinguistics. I. Vaina,
Lucia, 1946–   . II. Hintikka, Jaakko, 1929–   . III. Series.
BF637.C45C63 1983   153.6   83–9490
ISBN 90–277–1456–8

Published by D. Reidel Publishing Company,
P.O. Box 17, 3300 AA Dordrecht, Holland

Sold and distributed in the U.S.A. and Canada
by Kluwer Academic Publishers
190 Old Derby Street, Hingham, MA 02043, U.S.A.

In all other countries, sold and distributed
by Kluwer Academic Publishers Group,
P.O. Box 322, 3300 AH Dordrecht, Holland

Printed in The Netherlands

TABLE OF CONTENTS

INTRODUCTION

Communication is one of the most challenging human phenomena, and the same is true of its paradigmatic verbal realization as a *dialogue*. Not only is communication crucial for virtually all interpersonal relations; dialogue is often seen as offering us also a paradigm for important intra-individual processes. The best known example is undoubtedly the idea of conceptualizing thinking as an internal dialogue, "inward dialogue carried on by the mind within itself without spoken sound", as Plato called it in the *Sophist*.

At first, the study of communication seems to be too vaguely defined to have much promise. It is up to us, so to speak, to decide what to say and how to say it. However, on closer scrutiny, the process of communication is seen to be subject to various subtle constraints. They are due *inter alia* to the nature of the parties of the communicative act, and most importantly, to the properties of the language or other method of representation presupposed in that particular act of communication. It is therefore not surprising that in the study of communication as a cognitive process the critical issues revolve around the nature of the representations and the nature of the computations that create, maintain and interpret these representations. The term "representation" as used here indicates a particular way of specifying information about a given subject. The same subject may be described in many different representations, using structures as different as predicate calculus, generative grammars, mathematical set-theory techniques, semantic networks, and so forth. The different representations differ greatly in what information they make explicit. Usually one mode of representation is more suitable than another for a specific information processing task. Hence it is desirable to establish first what the information processing task is that a system is designed to carry out. One set of questions we shall ask accordingly aims at delimiting the goal of the information processing task under study, and an important type of constraint which we consider deals with maintaining the goal during a communication process, such as distinguishing primary from secondary goals.

For example, in Solomon Marcus' article the topic is diplomatic communication. He places it in a more general framework of a communication theory and presents two different sets of constraints, one on the participants

vii

L. *Vaina and J. Hintikka (eds.), Cognitive Constraints on Communication*, vii–xvii.
Copyright © 1983 *by D. Reidel Publishing Company.*

and the other on the message. The question he raises is what it is that characterizes a type of communication and avoids its degeneration in another type, such as a conflict, for example.

Stanton's article deals with the issue of the secondary goals of communicative activity. He takes as a specific example psychotherapeutic activity with schizophrenic patients. Schizophrenia is identified and considered almost entirely through its interpersonal and symbolic characteristics, that is, through the ways in which the patient tells the therapist about himself. The primary goal of psychotherapy is the achievement of an insight. Insight as used by Stanton means new information or new interpretation about himself which a patient achieves during the psychotherapy, information which affects and changes the patient's self-representation. The secondary goal of this communication is that of providing the therapist with new knowledge about the structure of the patient's mind. Common to the two goals is that they both produce modifications in the previously interfaced representations. Thus the types of processes that are to be studied here are those that produce modifications on the input representations. An important constraint on the goal of the communication is the preservation of the shared focus of attention between the participants. Any transgression leads to a communication deviance.

Sass in his article examines the conceptual issues pertaining to the so-called communication deviance hypothesis of the etiology of schizophrenia. According to this hypothesis, a high degree of communication deviance on the part of the parents is an important causal factor which contributes to the development of schizophrenia in their offspring. Communication deviance refers here to a failure on the part of a speaker to use language in a way which adequately establishes a focus of attention shared with the listener. Sass provides a theoretical description of the nature of the hypothesized interaction between parental speech style and offspring symptomatology. The plausibility of ascribing an etiological role to parental communication deviance is thus argued from a cognitive development standpoint. After a theoretical analysis of the relevant aspects of schizophrenia focusing primarily on the relevant aspects of cognitive disorganization, Sass proposes a model of possible processes by which different forms of parental speech might mediate the development of the schizophrenic symptoms in the offspring, suggesting that communication deviance in parents is likely to be more directly associated with cognitive disorganisation than with schizophrenia per se.

Once the goal of communication has been formulated and the constraints on maintaining it are discovered, the problem of achieving this goal can be addressed. In this direction the study of communication merges with the study of information processing, especially the study of how linguistic information is processed.

One point to be stressed here is that our ability to solve information processing problems is closely coupled to how well the problem and the knowledge relevant to its solution are formulated. An information processing problem can be formulated by specifying its input and output representations and the relationships that must obtain between them. The relations between the input and output representations are specified by the algorithms that might be used by the communicational system in achieving the task in question.

The success of any approach to investigating a complex problem generally depends on how well one can decompose the problem into simpler sub-problems that can be studied independently. Benowitz et al., Jakobson and Lübbe-Grothues, and Vaina deal with empirical evidence from various types of impairment to the brain (focal brain lesions to the right or left hemisphere or various psychiatric disorders) for such modularity of the process of communication. For example, Benowitz et al. study in their article such communication between humans as is not mediated through verbal language, including expressions, gestures, and intonational qualities of the voice, all of which contribute to the transmission of social clues, to the classification of the verbal message and to the communication of one's emotional state. The authors seek to understand which brain structures might be critical for processing one's emotional, non-linguistic information. The right hemisphere appears to be particularly critical for evaluating facial expressions, which are one of the most salient channels for emotional communication.

Thus the main interest for this paper lies at the level of the mechanism, the hardware which is employed specifically for carrying out a specific information processing task, and its results indicate that overall sensitivity to nonverbal communication is more reliant upon structures in the right cerebral hemisphere than the left and is thus processed on the opposite side of the brain from verbal language.

Vaina's approach moves on the functional level and not on the anatomical one, as in the paper just discussed. Relying on evidence from brain injured patients (agnosics, anomics and Wernicke aphasics) she stresses the necessity of having a modular representation of the semantic information. Thus she proposes a model of semantic memory that contains three modules: a category module (containing class information, such as "an elephant is an animal"), a descriptional module (that represents perceptual information such as color, the size of an object, and so forth), and a functional module (that categorizes objects by their possible use in actions). Processes that access, make inferences, and store information in each of these modules are defined. Whenever semantic information is required, the module which has it stored in the convenient form for the task at hand is accessed.

Jakobson and Lübbe-Grothues analyse Hölderlin's poem 'Die Aussicht' and show that in this creation of the schizophrenic poet the architectonic cohesiveness proves to be impressive despite the peculiarities in the systematic distributions of grammatical categories and their lexical analogues. Of special interest here is the observation that, although the confrontation with the environment usually realized through a referential use of the language, for instance the capacity for dialogue expressed through deictics, has been lost in the schizophrenic Hölderlin, nevertheless this competence for monologue remains. Thus we can hypothesize that the conversational form constrained by the use of deictics, reference and so forth might constitute a module which can be separately studied. Comparing the two poles in the language use of the schizophrenic poet we must emphasize, following Bühler, that deixis and naming are two acts that should be differentiated, and that designative words and naming words are two different categories to be kept separate. Hölderlin's late poetry, the Scardinelli poems, as opposed to his early poetic activity, is focused on reference-free naming.

Central to the cognitive science today is the assumption that the organization of cognitive processes is revealed through the dissociation of their function. On the basis of this idea, one tries to locate and to investigate the many functional modules that analyse, integrate, and produce information. The articles discussed above focus mostly on the modularization problem, this is to say on the question of how, by what means, one discovers modules in the information processing system under study.

It should be noted that a problem can be decomposed serially by identifying intermediate representations between the input and the output representations, or in parallel when several distinct computational problems can be formulated connecting the same input and output representations. Each of these separate computational problems has its own representation that will make explicit only the information relevant to that particular information processing task at hand. Implicit in this view is the assumption that each module has an important, active role in the overall solution to the communication process. The information these modules compute must then be integrated at some level. With regard to the serial and the parallel decomposition, we believe that although there are serially identifiable independent levels (modules) of the communication process, at each level there are also several modules working in parallel and differing either in the problem they solve (output) or the information they process (input). These issues are under analysis in the articles by Lehnert, Schank, Vaina and Minsky.

Wendy Lehnert's article on question answering in the context of a story understanding system constitutes a useful base for studying the range of semantic processing problems which must be present in human conversation. She differentiates three levels of analysis in the processing of questions and answers. The first stage concerns the social interaction among the participants. This can be analyzed through a study of the social context of dialogue. Hypotheses about what combinations of context classes occur and what not are put forth in the article and theoretically motivated. The next level concerns the understanding of language in its literal sense. The relation between the context and the processing of the language is established through focus. That is to say, when interpreting a question semantically the context often determines a focus of the question. Based on this assumption Lehnert proposes a semantic categorization of questions depending on the focus, as opposed to the usual classification by lexical features; thus she proposes categories such as enablement questions, quantification questions, instrumentality questions, procedural questions and causal-antecedent questions. Crucial in this classification is the kind of memory structures invoked by the question. This brings us to the third level taken into consideration in Lehnert's paper, the retrieval from memory. Retrieval mechanisms must guide memory search for correct responses. Then generation considerations must guide a selection process in the event that the memory search produces a choice of response. The rules that must be used in making a selection must enable an effective communication.

In his paper Roger Schank attempts to determine some of these rules that might be used for response creation in a conversational setting. He shows that a set of constraints on the communication is set up by the theme of the conversation which establishes the prior context of the situation, the legitimate expectations of the participants. The thematic constraints are important in that they provide a set of restrictions for the permitted interpretations of the message. Thus Schank isolates different levels that a conversation can take place on, e.g. the standard surface level, which contains the explicit response to what precisely was asked, the dominance games, the level describing the knowledge state of the hearer, the emotional states of the participants, the relationships between the participants, the argument strategy, and so forth. The point to make is that each of the levels proposed contains the information relevant for the information processing task resolved at that level, and that there are many different kinds of information exchanges going on at one and the same time. After differentiating among the various levels at which the conversation may proceed, Schank gives a set of rules for these levels which permits us to understand the computational problem resolved on each level.

In 'Jokes and the logic of the cognitive unconscious', Minsky is inspired by Freud's explanation of how jokes overcame the mental "censors" that make it hard for us to think "forbidden" thoughts. In his paper, Minsky argues that different forms of humor can be seen as being much more similar than we usually think, once we recognize the importance of "knowledge about knowledge" and in particular of those aspects of thinking concerned with recognizing and suppressing "bugs" (i.e. ineffective or destructive thought processes). His basic hypothesis is that the mind is a society of very simple agents who work in cooperation to solve problems, reason, learn, represent knowledge, and so forth. Of course the cooperation between agents, which are as a matter of fact simple processors, is not at all smooth. Agents send information to each other in a specific way, inhibit each other, instantiate a new and more knowledgeable agent, or control and censor other agents' activities. Using apparently trivial topics such as jokes and humor in general, Minsky aims at making a profound point. He is suggesting that it is Artificial Intelligence as a science that provides ways of dealing with many of the most central issues of intelligence, such as efficiency and effectiveness of reasoning, plans and goals, and their optimal structure for problem solving.

These are matters of a lesser concern for logic and philosophy, which focus more on such questions as the validity of proofs, the soundness of the arguments, truth values, and so forth. Of course Artificial Intelligence does not want to deny or ignore the issues of concern to the logician, but on the contrary it aims at expressing and dealing with these issues in a novel way so as to be useful for the understanding of how intelligent behavior is carried out, and subsequently for building devices that have intelligent behavior. The point we want to stress here is that Artificial Intelligence approaches do not reject the results of the "classical disciplines" but seek to integrate them critically in a new way of thinking. The best illustration of this point in our volume is William A. Martin's article 'A logical form based on the structural description of events'. Martin proposes a representation for natural language understanding suitable for the logical structure of the English sentences. For this purpose he introduces a set of constraints which permit a computational treatment of such phenomena as co-referential descriptions, definite descriptions, modifiers, quantifiers and so forth. The knowledge representation proposed by Martin is a form of network which has two kinds of nodes and three kinds of links. There are generic nodes, which are concepts or intentions, and individual nodes, extensions, which represent at most one entity, a particular instance of the concept. The description of a node is inferred from the rest of the network by tracing out the links. Nodes in the structural description of a given node are linked to this node by role-in links which for instance allow a natural modelling of phenomena related to context. Thus one starts with a node representing the world and structurally decomposes it in various ways. Each part of the decomposition can be indefinitely decomposed to any desired depth, thus producing a structural hierarchy of descriptions. In the most interesting way this structural hierarchy is complemented by an abstraction hierarchy produced by links such as "may-be-described-as". Thus the may-be-described-as links indicate an alternative description. The third type of link is the inheritance link which specifies the inheritance of all description which is not explicitly overridden. This article is particularly interesting because from a methodological point of view, too, it bridges two fields, philosophy of language and artificial intelligence, and provides a promising theory for language processing.

Taking in her article as a point of departure the language developed by Martin, Gretchen Brown uses an integrated representation for both verbal and non verbal activities of communicative behaviour. The advantage of using a uniform representation for different inputs is the fact that one can master and interface the various relevant parameters at once. The knowledge structures, called methods, are chunks of knowledge similar to Minsky's frames or to Schank's and Abelson's scripts.

Linguistically speaking, the typical form of a communicative process is a dialogue (in the wide sense in which it includes also poly-logues). Hence the linguistic and logical theory of communication is very closely related to the theory of dialogue and discourse. Cognitive constraints on communication will then appear in the form of logical, semantical, pragmatic and perhaps even psychological and sociological rules governing dialogues. Accordingly, a number of studies in this volume are devoted to the theory of dialogue, also known as the theory of discourse.

In his paper, Teun A. van Dijk poses the critical question as to what the features are that are needed in a satisfactory cognitive model of a dialogue. (These, of course, amount to so many "cognitive constraints on communication" in our sense.) He notes the failure of earlier models to integrate all the different aspects of dialogues, and offers a number of constructive proposals to overcome this fragmentation. In particular, he combines in an interesting way several factors from the social context (social act interpretations) with the more local conditions of discourse comprehension. He stresses the importance of interactional planning (interactional "strategies") in communication.

Arnold Günther goes further in one particular direction and proposes an actual formal model (representation) for dialogues. Here, as with all comparable models, many of the formal rules of a dialogue can be viewed as embodying various cognitive constraints on the dialogue process. Günther starts from the simple-minded idea of a dialogue as an ordered sequence of well-formed sentences (the sentences which are uttered in a dialogue), and introduces some of the other necessary parameters one by one. Strictly speaking, he considers two different types of representation which are distinguished from each other by the question whether one emphasizes the speech acts which the dialogue partners perform or their propositional attitudes. Günther's paper printed here is only a sample of the extensive studies of dialogues he has carried out with his associates. They are highly relevant to the theme of our volume, and we hope that the present paper by Günther will serve to introduce many of our readers to the rest of his work.

Anca Runcan's paper may be compared in intention with Günther's. One of the main differences in execution is that Runcan seeks to relate her model (framework of representation) with a number of ideas and concepts from the recent logical, philosophical and semantical theories, e.g. those of possible world, universe of discourse, proposition etc.

A third object of comparison is David Harrah's paper, for it is in scope and purpose roughly comparable with those by Günther and Runcan. His main conceptual tool is the formal message theory he has built in earlier publications. One of the distinguishing features of his approach is that he defines message-theoretical counterparts to several familiar concepts from formal logic, such as implication, consistency, assumption (presumption). Another important feature of Harrah's theory is that special attention is paid in it to questions and to replies to questions.

This forms a bridge from the papers by Günther, Runcan, and Harrah, to those by Hintikka and Carlson. They were originally motivated by an observation which is also made by Van Dijk. Far too often, linguists and logicians try to deal with dialogues by extending in some straightforward way the techniques of sentence semantics, sentence logic, and sentence pragmatics to dialogue (discourse). One linguist has gone so far as to suggest that we can deal with discourse by the simple trick of considering it as a conjunction of its several constituent sentences! It is not hard to see some of the things that are wrong with such suggestions. They imply treating all sentences of a discourse as if they were uttered by the same person against the same cognitive background. As Van Dijk puts it, the specific properties of dialogues (as distinguished from monologues) are frequently overlooked. As a consequence of this assumption of cognitive uniformity, many of the most important and most distinctive features of dialogues as cognitive processes get irrevocably lost.

A useful antidote to this oversight is the study of questions and answers. If a question and an answer to it were uttered against the same cognitive background, they would be pointless. Hence it is especially vital in the theory of questions and answers to hear the cognitive state of the different speakers and to see what constraints they impose on a question-answer dialogue.

An important such restraint is undoubtedly the question-answer relation. Jaakko Hintikka uses it to outline a logical model of question-answer dialogues, conceptualized in the form of question-answer "games" in the sense of the mathematical theory of games. (This is closely related to Van Dijk's emphasis on interactional strategies.)

One reason for the interest of question-answer sequences is that they can be used to model several different types of knowledge-seeking processes. (Cf. the old idea of the scientific method as a series of questions put to nature.)

In Hintikka's model, it turns out that the strategy selection in empirical information-gathering is extremely closely related to the selection of deductive strategies. This vindicates partly the old idea of logic as playing a major role in virtually all nontrivial knowledge-seeking, and constitutes a step towards integrating dialogue theory and the important theory logicians call *proof theory*. This suggestion may be compared with Marvin Minsky's ideas about the relationship between artificial intelligence and logic.

An especially significant restraint which Hintikka's model brings to the fore is the need of a restriction on the logical complexity of the questions that may be asked in question-answer "games". This restriction turns out to have close and interesting relationships to several apparently discrepant phenomena which logicians have noted from Aristotle's prohibition against "begging the question" to Gentzen's and John von Neumann's comments on the peculiarities of human information-processing as compared with that by automata. Here, and in the more general matter of modelling information-gathering by means of question-answer dialogues, we are approaching from a new angle the same information-processing problems as were dealt with in some of the earlier papers of our volume.

Lauri Carlson's ambitious paper enriches Jaakko Hintikka's model dialogues in several respects, especially in integrating them with another type of game that Hintikka has studied, the so-called semantical game. The result is one of the most realistic models for dialogues of several different sorts in the literature. The realism and the scope of Carlson's games are illustrated by the fact that they enable him to formulate an elegant and powerful theory of discourse-dependent stress in English.

Umberto Eco in his witty paper views the intellectual feats of that early precursor of Sherlock Holmes, Voltaire's Zadig, not as a series of questions put to a suitable source of information (with appropriate answers), but as unraveling a network of intensional relationships, an intricate system of symptoms and clues, plus a number of inferences based on them.

These connections are intentional in the sense that it matters how they are motivated. They are aptly contrasted by Eco to the extensional relations where only the end product of a referential process counts, not how it is reached.

One of the many suggestions of Eco's extraordinarily suggestive paper may likewise be compared with Hintikka's procedure. Eco views the speech-acts used in a dialogue as *world-creating devices*. This may be compared with a feature of Hintikka's model, viz. that in it each dialogue partner is thought of as being engaged in an attempt to construct descriptions of a number of suitable 'worlds', that is, of certain states of affairs or courses of events. In this respect, as in several others, there is probably a greater similarity between the two approaches than at first meets the eye.

Another paper that invites comparison with others is Steven Cushing's. He argues that the interpretation of discourse is a matter of model selection rather than model construction. This presumably places him squarely among Eco's extensionalists. It is no surprise to anyone who has witnessed the extraordinary power of the semantical methods based, as Cushing's ultimately are, on a Tarski-type approach to truth and satisfaction, that Cushing is able to reach several interesting results. An especially interesting facet of Cushing's paper is the attention he pays to relativized quantifiers. Their role in natural languages is one of the most important logico-semantical phenomena, and has long been unduly neglected.

Gheorghe Păun uses as his framework for modeling dialogues the theory of action systems he has developed earlier. This framework relies more on the theory of formal languages than on logic or conventional linguistics. Once again, the reader has an interesting opportunity here to compare with each other different approaches using different conceptual tools. It is our hope that such comparisons will eventually lead to a convergence of the different theories.

Yet another interesting recent theory is resorted to in the next paper, in which L. A. Zadeh brings the resources of the "fuzzy" languages he has developed (languages based on the concept of possibility distribution) to bear on the problems of human communication. He illustrates aptly by means of examples the uses of his language to help us understand the various phenomena of linguistic communication.

In developing models for communication, as different as the goals or the points of view here are, all the studies so far considered have explicitly one thing in common: they all take human performance as a paradigm case of communication. The article by David McDonald discusses how two programs talk to each other. He shows that when the matter is viewed abstractly, what a computer program does in trying to communicate with another computer program is no different from what people are believed to be doing when they communicate with each other. The programs, however, can be analyzed and altered to an arbitrary degree, which implies that it may be possible to look at programs as convenient model systems by which we can study human communication. This paper is partly didactic, explaining how it is that we can talk sensibly about a computer program using symbols or communicating. It then looks at different kinds of program to program communications, concluding that a common notion of levels of symbols and interpreters will explain the processes involved.

If there is a moral we want to draw from the materials we are presenting here, it is that in spite of their apparent differences the different papers often have more in common than might first seem to be the case. Computer scientists, psychologists, students of artificial intelligence, linguists, semioticians, logicians, and philosophers of language are often concerned with closely similar problems. We believe that this is an area where a co-operation and a dialogue between different disciplines is likely to prove especially useful. It is to further such interdisciplinary dialogues that we have brought the different papers together that the reader will find below. As far as their various points of contact and perhaps even their convergence are concerned, it was in the nature of our enterprise that we have to grant the joy of discovery to our readers in many cases in its entirety.

THE EDITORS

ACKNOWLEDGEMENTS

The paper by Alfred Stanton originally appeared in John S. Strauss et al. (eds.), *The Psychotherapy of Schizophrenia*, Plenum, New York, 1980, and is reprinted with the permission of the publisher. The Paper by Umberto Eco originally appeared in Italian as 'Il cane e il cavallo: un testo visivo e alcuni equivoci verbali', *VS (Versus)* 25 (1980), 28—43, copyright © Bompiani. The paper by Jaakko Hintikka contains material also included in a modified German version of his paper (jointly by Ulrike Leopold-Wildburger) which is forthcoming in *Conceptus*. The paper by Roman Jakobson and Grete Lübbe-Grothues is a translation of a chapter of their book *Hölderlin-Klee-Brecht: On the Verbal Art of Three Poems*, and is published here with the kind permission of Roman Jakobson, whose estate holds the relevant copyrights. It is with profound regret that we record the deaths of Roman Jakobson, William Martin and Alfred Stanton since they submitted their papers for this volume.

THE EDITORS

TEUN A. VAN DIJK

DIALOGUE AND COGNITION

1. PROBLEMS AND AIMS

1.1. Dialogues are verbal interaction sequences performed among language users. In order to be able to adequately accomplish their respective actions which constitute a dialogue, these language users must 'go through' a number of highly complex cognitive processes. It is the aim of this paper to briefly discuss some of the properties of the processes and representations involved in the cognitive management of dialogues.

The theoretical background of our discussion is the current work being done in the theory of discourse, and in particular the experimental research in cognitive psychology on processes of discourse production and comprehension. At the moment this kind of research is also done, from a theoretical point of view, in the domain of artificial intelligence. In the present paper we will have to see which additional properties must be postulated in a processing model for discourse in order to be able to account for specific aspects of dialogue. Our discussion will remain informal.

1.2. A cognitive analysis of dialogue indirectly involves many aspects of dialogues, e.g. structural properties on the one hand, and social and cultural conditions on the other hand (which also all need to be represented cognitively), which however cannot be discussed in the framework of one small paper. In order to stress that a complete cognitive model requires processes, operations, strategies, etc. which are linked to these structural and social properties of dialogues, we will nevertheless briefly list some of them:

1. phonetic and phonological relations between sentences, turns or moves of the verbal interaction sequence (intonation, stress, pitch, etc.); paraverbal activities;

2. morphological and lexical properties of sequencing (specific words as 'openers', 'closers', 'pass' indicators, pragmatic particles and other dialogue connectives)

3. syntactic properties and relations (incomplete sentences, completion of sentences by next speakers, phrasal boundaries of turns, repetitions, syntactic expressions of coherence phenomena, e.g. PRO-forms, etc.)

1

L. Vaina and J. Hintikka (eds.), Cognitive Constraints on Communication, 1–17.

4.   semantic relations, both intensional and extensional: local and global coherence (conditional relations between propositions expressed, establishment of topics of conversation, topic changes, etc.)

5.   pragmatic properties of the dialogue, taken as a sequence of speech acts: local and global pragmatic coherence (relative appropriateness of speech acts, global pragmatic 'point', etc.); schematic structures;

6.   interaction management of the dialogue taken as a sequence of 'moves' or 'turns' (turn taking and changing of turns, strategies and their rhetorical and stylistic devices, etc.)

7.   socio-cultural properties of the interaction sequence, the participants and the context (categorization of actions and agents, conventions of social 'frames', institutional constraints, cultural rules, etc.).

Clearly, this list is not complete and also does not show the multiple relations between the various 'levels' of analysis. The point is that language users in the dialogue are 'doing' many things at the same time, which requires cognitive planning, execution, monitoring, comprehension, storage and retrieval, etc. We will limit ourselves to only some of these cognitive operations, leaving the analysis of the further aspects to other approaches, e.g. those exemplified in the other contributions to this volume. We have already stressed above, however, that these other approaches, e.g. both the formal (game-theoretical or other) and the more empirical (e.g. the ethonomethodological analysis of conversation), may well have relevant results which may become components in a full-fledged cognitive model of dialogue.

2. THEORETICAL BACKGROUND

2.1. The theoretical background for our discussion features two large areas of research. The first is the general theory of discourse, including e.g. text grammars and other theories specifying various structures of discourse. The second is the psychological theory of discourse production and comprehension, which at some points is closely linked to the more 'linguistic' analysis of discourse structures.

2.2. The linguistic basis of a theory of discourse has been studied — e.g. under the label of 'text grammar' — first of all in the perspective of the extension of grammatical models towards structures 'beyond the sentence'. Apart from rather obvious generalizations of rules holding for clauses within complex sentences towards sentence sequences in discourse, this approach allowed that the focus of e.g. semantic analysis also became directed on phenomena, such as 'coherence', which were neglected before. Taking 'text' as the formal unit underlying a discourse utterance, it was also discovered that discourses should not only be analysed in terms of linearly or locally coherent sentence sequences, but also in terms of more global textual structures. Thus, the semantic characterization of 'themes' or 'topics' of a discourse in terms of 'macrostructures' appeared to be an important task of such a 'global' analysis.

2.3. Besides the crucial cognitive implications of this kind of linguistic analyses of discourse, to which we will turn below, the various categories, rules and levels of this linguistic theory also appeared necessary for a treatment of other, 'non-linguistic', structures of discourse. Thus, theories of narrative and argumentation for example feature global 'syntactic' categories which require global semantic 'content', viz. propositions at a macrostructural level of meaning.

Similarly, a characterization of stylistic and rhetorical structures and operations should not be limited to sentential structures alone, but also requires as their basis all kinds of sequential (inter-sentential) and more global textual units, rules and constraints.

In other words, the analysis of various kinds of discourse structures requires an integrated, interdisciplinary theory. It will be left open here in which respect the units (e.g. 'text') and rules involved belong to the domain of grammar or to a theory of language use and (other) communicative forms.

2.4. A theory of discourse also involves a pragmatic component, in which (utterances of) sentences are interpreted as speech acts of which the appropriateness is determined by conditions formulated in terms of certain contextual properties of the communicative situation (knowledge, beliefs, wants, evaluations and certain social relations).

Relevant here, especially also for a theory of dialogue, is the fact that, pragmatically, discourse can be defined in terms of speech act sequences. Parallel to the local and global coherence at the semantic level, speech act sequences also should exhibit local and global coherence. Thus, a given speech act may be appropriate only relative to certain preceding or following speech acts, of which it may function as a condition or consequence:

(1)   Could you please tell me the time? I have no watch.

In this example the assertion accomplished by the utterance of the second sentence of this discourse may sometimes (e.g. for a stranger) only be appropriate, and 'relevant', when following as an explanation for a previous request.

Similarly, sequences of speech acts may be globally coherent due to the accomplishment of a 'macro-speech act', such as a global request of a letter, global assertion of a newspaper article or lecture, or threat of a ransom note.

2.5. It should be noted that much of the work very briefly referred to above did abstract from the distinction between *monological* and *dialogical* discourses. Although mostly examples were used of monological discourses, many of the principles were — often tacitly — assumed to have a more general nature. Thus, semantic and pragmatic coherence, both at the local and global level, is a property which will hold both for monologues and dialogues. Without these notions it would even be difficult to have a theoretical distinction between different, e.g. subsequent, discourses of one or several speakers.

However, it should be admitted that much of the work on discourse analysis has neglected possible *specific* properties of dialogical discourses. And indeed, it has been the ethnomethodological analysis of conversation which, first in sociology and then in linguistics, has remedied this omission. Unfortunately, there has until recently been very little integration between the two areas of discourse and conversation analysis. Our contribution to this integration in this paper will only be very modest and take place in the domain of a cognitive model.

2.6. The second area of research which constitutes the theoretical background of this paper are recent developments in cognitive psychology and artificial intelligence. In the paradigm of 'semantic information processing' attention has been extended from sentential to textual materials. Models have been designed and experiments are being carried out about the processes and representations involved in the comprehension of discourses, e.g. of stories. The contribution of artificial intelligence in this area first of all pertained to the explication of the role of knowledge in understanding, both of 'real' and of textually represented states of affairs. Notions such as 'frame' and 'script' were developed in order to represent the organized and conventional nature of our conceptual knowledge of the world. At the same time it was shown in this approach that discourse comprehension depends on our knowledge about plans and goals of (represented) participants in interaction, and about other properties of action in general. Both in cognitive psychology and in artificial intelligence it was finally recognized that discourses may exhibit various kinds of 'schematic' structures, such as the categorical organization of a story or psychological paper.

The theoretical and experimental research has been focussing mainly on processes of comprehension. Discourse production has been little studied, probably because its properties are more difficult to assess experimentally. Comprehension was mainly tested in paraphrase, free or cued recall (reproduction), recognition, question answering and summarizing tasks. It was found that especially in delayed recall subjects will no longer be able to retrieve most propositions of a discourse. They will mainly recall macro-structures (main topics) and, personally varying, salient details. Summaries appear to feature the same properties. In both cases it was assumed that during reading and comprehension language users not only understand the respective sentences of a discourse and their semantic connections, but at the same time apply various 'macrorules' which construct the global topic or gist of the text. It is this macrostructure which organizes the representation of the text in memory and which is easier and longer accessible than the 'details' of the discourse.

Similarly, conventional schemata also play an important role in the global organization of the information of a discourse, both during comprehension and storage, and in (re-)production. Experiments have shown that the presence of well-known (narrative) schemata facilitate comprehension and recall.

Both in local and global comprehension of discourse it appeared that knowledge of the world (frames, scripts) play a decisive role, e.g. in the establishment of coherence and the formation of macrostructures.

3. SOME SPECIFIC PROPERTIES OF DIALOGUE DISCOURSE

3.1. In order to be able to see whether the cognitive models developed in these areas can simply be accomodated to also account for processes involved in dialogue interaction, we must briefly enumerate some of the properties which distinguish monologues from dialogues. In our first section we already summarized some main levels and domains of analysis for dialogues. The question now is where the properties involved are specific, so that extensions of the cognitive model would be needed at those points.

3.2. The obvious fact that dialogues require several participants as subsequent speakers has an immediate implication for experimental psychology. In current laboratory experiments textual materials are mostly used 'out of context'. That is, they are not produced, transmitted, understood and 'used' under normal pragmatic and social conditions. The pragmatic context is that of the psychological test situation, which has specific assumptions of readers/hearers, specific tasks and goals, etc. In other words, the results of experiments on discourse comprehension in this area are only an approximation of natural reading and comprehension processes. Now, in dialogues the hearer-comprehender must be at the same time a (real) participant which on a next turn becomes speaker. So, adequate experiments in this case would at least need a simulated context in which subjects engage 'naturally' in verbal interaction.

This is not only a difference and additional difficulty in experimental design but at the same time an aspect of the cognitive model itself: it needs both a comprehension and a production component, and these must be intimately related. Below we will assume for instance that in dialogues of certain kinds, e.g. daily conversations, processes of understanding and of planning for production may be mingled.

3.3. There are various kinds of dialogues, some of which may be close to *discourse sequences*, especially in written communication. Thus, a lecture would essentially have a monological character, but comments or questions should be considered as relevant subsequent verbal reactions to them. On the other hand, proper dialogues may consist of turns which have acquired a more or less independent nature, e.g. when we tell a story during a conversation.

Although there are several types of transitions between monologue and dialogue, we will provisionally establish dialogues as *global units of interaction*. Besides the various structural properties of the respective *utterances* constituting a dialogue (spatio-temporal continuity, grammatical connections and semantic coherence), we therefore should especially focus on the *action structure* of the interactional unit.

In the first place this means that the respective *speech acts* of the dialogue will be intended and performed on the basis of beliefs and purposes about subsequent speech acts of the hearer as the next speaker. In other words, both for speaker and hearer speech acts of a dialogue may each be planned or interpreted as a condition for the performance of speech acts in a next turn. And, similarly, each subsequent speech act will be planned and understood as a reaction to previous speech acts. So, at the pragmatic level dialogues are sequences of utterances which are *connected*. This pragmatic connectedness requires the semantic and grammatical connectedness of the (semi-)sentences expressed by these utterances.

This kind of linear connectedness of speech acts performed by subsequent speakers will in several kinds of dialogues, e.g. interviews, meetings, etc., be complemented by *global pragmatic coherence*. That is, for one or more participants involved, the subsequent speech acts are at the same time performed as instantiations of one or more *global* (speech) acts. In that case the dialogue may have one over-all intended result and one over-all purposed aim or goal, being the consequence of that result, e.g. as follows: 'B has been requested by A to borrow him thousand dollars' may be the global result of a successful global request, which may lead to the global consequence 'that B will (indeed) borrow him the money'. The same may hold in the perspective of arriving at a common decision or at a confession of one of the participants. In everyday conversation such an initial goal need not exist (small-talk) initially, or may have a very vague nature, such as confirmation of friendly social relationships.

We observe that dialogues are utterance sequences performed by subsequent speakers which are both locally and (often) globally coherent at the pragmatic level. Details of this pragmatic coherence, e.g. the relations between local and global coherence, will not be discussed here.

In the second place it should be noted that the local management of speech act sequences in subsequent turns may be different from monological discourse sequences (such as storytelling rituals). That is, speakers not always have control over the successful performance of their speech acts: they may be interrupted by other participants taking a turn, which may also lead to partial overlapping of utterances. The dialogical interaction, e.g. in conversation, is characterized by a distribution of rights and obligations of speaking, whereas in a monologue the speaker has (taken) the right to control the length of the utterance, although of course there exist socially accepted conventions which limit its length in practice (a lecture may not take 6 hours, say).

Finally, what has been said for speech act sequencing and local turn management holds for the further social implications of the unit of interaction. That is, not only the linguistic and pragmatic context are permanently changing, but also the social context. First of all, each speech act and its accompanying paratextual acts (face work, gestures, etc.) will in each *stage* of the communicative social context imply a number of *further social act interpretations*. Thus, an assertion may further be intended and/or interpreted as an attack, as 'showing confidence', as performing one's duty or compliance with a norm, etc. That is, each speech act or turn will change the social situation which will be the initial condition for the successful perform- ance and interpretation of the next social act of the interaction sequence: the speaker and/or hearer have different rights, obligations, their roles may change, and the social 'frame' may be changed. Again, these changes may take place both locally and globally. In a meeting we may have 'local' deliberations on one point, and at the same time make global decisions, whereas a trial will result in a final, globally intended social result, viz. a judgement, both having important social consequences. Whether initially planned or not, whether under the control of one or more speakers or not, this means that at the level of social analysis of dialogical interaction the dialogue can be defined in terms of identifiable differences between the initial social context and the final social context. This change is accomplished by a locally and globally coherent sequence of interactionally relevant actions of several participants.

Clearly, this is still far from an adequate definition, let alone theoretical framework, of dialogues. Our indications are not only very rough, but also were not specified for various types of dialogue, e.g. a daily conversation, a formal oral exam, a meeting, an interview, institutional 'exchanges' of various kinds (e.g. buying a ticket in the station or the movie theatre), etc. Yet, we now have some elementary insight into what might be needed in a cognitive model of dialogue.

4. COGNITIVE ASPECTS OF DIALOGUE

4.1. An empirically adequate cognitive model of dialogue, as we may guess from the previous indications, will not be a simple thing. First of all, it should contain a language processor and an (inter-)action processor. It must feature much social knowledge and knowledge of the world in general. It should have both a production and a comprehension component. It must have sets of textual and social strategies, and so on. In this stage of research in cognitive psychology there is no hope to come up with such a full-fledged model in the near future. So, we must try to model and experimentally test only some manageable parts of the model.

4.2. Therefore, let us start at a point where we *do* have some insight, viz. *discourse comprehension*. That is, at any point of a dialogue a hearer needs to understand the actual utterance of the current speaker. Moreover, he must link this utterance — or rather his interpretation of it — with previous utterances of the same speaker, and with his own previous utterances. That is, the internal textual structure of the current utterance must be understood, as well as the various coherence relations, both local and global, with the others of the dialogue. We will further assume that the understanding of the discourse is the decisive condition for the further understanding of the (speech or other) acts being performed by the speaker, and for the preparation of the (speech) acts of the hearer as a next speaker. Understanding of dialogue utterances, except for the first utterance, is therefore *relative*: all consequences of previous sentences and acts will count as presuppositions of interpretation.

The model, thus, first of all will contain the usual mechanisms for language processing, e.g. a parser analyzing surface structures and interpreting them as conceptual ('semantic') structures, e.g. propositions. Note that already at this point oral dialogue at the same time requires a mechanism for analysing and interpreting paratextual expressions. The terminal semantic interpretation may be the output of both analysers. We will further neglect the surface structure parsers and focus on the conceptual management of dialogues.

In a model of discourse comprehension it is assumed that, thus, sentences are 'translated' into structured proposition sequences. These are stored in *semantic working memory*. In order to connect sentences of a discourse these propositional structures must be linked, e.g. by conditional connections (cause, reason, enablement, situation-fact, etc.). This linear process of connection and coherence establishment has a *cyclical* nature: new propositions are being constructed whereas some 'old' propositions need to be stored elsewhere, e.g. in episodic memory. In this way, there takes place a gradual construction of a *representation* of the discourse in episodic memory. Since propositions as expressed by the discourse itself need not always be directly connected and coherent, world knowledge, as e.g. organized in frames or scripts in our semantic knowledge store of Long Term Memory (LTM), will supply necessary propositions to establish linear coherence.

However, the resulting representation is not sufficiently structured. During input comprehension in semantic working memory we are now able to link sentences with (previous) sentences, but not with the meaning of the discourse as a whole. That is, we do not know in which respect the sentence is relevant for the actual *topic* of the discourse. This means that *macrorules* must operate at the same time and construct from input proposition sequences one or more macropropositions which represent the actual topic, and which can be kept in the buffer store of semantic working memory. At the same time these macropropositions will further assign hierarchical structure to the discourse representation in episodic memory. The macrorules delete irrelevant propositions, make generalizations over sequences and construct propositions denoting normal conditions, components and consequences into a more global proposition denoting a more global fact. In all these cases, again, world knowledge must be activated in order to apply the macrorules. The resulting macrostructurally organized representation of the discourse may also be further structured by assigned *schematic* global structures, e.g. a narrative schema, or a dialogue schema.

Finally, it should at least briefly be mentioned that all these processes are controlled not only by a conventional knowledge system, but also by general values and norms, and further by the actually relevant opinions, attitudes, interests, tasks, etc. of the hearer. This collection of contextually operating and personally varying factors of processing will be called the *cognitive set* of the hearer. Note that at each point of the discourse (at each cycle) the cognitive set will change: the hearer knows more, may change opinions about the discourse or its author, form wishes, etc.

Against the background of this roughly sketched model of discourse comprehension we should see how utterances of dialogues are understood. First of all it should be recalled that such utterances will not always express complete sentences, and not even phrases or meaningful words (cf. frequent *Mmhmm*'s). Yet, hearers at least roughly make sense out of them. How conceptual representations can be formed on the basis of such grammatically incomplete input is a problem we cannot deal with here. Important in this case is the powerful system of inferences, which supplies missing information from both general world knowledge and knowledge and expectations about the context (including the speaker) and what has been said before, and from the global topic and global speech act now being 'carried out'. This does not mean that each utterance will be fully interpreted and represented by the hearer: we will have to account also for more or less frequent lacks of attention, e.g. due to own speech planning or contextual phenomena, which may make interpretations, *at least locally, partial.*

For longer utterances, expressing several sentences, the discourse comprehension mechanisms will operate which have been described above: macrostructurally organized representations will be constructed for each utterance and stored in episodic memory. These will be the basis for further interpretations and connections with previous and subsequent utterances.

We have seen at several points in our discussion that local comprehension is not sufficient. This means that the representations of each turn of the dialogue should be connected to those constructed for previous ones, both of one's own utterances and of those of other participants. Connections in this case, as we have seen before, will first be linear or sequential: propositions will be linked e.g. by conditional connections, co-reference will be established between expressions, etc. We may assume that in general this relevant 'previous information' must be taken from episodic memory, because the semantic working store has too limited a capacity to contain more than a few micro- and macropropositions. Moreover, as we will see below, turns not only exhibit different sentences but also different actions, which need both comprehension and planning, which cannot simply take place with the information stored in the short term buffer. Take for instance the following simple dialogue:

(2)   A: Are you coming?
         B: OK

In order to be able to semantically link both utterances we should be aware of the fact that B should understand A's utterance, first semantically, second pragmatically, viz. as a question or request, upon which a complex decision procedure will take place, finally resulting in B's utterance. Hence, although the two turns and sentences are contiguous, there is a considerable cognitive 'distance' between them in a complete processing model. This may mean that even previous propositions must be reinstated from episodic memory to the working store.

The establishment of coherence at a more global level of comprehension would imply that the hearer determines in what respect the propositions of the current utterance belong to the same topic. This actual topic may well be kept in the short term store, because it is permanently needed in order to semantically *monitor* the dialogue: 'what are we talking about?'. Of course, all kinds of interruptions, side sequences or other embedded turns or discourses, topic changes and topic 'losses' may occur, which presupposes that macropropositions are no longer available in the STM store.

4.3. The nature of verbal interaction, especially in dialogues, not only requires that hearers understand what the other is 'meaning by what he is saying', but also 'what he is meaning by what he is (thereby) *doing*'. In other words, the hearer will have to assign speech act concepts to the actual utterance, that is he must also *pragmatically comprehend* the actual utterance.

The cognitive processes of pragmatic comprehension are even more complex than those of semantic comprehension. That is, a sentence like that of A in example (2) above cannot simply be assigned the concept 'question' or 'request' by the form and the meaning of the sentence alone. Speech acts are defined in terms of various *contextual* properties, such as beliefs, wants and social relations of participants. Under specific conditions, then, (2,A) may also be a threat, an invitation, or an advice. It follows that the hearer must have or make an adequate *analysis of the relevant pragmatic context.* Speech acts, like other social actions, involve knowledge, beliefs, wishes, etc. of a speaker, and also conditions, purposes, etc. linking them to other (speech) acts. This means that the hearer has to check his representations of the previous utterances of the dialogue, of the actual context, the actual social frame, etc. in order to find the constitutive indices defining a possible pragmatic context in which some speech act may be expected and appropriate. This intricate process of comprehension will be both bottom up (given the utterance and its semantic interpretation) and top down (given previous knowledge and expectations of various kinds), and will result in a more or less firm *hypothesis* of what is meant by the speaker at this pragmatic level. Sometimes these data will be insufficient, which requires desambiguation questions: "Is that a promise or a threat?".

In the same way as sentences expressed by dialogue utterances are not comprehended in isolation, speech acts as we saw will be interpreted relative to other speech acts of the sequence. Thus, (2,B) may be interpreted by A as an adequate answer of consent. In order to be linearly connected and coherent, though, each speech act must satisfy the specific conditions which are defining the final state of the previous speech act (as in local question-answer pairs) *and* the actual global state of the global (speech) act now being performed:

(3)   A: Are you coming?
           B: OK. Let's go.

In the second turn of this dialogue, B not only gives a direct answer, but also initiates a speech act which is a possible next step in an interaction sequence in which the request-consent is embedded. Similarly, a hearer may produce or understand a speech act as a possible component, condition or consequence of a global speech act going on, e.g. thanks in a request ritual, or all kinds of preparations of such a request.

From this brief discussion it may have become clear that the processes involved in pragmatic comprehension are extremely complex; we know little about them and will therefore not discuss them further here.

4.4. The next component in the comprehension part of a cognitive model of dialogue is the proper *interactional* component: given the linguistic and pragmatic information of the utterance, and hence a representation of its meaning and speech act function, the hearer will at each stage of the sequence have to further establish a representation of the actual *social situation*. At least part of this analysis already takes place in order to be able to assign a pragmatic interpretation to the utterance. Some of the additional types involved however are:

(4)　(i)　social context type (formal/informal, public/private, etc.);
　　　(ii)　social (sub)system (public transport, education, etc.);
　　　(iii)　social frame or scripts (taking a bus, having a class, having breakfast, taking a drink in a bar);
　　　(iv)　participant categories (roles, functions, etc.);
　　　(v)　conventions of the frame or scripts (rules, norms, and their inferred expectations);
　　　(vi)　global social action now being performed;
　　　(vii)　previous local action(s) of the sequence;
　　　(viii)　dialogue schema categories ('opening', 'closing', etc.).

This list is not arbitrary. That is, we assume that the hearer, in order to manage the enormous complexity of data relevant for the full interpretation of the actual utterance will apply an analytic *schema*, with which the situation is analysed on crucial points for its type, (sub-)system, participant categories, etc. Again, the processes involved will be both bottom up and top down: very often the hearer already knows or expects what the relevant context and its properties are. In that case the observation and interpretation data need only be checked to the possible terminal categories of the social schema.

　　Note also that at this point we not only have a canonical analysis of the social situation, but also a representation of the *actual* interactional *strategy* of the speaker by which each utterance/turn is to be interpreted as a possible *optimal move* for the realization of a vague or precise goal. Again, we ignore the precise details of this process: here is another task of the model.

4.5. Having left many (also important) details aside we now have mentioned the major components in the comprehension part of the processing model. That is, we have discussed some properties of the first *stages* of that complex process of interpretation. We assumed that the various interrelated interpretations are represented in (episodic) *memory*. However, *what these*

representations look like has not been made explicit. We only assumed that
the representation of the utterances is a hierarchical propositional structure,
where macropropositions ('themes' or 'topics') are 'high' in the representation. The problem now is how the representation of the speech acts and
other social acts, as well as other properties of the communicative situation,
are represented and linked to the representation of the utterance. Is it the
case, for instance, that there is a complex representation of the action(s)
being performed by the speaker, e.g. 'giving an oral exam', 'asking questions',
in which the representation of the (semantic) structure of the actual
utterance is a functional part? Or do we have separate representations which
are only systematically linked at some points? At the moment this is merely
a theoretical problem for a cognitive model of comprehension, which might
be decidable if experiments can be designed to establish further data for
either one of these alternatives. Important though is the strong assumption
that the representations are *highly structured, hierarchically organized,* at
least *systematically* linked, and if possible organized according to existing
cognitive *schemata* of some kind (e.g. parts of some frame or script). Without
these assumptions it would, we think, not be possible for a hearer to organize
the amount of information which is relevant in the interpretation of moves in
dialogue sequences. Crucial in this respect is not only storage in memory but
especially *retrieval*, which constitutes a necessary condition for *appropriate
reactions*, i.e. for the *production of a next move.*

4.6. Although we possess little experimentally supported insight into processes of discourse and dialogue *production* — apart from some work in
psycholinguistics about sentence production — we may safely assume that
many of the general principles about complex information processing discussed above for comprehension also are valid for production. That is, a
discourse or dialogue fragment may be uttered after morphophonological
and syntactic formulation of underlying conceptual structures — taking into
account the various functions of words/sentences in the text and context.
Important for our discussion is that we should further assume that meanings
of sentences are planned under the *monitoring global plan* of a semantic
macrostructure or theme/topic. Of course this plan may be pre-programmed
or not, be rather stable for part or the whole of the dialogue, or not, may be
changed according to strategy, etc. The complexity of semantic coherence
makes such global conceptual planning necessary. At the same time it
establishes on the one hand a link with world knowledge (frames, scripts) and
on the other hand with the global plans of the social actions being carried out.

We may further assume that the global planning of actions is based on a complex motivational structure, involving decision making, intentions and purposes as determined by wishes, needs, knowledge and beliefs, attitudes and norms, etc. which cannot be discussed here. Given the global representation of certain (wished) goals and the representation of the (global) action to be performed to reach that goal, the action may be locally 'translated' into more specific (speech) acts, which are sequentially ordered and connected. Local data may of course change strategies and hence global plans.

Hence, whereas in comprehension global representations of meaning and action are gradually constructed in episodic memory after initial interpretation in STM, the production process first has global representations in episodic memory which by various processes (e.g. inverse macrorules and other semantic transformations) are given to working memory to be carried out. Again, the precise 'surface' details of speaking and acting will not concern us here: we first need a rough sketch of the model as a whole.

4.7. The comprehension and production processes do not simply 'follow' each other in a model of dialogue. Clearly, they are permanently interdependent. Representations resulting from comprehension are the input data for a process of action and utterance production. Important from a cognitive point of view are the striking *time limitations* in oral dialogue. A hearer cannot simply understand what is being said and what is being done, draw a number of relevant inferences, check upon his own wishes, etc., make decisions, form intentions and purposes for global plans of action or local executions thereof, etc. *after* the current utterance/doings. Answers mostly come right away, often in the middle of a current utterance. *Hence, comprehension and production planning must at least partly occur simultaneously*. This may be an obvious empirical fact, but the consequences for a cognitive model are not obvious at all. Short term memory is, as we observed, strictly limited in storage capacity. Although with the help of macrostructures and schemata of various kinds we are able to reduce and organize the complex information such that it can indeed be handled there, we have no insight yet in how *at the same time* details of action planning and its complex 'underlying' motivation may take place in the same working memory. This seems possible only if in each cycle of comprehension, information is not only linked to current world knowledge, but also to current other factors of the *cognitive set* (beliefs, attitudes, wants, interests, tasks, goals, etc.) and inferences drawn not only for the construction of what is being said/done by the speaker, but also what *must* be done by the hearer. Although schemata, fast strategies, macroplanning, etc. are relevant here too, it is still striking to witness that all this takes place in milliseconds. Compared to 'simple' syntactic analysis and production studied in psycholinguistics, the processes involved here seem vastly more complex, and in the near future we will at most be able to model some small fragments of it. A cognitive theory of dialogue is a challenge to psychology and artificial intelligence precisely because both production and comprehension, both language and action, and both cognitive and social contexts are involved, all being closely interrelated, and working under specific conditions of strategic, time-limited, interaction processes. This paper, therefore, is hardly more than a sketch of some of the future tasks and problems and hardly the beginning of possible answers or solutions.

University of Amsterdam

NOTES AND REFERENCES

The remarks in this paper about the structures of dialogues and conversation, are mostly due to results from current work in sociology, anthropology and linguistics about the analysis of conversation, e.g., as done by Sacks, Schegloff, Schenkein, Turner, Sudnow, Cicourel, Franck, and many others referenced in other papers contributed to this book.

Some more specific remarks about the strategical nature of conversational interaction are due to the work of Dorothea Franck, e.g., her thesis *Grammatik und Konversation* (University of Amsterdam, 1979).

For the theoretical background in the domain of discourse theory (text grammar and other theories), cf. e.g. Wolfgang Dressler (ed.) *Current Trends in Text Linguistics* (Berlin/New York: de Gruyter, 1977) and my *Text and Context* (London/New York: Longman, 1977), and the numerous references given in these two books.

The discussion of some of the assumed properties of a cognitive model of dialogue is an extension of my work, partly in collaboration with Walter Kintsch of the University of Colorado (Boulder), on discourse processing. For the current state of our processing model and for further references to (our and other's) earlier and further work in this domain, see: Walter Kintsch & Teun A. van Dijk, 'Toward a Model of Text Comprehension and Production', *Psychological Review* 85 (1978), 363–394.

The more general theoretical background in cognitive psychology and artificial intelligence constitutes the work by scholars such as Kintsch, Rumelhart, Frederiksen, Freedle, (Jean) Mandler, Meyer, Thorndyke, Bower, and others, on the one hand, and Minsky, Charniak, Schank and Abelson, and others, on the other hand, e.g. as appearing in the following recent books on discourse processing:

Roy O. Freedle (ed.), *Discourse Production and Comprehension* (Norwood, N.J.: Ablex, 1977).

Marcel Just & Patricia Carpenter (eds.), *Cognitive Processes in Comprehension* (Hillsdale, N.J.: Erlbaum, 1977).

Roger Schank & Robert Abelson, *Scripts, Plans, Goals and Understanding* (Hillsdale, N.J.: Erlbaum, 1977).

For relevant further references these books may be consulted. For an interdisciplinary treatment of global structures in discourse, interaction and cognition, as mentioned in this paper, see my *Macrostructures* (Hillsdale, N.J.: Erlbaum, 1980).

POSTSCRIPT (MAY 1983)

This paper was written nearly five years ago. In the meantime both conversation analysis and the psychology of discourse processing have undergone rapid developments, so that much of the general and programmatic observations in this paper could now be filled in with much more detail. Especially the *strategic* nature of both conversation and cognitive understanding can now be spelled out in more precise terms, as has been done in my book with Kintsch, *Strategies of Discourse Comprehension* (New York: Academic Press, 1983), in which also further details of the cognitive model have been specified which are relevant for the cognitive modelling of dialogical interaction. In that theory discourse monitoring (by macropropositions, goals, scripts, etc.) is not handled in STM, but by a separate Control System. Also, besides the proper representation of the discourse and the interaction in episodic memory, we now also postulate a separate *situation model*, i.e. an episodic representation of the fragment of the world a discourse is about, as well as a *communicative situation model*, which is a representation of the actual interaction context of the discourse/dialogue. This CSM is fundamental for the understanding of what 'goes on', e.g. socially, during conversation. CSM features previous dialogue experiences (of the same kind), and instantiated general schemata, such as specific dialogue scripts.

DIPLOMATIC COMMUNICATION

Our aim in the present paper is to analyze diplomatic communication from the viewpoint of a very comprehensive representation of the communication process. This representation will be obtained by a suitable combination of representations of this process due to Claude Shannon (the father of Information Theory), Roman Jakobson (with his well-known six-components-scheme of the communication process) and Colin Cherry (the famous specialist in Communication Engineering). We will obtain ten components of the communication process: the addresser, the addressee, the sender (or the transmitter), the receiver, the message, the referent (or the context), the channel, the code, the noise and the observer, with ten corresponding communicational functions: the expressive, the conative, the coding, the decoding, the poetic, the referential, the phatic, the metalinguistic, the noise function and the observer function. Each of these ten communicational functions deserves a special investigation. In the present paper, we accomplish this task only for some of them, a further paper being envisaged in order to continue this research. Although it is difficult to make a general hierarchy of these functions, our claim is that the most important communicational function, when dealing with diplomatic communication, is the phatic function. Thus, in some respect, diplomatic communication is similar to communication with children, where the phatic function has priority with respect to all other communicational functions.

Anatol Rapoport (*Fights, Games and Debates*, University of Michigan Press, Ann Arbor, 1960) has defined three types of conflicts which are considered by Karl W. Deutsch (*The Analysis of International Relations*, Foundations of modern political science series, Prentice-Hall, Inc., Englewood Cliffs, New Jersey, 1968, p. 112) as the three most important types of international conflict. This typology of conflicts is defined according to the various amounts and patterns of self-control and of mutual control of the actors involved in the conflict. In a *fight* type conflict the self-control and the mutual control of the actors decline rapidly. A *game* type conflict is characterized by strategy and by a rational control each actor maintains over his own moves, though not necessarily over their outcome. A *debate* type conflict is one in which the adversaries are changing each other's motives,

19

values, or cognitive images of reality. Fights tend to be automatic and mind-less, because the actions of each actor serve as starting-points for similar counteractions by the other actor. A dog meeting another dog in the street serves a good example in this respect. Unfortunately, arms races and confrontations of great powers follow this pattern. Strategic international conflicts are more rational than fights, but they still follow very often a line characterized by lack of cooperation and trust, like in the well known game of chicken or in the Prisoner's dilemma. The most rational form of conflict remain the debates. Terminology is misleading here, because the term *debate* in its technical sense as conceived by Rapoport and by Deutsch does not cover its everyday meaning. But, as Deutsch observes (op.cit. p. 131), debates in legislatures have a better chance of becoming genuine debates and so have negotiations among diplomats representing governments, and the debates of government representatives in international organizations. In contrast with the games, in a debate the outcomes most favorable to each, and perhaps jointly favorable to several or all of the parties concerned may yet have to be discovered, and if discovered, then presented for acceptance and agreement.

If genuine debates cannot be represented by game models, nor by fight processes, what is their real nature? "Adequate formal models for genuine debates have yet to be developed", as Deutsch observes (op.cit., p. 132). It is the purpose of the present paper to point out some aspects leading toward a better understanding of what international debates are and could be.

A world of peace is not a world without conflicts, but one where conflicts do not degenerate into fights and where the debate component of conflicts prevails over their strategic component. If the latter require only intelligence, the former is more exigent, being based on cooperation and trust, on research and knowledge. So, an acceptable combination of strategy and debate will be one where the strategy is not of a fixed-sum type, i.e., it is not one where the gains of any one actor necessarily must be always at the expense of other actors.

How can we start such an investigation? It is very important, in this respect, to take profit of the important research concerning communication and dialogue, from a linguistic, semiotic and informational point of view.

Human communication involves an *addresser* who is sending a *message* to an *addressee*. The message has a *meaning* and is sent through a *channel* by means of a *transmitter*, a code and a *receiver*. There is also a source of *noise* which may alter the message during its transmission. Such a description of the communication process is a combination of work done by Karl Bühler

('Die Axiomatik der Sprachwissenschaft', *Kant-Studien* **38** (1933), 19–90), Claude Shannon ('The Mathematical Theory of Communication', *Ball System Technical Journal* **27** (1948)), Roman Jakobson ('Linguistics and Poetics', in *Style in Language*, ed. Th.A. Sebeok, The M.I.T. Press, 1960) and Colin Cherry (*On Human Communication*, The M.I.T. Press, 1957–1966). The transmitter is sometimes identical to the addresser and the receiver is sometimes identical to the addressee (for instance during a direct talk between two individuals using a natural language); but they are different when an individual is sending a telegram to another individual: the transmitter in this case converts the message from a natural language into an artificial one, whereas the receiver proceeds in the opposite way. This change is obviously related to a change of channel. Different channels usually require different codes.

According to the above picture of human communication, various communicative functions are defined (see Roman Jakobson, op.cit.). Each of the constitutive factors of human communication determines a different function: the *referential* (or cognitive) function, oriented towards the meaning of the message, is concerned with the objective content of the message transmitted; the *expressive* function is focused on the addresser and aims a direct expression of the addresser's attitude towards what he is speaking about; the *conative* function is oriented towards the addressee (see, for instance, the vocative and the imperative); the *phatic* function serves to establish, to prolong or to discontinue communication, to check whether the channel works; the *metalinguistic* function permits the control of the functioning of the code; the *poetic* function is oriented towards the message (its intrinsic properties, for instance its metaphorical power). All these functions were described by Roman Jakobson (op.cit.). Let us observe that the metalinguistic function is concerned with three components of the communication process: the code, the transmitter and the receiver, whereas the poetic function is concerned with both the message and the noise. In a more detailed investigation we could define two more functions, oriented respectively towards the transmitter and the receiver. We can call them the *coding* and respectively the *decoding function*. They are very important during meetings of international organizations, where changing of codes and translation processes frequently occur. A third new function, the *noise function*, oriented towards the noise, could also be defined and investigated. The complexity and the importance of such a function for international communication follow from the fact that noise is not only what people usually understand by this common word; there is another noise, more abstract and more dangerous, consisting of various sources of ambiguity, imprecision, misunderstandings which a code may either contain in its internal structure or generate through its social use. We gave, in another paper ('A Dialogue about Dialogue', in the collective volume *Semiotics of Communication* no. 11 in the series KODIKAS/CODE, Gunter Narr Verlag, Tübingen, 1983) a detailed analysis of this abstract noise, so important in diplomatic talks and in international negotiations. The study of abstract noise has as one of its tasks the investigation of various types of distortion of a message and the possibility of diminishing them or avoiding them completely. An attempt of this type, for one of the simplest, but important types of communication – the smile – was made in our paper 'Smile and Suspicion' (in *Multimedial Communication*, vol. 1, editor Ernest W.B. Hess-Lüttich, Gunter Narr Verlag, Tübingen, 1981).

All the above communicative functions occur in any human communication process. But the way in which, and the extent to which, they occur are different for each type of communication. In a preceding paper ('Dialogue within International Organizations', *Revue Roumaine de Linguistique* 25 (1980), no. 5) we have analyzed the presence and the interrelation of these functions in the international dialogue. Crises occurring in this dialogue are directly related to the fact that one or several of these functions are blocked or distorted. Since the main functions (as we have argued in our papers quoted above) are here – in this order – the phatic, the referential, the conative and the metalinguistic function, the impossibility of developing them is one of the main sources of an international communication crisis. Why is the phatic function the most important? Because the fundamental condition of peace is the possibility of keeping the contact with all your partners, independently of their attitude and behavior. "Practice has proved that the capacity to keep the contact is *eo ipso* a way to substitute violent actions" says Mircea Malita (*Theory and Practice of Negotiations* (in Romanian), Editura politică, Bucharest, 1972, p. 150). The most dangerous symptom of deterioration of international relations is the ceasing of functioning of channels of international communication. Thus, keeping the peace is to a large extent the art of keeping at least some channels functioning at any given time.

But keeping the contact (with any price) may have some negative implications over the cognitive function of communication. Some requirements of a normal communication were formulated by H.P. Grice ('Logic and Conversation', in *Syntax and Semantics*, vol. 3, eds. P. Cole and J. Morgan, Academic Press, New York, 1975). He asserts a cooperative principle, having four aspects:

(1) *Quantity:* (1a) Make your contribution as informative as is required; (1b) Don't make it more informative than necessary;

(2) *Quality:* (2a) Try to make your contribution one that is true; (2b) Do not say what you believe to be false; (2c) Do not say that for which you lack adequate evidence;

(3) *Relatedness:* Be relevant;

(4) *Modality:* Be perspicuous; (4a) Avoid obscurity of expression; (4b) Avoid ambiguity; (4c) Be brief (avoid unnecessary prolixity); (4d) Be orderly. Some other norms, ethic, aesthetic and social, are also considered.

It is not difficult to observe that some of the above requirements, while improving the cognitive function of communication, may sabotage its phatic function. We have especially in view the requirements 1b, 4b, 4c. The most dangerous requirement is 4b. Ambiguity and generality are basic presuppositions of diplomatic talks, they make diplomatic life possible. Requirement 4c seems to work against one of the basic features of diplomatic communication: repetition. A lot of stereotypic expressions are again and again repeated, at various moments, in order to confirm that some principles, claims, requirements remain unchanged. Their presence may not be very relevant, but their absence would be significant. Repetitions have also an important role with respect to the phatic function of diplomatic communication. To what extent and in what form could ambiguity, generality, repetition be reduced without damaging other requirements of diplomatic communication? This question remains to be answered.

With respect to the conative function, difficulties occur when some wrong hypotheses with respect to the addressee are adopted. We may be wrong in various ways. We may not trust him when he deserves to be trusted (or conversely); we may attribute to him intentions and a capacity of sophistication other than the real ones; we may be wrong with respect to some semiotics of a higher order (the way in which the addressee appreciates the way in which the addresser is appreciating the addressee etc.). Johan Galtung's paper 'Expectations and Interaction Processes' (*Inquiry* 2 (1959), 213–234) and our already quoted paper about the smile as a basic way of contacting people are significant in this respect. Mistakes in this field generate, in a multiplicative way, other mistakes. A will to cooperate with the partner, a reciprocal tendency of trust, a better knowledge of the partner, a preoccupation to keep only those imprecisions of the message which are useful or which cannot be avoided (like some ambiguities of the smile) are a few of the possibilities for diminishing communication crises determined by a deterioration of the conative function. The game of chicken and the prisoner's dilemma are typical for this process of deterioration (see Karl W. Deutsch, loc.cit., pp. 118–121).

Of great importance are those communication crises which are determined by the deterioration of the metalinguistic function. We have to recall in this respect the "game without end" (Paul Watzlawicz, Janet Helmick Beavin, and Don D. Jackson, *Pragmatics of Human Communication*, Faber and Faber, London, 1968, pp. 232–236). Two persons decide to play a game consisting of the substitution of negation for affirmation and vice versa in everything they communicate to each other. Thus "yes" becomes "no", "I don't agree" means "I agree" and so forth. Once this game is under way, the players cannot easily revert to their former "normal" mode of communication. Indeed, the declaration "Let's stop playing" may mean "Let's continue". As the authors observe, to stop the game it would be necessary to step outside the game and so to have the possibility of communicating about it by means of a metamessage. Otherwise, the message "Let's stop playing" is undecidable, because it is meaningful both at the object level (as part of the game) and at the metalevel (as a message about the game), whereas the two interpretations are contradictory and there is no possibility of deciding on the one or the other meaning.

What could the players have done to prevent their dilemma? Watzlawick, Halmick Beavin and Jackson (loc.cit., pp. 234–236) discuss three possibilities: (1) The players, anticipating the possible need for communications about the game once the game has started, could have agreed that they would play it in English but would use French for their metacommunication; (2) The players could have agreed beforehand on a time limit of the game; (3) The players could take their dilemma to a third person with whom they have both maintained their normal mode of communication and have him rule that the game is over. The authors reject (1) (because in actual human communication it would be inapplicable, since there does not exist a metalanguage that is used only for communications about communication) and (2) (because the time-factor is not caught up in their game) and accept (3), in favor for which they bring, as a contrast, a new example, of the constitution of an imaginary country guaranteeing the right of unlimited parliamentary debate. But such a rule makes impossible any decision, by simply engaging in endless speeches. An amendment of the constitution is necessary, but the adoption of the amendment itself is susceptible of unlimited debate. But here, in contrast with the preceding example, there exists no mediator who would stand outside the rules of the game. The only possible change is a violent one.

Both the above examples illustrate what is called a *game without end*. We reach in this way the paradoxical dimension of some of today's global problems, where no outsider exists, capable of supplying what the system itself cannot generate: a change of its own rules. The contemporary world has to accept its self-referential situation: it must learn to cope with the para-doxical situation in which its object level is its own metalevel. This is one of the reasons why many analogies between politics and psychiatry fail; inter-national organizations may play the role of the outsider when dealing with local conflicts, with local confrontations and wars (even in this case, the therapeutic quality of the mediator's intervention is some times very low and the results are derisory), but they cannot remain outside "the rules of the game" when dealing with global confrontations. We are involved in a system which has to fight permanently against its condition of a game without end. The referential function as well as some other communicative functions are strongly affected by this situation. Some authors (see Colin Cherry, op.cit., p. 200) when describing the process of communication, introduce a supple-mentary actor: the observer. It is however important to point out the ambiguity of the observer. If I am the addresser and you are the addressee, then $they$ could be the observer. But the set A of individuals who are neither the addresser nor the addressee is heterogeneous. Some individuals in A may still be a part of the process of communication; for instance, they may belong to the context to which the message is referring, they may have a relevant influence when dealing with the pragmatic aspects of communication. Other individuals in A may look at the communication process by remaining outside of this process. For instance, Colin Cherry has in view an observer who is a researcher of the communication process. It only remains to see to what extent and in what conditions an observer could exist, fulfilling the condition of a mediator therapist. Otherwise, the communication process has to be its own therapeutist.

Many other sources of paradoxical situations occur in international com-munication processes. As Watzlawick, Helmick Beavin, and Jackson observe (loc.cit., p. 226),

"in human relations, all prediction is connected in one way or another with the pheno-menon of trust. . . . There is in the nature of human communication no way of making another person a participant in information or perceptions available exclusively to oneself. The other can at best trust or distrust, but he can never $know$".

This situation is a source of paradox. The drama of many human choices lies in the fact that, like in the situations of the Prisoner's Dilemma type, the safest strategy is not the most reasonable; but the latter can be reached only under conditions of mutual trust and this is just what is missing. But once reached, the "safest strategy" becomes unreasonable and the partners realize that another strategy is more reasonable; once the latter strategy is reached, the former seems again better. Such strategies of a higher order are beyond the possibilities of today's mathematical theory of games, but they are organically related to the pragmatic dimension of the social life.

Modern Speech Acts Theory developed by Austin, Searle and other authors considers the act of communication as a social action, where the interactive component is essential. According to this line of thought, Jürgen Habermas (*Communication and the Evolution of Society*, Beacon Press, Boston, 1979, p. 68) distinguishes four domains of reality (the world of external nature, the world of society, the world of internal nature and the language) and, with respect to the first three of them, three corresponding modes of communication: cognitive (objectivating attitude), interactive (conformative attitude) and expressive (expressive attitude). Whereas the first mode corresponds to the referential function and the third mode to the expressive function of communication, the second mode is mainly related to the conative function. The nature of the interactive mode of communication decides the nature of participants involved in the pragmatic dimension of the communication; particularly, it decides the possibility and the nature of an outsider. But the communicative action is only one of the two types of social action, the other being for Habermas (loc.cit., p. 209) the strategic action.

In Anatol Rapoport's terms, when dealing with conflicts, the communicative action corresponds mainly to the debate, whereas the strategic action is rather a game, although it contains, as a particular limiting case, the fight. But just as Rapoport pleads for the superiority of debates with respect to games and of the latter with respect to fights, Habermas shows the moral advantage of the communicative versus the strategic action. In the former a basis of mutually recognized validity claims is presupposed, whereas this is not the case in the latter. Habermas speaks of a *communicative attitude*, which allows us to reach a direct understanding oriented to validity claims, and of a *strategic attitude*, which, by contrast, permits only an indirect understanding via determinative indicators. The communicative action may be of two types: it can be oriented either to reaching understanding or to a consensual action (where agreement about implicitly raised validity claims can be *presupposed* as a background of consensus by reason of common definitions of the situations; such agreement, as Habermas observes, is supposed to be *arrived at* in action oriented to reaching understanding, when strategic elements may be employed under the proviso that they are meant to lead to a direct understanding). Habermas distinguishes two types of consensual action: *the proper consensual action*, where it is naively supposed that implicitly raised validity claims can be vindicated (or made immediately plausible by way of question and answer) and the *discourse*, where, by contrast, the validity claims raised for statements and norms are hypothetically bracketed and thematically examined. (As in the proper consensual action, the participants in discourse retain a cooperative attitude).

Following Habermas, the strategic action can be *open* (we would rather say *explicit*) or *latent*. Latently strategic actions can be of two types: manipulation and systematic distortion. Whereas in the latter at least one of the participants deceives *himself* about the fact that the basis of consensual action is only apparently being maintained, in the former the manipulator deceives at least one of the *other* participants about his own strategic attitude, in which he *deliberately* behaves in a pseudoconsensual manner.

It would be interesting to go deeper in comparing this approach with that of Rapoport, but their common point is anyway the superiority of the communicative attitude with respect to the strategic attitude.

What about the other six communicative functions? We will not discuss here the expressive, the coding and the decoding functions. But let us say a few words about the poetic, the noise and the observer function of international communication.

The stereotypes of the international communication may create some obsessions of ready-made expressions; attention could be so focused on some linguistic strings in divorce from their meaning. This is a way in which the poetic function could develop in a direction which is opposite to the common sense, intuitive understanding of poetic features. But there is another tendency, which works against the orientation towards the message. International communication is to a great extent realised by means of translation from some natural languages into other such languages. In this way, international messages are the result of some invariance properties of various linguistic structures through transformations by translation. What remains valid in the international communication is what succeeds in resisting translation. But this invariant part belongs less to the message and more to its meaning, its context, its referent. An important direction in modern poetry is incompatible with such a divorce between a message and its meaning. In this respect, we could say that international communication is like mathematics: every idea may be expressed in infinitely many ways. In other words, its synonymy is infinite. We could imagine that international communication is realized by means of an abstract language, which is the common denominator of various natural languages. But this abstract language is only a fiction. Each individual participating in the international communication process is using a concrete natural language which inevitably carries, with any message, a world of connotations, which could be a source of alienation and betraying, but which could also be a possibility of adaptation to some national realities. So, poetic function of international communication is an equivocal phenomenon, whose effects should be kept within reasonable limits; their deterioration could lead to some crises which deserve to be investigated.

The noise function is related to various obstacles the receiver and especially the addressee may meet in decoding, or understanding a message. One of the most interesting forms of noise in international communication is what we could call, with a generic term, *imprecision*. It may take various forms, like generality, ambiguity, fuzziness, randomness, variability, undecidability, incoherency, lack of cohesion, antinomy, ineffability, ignorance, mystery, openness etc. Only after having a typology of forms of imprecision can we proceed to an attempt to understand the equivocal role of imprecision in international communication, its dangers and its advantages. We intend to devote a special paper to such a typology. There is a tendency to use the term *ambiguity* for any type of imprecision. Lack of clarity and rigor in this respect does not permit the understanding of the way in which imprecision is both an obstacle and an advantage. Grice's requirement to avoid ambiguity should be understood as an invitation to avoid any type of imprecision. But there is a field where imprecision (under certain forms and to some extent) is a condition of validity; such a field is poetry and, more general, any artistic activity. The main forms of poetic imprecision are openness and ineffability. This tendency to imprecision is balanced by another, opposite, tendency to precision. Let us recall Mallarmé: the poetic work generates imprecise feelings, but the means it is using are precise. Indeed, openness and ineffability are concerned with the perception of poetry, with the way in which the reader understands the poetic work. It could seem paradoxical that openness and ineffability increase when the precision of some poetic techniques is improved. For instance, prosodio rigor is a way to improve poetic imprecision. With all these facts in mind, let us try to understand how deliberate imprecision could improve international communication and how the lack of imprecision could block this communication and lead to communicational crisis.

One of the main sources of imprecision in international communication is the asymmetry between its semantic and its pragmatic component. Whereas the semantic component is oriented towards a high degree of generality, the pragmatic one is subjected to an opposite tendency, towards testing some very particular circumstances. A typical example in this respect is the definition of aggression, adopted in December 1974, at the XXIXth session of the UN General Assembly. This definition distinguishes seven types of activity having the status of an aggression; they correspond to a large extent to the common intuition of this phenomenon. It would be difficult to imagine how one could disagree with such a description of an aggression. However, if from a semantic viewpoint things are very clear and non-susceptible of controversy (at least in their meaning if not in their formulation), they are less clear from a pragmatic viewpoint. As soon as we have to test whether a particular, concrete activity is of one of the considered seven types labeled as aggression, we have to face great difficulties. Where are they located? Let us take for instance the last one of the seven types. It deals with the situation when a state is sending some armed groups, some irregular forces or some mercenaries to perform some acts of force against another state, and these acts are of such a gravity that they are equivalent to one of the preceding six types of activity labeled as aggression. Such a description involves many gradual properties and actions such as "some", "armed groups", "acts of force", "is sending", "equivalence to one of the preceding types" etc. It is very difficult to test them because it is not specified for what degree (of fuzziness) such properties or actions are considered as real. Such a specification would be in contradiction with the gradual nature of the considered entities. If a minimum of the degree of fuzziness could be given, beginning with which property would be considered as real, then this property could be transformed in a nongradual, i.e. in an exact property. Other forms of imprecision like probability, ambiguity etc. can also be identified, but we will not do it now. However, it is important to stress the tension existing here between the semantic and the pragmatic component of the communication. The need to reach an agreement leads to an increase in imprecision of various types (especially generality, fuzziness and ambiguity). But this fact deteriorates the pragmatic component, which becomes less and less operational. It would be interesting to investigate how and what types of semantic imprecision increased during the long talks about the definition of an aggression. Two processes take place here, one of transfer and the other of compensation between semantics and pragmatics. When semantics improves, (i.e. when partners are nearer to an agreement), pragmatics becomes less operational. At the same time, some semantic imprecision is extended to the pragmatic component. When we want to improve the latter, we deteriorate the former. This is a dilemma of international communication. The needed imprecision comes in conflict with the unwanted imprecision.

Let us now say a few words about the observer function. It is essentially related to the metalinguistic function, but they are not to be identified (a similar problem arises with respect to the conative and the phatic function, which are closely related, but not identical). The metalinguistic function is fulfilled, to a large extent, by the addresser and the addressee, by the transmitter and the receiver. In the examples we recalled above, it was showed that some social systems may sometimes be unable to carry some metalinguistic functions they need. Such a task is transferred then to an observer who is outside the considered system. The problem we raised was whether such an observer could exist when dealing with global systems and our answer was negative. Like readers of poetry, who belong to the poetic work as an organic component of it, participating in the infinite creativity of art (the openness of modern art), the observers of the contemporary global processes belong to these processes and influence their orientation. We have to learn to cope with this paradox, we cannot avoid it and we cannot solve it. This is an objective limitation of our world, just as the impossibility of the set of all sets is one of our logical limitations. The observer function is then a permanent alternation of attempts and failures, because we always have the tendency to overcome our global closed system and we always fail to do it. Maybe this is one of the reasons why a dominant imperialistic strategy today is to avoid a big, global war, by replacing it by several small wars. There is then a hope to keep or to recuperate the observer function as a therapeutic one. Such attempts to transfer to an observer some basic metalinguistic functions deserve to be investigated, in order to understand to what extent our closed global system may contain some partial open systems. A particular topic in this respect is the role of international organizations as therapeutic observers.

International relations are to a large extent of a semiotic nature. All case studies are relevant in this respect. Let us take, for instance, Edward E. Azar's paper 'Conflict Escalation and Conflict Reduction in an International Crisis: Suez, 1956' (in *Analyzing International Relations,* eds. W.D. Coplin and Ch.W. Kegley, Jr., Praeger Publishers, New York, 1975, pp. 182-204). Let us quote Azar (op.cit., p. 183):

International actors tend to express their policies toward one another in the form of verbal and/or physical *signals.* An international signal is an inter-national *event* which has the following characteristics. On a specific *date* a specific *actor* directs an activity toward a specific *target* regarding an *issue* of mutual concern. The date is the day on which the signal is reported by a reputable and publicly available source; actors and targets are nations, organizations, or movements which have attained international or regional significance; activities are verbal or physical actions, reactions, and interactions; and issue-areas include the items about which actors and targets interact or signal one another.

Azar used 835 signals exchanged between Egypt and its opponents (Britain, France, Israel) from July 26, 1956 (the day Nasser nationalized the Suez Canal Company), through January 11, 1957 (about the time when all occupying forces had either withdrawn or were about to withdraw from Egyptian territory). We had the opportunity to examine the (unpublished) *Codebook of the conflict and peace data bank (COPDAB): A computer-assisted approach to monitoring and analyzing international and domestic events* (The University of North Carolina, Chapel Hill, 1971), which was one of the main sources in identifying the 835 signals and we discovered that about 80% of these signals were of a linguistic nature. So, a semiotic approach is strongly recommended. Even the nonlingustic signals are endowed with semiotic functions.

An important task remains to combine the strategic (game-theoretic) with the semiotic approach of international communication. We hope to attempt it in a further paper.

University of Bucharest

ALFRED H. STANTON†

INSIGHT AND SELF-OBSERVATION: THEIR ROLE IN THE ANALYSIS OF THE ETIOLOGY OF ILLNESS

1. ON READING MINDS

The subheading 'On Reading Minds,' is not without risk in a symposium of experts on schizophrenia, particularly if it suggests a cookbook set of directions. However, the way one reads minds is clear; it is similar to the way one reads books. One listens to what someone else has to say and hears what that person has in mind; not everything in his mind, and not necessarily accurately what is in his mind, but something of what he has in mind. This is a wonderful and improbable set of phenomena; that thoughts are quickly transferred back and forth between two organisms in a universe which, at first glance, would not seem to be a likely place for such an occurrence.

The phenomenon has not been overlooked. The special character of the humanities — those disciplines which develop upon the basis of understanding human communication: history, linguistics, the social sciences (including psychology) — distinguishing them from the natural sciences, continues to be a source of much concern and study. The most recent in our area of interest is perhaps that of Ricoeur [1] in his analysis of the nature of proof in Freud. The humanities represent systematic disciplines aimed at the fullest possible understanding of what people say, write, or paint; in contrast, the methods of the natural sciences are heavily based upon explanation — developing and testing hypotheses and theories which provide causal and predictive information.

Ricoeur emphasizes that we must use both methods of analysis together, even though various scholars have tried to assert that they are discontinuous, a non-intersecting language game; indeed, the usual American solution is to divide what an interviewer does into two parts — a scientific one and the clinical one, the clinical taking usually a second-class status. While the psychoanalyst may insist that his psychoanalysis is indeed research, he often does so with an inner reservation, and he is not likely to be widely accepted in this role. The systematic elaboration of the semantic precision, organization, stability and coherence of generalizations — which would move the individual experience of understanding someone toward a more stable and generalizable knowledge — has indeed proceeded within psychoanalysis, but the process is discouragingly complex.

L. Vaina and J. Hintikka (eds.), Cognitive Constraints on Communication, 33–47.

Ricoeur emphasizes that even Freud found himself using increasingly unsatisfactory metaphors when he arrived at an intersection between the elaboration of his analysis of understanding and the provision of explanation with its cause and effect formulations; his metapsychology never did illuminate his technical papers. But, however unsatisfactory, the metaphors were unavoidable for Ricoeur, uniting the processes of understanding and of explanation in an ongoing complex process of "interpretation."

There are two reasons for the appropriateness of this topic. First, the contributions of Ted and Ruth Lidz are excellent examples of clinical and investigative application of the methods of the humanities in a medical discipline. In a singularly clear way, the work of Lidz, Fleck and Cornelison changed the conception of schizophrenia. There had been smoke before, of course — discussions of the mothers of schizophrenics, the relation of the disorder to social disorder in general, and social class relations were being established, but with the Lidz work it was clear that the family, not one particular member, was the proper subject — that the family structure and the structure of the patient's disorder were systematically related to each other in ways which could not be seen unless one looked at it the way they did. Experimental methods were not only impossible — had they been possible they would have been wrong. Their work was a significant underpinning of a whole new method of treatment which has grown in importance, and their work is known to everyone, even to those who are so resistant to the humanities that they cannot bring themselves to examine exactly what the Lidz study reported.

A second reason for discussing the issue is its pertinence to the topic of research in psychotherapy, a field where many think of research method versus the clinical. There has recently been a spate of discussion about why the practice of psychotherapy has benefitted so little from research in psychotherapy. It is the case that most psychotherapists believe that what they have learned about patients comes primarily from clinical rather than from organized research efforts. If one pushes hard for more objective procedures in psychotherapy, he will be certainly thought of by many of his colleagues as abandoning psychotherapy, at least to some extent. And psychotherapists do tend to stick to their work, and their convictions. At the same time, those students most emphatically skeptical of the effects of psychotherapy on "research" grounds seek to find indirect ways to recommend it clinically.

This is not a sign of chaos, gullibility or cupidity. The coherence and intelligibility of the events of psychotherapy and of the emotional disorders studied in psychotherapy act as continuing reinforcers for psychotherapists. After it was first shown that schizophrenic patients were understandable, and something of how to do it, psychotic patients have never been left alone in the same matter of fact way they were before. This is, in principle, the same kind of coherence which Lidz showed in the families he studied, which Roman Jakobson brought to the distinctive features of phonemes, Champollion to the grasp of the nature of hieroglyphic writing, or Turner on the influence of the frontier on American life — it is the observation of a coherent structure, in every case derived from the human understanding of the scholar.

2. INSIGHT

Insight, the goal of psychoanalysis and of much of dynamic psychotherapy, condenses into itself both the values of therapy and those of research. The identification and analysis of relationships, of structures previously un-recognized, represent insight, for instance, into family structure and psychotic limitation. I should like, however, to restrict the term insight, here, sharply, to any new grasp *by the patient* of his own inner life, reserving other terms for anything learned by the therapist or others. Insight, in this sense, is particularly pertinent to our topic of schizophrenia. But the concept has a long history in psychology, especially among the gestalt psychologists (Wertheimer) and in psychoanalysis. For some time the attaining of insight was not often mentioned directly in psychoanalytic writing, but was indicated, for instance, in the term to "analyze" a symptom — leaving unspecified whether "analyzing" meant the analyst's putting a problem together, telling the patient, having the patient hear and accept it, have the patient put together some observations about himself, or some uncertain mixture of these.

Refinements in understanding insight have grown since the thirties, a growth which has been reviewed by Richfield [2] and by Hatcher. [3] The old problem of intellectual insight (where the patient decides something *must* be so on logical grounds) and the complementary confusing concept of emotional insight have been replaced on the basis of Bertrand Russell's [4,5] distinction between knowledge by acquaintance (where one knows something by direct cognitive grasp of it) and knowledge by description (where something is defined or described for one). Insight, of the acquaintance sort, is never "admitted", "confessed", or "proclaimed"; it is recognized, seen, taken as something one has always known, or should have always known; although it may be lost by the next hour, it is likely to return. It is non-controversial. In contrast, apparent insight (based on knowledge by description) may result from a patient's more or less thoughtful conclusion something must be so. Insight may occur dramatically, but much more often it is progressive and gradual. A few examples will illustrate:

> A sophisticated male patient in analysis had been stopped by a policeman for speeding on the way to his hour. Even later than he would have been, he was furious, a not unusual state for him regarding the police. As he was expressing himself violently, he started the sentence, "God, how I hate them" but it came out, fluently, "God, how I love them". A several minute pause, while he seemed to be thinking furiously, led to his recognizing his long-standing, ambivalent, not purely hostile, wishes, not only regarding the police, but proctors at school, and other authorities of importance. The analyst was substantially silent. This type of event is a somewhat unusual moment of insight.

> After months of talking often about his sister as a demanding and overbearing woman spreading gloom about her, a sophisticated male patient remarked to himself one hour: "You know, I guess I really don't like her," said with a mild tone of wonder and surprise. After recognizing his dislike, he proved much more able to deal with her, changing his automatic avoidance tactics, and recognizing, again with some surprise, that she was chronically depressed. (His choice of the phrase "I really don't like her" rather than speaking of his "hostility" or his "angry feelings" help to show that this type of insight was by acquaintance, not an intellectualized conclusion about himself).

> A year after an acute schizophrenic panic in which a patient drove up and down the streets of Boston in terror of either her or her family's being shot by foreign agencies, the patient had completely cleared except for recurrent periods of short-lived suspicions, each of which she quickly brought to the hour. She had broken down in the service of the state, and her fees were being paid by the state. She first connected the fears with times when the continuity of the treatment was interfered with, a discovery she made away from the hour and then brought in to review it, as it were, and see if it passed inspection. The fears

were related to the ever-present anxiety that something would interfere with the treatment and she would lose her therapist and have an unmanageable recurrence. Two months later, she brought the same problem back, saying she had found that the fears were also related to money — not only did she need money for her treatment, but she had in fact been very poor as a child, and had had many situations where she could have quite reasonably feared the loss of her father; her mother had died when the patient was at an earlier age.

These examples illustrate the variation of incidents of insight; they will also suggest certain ideal-type images of insight are never so and are often misleadingly expressed. Insight is never complete; it encompasses only one area in a patient's experience although a sense of wholeness may accompany a formulation. Insights vary in importance and in depth — Bibring's clarification may lead to a superficial (not necessarily unimportant) insight if it refers to oneself. I recently reported [6] a hierarchy of depths of insight into illness which is being used as the basis for a scale to measure it in typescripts of interviews with psychotic patients.[1]

One especially important aspect of the development of insight is the way the patient manages the discovery. We have oversimplified the patient's mental activity in a way which is all too usual. A patient's most effective use of insight, indeed its actual occurrence, depends upon his being able to observe his own mind effectively. This entails some distance from himself conceptually, some reasonably discriminating critical facility, some awareness of things missing, and of potential relationships in his mind, some interest, and a modicum of self-confidence. It is in this area that some of the most critical issues in the psychotherapy with schizophrenic patients occur, and differently than among psychoneurotic patients.

A "post-psychotic" patient came into the office in a frenzy of despair and agitation — he noted that months before he had "wanted to kill Julie", his girlfriend. What was he to do when he was terribly dependent upon her, loved her, and still was this sort of man? Questioning showed that he had been reflecting upon his earlier delusional fears of his family's being killed, including the girlfriend, and had assumed that this meant he had wanted her dead. Questioning and reflection on his fears of the rest of his family's deaths led to the observation that this was another manifestation of an anxiety over the control of his own mind.

The silence of the analyst with the patient angry at the policeman was possible only because the general condition of the patient and the therapist's knowledge of it made it almost certain that he was managing his insight by altering his self-conception. But he could have been pictured as wondering who put that thought into his head, or into his mouth, or that he was homosexual and hopeless (with suicidal thoughts developing), or a host of other possibilities.

When a patient achieves an insight, either with the therapist's interpretation or without it, it is instructive to note quite carefully how the patient deals with the information. He may agree with a therapist's interpretation, nod politely, and go on. He may admire the therapist's presentation and go on. He may agree, with some reservations, and go on. He may occasionally say "Oh, yeh", pause, and then go on. He may blush, stammer, and "confess". He may receive the interpretation with some appreciation as his due. He may openly or quietly resent the implications of the comments, he may withdraw into a suspicious regard of the therapist, and all but ask what he is doing here, etc. Each of these behaviors might be explored — they only hint at his management of the insight. It is unusual for a therapist to catalogue the patient's reception of an idea as carefully as he does what led up to his own remarks. If he does, he uses the remarkably general and vague criterion, does it lead to new material. How soon? How is new material different from changing the subject? Few therapists settle as a matter of course into an unreserved study with the patient of his reception of the interpretation, of what the interpretation signified to him, what it brought to mind, does he think it is so, and if so what difference does this make to his thinking about himself and the treatment. And, by the way, exactly what did the patient understand the therapist to say? If the patient grasped only half of what was said, and got that partly wrong, it would be understandable since, if the patient is psychotic, he suffers a combination of difficulty in cognitive function, often great social anxiety, and a moderate to profound disinterest in what is said, be this for defensive or other reasons. Understanding how the patient manages new information is usually overlooked in the literature but is often a most rewarding topic to explore.

One patient, some months out of a paranoid break, had profitably noted her tendency to defend particular beliefs as if they were challenged when she was in therapy. She began to use this to gain perspective, and many times aborted what she feared might otherwise be an overwhelming return of psychosis. She had attended this process aspect of her reception of alternative suggestions with persistent, up-hill hard work, which gained her mastery over this particular defense, and incidentally over the formation of delusions.

Pressman [7] has emphasized the implications of the earlier heavy reliance upon free association in psychoanalysis as if insight were simply given, came from someplace in a finished and final form, and was then used. This picture of a spontaneous and more or less effortless non-cognitive process, he believes, is inadequate; in fact it has never been the way patients understood themselves. He describes a "cognitive attitude", indicated by the style of the patient in which the patient is scanning his mental content while reporting it to the analyst and at the same time integrating his newly discovered material, combining his experiencing ego and integrating ego, primary process and secondary process. He emphasizes the patient may need to be taught, not only free association but also how to understand himself and his associations, how to increase his attention and his grasp not only of what he has said but of what its implications and contexts are. Pressman's emphasis is upon the indispensability of education and cognitive working into the insight for maximum effect.

Pressman's recommendations are timely and accurate for psychoanalysis — they are, however, particularly appropriate for our consideration of psychotherapy with schizophrenic patients, where ego processes counted upon by the therapist with psychoneurotic patients cannot be taken for granted. The ways psychotic patients observe themselves are often different from those of non-psychotic patients in many unpredictable ways. They include particular difficulties in taking emotional distance from oneself, unexpected rigidities in interpretation, obscure difficulties in recognizing contexts which lead to failures in appreciating figurative remarks — all have their effects upon patients' interpretations of themselves as well as of others. They can only be suggested here, but their frequency and importance underscore the value of noting the way patients incorporate new insights.

3. SELF REPRESENTATION

The special difficulties in interpretation mean, necessarily, resulting difficulties in self representation.

Here I must pause for semantic clarification needed since crucial terms are used differently by experts, and may lead to different conclusions because of these different usages. These usages also have significant effects clinically and in the understanding of clinical phenomena as sources of scientific information.

Much difficulty stems from the early psychoanalytic use of "ego" interchangeably with "self" and with "self representation." As the concepts are now used most helpfully, the two concepts are from entirely different levels of discourse. The ego is a pattern of processes controlling perception, action, defense, thought — a structure in the mind — while the "self representation" is the (reflexive) image each person has of his own person. The "self" *is* one's own person, everything of one's own person. This usage follows that of Hartmann [8], Jacobson [9], Sandler and Rosenblatt [10], and contrasts sharply with usages of Kohut [11] (who seems to have proposed a new department of the mind to be called the "self"), with usage by Sullivan (who uses the term "self" and "self system" in an entirely different way) and with many others. Hartmann's usage has the advantage of clarity and consistency, and unravels a number of tangles in the theory of narcissism.

Self observation then means only the perception, study, observation of some aspect of the self, of one's own person. While usefully heightened in some circumstances — psychotherapy for instance — it may be assumed to be going on a great deal of the time in a less focused way, contributing to the development of a self representation — the (reflexive) representation of one's self to one's self — an interpretive construct, more or less clear, more or less consistent, more or less a unit, more or less satisfying. Some aspects of the representation of the self are subjectively felt to be more real, solid, fixed, more essentially part of oneself, whereas others are felt as less part of one's core self. One's subjective impression of the homogeneity of one's self representation is usually high, but psychotic experience often jars this confidence.

The self representation is not only a part of one's perceptions, it has a motor function. It is part of the mechanism of control of behavior and of shaping it, so that we speak and act according to what we believe ourselves to be; personal integrity may refer precisely to the degree to which we perceive our behavior to be in accord with our background assumption of what we are. In psychotherapy we take for granted that the patient expresses himself in how he says something as well as in what he says, but the place of the self representation in this is rarely made explicit. A recent study by Fontana and Klein [12] showed the way a prolonged reaction time, classically the deficit of schizophrenic patients, could be eliminated in a setting appropriate to a different type of self presentation. I believe we would profit greatly by much more attention to the self representation of the patient, as such, and certainly not by confusing it with the patient's self.

Schizophrenic patients tend to oversimplify their self representation.

Observation and full acceptance of contrasting or contradictory themes of experience in oneself is a luxury usually of complex and generally sophisticated minds, where contrast can be counterpoint, not inconsistency or insanity, where discontinuities can be sources of interest and potential growth, not threats of tearing the fabric of the mind apart. This state of mind was not available to the patient who knew he wanted to kill his girlfriend, and for many others who can hardly wait to notice the actual complex content of their mind when threats arise.

But therapists often — usually? — reinforce patients in this type of misleading interpretation. We so usually use the shorthand "ego" or "self" for self representation, even to ourselves, that we often compound anxiety with confusion for our patients.

> A patient slowed in his therapy, with progressively less to say. Finally the therapist said, "Are you afraid of my going away on vacation?" The patient reluctantly said he was — and lapsed into silence. After reassuring him that he, the therapist, would be back, the matter ended.

The therapist had actually misled this patient, I believe, by oversimplifying his experience. He overlooked the degree to which the patient wanted not to be afraid of the vacation, what his fear meant to him, and had ended by simply underlining to the patient that he was dependent.

The occurrence of a conflicting wish in partial awareness is often interpreted by "What you really want to do is to get even with me" or whatever — the statement being made that the patient "really wants" only one of the two or more wishes at conflict in his mind. On a broader scale, the continuing activity during psychosis of the residual intact ego of psychotic patients took many years to identify, and the degree to which patients work with their therapists even while "out of contact" is only still partly known and accepted.

> The patient mentioned earlier who had recurrent controllable fears, usually mild and transient but reminiscent of, and fitting in with her earlier paranoid delusions, learned to note her own motivation in defending the suspicions and their reasonableness. Although at first discouraged over what she could do about recurring fears of this sort which required, she thought, the physician or her boyfriend to banish them — she came to note her own argumentativeness and used it as a cue to examine the origin of the fear. While she has succeeded only once or twice, the maneuver itself now often suffices to banish the fears.

This represents a great increase in the awareness of, tolerance of, and use of, the complexity of her mind, a complexity quite inconceivable to her while sicker. The change shows insight at work.

One special relationship should be mentioned: insight, inasmuch as it is new, is likely to occasion some surprise and, corollary to this, to mean a change in the self representation of some significance. A new feature of the self can be brought out by the patient in relationship to it. These are all aspects of the patient's readiness for insight and for interpretations. Ego activity is more handicapped, and in different areas, with psychotic patients than is often obvious or expected. Testing by finding out what the patient's response to one's interventions is an obvious and practical way of watching the growth in the patient's competence in self observation, in cognitive processing of insight, in maturity and sophistication of self criticism, in freedom of exploring alternative consequences, imagery, and possibilities — and, together, they indicate his level of competence in managing insight.

The absence of information in the case of patients treated with early deep interpretations about the patient's attitudes toward the interpretations shows one aspect of the therapist's oversimplification. His attention to only one side — the primitive fantasy or image — and not to its meaning to the patient, implies, I believe, that much of this "insight" (in the patient) is either a panic-driven incorporation of the therapist's apparent ideas, or actually a special form of schizophrenic intrusion or delusion which may replace delusional self interpretations.

4. THE VALUE OF INSIGHT IN EXPANDING KNOWLEDGE

I should return here to the nature of the self representation. We must assume that, however, "genuine", "honest" or "accurate" a patient's picture of himself, it cannot be more than a very partial and specially oriented image. Not only is there no possible "complete" self representation, it is *systematically* incomplete — no matter how deep the insight, it will never reveal that the patient has a cerebellum although the cerebellum plays a part in the overall activity which comprises his person. A highly informative account of the image of the mind was offered some years ago at the Ernest Jones Lecture in London by Richard Wollheim [13]. He concludes with some considerations on the spatial image of the mind, its having an inner and an outer aspect, borders, and other geographical characteristics, which are relevant to such imagery as that of Federn (and others) regarding "ego boundaries." Certainly patients do have various disorders in their representation of the boundaries of their self, and the elements which give rise to or maintain these alterations in self imagery are, potentially, open to patients to study. But are these "boundaries" themselves real, aside from the patient's representation of them? When splitting occurs, what is split? The patient's representation of himself, or his mind, or him, his "ego" — or simply his image of himself?

This type of question cannot be answered categorically and immediately. To accept as fact an honestly achieved insightful reorganization of the patient's self representation is to ignore that it still represents, as it were, only the opinion of the patient, however honest, and probably only one of several possible opinions at that. To discard it as "mere opinion" is to ignore its observable effect on the patient's behavior as real, its consistent immediacy as "real" to the patient, and, almost certainly, ignore selectively those aspects of the patient's report which do not fit our own pre-conceptions, retaining those which do. What is required is that the place of the insight in the patient's experience, or in his disorder if you will, be as accurately outlined as possible, using both humanistic and natural science types of analysis. To ignore the first is to risk missing the problem, or analyzing a miscast problem; to ignore the last is to risk being lost in a nightmare which just possibly might turn out to be psychotic.

5. EXPLANATION, UNDERSTANDING, INTERPRETATION

Ricoeur [14] examines this apparently dichotomous dilemma in some detail. The search for understanding (Verstehen of Dilthey) characteristic of the humanities — and of the psychological side of psychiatry — rests upon our ability to found understanding on our ability to transfer ourselves into another's psychic life on the basis of signs the other gives us, but it must be elaborated beyond this to become part of a science, into an organized body of knowledge, with some stability and coherence.

Specifically, in the study of action of persons, the problem of the nature of causation and of motives for action become significant. Analysis of causation has rested heavily upon Hume's type of "cause" where the cause must be logically separable from the rest of the effect — as a match is from the cigarette. The interpretation of violence in Freudian terms fits with this definition fairly well — what incited the behavior, what drives "caused it"; in contrast, many actions — of which a move in chess is offered as a clear example — have to be analyzed in terms of their "reasons": which are not separable from the action itself. Most human behavior falls between these two extremes — the tacit concept of cause is more Aristotelian than from

Hume since the cause is formally a part of the action — a motive, a sense of desirableness or a similar concept.

For our purposes what this entails is the necessity of retaining analytic abilities of both sorts — explanatory and understanding — and to note that where they meet, they need both to be submitted to an interpretation which is not the prisoner of one or the other form of thought.

A hypothetical example will permit clarification of the nature of the interpretation required. One type of emotional disorder is featured by a child's compulsively repeating, in "play", some terrible experience he has had; the experience, usually a single one but of hideous intensity, is reenacted by the child, in the usual interpretation, in order to experience the event as under his own control, and often therefore to make it come out differently and better, at least in fantasy. The recall and reporting of the experience may often be followed by a rapid disappearance of the behavior; there is usually a convincing similarity between the original experience and the reexperienced fantasy.

It would be quixotic to discard this insight into the child's disorder and its cause until one could subject some twenty children to the experience and a matched group of twenty to a similar but not unpleasant experience and examine the outcome. It would even be misleading to ask whether, if the event had not occurred, the child still might have had an emotional disorder — he would not have one of the particular form he did. "Understanding" is the principle tool of the investigator in this case and any "explanatory" description of repression, the nature of a traumatic experience and its effects will have to *include* the fruits of our "understanding" in its material. The relation between the two types of analysis of the cause cannot be reduced, even in thinking about it, to such empirical formulae as how much of the variance is accounted for by one or the other; their relations are not of this alternative type.

It would be dangerous also, if not quixotic, to ignore the manifold possibilities of suggestion, hypnotic states, anxiety to please the therapist, selective attention of the therapist, folklore and myth, parental guidance, possible law suits and similar phenomena as contributors to the disorder. The methods of the humanities require methodical and skeptical therapists whose sensitivity and ingenuity are encouraged but also controlled and directed. The development of quantification and rigorous methods of testing statistical inference is a major successful development in empirical scientific method; it is not adequately in place as a method for the humanities, nor is an equally satisfactory substitute. Many efforts to make the humanities scientific have involved the deliberate sacrifice of the understanding characteristics of our work — the superficial operationism, the emphasis upon repeatability (reliability before validity), have meant that the motivation and intentions of our patients have often been relegated to either non-existence, redefinition into something else, or into a never-never land some centuries away when we hope to be ready for it.

One of the better methods of controlling the study of "understanding" is the development of intensive psychotherapy, with its greatly extended interview, the special training of the therapist, the detailed study of the ways of deception and self deception among humans and how to help recognize and avoid them. Erikson [15] has described this method and its advantages, limitations, and techniques with some care not to abandon the analysis of understanding in the process of trying to describe it.

Erikson emphasizes appropriately the receptivity of the therapist, the "disciplined subjectivity" as he participates in a free floating attention

which turns inward to the observer's ruminations while remaining turned outward to the field of observation and which, far from focusing on any one item too intentionally, rather waits to be impressed by recurring themes. These will first faintly but ever more insistently signal the nature of the patient's distress and its location. To find the zone, the position, and the danger, I must avoid for the moment all temptations to go off on *one* tangent in order to prove it alone as relevant. It is rather the establishment of strategic intersections on a number of tangents that eventually makes it possible to locate in the observed phenomena that central core which comprises the 'evidence'.

He returns several times to "disciplined-awareness", to the full use of the therapist's personal responses to the patient's presentations and includes the importance of the patient's efforts as a collaborator with the therapist in assessing the interpretations of the observations. The paper is an excellent introduction to the nature of a therapist's experience as it contributes to the development of science. It is not possible here to follow these methodological problems beyond calling attention to the need for their further analysis.

The subjective experience of psychotic patients presents a specially interesting and promising area for such clinical analysis and for understanding the nature of illness and recovery.

A non-psychotic physician patient returned to an hour with a complaint I have almost come to regard as characteristic of physician patients — he had had a bad migraine at the beginning of the last hour and when he left, it had completely disappeared. He was annoyed and felt slightly cheated because he did not know why it had left — and made some penetrating remarks about my profession, ending with "It's like the old cultist folklore: you think you have that headache but you're wrong; it isn't really you."

There are reasons to suspect that he had begun to answer his own question with his fable, but, if so, how different his experience from that of a psychotic patient facing the same problem.

Harvard Medical School
and McLean Hospital, Belmont

NOTE

[1] A group of us in Boston are studying intensive psychotherapy with schizophrenic patients. The group includes Peter Knapp, M.D., John Gunderson, M.D., Robert Schnitzer, Ph.D., Howard Kataz, M.D., William Boutelle, M.D., Beverly Gomes-Schwartz, Ph.D., Marsha Vannicelli, Ph.D., and Norbett Mintz, Ph.D. It is supported by grant #MH 25246—05 from the N.I.M.H.

REFERENCES

[1] Ricoeur, P.: 'Explanation and Understanding,' in Regan, C.E, and Stewart D. (eds): *The Philosophy of Paul Ricoeur, An Anthology of His Work*, Boston, Beacon Press, 1978, p. 181.

[2] Richfield, J.: 'An Analysis of the Concept of Insight,' *Psychoanal. Quart.* 23 (1954), 390—407.

[3] Hatcher, R.L.: 'Insight and Self Observation,' *J.Am. Psychoanal. Assoc.* 21 (1973), 377—398.

[4] Russell, B.: *Human Knowledge, Its Scope and Limits*, New York, Simon & Schuster, Inc., 1948.

[5] Russell, B.: *Mysticism and Logic*, New York: W. W. Norton & Co., 1929, p. 209.

[6] Stanton, A.H.: 'The Significance of Ego Interpretive States in Insight Directed Psychotherapy,' *Psychiat.* 41 (1978), 129—140.

[7] Pressman, M.D.: 'The Cognitive Functions of the Ego in Psychoanalysis: I, The Search for Insight,' *Int. J. Psychoanal.* 50 (1969), 187—196.

[8] Hartmann, H.: 'Comments on the Psychoanalytic Theory of the Ego,' *Psa. St. Ch.* 5 (1950), 74—96.

[9] Jacobson, E.: *The Self and the Object World*, New York, International University Press, 1964, p. 6 and pp. 19—23.

[10] Sandler, J., Rosenblatt, B.: 'The Concept of the Representational World,' *Psa. St. Ch.* 17 (1962), 128—145.

[11] Kohut, H.: *The Restoration of the Self*, New York, International University Press, 1977.

[12] Fontana, A. A., Klein, E. G.: 'Self-Presentation and the Schizophrenic "Deficit",' *J. Consult. and Clin. Psychol.* **32** (1968), 250–256.

[13] Wollheim, R.: 'The Mind and the Mind's Image of Itself,' *Intntl. J. Psychoanal.* **50** (1969), 209–220.

[14] Ricoeur, P.: 'Explanation and Understanding – On Some Remarkable Connections Among the Theory of the Text, Theory of Action, and Theory of History,' in Regan, C.E. and Stewart D. (eds.): *The Philosophy of Paul Ricoeur: An Anthology of His Work,* Boston, Beacon Press, 1978, chap. 11.

[15] Erikson, E. H.: 'The Nature of Clinical Evidence,' in Lerner, D. (ed.), *Evidence and Inference,* Free Press of Glencoe, Illinois, 1959, pp. 73–95.

LOUIS A. SASS

PARENTAL COMMUNICATION DEVIANCE
AND SCHIZOPHRENIA:
A COGNITIVE-DEVELOPMENTAL ANALYSIS

INTRODUCTION

The form of psychopathology which has probably occasioned the most extensive study of thought and language is schizophrenia. The deviant and sometimes bizarre ways in which such patients use language are among their most striking symptoms, and it has long been orthodox to locate the core of their symptomatic constellation in disorders of cognition. In recent decades, the interest in thought and language has extended beyond the study of the patients themselves to the study of other family members and of the family conceptualized as a system. The examination of forms of thinking and language has subsequently come to be central not just to issues involving diagnosis and the interpretation of symptoms but also to the attempt to understand the etiology of the illness. This tendency is exemplified in the research by Margaret Singer and Lyman Wynne concerning the communication patterns of parents of schizophrenics, probably the most influential and empirically best supported work concerning environmental factors in the etiology of schizophrenia.

These authors consider the "communication deviance" (CD) of the parents to be a contributing cause which, when combined with other factors such as a genetic predisposition and a stressful environment, will lead to the development of schizophrenia in the offspring. "Communication deviance" is defined as a failure on the part of the speaker to "establish and maintain a shared focus of attention" with one's listener. Such deviance manifests itself in a higher than usual incidence of a wide variety of different features of speech, including semantic misusages, syntactic errors, referential vagueness, a tendency to equivocate concerning one's commitment to one's statements, and a tendency to vacillate concerning the content of one's statements, (cf., Singer and Wynne, 1966). The offspring of persons who manifest a high degree of such deviance are said to be given a virtual training in irrationality by parents whose egocentric, unorganized, amorphous, or inconsistent modes of transmitting meaning make it difficult for their children to learn either to interact with other persons in adequate ways or to process information in a cognitively advanced fashion (cf., Wynne and Singer,

49

L. Vaina and J. Hintikka (eds.), Cognitive Constraints on Communication, 49–74.
© 1984 by D. Reidel Publishing Company.

1963a; 1963b; Singer and Wynne, 1965a; 1965b; Singer, Wynne, and Toohey, 1978).

Singer and Wynne argue that CD is a variable with much plausibility as an important causal factor because it is able to account for the origins of the core or structural features of the schizophrenic syndrome. Presumably, they consider other aspects of family functioning, such as affect expression, power relationships, or sexual identity issues, as less likely to be significant determiners of the central ego deficiencies of schizophrenic offspring, those deficiencies of perception, attention, conation, and language which are usually viewed as constituting the central symptoms of the disease. A feature of family functioning such as "communication deviance" does indeed seem to have a great deal of intuitive compellingness as a possible etiological factor in the development of schizophrenia, the psychiatric disturbance which is often taken to be the communication disorder par excellence.

To argue in this fashion is to implicitly presuppose the importance of the criterion of there being some kind of reasonable connection between purported causes and effects. This point of view is expressed in the succinct if somewhat cryptic statement of Aquinas that "an effect must resemble its cause" (quoted in Richards, 1932). Such a perspective, which treats causality as interaction rather than as mere cooccurrence or correlation, could be considered to be in the neo-Aristotelian rather than in the Humean or positivistic tradition (cf., Bernstein, 1971). The latter tradition, which informs much of contemporary American psychology and which, in my view, unfortunately dominates past arguments concerning communication deviance and schizophrenia, can be interpreted as mandating a neglect of conceptual in favor of empirical issues (and also as justifying the more fundamental presupposition that these two kinds of issues can be meaningfully separated). Obviously, it is not possible or appropriate to argue such fundamental philosophical differences here. I merely wish to locate the position of the present essay, which makes no bones about accepting the importance of the criterion mentioned above in Aquinas' dictum. This essay is an attempt to show that the criterion of reasonable connection is fulfilled by the communication deviance theory of the etiology of schizophrenia.

Most of the papers which have argued either for or against the communication deviance hypothesis have concentrated on issues of a methodological or empirical kind, such as the degree of standardization of the diagnostic criteria used to select samples, the appropriateness of the methods used to measure CD, the degree of differentiation found between experimental and control groups of parents, and various issues of reliability and statistical signifiance (cf., e.g., Hirsch and Leff, 1971; 1975; Jacob, 1975; Doane, 1978). There has been a related tendency to ignore conceptual issues, such as the interpretation of the nature of speech characterized as high in communication deviance, the determination of the aspect of schizophrenia which is related to such speech in parents, and the development of theoretical models of the probable impact of such speech. While in no way wishing to belittle the importance of the empirical and methodological issues, I would argue that the conceptual issues are equally important. This is not only because, as is suggested above by Singer's and Wynne's claims regarding plausibility, the intuitive compelling-ness of a hypothesis will often be (and should be) as important in determining its acceptance as is empirical data, but also because scrutinizing conceptual issues may well lead to needed refinements and further specifications of a hypothesis as it stands.

In my opinion, there has been a tendency to reify the variables studied in the tradition of research on family interaction and schizophrenia, and this is not conducive to the making of such refinements and specifications of hypotheses. There has been a tendency to take at face value the variables as they have been labelled and to neglect the conceptual analysis of these variables. CD itself, for example, has often been treated almost as if it were a monolithic and non-problematic phenomenon, the underlying nature of which is not in question. Neither the nature of its implications about the speaker nor the nature of its impact on the listener has been explored in much detail. There has been a similar tendency to fail to examine with appropriate care the "effect" variables. I.e., writers have not been very clear about just what it is in the offspring to which high parental CD is supposed to lead. Is it to schizophrenia in general? To severe pathology of any kind? To thought disorder? The present essay concerns itself almost exclusively with such conceptual issues.

In the course of analyzing the relevant phenomena, one major revision of the CD hypothesis as it has traditionally been stated will be offered. This will concern certain paranoid schizophrenics, cases who can be both definitely and severely schizophrenic despite failing to manifest primarily symptoms which fit the common characterization of schizophrenia as involving significant cognitive deficiencies. Such patients, who manifest very little or no formal "thought disorder" and whose most salient symptoms, at least in the cognitive realm, appear to be more defensive than deficient, would appear to fall outside the general rationale that has usually been given for the communication deviance hypothesis. Singer and Wynne have, using a classification system they devised based on cognitive-developmental principles, labeled such patients as "constricted", but they have paid little attention to such patients in their writing and research, and they implicitly include such patients with disordered schizophrenics in their statement of the CD hypothesis. I will argue that the statement of the hypothesis should be revised such that parental CD is considered a contributing cause not for schizophrenia in general but rather for schizophrenia with clear formal thought disorder.

But the major purpose of the present essay is to argue for the plausibility of the etiological significance of communication deviance through articulating in greater detail than has previously been done the nature of the hypothesized interaction between parental speech style and offspring symptomatology. I will attempt to delineate the ways in which parental CD and certain crucial symptoms of schizophrenic patients may "resemble" each other and be causally related. Implicitly, I will be countering a view that I suspect is not uncommon, the view which considers CD to be implausible as a significant etiological factor on the grounds that CD is too specific, superficial, and circumscribed a phenomenon to account for the myriad and profound symptoms which characterize schizophrenia and which would, on these grounds, tend to dismiss the significance of the communication deviance variable.

What is required for this task is a theoretical analysis of the significant relevant dimensions of schizophrenia, a theoretical analysis of the nature and significance of CD, and the presentation of a sufficiently clear and compelling model of the possible "mechanisms" of the impact of CD. Such analyses will inevitably involve us in the consideration of two kinds of relationships between thought and language or between cognition and dialogue: 1, speech as a reflection of cognition, and 2, the impact of linguistic and social experience on cognitive development. But this will require adopting some overall theoretical perspective. Only by viewing the two realms of phenomena with which we are concerned, parental speech style and schizophrenic symptomatology, through the same theoretical lens, only by framing our interpretations of them in the terms of similar categories of understanding, will it be possible to see the relevant resemblances and contrasts emerge. For a variety of reasons which cannot' be considered here (cf., Sass, 1979), the perspective adopted is the cognitive-developmental perspective of Vygotsky, Werner, and Piaget.

The essay has the following sections:

1. Schizophrenic symptoms: including a brief summary of Wernerian and Piagetian concepts relevant to the description of schizophrenic modes of

cognition, a presentation of a classification system of thinking styles developed by Singer and Wynne and based on Werner's theories, and a further elaboration of this classification system as it applies to different forms of schizophrenic pathology.

2. Parental communication deviance: including a theoretical analysis of the nature of CD which suggests the importance of distinguishing between two important subtypes of deviance, termed "deficient" and "defensive".

3. Etiological models: including a consideration of the probable impact of these variant forms of CD and of their relationship to differing forms of schizophrenic pathology, and a brief reference to some confirmatory empirical findings.

1. SCHIZOPHRENIC SYMPTOMS

Concepts from Werner and Piaget

Werner, the developmental psychologist, considered schizophrenic cognition to be a manifestation of a developmentally "primitive" form of functioning. The "orthogenetic principle" — according to which all developmental phenomena, whether phylogenetic, ontogenetic, or microgenetic, involve a movement in the direction of greater differentiation, integration, and hierarchization of processes and elements — is the core of his point of view. He and his students have pointed out how in a wide variety of different forms of functioning schizophrenic individuals manifest either undifferentiated or unintegrated modes of cognition (Storch, 1924; Baker, 1953; Werner, 1957; Slepian, 1959; Goldman, 1960; Goldman, 1962; Werner and Kaplan, 1963; Feffer, 1967).

A closely related description of the course of cognitive development is offered by Piaget via the notion of increasing "decentering" or of the transition from "egocentrism" to "perspectivism" (Flavell, 1963). Langer (1969, p. 79) defines these latter two terms as follows:

Briefly, egocentricity is the child's cognitive state early in development when he doesn't differentiate between himself, his action, other things, and their action in an event. Perspectivism is the child's progressive capacity to differentiate cognitively between these aspects of an event and between his own and others' points of view, then to reflect upon these differences, and eventually to integrate his reflection into a personal 'theory' of the relationship of himself to other things and people in a given event.

Decentration has a number of different manifestations, of which at least

two are relevant here. In the impersonal sphere, decentration or the acquisition of perspectivism refers to the increasing "distance" of the perceiver or
thinker from the objects of his experience. With this "distance" comes a kind
of control, an ability to selectively attend to various aspects or facets of a
phenomenon in a voluntary way. "Concrete" forms of functioning as
described by Goldstein (Goldstein and Sheerer, 1941) might be also described
as "centered" or egocentric, meaning that the experiencer under such conditions is not able to imagine a variety of different potential points of view
which might be taken re. a phenomenon. To be capable of "abstract" categorization implies such a capacity to shift point of view in the sense that such
a capacity would imply the understanding of the fact that a given mental
object could be classified into any number of different categories depending
on what aspect of it one were to focus on (i.e. depending on which point of
view one were to take, for an "aspect" is but the object pole of a cognitive
act, which always involves a particular point of view). Without at least a
modicum of decentration, there can be no concept of a truly external real
world for there would be no differentiation between the self and the world.
One manifestation of such un-differentiation would be the failure to
recognize that an object is more than merely the appearance it contingently
has at the present moment. In an article concerned with such questions,
Schachtel (1959) describes the outcome of the development of selective
attention, which is akin to the development of perspectivism, to be the very
"emergence of reality".

A point of view which is conceived of as the perspective taken by another
human being involves a form of decentration or perspectivism of special
importance. The gradual process of interpersonal decentration results in a
conception of the interpersonal other as being in many respects like the self
(i.e., the other is a consciousness) yet in other respects not like the self
(i.e., the other's consciousness is not coextensive with that of the self either
with respect to its content, i.e., what information is available to it, nor even,
under some circumstances, with respect to its form, e.g., when an adult
speaks with a child). Essential to this awareness is the ability to conceive of
oneself as both an object among objects and also a perspective among
perspectives. It seems that the fragile and fleeting qualities of a full lived
realization of such an advanced conception of the other may tend to be overlooked when one takes a cognitive-developmental perspective, which
emphasizes relatively permanent underlying structures. However, there is
nothing at the core of a cognitive-developmental perspective which would be
at odds with the following statements of a phenomenologist writing about

the relationship between self and other involved in speaking. These statements capture the prodigious strangeness of all speech situations. Even among normals there is of necessity an inherently unstable balance between the sense of the other as both different and separate from the self yet also, in other senses, similar and coextensive with the self (for both speaker and listener must imaginatively project themselves into the other):

... speech concerns us, catches us indirectly, seduces us, trails us along, transforms us into the other and him into us, abolishes the limit between mine and not-mine, and ends the alternative between what has sense for me and what is non-sense for me, between me as subject and the other as object ...

The happy writer and the speaking man ... cross bridges of snow without seeing how fragile those are, using to the very limit that extraordinary power given to every mind of convincing others and entering into their little corner when it believes itself to be coextensive with the truth ...

Myself and the other are like two nearly concentric circles which can be distinguished only by a slight and mysterious slippage .... Nevertheless, the other is not I, and on that account differences must arise. (Merleau-Ponty, 1973, pp. 134, 145.)

Egocentrism is the state when the circles are merged, when they are no longer, or never were, two.

The abnormalities of schizophrenic language and cognition have often been thought of as manifestations of earlier, more primitive, levels of functioning, a point of view which is of course implied by any description of schizophrenia as a form of "regression" or developmental "fixation". The Wernerian and Piagetian perspectives, according to which schizophrenic cognition is "egocentric" or "centered", are only two of several major theoretical perspectives which view the illness in a developmental context. The treatments of schizophrenia as indicative of primary process thinking (Freud), of concrete rather than abstract cognition (Goldstein), and of predicate logic (Von Domarus, 1964) also imply such a perspective. It is the cognitive-developmental approach which will be of central importance for the present essay, however, not only because Singer and Wynne use Wernerian ideas for their own classification of forms of schizophrenic thinking, but also because a cognitive-developmental orientation is the most useful for the construction of an adequate etiological model of the impact of communication deviance.

AMFC Classification of Forms of Cognition

Wynne and Singer (1963b) have developed a system for the classification of forms of thinking based on Werner's orthogenetic principle. The four forms of thinking which this system recognizes are listed below, ordered from most to the least primitive. It should be apparent that, as Singer and Wynne have pointed out, the term "thinking" is not being used in an exclusive sense, and the various forms might more appropriately be called forms of "experience disorder".

Amorphous style: Global and undifferentiated forms of functioning. Wooly, indefinite, impoverished vagueness with loosely organized and blurred attention and perception. Communication would be marked by indefiniteness and vagueness, sometimes with the usage of words which are but vague approximations. Patients with the amorphous style have the general appearance of a deficiency disease and of "underinclusive" thought disorder.

Mixed style (i.e. both amorphous and fragmented): Less pervasively amorphous forms of thinking and experiencing with islands of perceptual and cognitive clarity.

Fragmented style: "Loosening of associations" or "fragmentation of thought processes" (Bleuler), with relatively well-differentiated percepts or ideas which are not adequately integrated or logically related. Often there would be intrusions of primitive primary process material and the general appearance of "overinclusive" thought disorder.

Constricted style: Characterized by rigid, constricting defenses which seal off potential cognitive disorganization and primary process intrusions. Usually such patients would be guarded, circumspect, and would tend to impose logical structure or interpretations on experience in a rigid and paranoid fashion.

Incidentally, the AMFC method of classification does not involve merely a renaming of the traditional paranoid-versus-nonparanoid distinction. This is because, although constricted schizophrenics are almost invariably diagnosed as paranoid, paranoids are also found among the fragmented, amorphous, and mixed groups. By separating the non-thought-disordered paranoids (C group) from thought-disordered schizophrenics (A, M, and F groups), paranoid or otherwise, this system avoids two inaccurate conflations which are common in the literature on schizophrenia.

One of these is the conflation between the paranoia dimension and the dimension of lack of ego-disorganization (or, absence of thought disorder,

TD), a mistaken equation since there are numerous schizophrenics who are both very paranoid and very disordered. It is these patients who make it clear that there are at least two different criteria on the basis of which a schizophrenic is considered of the paranoid type, thought content (i.e., paranoid or grandiose preoccupations) and cognitive style (i.e., a characteristic vigilant, articulated, detail-oriented, selective, and, in the paradigmatic case, intellectualizing and integrated mode of cognition). It is the paranoid (in terms of thought content) but cognitively disorganized patients whom different psychiatrists diagnose differently, as "paranoid" or as "chronic undifferentiated", depending on whether thought content or cognitive style happens to be the dimension taken as criterial by that diagnoser.

The constricted schizophrenic might be thought of as the paranoid schizophrenic par excellence for only he qualifies unequivocally as a paranoid on both the important criteria. Among the amorphous, mixed, and fragmented groups, a diagnosis of paranoid schizophrenia must either have been based solely on the salience of paranoid themes in the content of the patient's thought (as is probably the case with an amorphous schizophrenic diagnosed paranoid) or, where the diagnosis has involved some features of cognitive style, there will have been other features less consistent with the paranoid designation. An example would be a fragmented schizophrenic who may well manifest both a preoccupation with paranoid themes and an articulated attentional style (focus on details) of the typical paranoid, but who will also manifest a somewhat high degree of cognitive disorganization. Only the constricted patient has both the preoccupation with paranoid content and a cognitive style characterized by all the classic features (vigilance, articulated attention, organization and integration, need for consistent explanatory system, etc.).

The other common conflation is the conflation of schizophrenia and formal thought disorder involved in treating the latter as the defining essence of schizophrenia and in implying that amount of TD is equivalent to severity of schizophrenic illness. Significant formal thought disorder cannot be a necessary condition for the presence of schizophrenia if one wants to consider as schizophrenic certain severely paranoid, constricted individuals.

Incidently, one important distinction to be borne in mind is that between thought disorder of the content and thought disorder of the form of thought. The phrase "thought disorder" can and is used to refer to either or both variants. However, it is disorder of the form of thought which is being referred to when "thought disorder" is considered the criterial symptom of schizophrenia, when Singer and Wynne refer to TD, and in the present essay.

These are disorders in the form, structuring, or interrelationships of ideas and of language, as opposed to mistaken, bizarre, or in any way inappropriate particular beliefs or ideas.

In the light of the considerations discussed above, the AMFC method of classification seems especially appropriate since the specification of the constricted group involves a recognition of the facts that: 1, not all schizophrenics have significant formal thought disorder, and 2, only certain paranoids are characterized by a low degree of thought disorder or ego disorganization. (Incidently, McConaghy, 1960, makes a distinction similar to the constricted versus disordered one.)

Forms of Schizophrenic Cognition

According to the orthogentic principle, the amorphous form of thinking and experience is more primitive than is the fragmented, which itself is more primitive than either the constricted or the normal modes. Let us consider some of the ways in which these various modes manifest the quality of relative primitiveness.

The amorphous mode of experience is both undifferentiated and unintegrated. Both the thoughts and the perceptions of such persons are vague and relatively unarticulated, and it would be typical of such persons to have difficulty elaborating upon or interpreting their stimulus environment in complicated ways. Thus they are unlikely to take up several different perspectives or orientations concerning any given thought or perception, and even the one orientation they do adopt is likely to be a relatively stimulus-bounded and impoverished one. The concept of the interpersonal other is not likely to be highly differentiated, as if there is a failure to recognize the "otherness" of the other. This will manifest itself in vague, amorphous, overly general and laconic modes of speech which fail to adequately take into account the informational needs of the listener in conversation.

The fragmented mode, though unintegrated, is relatively more differentiated than is the amorphous. The thoughts and perceptions of such a person are likely to be rather specific and highly elaborated, and such a person is likely to be able to take more than one perspective on a given thought or perception, though perhaps not to shift among these perspectives in a coordinated and clear fashion. There is not likely to be an adequate integration among the various specific thoughts, perceptions, and perspectives, and the person may appear to career from idea to idea in a confusing, disorganized manner. The mental contents elicited from such a person on some topic will have the quality of a loosely-linked "heap" rather than of a hierarchically organized systematic structure, and this will manifest itself in terms of a verbal style more characterized by parataxis than by hypotaxis. Although there will be more of a differentiation between self and other than in the amorphous mode — this is ensured by the very possibility of taking different perspectives toward a mental object, absent in the amorphous mode — for the fragmented as for the amorphous person, the concept of the interpersonal other will fall far short of the most advanced form. The most advanced concept would involve a relatively stable, integrated, differentiated-from-the-self "generalized other" (G.H. Mead) recognized as a consciousness both analogous to yet separate from the self and used in communication as a way of monitoring speech to ensure that the informational requirements of the other are met. Perhaps a statement by one of Searles' patients reflects the combination of a separate other yet without stability and integration characteristic of the fragmented patient: "Every time I hear the word 'mother', I see a whole parade of women, each with a different point of view" (Searles, 1967). A study in the Wernerian tradition (Slepian, 1959) illustrated the tendency among schizophrenics for speech for others to fail to be very different from speech for the self, which would reflect the relative absence of interpersonal perspectivism.

One manifestation of relative primitivity characterizing both the fragmented and the amorphous patients which is worth mentioning concerns the relationship between symbol and referent. It would seem that for all thought-disordered schizophrenics (i.e., F, M, and A types) there is a failure to consistently recognize the particular quality of separateness yet relatedness of a symbol and referent. This is manifest in various deviances in the use of language, including the tendency to treat the sounds of words, or the referents they have when heard as puns, as indicative of their meaning, and it seems related to what Freud referred to as the schizophrenic tendency to cathect the "word-representation" rather than the "thing-representation" (Freud, 1965).

In none of the respects mentioned above does the constricted schizophrenic appear to qualify as primitive in his cognitive functioning. Far from being undifferentiated or unintegrated, his mental contents are likely to be highly specific and systematically organized, perhaps even more ordered than reality justifies. The constricted person does not confuse symbol and referent or evince any of the deviant forms of language usage to which that confusion gives rise. His extreme concern with figuring out underlying truths involves a style of cognition in which there are careful differentiations between such "levels" of experience as appearance versus reality, motive versus behavior, relevant versus irrelevant fact (i.e., that which does versus does not qualify as evidence). This would seem in many ways to be the polar opposite of the "lived world" evoked by the following statement made by one of Searles' disorganized patients: "I don't know, when I talk to you, whether I'm having an hallucination, or a fantasy about a memory, or a memory about a fantasy" (Searles, 1967). Far from being unable to take up or coordinate various perspectives on a given topic, the constricted schizophrenic is liable to indulge himself in elaborate speculations concerning the variety of possible meanings which a given event could have. In addition, the constricted person is hardly liable to lapse into an unawareness of the separateness of the other. As Schwartz (1963) puts it, "Where the autistic schizophrenic denies the meaningful existence of others, the paranoid patient creates others in a meaningful context where they do not exist in reality."

Psychoanalytic schools of thought appear to be recognizing the lesser primitiveness of the constricted as compared to the thought-disordered patient when they describe the disordered schizophrenic as fixated at an earlier stage of psychosexual and ego development, a stage prior to the differentiation between self and other (stage of "primary narcissism"), whereas the paranoid is seen as fixated at a later stage, usually considered to be that of "secondary narcissism" (e.g. Schwartz, 1963; Freemen, Cameron, and McGhie, 1958, pp. 25–28; both in the ego-psychological tradition). European writers influenced by Lacan's fusion of psychoanalysis and structuralism are saying much the same thing when they state that the paranoid is fixated at the "mirror stage" and the disordered schizophrenic at an earlier stage (Deleuze and Guattari, 1977; De Waelhans, 1978).

Fragmented and amorphous modes are clearly more primitive than either the constricted or non-schizophrenic modes of thinking. The hierarchical placement of the constricted group of schizophrenics in relationship to non-schizophrenic modes of cognition seems more problematic however. If one wants to consider constricted psychotics as schizophrenics, in fact, it may seem necessary to shift the criterion of schizophrenia from the dimension of disorganization/dedifferentiation to that of the adequateness of reality-testing, since only the latter criterion captures the pathological quality of the delusions and inordinate suspiciousness of constricted persons. What seems pathological about constricted thinking does not appear to have to do with the form of thinking so much as with the content of the thinking, i.e. with the fact that a rigid selectivity is imposed on the possible contents of consciousness.

On the other hand, one could argue on the basis of the statements regarding developmental fixation points discussed in the last paragraph that there is something structurally pathological about the constricted mode and that this can be understood in the light of the notion that the paranoid is fixated at the stage of narcissism. According to psychologists influenced by Lacan, for example, this means that the paranoid, though always able to conceive the separateness of the other, can be unable to experience what one might call the "differentness" of the other, i.e., the ways in which the real other's actual point of view might differ from the one projected upon him by the paranoid. This projected point of view is always, of course, a point of view held by the paranoid himself, even if some aspects of it are not recognized consciously. The other's attention, for example, is assumed to be primarily focussed on the constricted person, thus neatly mirroring the constricted person's self-consciousness, while seeming to cause and justify it. Whether one wishes to consider these aspects of experience to be characteristics of the form or of the content of cognition seems to be a semantic issue, one for decision by convention rather than argument (c.f. Goodman, 1978, re the ambiguities of this and related distinctions). However, if one does choose to conceive the constricted person's "secondary narcissism", propensity toward projective defense, and centrality as features of the form of thinking, this should not obscure the very significant differences between the obvious kind of primitiveness characteristic of fragmented and amorphous modes on the one hand versus that of the constricted mode on the other. It is this particular difference which is the subject of the present report. We will then hold in abeyance the question of the hierarchical placement on the developmental dimension of constricted modes as compared to non-schizophrenic modes of experience.

One further difference between the constricted as opposed to the other disturbed modes of experience should be mentioned. Paranoid symptomatology is usually described as characterized more by defensiveness, while nonparanoid (especially hebephrenic) symptomotology is seen as more characterized by deficiency. This difference would certainly apply to the most salient symptomatic features of cognition of the constricted as opposed to those of the F, M, and the A modes.

2. STYLES OF COMMUNICATION DEVIANCE IN PARENTS

But what of the other set of variables of concern to us? How, using a developmental perspective, is one to conceptualize the forms of communication discovered by Singer and Wynne to characterize the speech of the parents of schizophrenics? Singer and Wynne themselves have not devoted much attention to this issue, preferring for understandable reasons to stick to the

presentation of the empirical findings and to focus on the impact of these
speech styles rather than on the somewhat less immediately significant
question concerning the personality structures of the speakers (Singer,
1976b). Lidz, however, has explicitly characterized the parents of schizophrenics as being egocentric and thus primitive in the developmental sense
(Lidz, 1978), and the majority of the categories of communication defects
and deviances specified by Singer and Wynne would seem consistent with
such a characterization. Forms of speech such as the following, all classified
as deviances by the Singer-Wynne system, could certainly be construed as
indicating a rather high degree of cognitive primitiveness: lack of specificity
with regard to the referent, unexplained contradictions, peculiar reasoning
which has the appearance of nonsequitur inference, inappropriate responses
suggestive of a failure to grasp the intent of a question by the interlocutor,
a tendency to jump about confusingly among different topics, idiosyncratic
and consensually inappropriate word choice, a tendency to associate more to
the sound than the sense of one's own language, syntax which is odd and
disconcerting to the listener. In fact, some of these patterns seem suggestive
of speech styles which might well be dubbed "amorphous" or "fragmented".
The developmental primitiveness is indicated by the fact that many of these
features of speech are reminiscent of the speech of children as described by
a variety of studies in the cognitive-developmental tradition (Piaget, 1955;
Flavell, Botkin, Fry, Wright, and Jarvis, 1975; Werner and Kaplan, 1963;
Krauss and Glucksberg, 1969). Also, they are similar to patterns of language
which are considered to be typical of "inner speech", speech for the self
which, in adulthood, is usually not spoken aloud (Vygotsky, 1962; Werner
and Kaplan, 1963), and this suggests that speakers given to the use of such
patterns are likely to be failing to take into account the cognitive needs of
the listener experienced as a separate other.

On the other hand, there are a variety of forms of deviance found by
Singer and Wynne in the parents of schizophrenics and considered to contribute to an impairment of shared focus of attention which do not seem to be
likely to stem primarily from an egocentric/primitive cognitive style. These
include disqualifications of what one has said, retractions and denials,
responses in negative form (which state what is not the case), responses in
subjunctive form (where speaker says what would have been his interpretation, but only if something were the case), and vacillations (where the speaker
refuses to choose among several different interpretations of a given stimulus
which he is describing). In fact, some of these forms of CD might even imply
a rather advanced cognitive orientation in that some of them seem to imply

a kind of conceptual "distance" from both the referent and the interlocutor, and this suggests the very opposite of the forms of concrete functioning as described by Goldstein, of egocentricity as described by Piaget, or of de-differentiation as described by Werner. Responses in negative form, for example, involve the stating of what is not the case, and this implies the ability to conceive of something that might have been the case but in actuality is not, a perspective suggestive of Goldstein's abstract attitude. The giving of several alternatives may suggest an ability to flexibly shift from one interpretation of a given stimulus to another and therefore probably involves a high degree of perspectivism since the speaker is describing what might be seen if one chooses to take a certain point of view.

Also, the speech of persons who are primarily defensive in their communication deviance often involves a rather elaborate and explicit logical structure in which the various details mentioned have a clear role in a structured argument. Therefore such speech often has a hypotactic quality, i.e., it is highly structured in a hierarchical manner, as opposed to the rambling quality more characteristic of primitive/deficient communication.

From another perspective, these latter forms of CD could be considered to be indicative of defensiveness (i.e., they are intentionally determined) rather than of deficiency or primitiveness. This would be an especially likely interpretation if the speech is elicited in a situation where the speaker might be motivated to try to avoid a feared revelation of the self, such as is likely to be the case for some subjects taking projective tests, which is the speech situation on which the majority of research has been done. Being aware that the interpretation they offer of a Rorschach or TAT card may well be used to draw conclusions of some kind about them, many speakers might attempt to avoid committing themselves to a single interpretation, and this can be achieved by describing what one does not see (negative responses), or what one might have seen (responses in subjunctive form) or the several different things that one can see. Such speakers would obviously be well aware of the other as a separate consciousness since they are doing their best to thwart what they imagine, rather accurately, to be the scrutinizing attitude on the part of the listener/tester.

One might wish to belittle the significance of the distinction just made between these two forms of CD on the grounds that, after all, what really matters is the interpersonal impact, and that the blurring of a shared focus of attention results equally from either form of deviance, whether deficient or defensive. It seems to me, however, that one must not lose sight of the fact that a speech situation is always interpersonal as well as cognitive, i.e., that the participants are constantly involved both in attempting to grasp the content of their interlocutor's words but also in attempting to ascertain the attitudes of their interlocutor, not only toward the subject of their conversation, but also toward the conversation itself and toward themselves. As much recent work in speech act and pragmatic linguistics as well as in experimental psycholinguistics emphasizes, the hearer of speech always works down from a global grasp of the meaning of a sentence as an act embedded in a context which is interpersonal to the dissection of the meaning of separate clauses and words, rather than the other way around (Lakoff, 1972; Gordon and Lakoff, 1971; Bates, 1976; Searle, 1975; Rommetveit, 1974; Searle, 1969; Grice, 1967). We understand sentences from the outside-in rather than from the inside-out (Wanner, 1973). Since a linguistic interaction involves such a total situation which includes the listener's attempts to assess the intentions of the speaker, it would seem that a failure to be clear which results from a motivated defensiveness may well have a very different impact than does a failure to be clear which is experienced as the result of the speaker's inability to be clear.

Also, one must keep in mind the fact that the speech samples studied in all research concerning CD are of course taken to be exemplars of the quality of speech in other situations as well. Yet it would seem that a speaker who is unclear in his interpretation of a Rorschach or TAT card because of primarily defensive reasons is likely to be much clearer in other situations where the topic or the nature of the interaction is less likely to elicit this defensiveness. Such variability in degree of clarity would be considerably less in the case of a speaker whose CD stems primarily from deficiency/primitivity. Clearly, the impact of these two kinds of speakers on a child growing up with them would be quite different.

3. ETIOLOGICAL MODELS

In discussing the two realms of phenomena, schizophrenia and parental communication, we have located two significant exceptions to what appear to be overly generalized characterizations. These are: the existence of the constricted schizophrenic who does not manifest a significant degree of TD, and the existence of the defensive form of communication deviance. Now we turn our attention to the purported connections between these two realms. How is one, in a cognitive-developmental framework, to characterize the "mechanisms" by which deviant communication styles might bring about or elicit the varied forms of symptomatology with which, according to our hypotheses, they are connected? The following then should serve as an answer to the argument that criticizes the communication deviance hypothesis regarding the origins of schizophrenia on the grounds of its intuitive implausibility.

The Impact of Deficient/Primitive Communication

Singer and Wynne have not written extensively on the nature of the connection between CD and schizophrenia for they have been more concerned with demonstrating the existence of the empirical correlations. However, their somewhat sketchy discussions of this topic do suggest that in confronting this issue they are thinking primarily of the disordered forms of schizophrenia, which is not surprising, given that virtually all of the subjects in their research were of the F, M, or A types. They defend the plausibility of their hypotheses on the grounds that CD does seem a reasonable predecessor to the core structural deficiencies of schizophrenia, i.e., the disturbances of thought, attention, conation and language which constitute the ego deficits of the illness. It seems also that they are primarily thinking of the primitive/deficient forms of CD. It is indeed plausible that the deficient and primitive forms of CD could be significant contributors to the development of these core ego deficiencies in the child. Singer and Wynne say that they view the ego deficiencies of the offspring as in certain respects the result of the "internalization" of interactional patterns in the family. Let us attempt to describe in more specific detail the nature of this "internalization".

The view that thought is to a large extent an internalization of various forms of interpersonal experience, particularly linguistic, is taken by a number of psychologists, including Werner (Werner and Kaplan, 1963) and Piaget (Flavell, 1963; Langer, 1969), and, in even stronger terms, by Vygotsky (1962) and Luria (1976; Toulmin, 1978). Vygotsky and Luria give special emphasis to the impact of social experience on the structuring of consciousness. It seems that a meta-psychological perspective such as they would share with Piaget and Werner is most appropriate for the conceptualization of the phenomena at hand. Such positions, being neither extremely nativist nor extremely environmentalist, are free to study the social evolution of "mind", i.e., to attempt not merely to describe (in the way in which the nativism of Kant or Chomsky seems to require) but to account for, i.e., to trace the developmental process of the acquisition of, the actual "forms" of consciousness. The very concept of such "forms" is inconsistent with extreme environmentalist, e.g., behaviorist, positions. Thus, such cognitive-developmental approaches seem ideally suited to the study of the acquisition of forms or structures of thought and cognition via social/linguistic experience.

In the normal case, the individual learns to employ a variety of the essential functions of thought largely through his experience with other individuals, for it is other people who provide the impetus and to some extent the means whereby he manages to actively rethink his own point of view and thereby overcome the cognitive egocentrism and centration characteristic of the earlier stages of cognitive functioning. It is the speech of the parents which ideally provides the necessary models of advanced cognition and constitutes the basis for the acquisition of the capacity for dialectical reasoning and various logical problem-solving processes. As developmental research has shown, such models provided by adults are maximally beneficial to stable cognitive growth when they are only somewhat discrepant with the child's current stage of development. It seems plausible that a parent who is egocentric and primitive in his own functioning is less likely to provide the optimal opportunities for such growth. It would also seem likely that one tendency on the part of a child growing up with such parents would be to turn to inner resources and private fantasies as a source of intellectual stimulation and emotional comfort.

The decentrations in the normal course of development culminate in the ability to flexibly and appropriately use a number of the essential functions of thought in which the disorganized (A or F) schizophrenic is often deficient or abnormal. These functions include categorization, implication, and the ability to shift point of view (an ability critical to the monitoring of one's own speech so that it will be comprehensible from the perspective of someone else). A closely related ability is the capacity to be self-critical, i.e., to think about thinking itself. Several of these functions might be thought of as requiring the acquisition of a model of the "generalized other" described by George Herbert Mead, and it is precisely such an acquisition which the primitive/deficient communication deviance studied by Singer and Wynne would seem likely to vitiate. It would seem likely that the ability to have a stable but appropriately flexible concept of the "generalized other" would be hindered if the child grows up around parents who fail to communicate a consistent point of view on a given topic — as Singer and Wynne have found appears to be the case with the parents of schizophrenics.

It should be emphasized that concepts and cognitive capacities that seem less obviously interpersonal in nature would also be affected by such experience since parents with high deficient CD will fail to provide a clear description of their own mental contents and thus will fail to aid the child in the acquisition of linguistic concepts of relevance to the non-interpersonal world. Vygotsky states that, "The child's intellectual growth is contingent on his mastering the social means of thought, that is, language" (Vygotsky, 1962, p. 51). According to him, the earliest experience with language, i.e., the egocentric speech indulged in and the quasi-dialogues engaged in during the early stages of development, eventuate via two different lines of development in both advanced socialized speech and inner speech, the latter including both autistic as well as logical variants. According to his view, children use the latter forms of subvocal inner speech in the mastery of intellectual skills and thus such inner speech mediates secondary process thinking. Language of both the public and inner kinds thus provide a kind of scaffolding for the mastery, consolidation, and memorization of ideational complexes (Toulmin, 1978). Given this view, it would seem plausible to discover part of the origin of schizophrenic abnormalities of thought, language, and social cognition in the abnormal patterns of linguistic communication in their families, which would be conducive to the deficient and deviant acquisition of such a linguistic scaffolding.

Incidentally, Singer and Wynne argue that the relationship between parental CD and the cognitive abnormalities of the offspring should probably be thought of as symmetrical and complementary. To some extent, and in some cases, parental CD of a particular type might mediate the development of a similar mode of speech and cognition in the child via a modeling effect. But there will also be instances in which the style of language and thought of the child will contrast sharply with that of a parent. (Eg., where an extremely withdrawn and linguistically vague parent might elicit an over-inclusive, over-ideational style in the offspring.) One kind of complementary outcome which would seem highly unlikely, if not impossible, however, is a case where two primitive/deficient parents would foster a child without evidence of analogous cognitive deficiency, for the acquisition of non-deficient/advanced cognition would seem to require a model that such parents could not provide.

It would seem plausible to suggest that experience with such deficient parents could result in either a general deficit in many important cognitive faculties or in a greater vulnerability to the loss of such faculties under situations of stress or in a propensity to use such disorganization when it can serve certain personal goals, such as avoiding interaction, responsibility, or the necessity of choice in what is experienced as a double-bind situation. This last possibility is suggested by Arieti's concept of "progressive teleological regression" (Arieti, 1974). Probably, however, these several potential outcomes are not so clearly differentiated one from another as the above list would suggest. The overdrawn but, it sometimes seems, unavoidable casual-versus-intentional dichotomy (and, in this case, the related contrast of state-versus-trait) tempts one toward a too-simplified set of choices (c.f., Peters, 1958; Bernstein, 1971). Most likely of all is probably some combination of all these outcomes. However, schizophrenics with thought disorder would seem to differ on the basis of how variable according to the situation is their disorganization and also according to the degree to which it is under the control of teleological goals.

There are several studies which might indirectly bear upon this purported link between deficient communication in the parents and disorganization in the offspring. Muntz and Power (1970) found a relationship between TD in parents and TD in their child. One would expect that parents who showed TD would for the most part be those likely to manifest deficient CD. McConaghy and Clancy (1968) have reported on a significant tendency for at least one parent to evince allusive thinking (akin to Bleuler's concept of loosening of associations) if the offspring, whether schizophrenic or not, manifests it. Strauss, Harder, and Chandler (1979) have reported that the offspring of psychiatrically ill parents manifest egocentricity in proportion to the degree of illness of their parents. None of these studies employ exactly the variables we are treating in the present essay, yet all three are consistent with the prediction of a relationship between the degree of primitiveness and dis-organization of the parent and that of the offspring.

The Impact of Defensive Communication

The situation of children who grow up with parents who manifest primarily communication deviance of the defensive sort should be altogether different. For one thing, such parents should, at least when engaged on topics in con-nection with which they do not fear revealing themselves, manifest adequate models of advanced cognition and language. For another, such parents should have more or less the normal capacity for gauging the needs of their listener and making their communication appropriate to the cognitive capacity and informational requirements of that listener. In fact, since a defensive orienta-tion involves speculation regarding the thoughts and intentions of the listener, one might even expect that such a style of communication, far from being egocentric, would sometimes involve even more than the normal tendency to attempt to ascertain the listener's point of view. Consequently one would not predict the overall deleterious effect on general cognitive competence such as might result from growing up with deficient/primitive communicators.

Even when engaged on topics concerning which such parents do feel threatened and consequently obscure shared focus in defensive ways, the impact of the resulting impairment of shared focus is likely to be quite different from that deriving from deficient communication. This is because a person listening to defensive patterns of communication is more likely to realize that the speaker has not transmitted an unambiguous and clear message, whereas a person listening to deficient communication is inclined to wonder whether or not he ought to be able to extract such meaning from the speech he has heard. Defensive communication, then, would be not nearly so confusing and not nearly so liable to encourage in the listener a failure to differentiate his own perspective from the speaker's. It is also, of course, possible that a given speaker might at times manifest deficient communication, but that this would occur only when the topic was anxiety-provoking or threatening while on other topics the speaker would be relatively clear. In such a case also, the deleterious impact on the cognitive development of the child should be less than in the case where the deficient communication occurred with regard to almost any topic and in almost any situation. So far I have discussed only the ways in which defensive communication would *not* have the same deleterious effect as deficient communication. However, one ought also to consider how a propensity toward defensiveness on the part of the parent might give rise to certain symptoms in the offspring.

The very fact of defensiveness itself conveys the implicit messages that the speaker is wary and mistrustful and that the world is fraught with danger. Surely such an attitude of fear and suspicion could encourage the same orientation in a child, whose world-view is as yet inchoate and plastic. Defensive communicators often have a kind of "evidential attitude" toward a situation like a projective test. They attempt to bolster their interpretations by means of finding a kind of evidence in the stimulus or environment, as if to thereby convey that the meaning they offer cannot really be attributed to them but is merely given by the stimulus. Such communicators also tend to offer multiple possible meanings when they describe an ambiguous stimulus. It is not hard to imagine how growing up around parents whose orientation under certain circumstances involves the seeking of clues or the suggestion of the existence of a slew of potential meanings underlying the observed could contribute to an attitude in the child such as that described by Shapiro (1965) as the paranoid style of relating to the world by means of scanning widely for specific clues to an underlying and hidden meaning (the paranoid "loss of reality").

Thus, it would seem plausible to argue that defensive communication could give rise to the two main attributes of the classic paranoid style since the capacity on the parents' part for providing adequate cognitive models would be conducive to the capacity on the part of the offspring to cognize the world in an adequate and advanced manner and because the defensiveness might well give rise to the suspiciousness characteristic of such persons. It is the combination of such adequate intellectual faculties with an attitude of distrust and suspicion toward the environment that forms the essence of the paranoid orientation.

Incidentally, Arieti (1955) reports clinical observations in accord with these hypotheses. He states that the parents of paranoid patients tend to blame their children concerning their intentions and thoughts, whereas the parents of other kinds of schizophrenics, especially catatonics, are more likely to blame their children for their actions. This characterization of the parents of paranoids would certainly be consistent with suggesting that they have a defensive style of communication for it seems that the defensive style of communication would go along with a tendency to scrutinize the environment for hidden meanings. Such scrutiny, when the environment is other persons, involves scrutinizing the other for hidden motives.

Although there is some evidence which might indirectly suggest that the communication styles of different members of the same family tend to be similar to each other (Wild, Shapiro, and Abelin, 1977), it is certainly possible and probably likely that in some cases the father and mother will have quite contrasting styles. One might well expect on the basis of the etiological model presented here that such differences would have interesting consequences concerning the cognitive style of the offspring. One possibility for example is that, in the case of a family where one parent has an extremely deficient style whereas the other is capable of great clarity at least on certain topics, the offspring would evince some thought disorder, but its manifestation would be far more variable than in the case of a child both of whose parents manifested primarily the deficient style.

It is interesting, given the above speculations concerning differential etiological patterns, that there is some evidence that when more than one member of a given family is schizophrenic, there is a tendency for those members to be of the same subtype (e.g., hebephrenic versus paranoid; Tsuang, 1975; Winokur, 1975; Winokur, Morrison, Clancy, and Crowe, 1974).

CONCLUDING REMARKS

The above theoretical treatment suggests certain empirical hypotheses. One would expect to find that the styles of communication of parents of thought-disordered patients would be primarily of the deficient kind and would, relatively speaking, be manifest across a broad variety of tasks and inter-personal situations. Furthermore, the more disordered the schizophrenic, i.e., the more severe or constant his thought disorder, the more deficient the communication style of his parents would be likely to be. The communication of parents of constricted, i.e., non-thought-disordered paranoid patients, would on the other hand be much more dependent on task or situation involved, such that they would be liable to be clear on tasks which do not threaten revelation of the self. On tasks which do threaten such revelation, the style of their communication deviance would be likely to be of the defensive rather than of the deficient/primitive kind.

In research carried out by the author (Sass, 1979), these hypotheses were, in the main, confirmed. Such empirical findings, which cannot be summarized in any detail here, lend credence to the theoretical arguments presented above concerning the appropriateness of making certain qualitative distinctions in the two realms of phenomena whose relationship is at issue. It appears that constricted and thought-disordered schizophrenia are quite different forms of illness, at least with respect to the role which communication deviance plays in their genesis. It also appears that communication deviance should not be thought of as a unitary phenomenon (rather, as a disjunctive concept) since it includes at least two forms of deviance which stem from quite different sources. It was found, incidently, that the CD variable measured primarily the presence of deficiency deviance.

Since the previous studies by Singer and Wynne included very few constricted schizophrenics, there is no contradiction between the empirical results of those studies and the findings of my research. I would dispute only those past interpretations which take their findings as indicating the importance of CD for the etiology of schizophrenia in general. On the basis both of my findings and of the theoretical analysis presented above, I would argue for revising the communication deviance hypothesis to state that CD is a necessary condition in the etiology only of clearly thought-disordered schizophrenia. It seems clear, in any case, that both in evaluating and in further extending the seminal work by Singer and Wynne concerning communication patterns of parents and offspring psychopathology, it may be important to pay greater attention to significant questions involving the proper theoretical conceptualization of the phenomena at issue.

McLean Hospital/Harvard Medical School

REFERENCES

Arieti, S.: 1955, *The Interpretation of Schizophrenia*, Brunner, New York.

Arieti, S.: 1974, *Interpretation of Schizophrenia* (2nd edition), Basic Books, New York.

Baker, R.: 1953, *The Acquisition of Verbal Concepts in Schizophrenia*, unpublished doctoral dissertation, Clark University.

Bates, E.: 1976, 'Pragmatics and Sociolinguistics in Child Language', *Language Deficiency in Children: Selected Readings*, D. Morehead and A. Morehead (eds.), University Park Press, Baltimore.

Bernstein, R.: 1971, *Praxis and Action*, Univ. of Penn. Press, Philadelphia.

Deleuze, G. and Guattari, F.: 1977, *Anti-oedipus, Capitalism and Schizophrenia*, Viking, New York.

De Waelhens, A.: 1978, *Schizophrenia, a Philosophical Reflection on Lacan's Structuralist Interpretation*, Duquesne University Press, Pittsburgh.

Doane, J.: 1978, 'Family Interaction and Communication Deviance in Disturbed and Normal Families: a Review of Research', *Family Process* 17, 357–376.

Feffer, M.: 1967, 'Symptom Expression as a Form of Primitive Decentering', *Psychological Review* 74, 16–28.

Flavell, J.H.: 1963, *The Developmental Psychology of Jean Piaget*, Van Nostrand, Princeton.

Flavell, J., Botkin, P., Fry, C., Wright, J., and Jarvis, P.: 1975, *The Development of Role-taking and Communication Skills in Children*, Krieger, New York.

Freeman, T., Cameron, J.L., and McGhie, A.: 1958, *Chronic Schizophrenia*, International Universities Press, New York.

Goldman, A.E.: 1960, 'Symbolic Representation in Schizophrenia', *Journal of Personality* 28, 293–316.

Goldman, A.E.: 1962, 'A Comparative-Developmental Approach to Schizophrenia', *Psychological Bulletin* 59, 57–69.

Goldstein, K. and Sheerer, M.: 1941, 'Abstract and Concrete Behavior: an Experimental Study with Special Tests', *Psychological Monographs* 53, (2, Whole No. 239).

Goodman, N.: 1978, 'The Status of Style', *Ways of Worldmaking*, Hackett, Indianapolis and Cambridge.

Gordon, D. and Lakoff, G.: 1971, 'Conversational Postulates', *Papers from the Seventh Regional Meeting, Chicago Linguistic Society*, Chicago Linguistic Society, Chicago.

Grice, H.: 1967, *Logic and Conversation*, circulated manuscript (Delivered as the William James lectures at Harvard).

Hirsch, S.R. and Leff, J.P.: 1971, 'Parental Abnormalities of Verbal Communication in the Transmission of Schizophrenia', *Psychological Medicine* 1, 118–127

Hirsch, S.R. and Leff, J.P.: 1975, *Abnormalities in Parents of Schizophrenics*, Oxford U. Press, London.

Jacob, T.: 1975, 'Family Interaction in Disturbed and Normal Families: a Methodological and Substantive Review', *Psychology Bulletin* 82, 33–65.

Krauss, R. and Glucksberg, S.: 1969, 'The Development of Communication Competence as a Function of Age', *Child Development* 40, 255–266.

Lakoff, R.: 1972, 'Language in Context', *Language* 48, 907–927.

Langer, J.: 1969, *Theories of Development*, Holt, Rinehart & Winston, New York.

Lidz, T.: 1978, 'A Developmental Theory', *Schizophrenia, Science and Practice*, J. Shershow (ed.), Harvard University Press, Cambridge.

Luria, A.R.: 1976, *Cognitive Development, its Cultural and Social Foundations*, Harvard U. Press, Cambridge.

McConaghy, N.: 1960, 'Modes of Abstract Thinking and Psychosis', *American Journal of Psychiatry* 117, 106–110.

McConaghy, N. and Clancy, M.: 1968, 'Familial Relationships of Allusive Thinking in University Students and Their Parents', *British Journal of Psychiatry* 114, 1079–1087.

Merleau-Ponty, M.: 1973, 'Dialogue and the Perception of the Other', *The Prose of the World*, Northwestern U. Press, Evanston.

Muntz, H.J. and Power, R.P.: 1970, 'Thought Disorder in the Parents of Thought-disordered Schizophrenics', *British Journal of Psychiatry* 117, 707–708.

Peters, R.S.: 1958, *The Concept of Motivation*, Routledge and Kegan Paul, London.

Piaget, J.: 1955, *The Language and Thought of the Child*, World, Cleveland.

Richards, I.A.: 1932, *Mencius on the Mind*, Harcourt Brace, New York.

Rommetveit, R.: 1974, *On Message Structure – a Framework for the Study of Language and Communication*, Wiley & Sons, London.

Sass, L.A.: 1979, *Styles of Communication Deviance in the Parents of Thought-Disordered and Non-Thought-Disordered Schizophrenics*, unpublished doctoral dissertation, University of California at Berkeley.

Schachtel, E.: 1959, 'The Development of Focal Attention and the Emergence of Reality', *Metamorphosis*, Basic Books, New York.

Schwartz, D.A.: 1963, 'A Re-view of the "Paranoid" Concept', *Archives of General Psychiatry* 8, 349–361.

Searle J.: 1969, *Speech Acts*, Cambridge U. Press, Cambridge.

Searle, J.: 1975, 'Speech Acts and Recent Linguistics', in D. Aaronson and R. Rieber (eds.), *Developmental Psycholinguistics and Communication Disorders*, New York Academy of Sciences, New York.

Searles, H.: 1967, 'The Schizophrenic Individual's Experience of His World', *Psychiatry* 30, 119–131.

Shapiro, D.: 1965, *Neurotic Styles*, Basic Books, New York.

Singer, M.T.: 1976, 'Impact Versus Diagnosis: a New Approach to Assessment Techniques in Family Research and Therapy', circulated manuscript.

Singer, M.T.: and Wynne, L.C.: 1965a, 'Thought Disorder and Family Relations of Schizophrenics: III. Methodology Using Projective Techniques', *Archives of General Psychiatry* 12, 187–200.

Singer, M.T. and Wynne, L.C.: 1965b, 'Thought Disorder and Family Relations of Schizophrenics: IV. Results and Implications', *Archives of General Psychiatry* 12, 201–212.

Singer, M.T. and Wynne, L.C.: 1966, 'Principles for Scoring Communication Defects and Deviances in Parents of Schizophrenics: Rorschach and TAT Scoring Manuals', *Psychiatry* 29, 260–288.

Singer, M.T., Wynne, L.C. and Toohey, M.: 1978, 'Communication Disorders and the Families of Schizophrenics', *The Nature of Schizophrenia*, Wiley, New York.

Slepian, H.: 1959, *A Developmental Study of Inner Versus External Speech in Normals and Schizophrenics*, unpublished doctoral dissertation, Clark University.

Storch, A.: 1924, *The Primitive and Archaic Forms of Inner Experience and Thought in Schizophrenia,* Nervous and Mental Disease Publishing Co., New York and Washington.

Strauss, J.S., Harder, D.W. and Chandler, M.: 1978, 'Egocentrism in Children of Parents with a History of Psychotic Disorders', *Archives of General Psychiatry* 36, 191–196.

Toulmin, S.: Sept. 28, 1978, 'The Mozart of Psychology', *New York Review of Books.*

Tsuang, M.T.: 1975, 'Heterogeneity of Schizophrenia', *Biological Psychiatry* 10, 465–474.

Von Domarus, E.: 1964, 'The Specific Laws of Logic in Schizophrenia', *Language and Thought in Schizophrenia,* J. Kasanin (ed.), U. of California Press, Berkeley.

Vygotsky, L.S.: 1962, *Thought and Language,* M.I.T. Press, Cambridge.

Wanner, E.: 1973, 'Do We Understand Sentences From the Outside-in or From the Inside-out?', *Daedalus,* 163–184.

Werner, H.: 1957, *Comparative Psychology of Mental Development,* International U. Press, New York.

Werner, H. and Kaplan, B.: 1963, *Symbol Formation,* Wiley, New York.

Wild, C., Shapiro, L. and Abelin, T.: 1977, 'Communication Patterns and Role Structure in Families of Male Schizophrenics', *Archives of General Psychiatry* 34, 58–70.

Winokur, G.: 1975, 'Paranoid Versus Hebephrenic Schizophrenia: Clinical and Familial (Genetic) Heterogeneity', *Psychopharmacology* 1, 567–577.

Winokur, G., Morrison, J., Clancy, J. and Crowe, R.: 1974, 'Iowa 500: the Clinical and Genetic Distinction of Hebephrenic and Paranoid Schizophrenia', *Journal of Nervous and Mental Disease* 159, 12–19.

Wynne, L. and Singer, M.T.: 1963a, 'Thought Disorder and Family Relations of Schizophrenics: I. A Research Strategy', *Archives of General Psychiatry* 9, 191–198.

Wynne, L. and Singer, M.T.: 1963b, 'Thought Disorder and Family Relations of Schizophrenics: II. A Classification of Forms of Thinking', *Archives of General Psychiatry* 9, 199–206.

LARRY I. BENOWITZ,[b] DAVID M. BEAR,[c] MARSEL-M. MESULAM,[d]
ROBERT ROSENTHAL,[e] ERAN ZAIDEL[f] AND ROGER W. SPERRY[f]

CONTRIBUTIONS OF THE RIGHT CEREBRAL HEMISPHERE IN PERCEIVING PARALINGUISTIC CUES OF EMOTION[a]

Discoveries in neurology and linguistics indicate that many aspects of human language are determined by specific structural features of the brain, a notion which differs radically from the more prevalent idea of language being an arbitrary, culturally evolved set of symbols and combinatorial rules which during development somehow become represented upon an infinitely malleable nervous system. The present study has attempted to examine whether such neurological specification might extend to other aspects of our social interactions as well, particularly the communication of affect through paralinguistic cues. But before describing the rationale for our own studies, it might be best to mention a little more about spoken language.

Through postmortem studies of people who, during their lives had lost linguistic fluency after stroke, the French neurologist Paul Broca discovered that it was the left inferior precentral cortex whose destruction caused speech production to be very labored, with most grammatical elements omitted. In this disorder, now commonly known as Broca's aphasia, the principal content words remain appropriate but are produced with difficulty. Full sentences are seldom used, and surprisingly, reading or repetition of text material follows the same pattern. Singing remains intact, however, showing that the dysfunction is not general to all vocal control. Rather, it has been postulated that Broca's area is involved in transforming intentions or ideas into spoken utterances according to the appropriate grammatical rules.[1] A few years after Broca's discovery, the German neurologist Carl Wernicke found that damage to another portion of the left hemisphere, adjacent to the primary auditory area in the temporal lobe, is associated with a disorder in which speech production is fluent but often makes little sense. Nonsensical words are included, incorrect syllables are substituted in otherwise correct words, and ideation is sometimes aberrant. Grammatical form is intact, however, and even the inappropriate words take on a syntactic form suitable to their place in the sentence. Phrase length and melody of speech are preserved, so that someone not familiar with the language being spoken would have the impression that all is normal. Comprehension of spoken or written language is

---

[a]Adapted from an article written for the *McLean Hospital Journal* **3**, 146–167, 1980.

L. Vaina and J. Hintikka (eds.), Cognitive Constraints on Communication, 75–95.
© 1984 *by D. Reidel Publishing Company.*

likewise impaired, and it is believed that Wernicke's area may play a role in processing semantic and ideational aspects of language. Other types of language disorders, including selective losses in reading, repetition, and naming, have likewise been associated with the loss of particular left brain regions, supporting the idea that human language is inexorably related to specific anatomical features of the brain. Moreover, recent studies now indicate that portions of the posterior temporal cortex, which includes the Wernicke's area, are asymmetric between the two sides of the brain at birth.[2] Thus, it may be the case that the neurology may even prefigure where and how language becomes represented in the brain, or, in other words, our linguistic abilities may actually be the product of highly specialized, predetermined circuits in the brain. A similar conclusion has been reached by linguists impressed with the many stereotyped features of language development in the child and with the universality of formal aspects of syntax.[3,4] Language develops without the child needing any explicit instruction as to rules of phoneme production or syntax, a phenomenon which Chomsky[3] has argued can only come about by linguistic competence being predetermined by the neurology of the human brain. Chomsky has also argued that other domains of human cognition which are similarly acquired spontaneously in childhood and which are universal in their manifestation must likewise reflect well-defined neural determinants. One faculty which may be of this nature would be the ability to evaluate the significance of paralinguistic cues in communication.

As demonstrated in numerous studies, a great deal of the information which is exchanged in human interactions is not contained in the words alone as they would appear in a written text: facial expressions, body movements and intonational qualities of the voice all serve to structure and qualify the verbal message, influence the social relationship between speaker and listener, and convey information about one's emotional state.[5-10] The thesis that competence in evaluating these cues may be specified by our biological inheritance was first put forth in 1872 by Charles Darwin.[11] 'The Expression of the Emotions in Man and Animals,' presents a series of observations, arguments, and proposals for further research which stand today as the most thorough analysis of the biology of affective communication. Darwin was particularly impressed with the observation that the facial expressions that appear during such states as anger, disgust, and pleasure appear in infancy and are universal to all cultures. He carefully analyzed the groups of facial muscles involved in the formation of these expressions, then reasoned how such activational patterns might have selectively come to be "hard-wired" because of their functional advantages in our evolutionary past. And while their actual utility would have long since disappeared, the patterns of expression may have been retained for their communicative value. However, for this to be of any significance, not only the expressive capacity, but also the ability to perceive the significance of these signals would need to be specified biologically. By analogy with spoken language, where some 2000 distinct tongues exist and where almost no words are universal, the issue is not whether the particular signals used are common, but whether formal features of the communicative system are. Yet unlike spoken language, many facial expressions, body movements, and vocal intonations used to express particular emotions are indeed identical between cultures that have been separated from one another for thousands of years, presumably because the fixed neuromuscular patterns that are involved. But aside from these instances of emotional expression, much of nonverbal communication is quite culture-specific, composed, according to Birdwhistell,[9] of a hierarchy of elements which can be compared to phonemes, words and sentences.

In the present study we examined whether the ability to evaluate the emotional significance of paralinguistic cues might be associated with specific cortical regions. Subjects having well-defined patterns of brain damage, including either lateralized lesions or surgical commissurotomy, were given a standardized test in identifying facial expressions, body movements and intonational qualities of the voice. The principal question was whether these abilities are well localized, as is the case for spoken language, or whether instead they are more diffusely represented in the brain. A priori, one might imagine that nonverbal communication could be closely allied in the brain to language, since paralinguistic cues accompany the verbal message and, like it, require the interpretation of discrete symbols. Alternatively, it might be anticipated that nonverbal communication might be more a function of the right cerebral hemisphere, since it is that side of the brain which is dominant for such functions as distinguishing faces, apprehending spatial relations, processing certain features of music, and perhaps even responding appropriately to emotional situations.[12] Another question was whether the various aspects of nonverbal sensitivity were dissociable from one another, i.e., whether each represents a discrete function unto itself, and further what other cognitive faculties these abilities might be related to.

SUBJECTS

The 11 subjects used in the first set of studies had predominantly unilateral brain lesions which had been verified radiographically (10 by CT scan and

TABLE I
Profile of neurological subjects

Subject	Age	Sex	Pref. Hand[a]	Lesion Site	Cause of Pathology	Time Elapsed	Neurological Signs	Neuropsychiatric Profile
R1	56	M	R	CT:[b] infarction of R. temp., inf. parietal lobe	Hemorrhage from an aneurysm of R. MCA	6 mos.	Mild, transient L. hemiparesis; L. inf. quadrantopia; resolving L. VF neglect	WAIS VIQ 134, PIQ 102. Difficulties with colors, spatial relations, faces; object agnosia. Inappropriate irritability, joking. Minimization of deficits.
R2	41	M	L	CT: low density throughout R. hem.; gross enlargement R. lat. ventricle, porencephaly	Traumatic encephalopathy	8 yrs.	L. hemiparesis, hemaesthesia; rotational nystagmus	Agraphia. Poor calculations. Speech fluent but production aprosodic; minimization of deficits; inappropriate irritability, familiarity, jocularity.
R3	39	F	R	CT: dilatation of R. cerebral ventricle, extensive atrophy. EEG: sharp and slow waves over R. hemisphere	Intracerebral hemorrhage from AVM of R. MCA. Surgical resection of AVM, implantation of shunt	31 yrs. 19 yrs.	Spastic L. hemiparesis, mild hemaesthesia. LVF neglect	WAIS verbal "superior". Concrete. Unable to distinguish major from minor features of stories. Poor block design, picture arrangement, constructions. Minimization of physical, intellectual deficits. Alternating irritability and submissiveness; socially imperceptive.
R4	24	M	R	CT: bilateral enlarged ventricles. General hydrocephalus. EEG: slow waves, decreased voltage over whole R. hem.; some slowing over L. temp.	Traumatic encephalopathy. R. subdural temporal hematoma, brainstem contusion (motorcycle accident)	8 yrs.	Hemaesthesia, hemiparesis of L. side. Weak, atrophied L. hand, thigh. Circumduction of L. leg. R. hypotonia, R. eye deviated	Poor interpersonal relations, perceptions. Delusional denial of disabilities. Continuous irritating comments. Unmotivated. Increased religiosity. Obsessional orderliness. Excellent language usage but misses gist of stories.
R5	59	M	R	CT: focal atrophy, R. parietal. Dilatation of R. lat. ventricle and temporal horn. EEG: seizure activity, R. hem.	Local infarcts from 2 CVA's	5 yrs. 8 yrs.	L. hemifield inattention	Poor memory for faces, personalities, spatial orientation, designs. Copies figures well. Decreased motivation.
R6	52	M	R	CT: arteriogram: infarcted R. temporal lobe	AVM, R. mid. cerebral artery		L. homonymous hemianopia; mild L. hemiparesis	WAIS VIQ 110, PIQ 93. Poor digit-symbol, object assembly, memory for geometric designs. Occasional outbursts of anger; insensitivity to others' feelings. Alternating exuberance and depression. Suicide attempts.

	Age	Sex		CT[b]	Etiology	Duration	Neurological	Clinical
R7	71	M	R	CT: severe atrophy of R. temporoparietal area	2 infarcts in distribution of R. mid. cer. artery	10 mos.	Dense L. hemiplegia, hemaesthesia, LVF neglect	WAIS VIQ 148, PIQ 89. Reading intact, some pseudoalexia. Verbal output rich in detail, humor, but production monotonous. Poor verbal abstraction, block design, picture arrangement, object assembly, drawing. Poor facial mimicry. Immodesty on ward. Unaware of cognitive deficits.
L1	27	M	R	Angiography: occluded L. carotid artery. General atrophy of L. hemisphere	CVA	21 yrs.	Dense R. hemiplegia; R. arm spastic and atrophic	WAIS VIQ 100, PIQ 103. Good visuospatial constructional abilities. Deficits in motor organization, sequencing. Fluent aphasia, poor reading, writing, spelling, calculations. Grammar, vocabulary somewhat restricted.
L2	48	F	R	CT: infarct of L. posterior frontal, parietal areas	CVA after auto accident	8 mos.	Transient R. hand weakness, difficulty performing bucco-facial motions	Broca's aphasia. Labored oral expression with some agrammatisms, word-finding pauses; mild comprehension difficulty, difficulties making logical inferences.
L3	61	F	R	CT: marked lesion of L. frontal insular areas: Gen. cortical atrophy	CVA	1 yr.	Transient R. hemiparesis	Conduction aphasia (speech fluent, paraphrasic; some word-finding pauses). Requires repeated readings for comprehension. Poor repetition ability. Writing impaired.
L4	49	M	R	CT: infarct in distribution of L. MCA	Aneurism of L. internal carotid artery; embolus to L. MCA	2 yrs.	Slight R. sided weakness	Recovering Wernicke's aphasic; impaired auditory comprehension: fluent speech with paraphrasias, agrammatisms, circumlocutions. Poor repetition. WAIS PIQ 144.

[a] Handedness prior to surgery indicated

[b] CT: Computer-assisted tomographic data

Other abbreviations: AVM – arteriovenous malformation
MCA – middle cerebral artery
VF – visual field
WAIS – Wechsler Adult Intelligence Scale
inf. – inferior
sup. – superior

one by angiography): EEG data were also available in several cases. Table I summarizes the neurological and behavioral data on these subjects, obtained by staff members of the Beth Israel and Boston Veterans' Administration Hospitals.

THE PONS TEST

The test used for these studies, the Profile of Nonverbal Sensitivity (PONS), was developed by Professor Robert Rosenthal and his colleagues in the Department of Psychology, Harvard University.[13] The PONS is a standardized scale designed to assess competence in interpreting various types of emotional scenes presented through facial expressions, body movements and intonational qualities of the voice. The test has been administered to several thousand people in this country and elsewhere, providing extensive normative data against which the performance of our neurological subjects could be compared.

The PONS consists of a 16 mm black-and-white film containing 220 items to be discriminated. Each item runs for two seconds and portrays one of 20 different scenes presented through one or more channels of nonverbal communication. The 20 scenes used in the PONS test were portrayed by a young woman and vary in emotional tone along two dimensions, positive-negative and dominant-submissive.

Each of the scenes is presented in 11 different ways, varying according to the channels of information available. Five of these contain only "pure" visual or "pure" audio information: (1) face alone, no voice; (2) body from neck to knees, no voice; (3) face plus body, no voice; (4) random-spliced (RS) speech, no picture; (5) electronically filtered speech (called CF, or content filtered). The remaining six modes represent combinations of these: (6) face plus random-spliced speech; (7) face plus content-filtered speech; (8) body + RS; (9) body + CF; (10) full figure + RS; and (11) full figure + CF. Items depicting various emotional scenes through different channels appear in random sequence on the test.

To prepare the random-spliced speech, the two-second audio tape was cut into small segments and randomly reassembled. When played back, tonal qualities of the voice are retained but the sequence of individual sounds is disrupted. In content-filtered speech, selected bands of frequencies are removed and the audio signal is clipped. Although the voice sounds muffled and unintelligible, the intonation, rhythm, tempo and loudness of speech are preserved. In a sense, the random-spliced speech and the content-filtered speech can be viewed as being somewhat complementary. The random-spliced speech retains tone and timbre but degrades the rhythm, while the content-filtered speech loses the tonal qualities of the voice but retains the rhythm or sequence.

After ascertaining that the oral instructions for the test were understood, visual functioning was demonstrated by having subjects read the film credits on the screen and, intermittently during the test, asking them to describe the actress's poses. For the test items, the viewer selects one of two alternative choices which best describes the scene presented. These two choices — the correct one and a randomly selected incorrect one — normally appear on an answer sheet. However, since many of the neurological subjects were either dyslexic, hemianopic, or suffered hemifield neglect, the choices were read aloud to them before the scenes appeared. When requested to do so by the subjects, the choices were again repeated after the scenes, though this was kept to a minimum to avoid possible cueing by the experimenter's voice intonation. General alertness and attention to the test were monitored throughout. The strongest assurance of adequate comprehension and response set, however, was the observation that each subject was able to obtain normal scores on one or more portions of the test.

Data

Test results are reported in terms of percentile rankings, obtained by comparing subjects' raw scores with the published normative data.[14] On the various channels of nonverbal communication, data are pooled together to increase the size of the item samples. Thus, for the first channel presented in Table II, "Audio only," the score for the 20 items in which CF speech was presented without any visual information plus the score for the 20 items in which RS was presented without any visual information are pooled together. Each of the next two columns, RS and CF, combines the score for the 20 items in which the audio channel was presented alone plus the 60 in which it was combined with either the face, body, or whole figure. On the visual items, "Face" includes the 20 items in which the face was shown alone plus the 40 items in which it appeared together with RS or CF speech. "Body" and "Figure" are similarly derived. "Video only" shows the score for the 60 items in which the face, body, and full figure were presented without any audio information. The right side of Table II presents subjects' performance analyzed by the type of scene: scores are based upon the 55 items for each emotional quadrant (i.e., positive-

TABLE II
Performance of neurological subjects on the PONS Test: Percentile ranking scores

| | | Subjects | Total | Channels (pooled data) | | | | | | | | | | | |
| | | | | Auditory | | | Visual | | | | Type of scene | | | |
				Audio only	RS	CF	Face	Body	Figure	Video only	Pos.-sub.	Pos.-dom.	Neg.-sub.	Neg.-dom.
Right hemisphere damage		R1	0.2	30	0.1	6	<0.1	11	1	2	0.1	5	1	9
		R2	1	11	4	3	4	4	2	3	1	2	26	3
		R3	5	37	8	24	3	27	9	8	6	21	26	9
		R4	12	19	13	26	5	38	19	12	14	75	16	1
		R5	12	2	13	10	52	23	19	40	6	5	22	69
		R6	42	98	30	69	8	38	42	40	89	21	30	39
		R7	0.1	(76)*	4	1	2	0.1	<0.1	0.1	0.1	14	2	<0.1
	Average		4	39	6	12	3	12	5	8	5	15	13	8
Left hemisphere damage		L1	62	19	65	39	77	72	69	86	59	36	94	29
		L2	12	30	18	9	52	16	4	40	6	5	69	15
		L3	24	67	48	42	30	28	22	11	14	51	46	24
		L4	37	30	24	45	44	46	52	66	59	21	22	79
	Average		34	35	38	29	50	40	34	50	29	24	61	34
	Number of items		220	40	80	80	60	60	60	60	55	55	55	55

*Subject completed only ½ of test; scores statistically unreliable for "audio only".

submissive, positive-dominant, negative-submissive and negative-dominant).

Several of the most interesting cases will first be presented individually; general comments about the overall performance of right- vs. left-brain-damaged subjects follow.

A. Right-Brain-Damaged Subjects

R1. This 56-year-old man suffered a stroke of the right middle cerebral artery six months prior to testing, which resulted in an infarct of the right temporal and inferior parietal areas. He had previously held a position of considerable responsibility in a large company, while also finding time to read several books a week. After the stroke, R1 was no longer able to get the gist of what he was reading, but described this simply as a "vision problem." Subsequent tests showed his acuity to be normal, although a left inferior quadrantanopia and some left visual field neglect were noted. Deficits were found in color-naming, judgment of distances, and object recognition. A striking personality change was also noted: his formerly reserved, gentlemanly demeanor disappeared and he became quarrelsome, joked continuously, often about sexual subjects, and was noted as acting inappropriately familiar with staff members. Language usage remained rich; his posttraumatic verbal IQ was 135, performance 102.

On the PONS test, R1's overall score fell three standard deviations below normal. Performance was particularly impaired on the items involving facial expressions, and when only the face was shown he scored randomly. In striking contrast, he was normal on items requiring judgment of body gestures alone. An extraordinary feature of this man's performance was that, despite his inability to evaluate facial items, the face nevertheless appears to have remained magnetic to him and stood in the way of his making use of other cues whenever it was present. If we consider the test items in which the face was absent (i.e., body alone, tone-only items, BO + CF speech, etc.), this subject actually scored fairly well, performing only 0.83 standard deviation below normal; however, when the face was added on to these channels his performance fell another two standard deviations.

On audio items, R1 was 3.2 standard deviations below normal on items containing random-spliced speech alone, but only 1.6 standard deviations below normal for content-filtered items. When his performance was analyzed across the different types of scene, a very skewed profile appeared: while he was only one standard deviation below average in recognizing dominant items, particularly negative-dominant ones (e.g., expressing anger), he was practically incapable of properly identifying positive-submissive items (e.g., asking forgiveness).

R5. This 59-year-old man suffered two strokes five and eight years ago: CT scans reveal focal atrophy in the right parietal area, along with some dilatation of the right lateral ventricle and temporal horn. Continuing seizure activity in the right hemisphere was revealed by an EEG. Formerly a factory owner and manager of two restaurants, R5 lost much of his drive after the two strokes. However, he remains articulate and continues to speak three languages fluently. He is very sociable, humorous, and warm.

Striking visuospatial deficits are apparent: though he can copy figures well, he has poor memory for designs and is highly disoriented spatially. He has little ability to remember faces; he reports having spoken to people for hours, then having no memory of them or of the conversation the next day. A left hemifield inattention was noted in the neurological exam.

On the PONS test, R5's overall performance was a little over one standard deviation below normal. Unlike R1, his ability to identify facial expressions was fully intact. He scored less well on items showing the body only, and was extremely poor in judging intonational qualities of the voice (on items that included the voice only, he scored at a nearly chance level). Across the various types of emotional scenes, he showed a skewed performance profile reminiscent of R1's. R5 was adept in identifying negative-dominant items, but was poor in evaluating positive emotional scenes.

R6. Ten months previously, this 71-year-old man suffered two massive strokes in distribution of the right middle cerebral artery, resulting in a severe atrophy of the temporoparietal area. A dense left hemiplegia and hemaesthesia remain, as does a neglect of the left visual field. This eminent surgeon had been admitted to college in his youth on the basis of having one of the highest Stanford-Binet scores in the country. His WAIS verbal IQ remains 148 after the stroke, although his performance score is down to 89. Writing and reading remain intact, although inconsequential words in the left hemifield are occasionally omitted. Language usage, especially in describing remote events, is rich in detail and humor, though produced in a somewhat deadpan, monotonous manner. Digit span and simple arithmetic are normal. However, verbal abstraction is poor. Performance on block design, picture arrangement, object assembly and digit symbol tasks are all severely compromised, as are copying and drawing from memory. A left hemineglect is dramatic, although this is more marked for designs than for reading words. Recognition of famous faces is somewhat impaired, but faces on the ward are recognized. Facial mimicry is poor. Singing is monotonous with rhythm preserved. The subject has been incontinent and has occasionally been seen exposed on the ward. He is unaware of his visuospatial and other cognitive problems.

R7 was only able to complete half of the PONS test, and consequently the scores reported in Table 2 represent extrapolations which are somewhat less statistically reliable than for the other cases. Overall performance was 3.5 standard deviations below the norm ($0.02°$ percentile), with the deficit being greater for video than for audio channels. Across the various types of scenes, identification of positive-dominant items was just outside the normal range; in contrast, negative-dominant items, normally the most salient on the test, were barely recognized at all.

B. Subjects with Damage to the Left Hemisphere

L1: This formerly right-handed, 27-year-old man suffered an occlusion of the left carotid artery at the age of six which resulted in a dense right hemiplegia and a severe language deficit. The right side remains spastic and atrophic, and the subject now relies upon his left arm. However, no right hemianopia or loss of sensation are observed. The subject reads at a grade 4 level, writes at a primer level, misspells the simplest words and cannot do simple arithmetic operations. Vocabulary is at a grade 6 level. Grammar is somewhat restricted but correct. Some difficulty in word-finding and in pronunciation remain. Prosody is good. Moderate to severe deficits are seen on tests of motor organization and sequencing. Constructional ability and recall of complex figures are good. WAIS verbal IQ is 100, performance 103. Dilantin and pentobarbitol are taken to control seizures.

The subject's overall performance on the PONS test was slightly above average. Excellent scores were obtained on video items, particularly those involving the face. Performance for items with audio information only was considerably inferior, although all scores fell within one standard deviation of the mean. For the different types of scenes, the negative and submissive items were perceived exceptionally well, the others within the normal range.

L4, a 49-year-old right-handed man, suffered an aneurism of the left internal carotid with a cerebrovascular infarct in distribution of the left middle cerebral artery two years ago. Shortly after the stroke, speech was fluent but empty of content. The subject could follow orders but could not point to objects or repeat even single words or numbers. Comprehension has improved markedly, although a few words are still missed. Speech is halting, contains paraphasias of phonetically or semantically related words, along with circumlocutions, agrammatisms, and some neologisms. Intonation of speech is good. Visuospatial and constructional abilities are unimpaired. Performance IQ on the WAIS is 144, and even shortly after the stroke, the subject scored in the 95° percentile on the Raven's progressive matrices test.

Overall performance on the PONS test was just below average (38th percentile), and scores on all items fell within ±1 standard deviation of the norm. Across the various types of scenes, scores range from the upper quartile for recognition of the negative-dominant scenes to the lower quartile for both positive-dominant and negative-submissive items.

C. General Comparison of Right- and Left-Brain-Damaged Groups

The left- and right-hemisphere groups both comprise heterogeneous populations, not only in terms of the subjects' age, sex, background, and native intelligence, but also in terms of the specific loci of damage within the hemisphere. Nevertheless, certain between-group differences stand out markedly. In overall scores, the subjects with right-sided damage averaged 1.86 ± 0.40 standard deviations below the mean, the subject with left-sided damage 0.48 ± 0.33 standard deviation below; these differ at a level of $0.05 > p > 0.01$ (2-tailed). Comparing the two groups' performance on the various channels, the subjects with right-sided damage were significantly poorer in interpreting random-spliced speech ($p \sim .02$), and, most strikingly, facial expressions ($p \sim 0.01$). No reliable between-group differences were found for recognition of body expressions ($p \sim 0.15$), content-filtered speech ($p \sim 0.25$) or tone only.

Differences between the two groups were marginally significant for items involving the whole figure ($p \sim 0.08$) and video alone ($p \sim 0.07$), effects very likely attributable to the inclusion of facial expressions in both of these categories.

The scoring profiles of the two groups suggest a complementarity in their patterns of deficits. On visual items, subjects having right hemisphere damage did relatively better in discerning emotions from the body gestures than from the face; with audio input, they were relatively better with content-filtered than with random-spliced speech. The data from the left-hemisphere subjects suggest just the opposite pattern: better performance of items of facial expression than for body gestures, and higher scores for RS vs CF speech.

In comparison with the subjects having left-sided damage, the right hemisphere group's relative impairment in discerning facial emotions more than body gestures is significant at a p value of 0.08 (2-tailed), and for audio information the relative impairment in interpreting random-spliced more than content-filtered speech is reliable at the $p = 0.07$ level (2-tailed).

While most individuals in both groups tended to show highly skewed profiles across the different types of emotional scenes, no overall between-group differences stood out when scores were pooled.

D. Studies in "Split-Brain" Subjects

Working in the laboratory of Dr. R.W. Sperry at Cal Tech, we administered the PONS test to several "split-brain" patients, people whose two cerebral hemispheres function in isolation from one another following surgical resection of the tencephalic commissures.[12] Studies in these subjects have of course already provided us with invaluable information about the contributions of the two hemispheres in many cognitive domains, and we felt that these people would allow us an extraordinary opportunity to further examine the cerebral lateralization of nonverbal communication.

In these subjects we used a shorter version of the PONS containing 80 items: a film showing the 20 "face only" items and the 20 with body alone; and an audio tape which presented the 20 RS and 20 CF speech items.

Very dramatic results were obtained from subject LB, a 24-year-old right-handed man who had been commissurotomized at the age of 13 for intractable epilepsy. His WAIS verbal IQ is 110, performance 100. On visual items of the PONS test, each hemisphere was tested separately using the newly developed "Z-lens."[16] This system is composed of a collimator attached to a contact lens. By covering one eye and occluding either the nasal or the temporal half of the collimator, complex visual stimuli can be presented over long periods of time to only one hemisphere, an advance which for the first time allows the limits of competence of each side of the brain to be studied in isolation. The right hemisphere was tested first so that any practice effects, though unanticipated, would be to the advantage of the left hemisphere. To obtain the response of the mute right hemisphere, the subject was asked to use left hand signals to indicate which of the two choices read to him he preferred. On video portions of the PONS test, LB's right hemisphere scored perfectly normally on the items showing facial expressions (i.e., in the 50° percentile); but only at the 5° percentile level for body movements. The isolated left hemisphere showed just the reverse pattern: using verbal resposes

to indicate his choices, LB now scored in the 26° percentile for body movements but only at the 4° percentile level on facial expressions.

Since audio information presented to either ear gets projected to both
cerebral hemispheres, it was not possible to lateralize the vocal items of the
PONS test. We nevertheless attempted to assess each hemisphere's performance, either by having the contralateral hand use finger signals to indicate
which choice was preferred, or in some cases, by allowing the hand to select
by touch a plastic number 1 or 2 from an array of six plastic numbers. With
this method, subject LB scored very well on both RS and CF items using
either his left hand or a verbal response to indicate his choice.

In three other split-brain subjects who were studied, it was not possible to
lateralize the video portion of the test (contact lenses have not been made to
fit two of these subjects, and a third who does have a lens was completely
inattentive when the right hemisphere was tested). Viewing the test in free
vision and making verbal responses which presumably reflect the choices of
the left hemisphere, two of the three scored equally poorly on both face and
body; the third subject scored normally on body movement items but in the
bottom percentile on facial expressions. On audio items, one subject showed
a striking superiority for CF speech over RS, while the other two did not
show much of a difference between RS and CF when giving verbal answers.

Another remarkable subject tested at Cal Tech was DW, a 20-year-old man
who underwent a right hemispherectomy at the age of eight. His WISC verbal
IQ has been measured as 80, performance 60. On the PONS test, he scored at
a purely chance level on facial expressions, but in the 26° percentile on body
movements. On audio portions of the test, DW scored in the 82° percentile
on content-filtered speech items, but only in the 16° percentile for RS
speech. Since this subject only possesses a left hemisphere, these results are
quite unambiguous with respect to which side is controlling the response.

DISCUSSION

The first conclusion to be drawn from these results is that sensitivity to nonverbal communication is largely dissociated in the brain from verbal abilities,
the two domains essentially requiring opposite hemispheres. This dissociation
is particularly evident in right-brain-damaged subjects R1 and R7. Both of
these men scored nearly three standard deviations below normal on the PONS
test, but retained posttraumatic verbal IQ's more than two standard deviations
above normal. In contrast, subject L1, whose extensive left hemisphere
damage early in life left him with a number of severe language-related

problems, scored above average on the test. It might be noted that despite the relatively small population tested here and the variability among the sites of damage, the performance difference between the right and left hemisphere groups nevertheless achieved statistical significance, a testimony to just how clear a right hemisphere function overall sensitivity to nonverbal communication is.

Facial expressions normally convey the greatest amount of information in nonverbal communication[10,17,18] and it is their inability to evaluate these signals which presents the greatest problem for most of the right-brain-damaged subjects. Five out of seven patients in this group scored in the 4° percentile or below on items showing facial expressions alone.

The right hemispherectomy patient also scored at a chance level on these items, while the split-brain subjects tested with their left hemisphere did only slightly better. Conversely, the one split-brain subject who was tested with his right hemisphere alone performed quite well on facial expressions, as did all of the neurological subjects having left-sided lesions but an intact right hemisphere. Thus, all of the data indicate that it is the perception of facial expressions which is particularly lateralized to the right hemisphere. In the right hemispherectomy patient, the persistent inability to evaluate facial emotions despite the passage of 12 years since surgery would further suggest that the left hemisphere may possess little potential to acquire facial emotional recognition. Further support for this thesis would require studies in cases where right hemispherectomy had been done even earlier than age eight.

A superiority of the right hemisphere in the recognition of different faces is well established[19,20] involving in particular the right occipitotemporal region,[21,22] and for learning new faces, the hippocampal and parietal areas as well.[23,24,25] Prosopagnosia, a relatively pure inability to recognize faces but not other familiar visual objects, has been associated with lesions of the right occipitotemporal area (lingual and/or fusiform gyri), combined with damage to related (usually homologous) structures on the left side of the brain.[26]

In the present group of subjects, the region that appeared to be the most critical for identifying facial emotions may be somewhat coextensive with that involved in facial recognition: a comparison of the lesion sites for subjects who did relatively well or poorly in judging facial expressions would suggest that it may be the right temporal area that is particularly important for "reading the face." This raises the question of whether the deficit reported here may not be part of a general prosopagnosia. However, among the subjects who scored poorly in evaluating facial emotions, all but one were clinically unimpaired in distinguishing faces; conversely, the one right-brain-damaged subject who did well in recognizing facial expressions (R5) reported great difficulties in remembering new faces. Differential impairments in physiognomic vs emotional recognition of faces have also recently been reported in another study of right-brain-damaged subjects.[27]

In normal subjects, studies using tachistoscopically presented faces suggest that the perception of facial emotions is more strongly lateralized as a right hemispheric function than is the ability to identify individual faces. Several earlier studies had shown that faces presented tachistoscopically to the left visual field (i.e., directly to the right hemisphere) are recognized somewhat faster than when presented to the right visual field, although this difference is minimal for familiar faces.[28,29,30] When the task is to recognize *emotions* in the face, however, the superiority of the right hemisphere becomes considerably more pronounced. For facial emotions, the reaction time difference for the right vs the left hemisphere is twice that obtained when the faces are nonemotional,[31] and another study reported that the right hemisphere's superiority over the left increases systematically with the intensity of the emotions depicted.[32] Also, in split-brain subjects, Levy et al[20] have shown that while the right hemisphere is superior to the left in distinguishing different faces, the left side is quite competent as well, particularly when readily nameable features are available (e.g., glasses or a moustache). In contrast, the present studies, some of which were done in the same split-brain subjects, indicate practically no left hemispheric ability at all for recognizing facial emotions.

In contrast to facial expressions, the evaluation of body movements does not appear to be lateralized as a right hemispheric function. Four of the right-brain-damaged subjects scored at least 1.5 standard deviations higher in judging body movements than facial expressions, and in the split-brain and hemispherectomy subjects, the left hemisphere showed a far greater ability in judging body movements than facial emotions. Conversely, in the one instance where the right hemisphere was tested alone, it did much poorer with the body than with the face. At this point, the basis for a differential lateralization in judging facial expressions and body movements can only be a matter of speculation. Perhaps it is because the body movements are more conventionalized sequences of specific symbols in time, and thus more the métier of the left hemisphere. Other studies have shown that losses of gestural and pantomimic abilities are associated more with left than with right hemisphere damage,[33] as are deficits in interpreting gestures.[34] The perception of emotion-specific body movements seems not to have been explored as thoroughly, although it might be noted that losses in overt emotional expression have been linked with right parietal damage.[35]

On the audio items of the PONS test, the patterns of impairments shown by our subjects suggest the possibility that two distinctive qualities in the voice may be processed differentially in the two hemispheres. That is, the right hemisphere may be relatively more concerned with processing timbre and tonal contrasts of the voice (which are retained in RS speech), whereas timing or rhythmic qualities (which are preserved in CF items) may depend more upon the left side of the brain. Such a dichotomy would be consistent with the observation that in music, discrimination of tone and timbre are more sensitive to right than to left temporal lobectomy,[36] while rhythm appears to be better represented on the left side of the brain.[37] It should be emphasized, however, that counterexamples to this dichotomy can be found among the present group of subjects: e.g., several right-brain-damaged subjects scored as poorly on CF items as on RS, while one subject with a right temporal AVM scored very well on both RS and CF speech. Thus, any conclusions reached about the roles of the two hemispheres in processing various qualities of the voice must be considered very tentative. Previous studies in this area have generally not separated the contributions of tone vs timing, but have instead presented emotionally intonated neutral or foreign material, either to neurological subjects or to normals using dichotic listening. While most of these studies have suggested an overall right hemispheric superiority in judging emotion in the voice,[38-42] others suggest an equal involvement of the left hemisphere.[43,44]

The inability of right-brain-damaged subjects to assess the emotional significance of items on the PONS test is consistent with many earlier observations. Denial and unconcern about their illness, indifference to previously significant details or people, inappropriate reactions to abstract, emotional or humorous stories, continuous joking, and inappropriate social behavior have all been described in association with right-brain damage.[12,45-49] As noted in the descriptions of the individual cases here (Table 1), all but one of the right-brain-damaged subjects tested showed some of these characteristics. However, somewhat surprisingly on the PONS test most of our subjects appeared to have idiosyncratic patterns of emotional apperception selective to certain types of scenes. R4, for example, who was strikingly insensitive to his family's anger towards him, scored in the lowest 1% in evaluating negative-dominant scenes. R5, in contrast, scored in the 69° percentile for judging negative emotions but did poorly for all positive items. In all, five out of seven right-brain-damaged subjects had scores which spanned more than two standard deviations across the different emotional quadrants. And while subjects with left hemisphere damage generally scored higher overall on the PONS test, they too showed great variability in their perceptions of different emotions. At this point we are unable to determine whether these results reflect exaggerated aspects of subjects' premorbid personalities, interpretive problems resulting from each subject's particular pattern of perceptual changes, or differential alterations of neural substrates underlying various emotional associations.

Considering the importance of nonverbal communication for such things as mother-infant interactions, establishment of social hierarchies, minimization of physical conflict, and group coherence, it does not seem unreasonable to imagine that specific neural determinants have evolved to specify competence in this domain. In certain neurological patients, particularly those suffering lesions of the right hemisphere, damage to these centers could lead to major perceptual and behavioral limitations and may be related to the crippling interpersonal and emotional changes which have often been described after such brain damage.[50] It would seem that the routine inclusion of tests for nonverbal sensitivity in the neurological examination might help bring to light important dysfunctions, while also contributing to our general understanding of brain-behavior relations.

[b]*Department of Psychiatry, Harvard Medical School, Mailman Research Center, McLean Hospital, Belmont.*
[c]*Department of Psychiatry, Harvard Medical School, and Behavioral Neurology Unit, Beth Israel Hospital*
[d]*Department of Neurology, Harvard Medical School, Beth Israel Hospital*
[e]*Department of Psychology and Social Relations, Harvard University*
[f]*Department of Biology, California Institute of Technology*

ACKNOWLEDGEMENTS

We wish to thank Dr. S. Weintraub and Ms. Robin Baratz (Behavioral Neurology Unit, Beth Israel Hospital) and Dr. Edith Kaplan (Boston Veterans' Administration Hospital) for kindly providing us with subjects and with neuropsychological assessments. The research was supported by a Sloan Foundation Fellowship to the first author.

REFERENCES

[1] Benson, D.F. and Geschwind, N.: 'Psychiatric conditions associated with local lesions of the CNS', in Arieti, S. and Reiser M.F. (eds.), *American Handbook of Psychiatry*, Basic, New York, 1975, pp. 208–243.

2 Geschwind, N.: 'Specializations of the human brain', *Scientific American* **241** (1979), 180–202.
3 Chomsky, N.: *Reflections on Language*, Pantheon, New York, 1975.
4 Lenneberg, E.: *Biological Foundations of Language*, Wiley, New York, 1967.
5 Wolfgang, A. (ed.): *Nonverbal Behavior: Applications and Cultural Implications*, Academic, New York, 1979.
6 Weitz, S. (ed.): *Nonverbal Communication* (2nd ed.), Oxford Univ. Press, New York, 1979.
7 Hinde, R.A. (ed.): *Nonverbal Communication*, Cambridge Univ. Press, New York, 1972.
8 Knapp, M.L.: *Nonverbal Communication in Human Interaction* (2nd ed.), Holt, Rinehart and Winston, New York, 1978.
9 Birdwhistell, R.L.: *Kinesics and Context*, Univ. Penn. Press, Philadelphia, 1970.
10 Ekman, P., Friesen, W.V., and Ellsworth, P.: *Emotion in the Human Face*, Pergamon, New York, 1972.
11 Darwin, C. (1872): *The Expression of the Emotions in Man and Animals*, Appleton, London, 1965.
12 Gardner, H.: *The Shattered Mind*, Vintage, New York, 1976.
13 Rosenthal, R., Hall, J.A., DiMatteo, M.R. et al.: *Sensitivity to Nonverbal Communication: The PONS Test*, Johns Hopkins Univ. Press, Baltimore, 1979.
14 Rosenthal, R., Hall. J.A., Archer, D. et al.: 'The PONS test: Measuring sensitivity to nonverbal cues', in Weitz, S. (ed.), *Nonverbal Communication*, Oxford Univ. Press, New York, 1979.
15 Sperry, R.W.: 'Lateral specialization in the surgically separated hemispheres', in Schmitt, F.O. and Worden, F.G. (eds.), *The Neuroscience: Third Study Program*, MIT Press, Cambridge, 1974.
16 Zaidel, E.: 'Concepts of cerebral dominance in the split-brain', in Bouser, P. and Rougeul-Buser, A. (eds.): *Cerebral Correlates of Conscious Experience*, Elservier, Amsterdam, 1977.
17 Buck, R.W., Savin, V.J., Miller, R.E. et al.: 'Communication of affect through facial expressions in humans', *J. Personal Soc. Psychol.* **23** (1972), 362–371.
18 Izard, C.E.: *The Face of Emotion*, Appleton-Century-Crofts, New York, 1971.
19 Hecaen, H. and Angelergues, R.: 'Agnosia for faces (prosopagnosia)', *Arch. Neurol.* **7** (1962), 92–100.
20 Levy, J., Trevarthen, C.B., and Sperry, R.W.: 'Perception of bilateral chimeric figures following hemispheric deconnexion', *Brain* **95** (1972), 61–78.
21 Yin, R.K.: 'Face recognition by brain-injured patients: A dissociable ability?' *Neuropsychologia* **8** (1970), 395–402.
22 Newcombe, F. and Russell, W.R.: 'Dissociated visual perceptual and spatial deficits in focal lesions of the right hemisphere', *J. Neurol. Neurosurg. Psychiat.* **32** (1969), 73–81.
23 Milner, B.: 'Visual recognition and recall after right temporal lobe excision in man', *Neuropsychologia* **6** (1968), 191–209.
24 DeRenzi, E. and Spinnler, H.: 'Facial recognition in brain-damaged patients', *Neurology* **16** (1966), 145–152.
25 Warrington, E.K. and James, M.: 'An experimental investigation of facial recognition in patients with unilateral cerebral lesions', *Cortex* **3** (1967), 317–326.

26 Meadows, J.C.: 'The anatomical basis of prosopagnosia', *J. Neurol. Neurosurg. Psychiat.* **37** (1974), 489–501.

27 Cicone, M., Wapner, W., and Gardner, H.: 'Sensitivity to emotional expressions and situations in organic patients', *Cortex* **16** (1980), 145–158.

28 Rizzolatti, G., Umilta, C., and Berlucchi, G.: 'Opposite superiorities of the right and left cerebral hemispheres in discriminative reaction time to physiognomical and alphabetical material', *Brain* **94** (1971), 421–442.

29 Patterson, K. and Bradshaw, J.L.: 'Differential hemispheric mediation of nonverbal visual stimuli', *J. Exper. Psychol.* **1** (1971), 246–252.

30 Hilliard, R.D.: 'Hemispheric laterality effects on a facial recognition task in normal subjects', *Cortex* **9** (1973), 246–258.

31 Suberi, M. and McKeever, W.F.: 'Differential right hemispheric memory storage of emotional and nonemotional faces', *Neuropsychologia* **15** (1977), 757–768.

32 Ley, R.G. and Bryden, M.P.: 'Hemispheric differences in processing emotions and faces', *Language* **1** (1979), 127–138.

33 Goodglass, H. and Kaplan, E.: 'Disturbance of gesture and pantomime in aphasia', *Brain* **86** (1963), 703–720.

34 Gainotti, G. and Lemmo, M.A.: 'Comprehension of symbolic gestures in aphasia', *Brain Language* **3** (1976) 451–460.

35 Ross, E.D. and Mesulam, M.M.: 'Dominant language functions of the right hemisphere?', *Arch. Neurol.* **36** (1979), 144–148.

36 Milner, S.: 'Laterality effects in audition', in Mountcastle, V. (ed.), *Interhemispheric Relations and Cerebral Dominance*, Johns Hopkins Univ. Press, Baltimore, 1962, pp. 177–195.

37 Robinson, G.M. and Solomon, D.I.: 'Rhythm is processed by the speech hemisphere', *J. Exper. Psychol.* **102** (1974), 508–511.

38 Heilman, K.M., Scholes, R., and Watson, R.T.: 'Auditory affective agnosia', *J. Neurol. Neurosurg. Psychiat.* **38** (1974), 69–72.

39 Tucker, D.M., Watson, R.T., and Heilman, K.M.: 'Discrimination and evocation of affectively intoned speech in patients with right parietal disease', *Neurology* **27** (1967), 947–950.

40 Carmon, A. and Nachshon, I.: 'Ear asymmetry in perception of emotional nonverbal stimuli', *Acta Psychologica* **37** (1973), 351–357.

41 Haggard, M.P. and Parkinson, A.M.: 'Stimulus and task factors as determinants of ear advantages', *Quart. J. Exper. Psychol.* **23** (1971), 168–177.

42 Blumstein, S. and Cooper W.E.: 'Hemispheric processing of intonation contours', *Cortex* **10** (1974), 146–158.

43 Schlanger, B.B., Schlanger, P., and Gerstman, L.J.: 'The perception of emotionally-toned sentences by right hemisphere damaged and aphasic subjects', *Brain Language* **3** (1976), 396–403.

44 Zurif, L.B.: 'Auditory lateralization: Prosodic and syntactical factors', *Brain Language* **1** (1974), 391–404.

45 Denny-Brown, D., Meyer, J.S., and Horenstein, S.: 'The significance of perceptual rivalry resulting from parietal lesion', *Brain* **75** (1952), 433–471.

46 Gainotti, G.: 'Emotional behavior and hemispheric side of the lesion', *Cortex* **8** (1972), 41–55.

47 Gardner, H., Ling, P.K., Flamm, L. et al.: 'Comprehension and appreciation of

humorous material following brain damage', *Brain* **98** (1975), 399–412.
[48] Heilman, K.M., Schwartz, H.D., and Watson, R.T.: 'Hypoarousal in patients with the neglect syndrome and emotional indifference', *Neurology* **28** (1978), 229–232.
[49] Wechsler, A.F.: 'The effect of organic brain disease on recall of emotionally charged versus neutral narrative texts', *Neurology* **23** (1973), 130–135.
[50] Bear, D.M.: 'Personality changes associated with neurologic lesions', in Lazare, A. (ed.), *Textbook of Outpatient Psychiatry*, Williams and Wilkins, Baltimore, 1979.

LUCIA M. VAINA

TOWARDS A COMPUTATIONAL THEORY
OF SEMANTIC MEMORY

INTRODUCTION

Memory is one of the most important functions of the human brain, yet its understanding — why and how it does what it does — has so far eluded us. Research in memory has been a frustrating task not least because of the intimate familiarity with what we are trying to understand, and partly also because the human cognitive system has developed as an interactive whole; it is difficult to isolate its component modules — a necessary prerequisite for their thorough elucidation.

Before one embarks on a new research area its general demands and underlying theoretical hypotheses should be stated.

FUNDAMENTAL DEMANDS OF RESEARCH IN MEMORY

The first demand to the student of memory, and of cognitive abilities in general, is to attempt to separate those topics that appear capable of explanation by available approaches from those for which no ready explanation even in outline seems available.

The second demand concerns the properties and attributes of the human brain that the researcher must aim to account for. Some of these are:

(1) the redundancy and self-restorative nature of the brain mechanisms connected with learning and memory;

(2) the capacity to learn;

(3) the modification and refinement of the information already stored;

(4) the local character of computations (a local change shouldn't require large modifications);

(5) the existence of sensory-specific modules that independently convey information to the language module.

The third demand concerns to the evaluation of the research done and the choice of those methods that seem to lead to the most relevant results. It has become clear that the most reliable approach to the study of the brain

97

L. Vaina and J. Hintikka (eds.), Cognitive Constraints on Communication, 97–113.
© 1984 *by D. Reidel Publishing Company.*

activity is to regard it as a large and complex information processing system. Central to this approach is the belief that human cognitive capacity can fruitfully be viewed as some kind of symbolic system. Thus, much is to be learned by developing computational theories for aspects of human information processing and comparing the results of these theories and their implementations with human performance on the same tasks. Behavioral phenomena may suggest or constrain possible information processing tasks whose properties can be studied computationally, and thus might lead to the search for previously unrecognized behavioral consequences that they imply.

In an information processing approach, such as the one to which I subscribe, there is a distinction (pointed out by Marr and Poggio [6]) between the various levels at which our information processing device may be understood: at one level, there is the theory of computation, which is what is computed and why, and at the next level is the particular algorithm, or way in which the computation is carried out. My present goal is to elaborate the computational theories of some of cognitive abilities of the human brain. The particular implementation, although eventually important, plays only a secondary role at the moment.

THEORETICAL HYPOTHESIS OF RESEARCH

(1) To understand various disabilities resulting from lesions to the brain helps us to understand the normal function of the brain.

(2) Data are important for the process of developing the theory; ideas and hypotheses that are at the variance with the data have to be rejected.

(3) We should bear in mind that the facts that we deal with are soft and the working domain ill understood, so our intellectual resources would be misplaced if at the present they are spent on the construction of elaborate mathematical structures.

LEVELS OF RESEARCH INTO MEMORY

Memory may be studied at several levels. At the most physiological end one would study the neural basis of memory, how the hardware implements the storage process. Examples of theories at this level are the cerebellum [4], [8], the mathematical theory of associative memory devices [7]. Although such research can provide us with illuminating insights into the functioning of the brain, and provides an essential component of an eventual understanding of memory, it is clearly not the whole story. Although studies at this level address the details of how to implement a certain kind of memory in a particular hardware, they unfortunately shed no light on what information should be stored in the memory or how it should be represented there. The underlying reason is that studies at this level contain no analysis of the uses of memory in the broader context of day to day information processing tasks.

Memory cannot be studied in isolation, since it is essentially only an adjunct to the proper execution of our ordinary information processing tasks. In order to try to formulate specifically some of the basic requirements of memory we must therefore examine the structure of the processing tasks for which it is used. A first division in central processing, although a rough one, would be between *modality specific* and *modality unspecific* analysis. Examples of modality specific analysis include the tasks of visual analysis, tactile analysis, auditory analysis, etc. It is clear that these different types of analysis must be taken at least some way before cross-modal interactions of any complexity could be useful, and in fact clinical evidence from neurology suggests that these analyses can proceed a substantial way before their combination. Thus in vision, for example, a sophisticated representation of the shape and disposition of a viewed object can be derived by patients whose realization of the shape's use or purpose is severly impaired.

Each of these modality-specific analyses poses its own self-contained memory problem, whose primary purpose will be to aid the recovery of a structural description (in the case of vision, of the shape of the viewed object from images of it). One might call such memories *modality specific recognition memories* (MSRM). Thus in vision, for example, the MSRM which Marr and Nishihara [5] used to organize and store their 3-D models, (see Figure 1), is deployed during the construction of a specific, arbitrarily detailed, object-centered description of the shape of the viewed object. According to current thinking, visual processes preceding this step do not usually involve the deployment of a learned catalog of shapes; they consist almost exclusively of memory-free perceptual processes, like stereopsis and structure from motion, and can usefully be thought as pure perceptual processes.

If this were generally true, one could view the different recognition modules as roughly consisting of two parts: the first, which one might perhaps call pure perception, consists of essentially memory-free analysis of

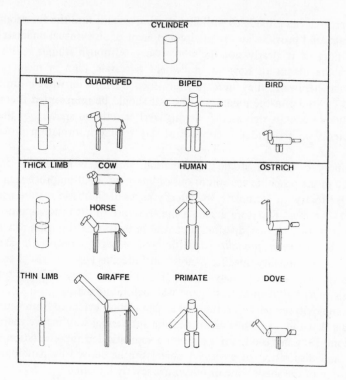

Fig. 1.

the incoming sensory information; and the second involves the use of
memory of stored descriptions during the construction of a representation of
the incoming information. Thus in vision, for example, a patient lacking his
visual recognition memory but retaining his perceptual apparatus should still
be able to perform simple visual tasks, like discriminate two lines at different
orientations, or two points at different depths, even though unable to
describe the shape of the viewed object. The descriptions supplied by the
different MSRM, are potentially complex, since they are capable of representing exhaustively all the information that can be acquired via that particular
sense. For example the description from vision of even a fairly simple shape
can include 3-D models for aspects of the shape at several different scales, as
illustrated in Figure 2.

Yet rich as these individual modality specific descriptions can be, we know

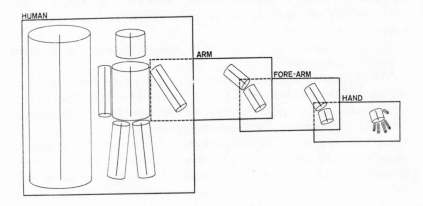

Fig. 2.

from our own experience that the comprehension of what we see, touch, hear, involves more than each one, and more even than their combination. For example, our comprehension of an object includes a knowledge of its use and purpose, to which there are often several aspects, and its name. The organization and representation of this information involves a different category of memories that are not modality specific. To distinguish them from the MSRM, let us call them Cognitive Memories. These memories are our research interest.

How is one to discover the computations performed by the cognitive memories? One possibility would be to consider what tasks are accomplished by the cognitive memories in order to investigate the computations they perform. In this case we have to define the goals of cognitive memories, and once we know them we can define the problems involved in attaining these goals. Naturally, it is very important during the formulation of the goals to rely on the right kind of data. Once the computational problems have been formulated, and we have a computational theory it is useful to develop a program. A strong theoretical motivation for having an implementation of a theory is that it helps one to appreciate problems that otherwise risk being passed unnoticed.

The memory whose task it is to process, store and retrieve upon request information about the meaning of words, concepts, facts, etc., was called Semantic Memory by Tulving [9], and my present concern is exactly this. I shall discuss a model of semantic memory called THREAD MEMORY. But before talking specifically about it, some general features of semantic memories need to be mentioned.

Semantic memory, in contrast with episodic memory, has a strong inferential mechanism.

The information in semantic memory is organized and can be modified, and the modifications in semantic memory are caused by interaction with the environment, for example through the Modality-Specific Recognition Memories and probably other Cognitive Memories, and they are produced by various internal processes, for example by inference. Because of this, semantic memory must be organized so as to allow modifications without requiring dramatic changes in its overall structure; that is, modifications for the most part to be local, without entailing global consequences. This requirement could be formulated as a principle of the *modularity of the representation*. The computational investigation of semantic memory enquiries about the nature of the representations used by the cognitive system for storing knowledge about the world, their structure, and the processes by which they are derived, accessed, and preserved.

THEORETICAL FOUNDATION AND DESCRIPTION OF THREAD MEMORY

The direct motivation for thread memory was a paper by E. K. Warrington, entitled 'The selective impairment of semantic memory' [11]. Warrington studied in detail three patients, selected on the basis of a failure to recognize or identify common objects on visual confrontation. This deficit, called by Lissauer "associative agnosia", manifests itself by the patient's being generally capable of describing, copying and representing the stimulus item, yet having no knowledge of its use or purpose. Warrington argued that this is a deficit of semantic memory, characterized by the degradation of stored information, knowledge of subordinate categories being more vulnerable than knowledge of superordinate categories.

Another set of data comes from clinical studies of anomia. Anomia is a failure of naming on confrontation. As Geschwind [1] pointed out, one must make sure that the failure to name an object is not the result of a failure of perception, or comprehension. Poor naming is a characteristic of aphasics in general and it is manifested most dramatically in anomics. In general when confrontation naming is impaired, the patient, while his speech is fluent, uses many circumlocutions or over-general words, such as "thing", "place", etc. Anomia is generally present for all stimulus modalities, but the intensity of the disturbance [2] is not necessarily equal for them all. A question that naturally arises here is to what extent is anomia due to a failure in the individual recognition memories and to what extent is it independent of them.

In a collective study by Goodglass et al. [2], it was shown that preservation of letter and number naming were more characteristic of patients with posterior speech zone lesions; these were patients in whom anomia, particularly for object names, was very characteristic. Broca's aphasics, patients with more anterior lesions, are characterized by telegraphic speech and lack of function words, yet they seem to be much better at naming. This observation, and other similar ones, lead to the question of whether there is a difference between naming errors for different kinds of objects (e.g. singular terms, mass terms, proper nouns, etc.).

In a recent study by Goodglass [3] it was shown that Broca's aphasics have a relatively high proportion of concrete or picturable words. Fluent aphasics, on the other hand, apparently preserve a higher proportion of abstract words. Goodglass conjectured that this was because fluent aphasics readily produce the grammatical context leading up to the key nouns in their messages. This pattern would be expected to give them an advantage over Broca's aphasics for the production of nouns that are highly context determined. Thus he supposes that the marked preference of fluent aphasics for abstract over concrete words relies on their facility for producing contexts that favour high frequency abstract words like time, year, week and so forth.

In their paper, 'Naming in Aphasia: Interacting effects of form and function' [12], Whitehouse, Caramazza and Zurif asked whether anomia was the same process in all states of brain damage in which it appears. They pointed out that the information-processing chain which generates the labels for a visually perceived object can be disrupted at different stages. They produced evidence that suggests that at least one source of difficulty in naming is a disturbance of the conceptual representation associated with a label. However it is also possible that brain damage spares the conceptual structures underlying lexical organization, but dissociates and disrupts mechanisms responsible for addressing and/or retrieving information from this structure. Another interesting question is how different categories of aphasics integrate different kinds of information. Broca's aphasics, for example, demonstrated a relatively intact understanding of lexical structures, and have a pretty normal ability to integrate perceptual and functional information. They also seem to be quite good at dealing with the fuzziness of conceptual boundaries. Anomics on the other hand, show evidence of lexical distortion, and manifest an inability to integrate perceptual with functional information. In addition to this, they seem to be insensitive to category boundaries.

THE RELEVANCE OF APHASIA TO THREAD MEMORY

The phenomena described in the last section together with my own experience with aphasic patients, have led to the following preliminary formulations of some principles of semantic memory.

(1) The existence of the different agnosias suggests the presence of several structurally distinct modality-specific representation systems. That is, a particular object is represented internally in several different memories.

(2) From the work done on visual-recognition memories, it appears that the description of an object is structured rather than unitary, and the units of description are organized hierarchically from the general to the particular.

(3) There are several ways of representing knowledge about an object: by its modality-specific descriptions, its functions or uses, and the categories to which it belongs. Each of these modes can be independently impaired. This suggests that semantic memory contains at least three modules, one for each of these modes of representation.

(4) Perceptual classifications and semantic classifications are separate, hierarchically organized systems and can be differentially impaired.

(5) Most concepts have both superordinate and subordinate categories. But at their most detailed level the representations of two different objects will be different.

(6) There is rarely an all-or-none response to an object; on the contrary, some semantic meaning is often preserved, and this is invariably of a general rather than of a specific nature. For example, an agnosic patient in Warrington's experiments would respond faster to "Is a duck an animal?" than to "Is a duck a bird?".

(7) From the comparative study of different types of patients (for example anterior vs posterior lesions) we see that the capacity for semantic categorization may be good, the recognition of functionality of objects may be good, and their perceptual description may also be good, yet some types

of objects may be easier to name than others. Some aphasics do much better with concrete than with abstract objects. This might be due to impaired access mechanisms rather than to the degradation of stored information. Thus we can begin to differentiate between processes that access information and processes that store and organize it, and there is some evidence that they can be independently impaired.

(8) We have seen that semantic memory as opposed to episodic memory relies on inferences. So, we can further differentiate the processes that store and organize the information, into processes of inference and processes of storage.

(9) From a comparison of posterior with anterior aphasics, it seems that the anterior lesions (Broca's) produce an impairment of the access processes (probably damaging control processes that deal with contextual differences) whereas posterior lesions may impair mechanisms that store and organize the information. Anomic patients can apparently retrieve a superordinate category of the object they are asked to name together with a correct description of its use. They are, however, apparently often unable to access a more particular representation. (e.g. for a rose, they may get "flower" but not "rose"). It seems then that the damage here is to the inference processes and not necessarily to the storage processes. Wernicke's aphasics, on the other hand, seem to have a general impairment of the memory itself.

(10) Evidence for the difference between impaired access mechanisms and damage to the memory itself has recently come, for example, from patients at the VAH-Boston. One of them initially had a severe inability to manipulate symbolic expressions, and showed no use of semantic memory. On re-learning the ability to manipulate symbols, some of his use of semantic memory returned. This suggests that his primary damage lay in his access mechanisms.

(11) Frequency and familiarity plays an important role in the case of impairment of semantic memory. Frequent or familiar terms are retrieved correctly more often than less frequent and unfamiliar terms.

THREAD MEMORY

The requirements formulated in the previous paragraphs have led us to formulate a new type of semantic memory, called "thread memory". A preliminary version of thread memory was introduced by Vaina & Greenblatt ([10] 1979), and the ideas behind it have been evolving over the past year.

I will now describe briefly the structure of the memory and some of the processes associated with it.

Structure of the Thread Memory

The basic element in the representation of objects in memory is called a thread, and it consists of a set of symbols (nodes), ordered according to precise rules. The relation between symbols might have different meanings, each of these meanings being associated with a module of representation. Three modules may be distinguished:

(1) a category module, which is a hierarchical organization of the symbols in memory, from the more general category to the more particular category. For example, mallard → thing → living-thing → animal → bird → duck → species-of-duck → mallard.

(2) a functional module, which contains information about the function, or the uses of the objects. In this module, actions and objects are represented in relation. Thus for example (S LEADS-TO) SEE → BOY → RUN.

(3) a descriptional module, which contains information about the component parts of an object, about its appearance. Each element of this module results in the creation of a thread. This module establishes relations between various threads that can be associated with a symbol. For example (BIRD FEATHERS) relates the thread keyed on FEATHERS to the symbol BIRD.

The first element in the thread, called the key, is the stimulus by which the thread is accessed. The threads end in the same symbol as the key. The difference is that when we reach the access symbol at the end of the thread it is loaded by then with all the meaning that is represented on the thread. The symbols in the thread are not unique to the thread, they might appear in several threads. This is a very useful property because it allows a leveled partitioning of information in the memory. So for example, most of the objects from the world could have as their most general representation a symbol like "thing". But that it would not tell us anything, we need to be more specific. The extent to which the memory gets specific can vary, but a semantic memory has to be able in principle to give a unique description to every object in the world.

Objects are represented by a set of threads that give a multiple description of the object and its functionality. The set of all threads associated with an object, or in other words, having the same key, constitute a *general thread* (Figure 3). There are many symbols in common among the threads in a general thread. Some of them are explicit and, some of them as we will see in

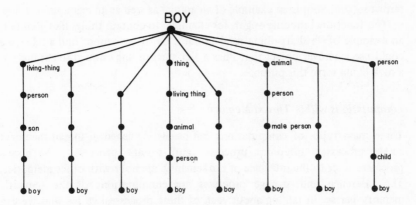

Fig. 3. Example of a general-thread.

the next section can be deduced by the application of the simple thread operation of deduction. A complete semantic representation of an object is given in all the modules of the semantic memory.

We call the more specific common node of two (or more) threads in the same module a *fork-point*. The fork-point of all threads in a general thread constitutes the most common knowledge that one has about an object and which is not dependent on its particular occurrence. In each general thread there are different fork-points, depending on the threads that one is looking at. At the fork point one has to decide which representations or descriptions might contain the needed specific information and choose that thread. The fork point of threads that belong to different general threads reveals what the compared representation have in common in a particular module of representation. For example, what is common between a chair and a table in the category module? The usual response is that they are both pieces of furniture. Fork-points obtained in the descriptional module might be misleading for interpretation in another module, like the categorial module for example. Thus a WHALE in the descriptional module is represented as LIVES-IN-WATER and its shape description is like the shape of a fish. From this, one might believe that a whale is a kind of fish. To avoid confusions, simple threads are formed to tell us that a whale is not a fish for example. Or specifying that IS-NOT-A PLANT ANIMAL enables us to distinguish all plants from animals by means of a single thread operation.

Sometimes we need to particularize an object. Thus, dog is a generic term that refers to all dogs in general, Spot a particular one. Animal is a generic term too, and Spot is an example of an animal as well as an example of a dog.

The functional module ought, for example, to contain things like a knife is an example of "a sharp thing used to cut". Or, if we cannot find a table, we could use whatever object that "has a flat surface, big enough to eat on", so a rock could serve this purpose.

Computations within Thread Memory

Three main types of computations can be distinguished in thread memory: access processes, inference processes and storage processes. The access processes refer to the interface of the semantic memory with other memories. The inference and storage processes are computations of the semantic memory per se. In talking about each of these processes we see that we can differentiate them further. Thus the access processes are of two types: the access processes themselves and processes that control them. By the general access processes a general thread is brought in the temporary buffer, and then the simple threads are examined one by one (by an operation called "advancing the thread" (Figure 4)). If one had to examine exhaustively every single thread of a general thread, the performance would be very slow and uneconomical. The access control processes and some inference process optimize this. The access control operations can "turn-on" or "turn-off" a group of facts. The context which is "on" at the time of accessing a thread is always specified; thus in advancing the thread we know that a specific-context, with its restrictions and requirement is needed. The specific context affects only the extraction or the choice of threads. Once a thread was chosen and activated in the temporary buffer, the specific context doesn't interfere anymore. We could suppose probably that the specific context is inherited or moved over from the episodic memory.

Another access control mechanism is the general context which allows the threads to be related. The information handled by the general context mechanisms is the information represented in the semantic memory. We can say then that the control access mechanisms control the interface between the information in episodic memory, the information in the semantic memory, and the temporarily active buffer.

INFERENCE PROCESSES

In the section about the structure of thread memory the fork-points were discussed as being special nodes on the threads. Finding the fork-point is a

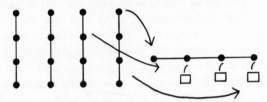

Fig. 4. Access processes: advancing the thread.

special inference process that deals with compare and contrast questions. Another inference process is the process of deduction. For example from the two following threads

ELEPHANT → ANIMAL → ELEPHANT
ANIMAL → LIVING-THING → ANIMAL

we can deduce the answer to this question: Is an elephant a living thing? The necessary one step deduction is performed by searching each thread whose semantic node is on the elephant thread, for the node living-thing. After the node ANIMAL is found, a storage operation is performed (the process of assimilation) to store the deduction. An interesting feature of deduction in thread memory is that the depth of deduction is not the distance between two nodes, as in most proposed semantic memories, but the number of jumps from one thread to another (Figure 5a). Thus a very modest search depth can find solutions to non-trivial questions.

There are several ways of optimizing the inference processes. For example,

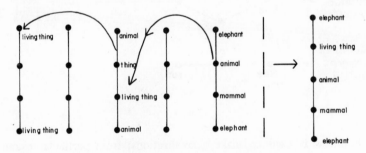

Through one step of deduction we obtain the answer, and at the same time the general thread of living-thing (the facts about living-thing).

Fig. 5. Deduction: Is an elephant a living thing?

we can define a measure of closeness between symbols in each module of representation called neighborliness. I think this may be important for problem solving or for improving the access process that advances the thread. If the result found is acceptable then the neighborhood is reinforced. The neighborliness is not a simple information processing task; it relies on many other operations. For example, crucial in the measurement of neighborliness is the number of threads in a general thread whose fork point is quite deep (we shall see in the storage processes that these threads are "bundled" together: Figure 6f). In the functional module the process of

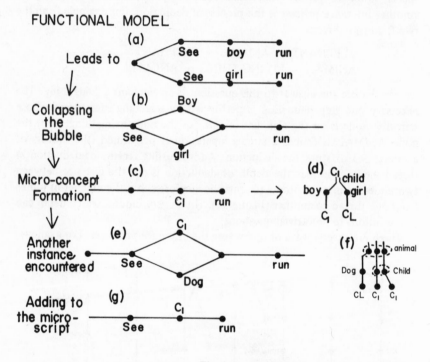

Fig. 6.

neighborliness is used to make generalizations; from particular examples inferences are made to more general categories. This is clearly an optimization process because it actually reduces the enormous number of particular examples of objects that are in the same relation with verbs, to their common fork-point in the category module. For example from

(S LEADS-TO) JOHN CRY
(S LEADS-TO) JANE CRY
(S LEADS-TO) DOG CRY
(S LEADS-TO) BABY CRY
(S LEADS-TO) BOY CRY
(S LEADS-TO) MOTHER CRY

By applying the neighborness process we obtain that (S LEADS-TO) ANIMAL CRY, and by that we would know, for example, that we can say ELEPHANT CRY as well as RABBIT CRY.

An interesting observation can be made, namely that the processes of inference are not simple processes, they presuppose processes of storage. (These remarks relate to a hypothesis made in the study of aphasic patients, that in the case of Wernicke aphasics probably all inference processes as well as the storage processes are impaired and yet in the case of anomic aphasics the impairment is of the inference processes. It is supposed in the literature that Wernicke's aphasics who improve usually recover to become anomic aphasics. This seems very much to support our hypothesis that the processes of inference are based on the processes of storage and the storage processes are first recovered.)

STORAGE PROCESSES

The simplest storage process is the process that creates a thread, a new representation in the memory. Usually new information is based on pre-existing information, or at least on the descriptional information that is given by the single modality recognition memories, or information from other cognitive memories. The module in which the new thread is created depends on the way in which the information is acquired. An important class of storage processes is assimilation processes. These assimilation processes chain together intermediate deduction steps so that the entire chain is available as a single deduction step. The assimilation processes build the thread, and make it more complex by storing the result of deductions (Figure 5b).

There are other types of storage processes, such as processes that optimize the thread. First, threads that share a number of common nodes constitute bundles of threads. These bundles are thicker on the upper part of the thread, where the information is less specific, but they divide into smaller and smaller bundles until they break down to single strands. Bundles have a way of recording their thickness. This recording is very important for the accessing of the information. Unless a special context instruction is given, usually the thickest bundle is looked up first. The thickest bundle in a general thread represents the prototypical representation of an object, and it is accessed first. The thickness of bundles is not fixed, for it changes with every incoming thread. Thus the prototype might change too.

Another optimization process is used when it appears that several threads are sharing a common part. Then it seems useful to make a rearrangement so that all the simple threads share a single pointer to the common part. In other words, the uncommon part constitutes a paradigm in the context determined by the common part. The elements in the paradigm behave as if they were the same. In that context we can replace the paradigm with a new, more general symbol. For example, in the functional module we can have different elements that have the same function: one can throw a rock, a ball, a plate, a pencil, a piece of wood, etc. These objects form a paradigm in the context of throw. We can replace them with a common symbol, such as small physical object. This new type of symbol, called *micro-concept,* will be represented in the descriptional module by the elements that the elements in the paradigm have in common. Thus we see that this new, more abstract concept is derived from particular examples of objects in the real world that can function in certain way (e.g., can be thrown). *Micro-concepts are representational units for the object in the real world* (Figure 6). They serve for their better understanding and manipulation. They also serve for the interface with other cognitive modules, such as the modules involving language.

Massachusetts Institute of Technology Cognitive Science Center and
Boston University Computer Science Dept.

ACKNOWLEDGEMENTS

I am grateful to David Marr, for many stimulating discussions and to Richard Greenblatt, with whom much of the overall framework of thread memory was developed. I thank Dr. Norman Geschwind for carefully reading my manuscript and for his illuminating observations.

Many thanks to the members of the Aphasia Research Center and the speech therapists of the Veterans Administration Hospital Boston, for making my experimental research possible. I especially thank M. Walsh and Dr. Harold Goodglass for their encouraging support.

REFERENCES

[1]   Geschwind, N.: 1967, 'The varieties of naming errors', *Cortex* 3, 97–112.

[2]   Goodglass, H., Hyde, M. R., and Blumstein, S.: 1969, 'Frequency, picturability and availability of nouns in aphasia' *Cortex* 5, 104–119.

[3]   Goodglass, H.: 1978, 'Disorders of naming in aphasia', Fellow's address, Division 6, American Psychological Association, Toronto.

[4]   Marr. D.: 1969, 'A theory of cerebellar cortex' *J. Physiol. (Lond.)* 202, 437–470.

[5]   Marr, D. and Nishihara, H. K.: 1978, 'Representation and recognition of the spatial organization of three-dimensional shapes', *Proc. R. Soc. Lond.* B 200, 269–294.

[6]   Marr, D. and Poggio, T.: 1977, 'From understanding computation to understanding neural circuitry', *Neurosciences Res. Prog. Bull.* 15, 470–488.

[7]   Poggio, T.: 1975, 'On optimal nonlinear associative recall', *Biol. Cybernetics* 19, 201–209.

[8]   Szentagothai, J.: 1971, 'Memory functions and the structural organization of the brain', *in Adam, G. (ed.), Biology of Memory, Symposia Biologica Hungarica* 10, 21–25.

[9]   Tulving, E.: 1972, 'Episodic and semantic Memory', in Tulving, E. (ed.), *Organization and Memory*, Acad. Press, New York.

[10]   Vaina, L. M, and Greenblatt, R.: 1970, 'The use of thread memory in anomic aphasia and concept learning', *AI Working Paper* 195.

[11]   Warrington, E. K.: 1975, 'The selective impairment of semantic memory', *Quarterly Journal of Experimental Psychology* 27, 635–657.

[12]   Whitehouse, P., Caramazza, A, and Zurif, E.: 1978, 'Naming in aphasia: Interacting effects of form and function', *Brain and Language* 6, 63–74.

ROMAN JAKOBSON[†] AND GRETE LÜBBE-GROTHUES

TWO TYPES OF DISCOURSE IN HÖLDERLIN'S MADNESS*

CONVERSATION

Hölderlin, who had already suffered schizophrenic attacks, became ill in 1802, i.e., in his thirty-second year — according to medical opinion, "with an acute schizophrenic psychosis."[1] Schelling described him in a letter to Hegel of July 11, 1803 as "with his mind completely shattered" and, although "still to a certain degree capable" of a few more literary works, "otherwise in a state of total oblivion."[2] In August 1806, Hölderlin's mother received a letter from his close friend, Isaak Sinclair, reporting that it was no longer possible that "my unhappy friend, whose madness has reached an advanced stage, remain any longer . . . in Homburg" and "that his continued freedom could even become dangerous to the public."[3] After a few agonizing months in a Tübingen asylum, the ill man, in keeping with his poetic pre-monition, remained for an entire "Hälfte des Lebens" [Half of One's Life] "Weh mir, wo nehm ich, wenn // Es Winter ist, die Blumen" [Alas, where shall I find, when // It is winter, the flowers][4] in the house of a Tübingen carpenter, Ernst Zimmer, "given lodgings and care" until the end of his life [1843 — Trans.]. According to the reminiscences of the pastor Max Effert (published in 1849), "the unhappy poet Hölderlin," the inhabitant of the little tower room in the carpenter's house near the old animal pen, "wandered . . . to and fro" "until a few years ago, out of his mind, en-gaged in an eternally confused conversation with himself."[5] According to Wilhelm Waiblinger, Hölderlin was not allowed to go out by himself, "but instead could walk about only in the enclosed area in front of the house."[6]

The numerous accounts of those who visited the poet in the carpenter's house, from K. A. Varnhagen's observations on December 22, 1808[7] until the year of Hölderlin's death, contain valuable information, which is now collected in the *Complete Stuttgart Edition*.[8] It draws our attention to the stubborn anger and agonizing inability of the madman to carry on a conver-sation with people and, as a result, to the "enormous gulf" between him and his human environment, as the attentive and detailed comments of the writer Wilhelm Waiblinger from the years 1822–1826 already make clear (disregard-

115

L. Vaina and J. Hintikka (eds.), Cognitive Constraints on Communication, 115–136.
©1976 *by Roman Jakobson.*

ing his all-too-subjective approach), and as later observers also confirmed repeatedly.

From the poet's early youth until the development of his acute illness, a "peaceful give and take" was a necessity of life, as Nussbächer noted correctly: "His dialogic nature sought out conversation, and from the conversation with another grew his poem. In the love-encounter with Diotima, Hölderlin experienced the inspiring and responsive other person, and from early youth until the years of his sickness, he was in dialogue with true friends."[9] It is precisely the loss of conversation that characterizes the entire behavior of the Tübingen recluse. He became embarrassed when spoken to as well as when addressing another or attempting to reply, so that "even his former acquaintances," in Waiblinger's words, found "such conversations too strange, too depressing, too boring, too meaningless." Newcomers were received by Hölderlin with a torrent of meaningless words: "One hears a few words that are understandable, but most of which it is impossible to respond to" and he himself usually remained "completely unresponsive to what one says to him."

When questioned pointedly, Hölderlin became very agitated and the questioner received from him "a terribly jumbled, meaningless torrent of words." Or Hölderlin simply preferred to refuse to answer: "Your Royal Highness, I may not, I cannot answer that." Finally, the reply could be turned back to the questioner: "You haven't been to France again for a long time?" — "Oui, monsieur, so you say." Another subterfuge was: "You may be right." His fear of being responsible for an independent affirmation or denial was evident in such comments as "So you say. So you assert. Nothing will happen to me." That was supposed to be Hölderlin's "favorite phrase." Hölderlin even managed to attribute to his companion his own refusal of suggestions. Thus there followed upon an invitation to take a walk an "extremely strange form" of affirming protest: "You order me to stay here."

Waiblinger had already observed [in the early 1820s — Trans.] "countless times" the regular conflict between yes and no in Hölderlin's way of speaking, as, for example, between the statement "Human beings are happy" and its retraction, "Human beings are unhappy." As Christoph Theodor Schwab noted in his journal from the year 1841, the ill poet is said to have thought up and preferred using the expression *pallaksch*, which one could take for either yes or no and which he used as a way of avoiding both.[10]

A similar uncertainty is reflected in the "polyglot flood of titles" and expressions of courtesy noted by observers on different occasions, which the ill man used all the time, especially to greet someone. According to a report by the editor Gustav Kühne (who in 1838 described his Tübingen impressions), Hölderlin interjected, "He receives a visit, with Your Highness and Your Grace near him, even with Your Holiness and Your Majesty he is generous,"[11] as if (according to an earlier hypothesis of Waiblinger's) he thereby tried studiously to keep everyone at an insurmountable distance — although one shouldn't think that he believed he was really dealing with kings. As master carpenter Ernst Zimmer asserted (according to Gustav Kühne), Hölderlin thus remained in himself a "free man, who didn't let anyone do harm to him."[12]

The "give and take" disappeared from the daily life of the schizophrenic. Stubbornly Hölderlin refused to accept any gifts of books, even editions of his own works, and Waiblinger's journal notes "a dreadful peculiarity of his": as soon as he had eaten, Hölderlin simply placed the dish in front of the door.[13]

His denial of his own name and his assumption of a borrowed or invented name is, above all, an attempt to exclude his self from conversation and later from writing as well.[14] He had already said to Waiblinger [in the early 1820s — Trans.] that he was now called Killalusimeno.[15] According to Johann Georg Fischer, the disturbed man disavowed the name Hölderlin on the title page of his poems and asserted that he was called Scardanelli or Scaliger Rosa.[16] When in 1842 students, drinking coffee near him, "called him by his name, he wouldn't accept it, but instead answered: 'You are speaking with His Excellency, Rosetti.' "[17] Compare Christoph Theodor Schwab's descriptions of Hölderlin's insistence on having his name Scardanelli recognized.[18] Apparently the mad poet was most concerned with avoiding every spoken or written use of his given name.

POETRY

Of the literary works from his last years only meager and quite accidental fragments have been saved, and yet a close look at them yields abundant and surprising information about the artist's creativity in the last decades of his "deep psychosis."[19] We possess substantial reports of the late stages of his nearly forty-year Tübingen confinement and the poems that the aged Hölderlin wrote down at the request of visitors — in their presence and *ex tempore* — and then handed over to them. Ernst Zimmer in 1835 informed a correspondent (whose name is unknown to us): "I asked him again to write something for me too. He just opened the window, looked into the distance, and in twelve minutes it was done."[20]

We find some noteworthy passages concerning Hölderlin's last creative efforts in the obituary written by the lyric poet Gottlob Kemmler:

When he, standing at his desk, sought to bring his thoughts together in a "written prayer," then all apprehensiveness fled from his gloomy brow, and a quiet joy spread over it; no matter how loudly one talked in his presence, even if one looked over his shoulder, nothing could disturb him there . . . He wrote poetry whenever one liked, perhaps also in order to isolate himself from the kindly, but pressing, companionship.[21]

The constrained dialogue and its participants disappeared before his delight in the creative monologue. The thought "Nothing will happen to me," a formula of exorcism in Hölderlin's conversations, here becomes a happy, welcome experience.

Johann Georg Fischer, a teacher and writer, tells how, at his last visit in April, 1843, he asked Hölderlin for a few stanzas as a remembrance, and the poet, ready to write, went over to his desk: "I will never forget the radiance of his face at that moment; his eyes and forehead shone, as if profound confusion had never passed over them . . . When he was through, he handed me the page, saying, 'It pleases Your Holiness?' "[22]

Christoph Theodor Schwab, who edited the posthumous edition of Friedrich Hölderlin's *Complete Works* (1846), claims that he never saw a meaningless verse from the ill poet, although he composed his verses right "after one hadn't heard a sensible word from him for days or weeks," and he wrote these poems "without reading them over or improving them in any way."[23] In any event, Christoph Theodor Schwab limits himself in his biography to including only quite short samples of the poems "from the period of Hölderlin's darkened mental state."[24]

Despite the enthusiasm that Waiblinger had felt for the "drunken, divinely-inspired human being" at the beginning of the 1820's,[25] he was still inclined to find meaningless verses, blunders, and evidence of a "terrible style" in Hölderlin's "latecomers," although the madman's creations were incomparably superior to those of his judge.

Only a few contemporaries of the suffering artist were able to comprehend and value his late poetry. Gustav Schwab (Christoph's father, who with Uhland edited the first edition of Hölderlin's poetry in 1826), even after reading the most recent poems of the ill poet in 1841, remained firm in his conviction that "Hölderlin's entire genius still reveals itself here." Gustav's wife, Sophie Schwab, added: "How splendid that with Hölderlin one sees, even after forty years of the darkest madness, that his mind is still present and still makes itself known after so long a time."[26]

In Bettina von Arnim's view during the same period, Hölderlin,

[suffering] under the unspeakable fate that weighs upon him, . . . has for forty years been lost to the ordinary life of human beings; only confused sounds come from his mouth and the presence of other people intimidates and oppresses him. Only the Muse is still able to speak with him and in odd moments he writes down verses, little poems, in which his earlier depth and grace of spirit are reflected, but these abruptly change over into word-rhythms that are inaccessible to the understanding.[27]

If even this bold enthusiast of the poetic quest believed that these poems "lead to the abyss where the word eludes the understanding,"[28] it is not surprising that the completely unexpected artistic forms of Hölderlin's late poetry evoked narrow-minded censure.

Thus one finds in the *Morgenblatt für gebildete Leser* for April 30, 1838 an essay by the journalist and poetaster Hermann Kurz (1813–1873) on Hölderlin's poems, which are characterized as "odd words, lumped together without plan, and of an awful unintelligibility."[29] In the obituary published in 1843 by the aesthetician Moriz Carriere (1817–1895), one learns the following: Hölderlin's poetic tones "wavered unsteadily between the meaningful and meaningless."[30] To this day, similar and even harsher criticism of Hölderlin's last poems continues. Thus they are reproached for showing "a deep disturbance of feeling for language," "failure of linguistic expression," and "helpless banality"; the author is said not to be able to grasp "the complete meaning" of his verbal signs any longer, and Hölderlin's last poems are described as being "completely devoid of any fruitful tension, mere organgrinding".[31]

As Böschenstein emphasizes with good reason, the studies of Hölderlin's last works are generally informed by the prejudice that the literary work of a mentally-ill person cannot be interpreted as anything other than proof of mental and verbal decline, whereas "mental illness and genuine poetry are by no means mutually exclusive."[32] According to W. Kraft, one should "finally begin to think about the artificial distinction between health and disease, which one has dragged about for such a long time – to the detriment of poetry."[33]

What is probably the cruellest attempt to devalue Hölderlin's poems "from the years of the final stage of his illness" was made by the Tübingen physician Wilhelm Lange in his *Pathography*, where he finds "a catatonic form of idiocy" in the creations of the mentally-ill man. This researcher's clinical judgment was apparently heightened by his artistic deafness. Those poems of the sick Hölderlin that have been preserved are dismissed here with the following comments:

Stiffness and constraint, stilted language, meaningless new words and word-mannerisms, and a childish tone are common to all of them, as well as absentmindedness, stereotyped phrases, and an idle playing with sounds, along with banal expletives and insertions. The poet has lost his ability to distinguish between the language of poetry and everyday speech. He has lost his feeling for style; in the place of clear concepts, one finds just empty words . . . The circle of his interests has grown narrow; only tenuous links to emotion shine faintly through his verses.[34]

As late as 1921, a similar viewpoint is heard again: "The systematic study of these would have at the most a pathological interest or that of a curiosity item."[35]

C. Litzmann's book (*Hölderlin's Leben in Briefen von und an Hölderlin* [Hölderlin's Life in Letters to and from Hölderlin]) already mentioned 'Die Aussicht' [The Perspective] in 1890: There are "a few matter-of-fact comments about nature, loosely strung together, that lead [the author] to an abstract idea, which, however, he is no longer able to grasp or express clearly."[36] It is in a completely different light that the poems Hölderlin wrote toward the end of his life appear to L. von Pigenot in his writings from the year 1923, where he gives prominence to 'Die Aussicht' as "that intellectually refined poem, solemn and full of forebodings, which we may well take to be Hölderlin's last poem."[37]

Since Pigenot's early outline, German literary scholarship has shown increased interest in the strange poetics that underlies Hölderlin's final works. It has thereby become more and more clear that the final phase of the poet's writings is to be distinguished sharply "from the first half of the last group of poems." Here too mixing of the vocabulary from the different poetic phases should be avoided, because it would result "not in clarifying but in blurring the contours of each semantic field."[38] It is significant that words characteristic of 'Die Aussicht' (as well as of other poems of the Scardanelli cycle) are foreign to the so-called period of hymns: *Aussicht* "perspective, view, outlook," *Vollkommenheit* "perfection," *ergänzen* "to complete," *vorübergleiten* "to pass by." In addition to statements of admiration for individual poems by "Scardanelli," there were, in the 1960's, a few attempts to discuss Hölderlin's verbal art in the last years of his life more thoroughly and either to trace the links to his earlier works[39] or to uncover the new and original characteristics of the last poetic phase, whereby this stage, instead of giving evidence of decline, "conforms legitimately to Hölderlin's development and, in fact, paradoxical as that may seem, as a genuine step forward," as Wilhelm Michel had already expressed it in 1911.[40] In 1964 the Polish Germanist

Z. Żygulski wrote: "The assertion may indeed seem absurd, but the mentally-ill Hölderlin wrote poetry more clearly than did the ostensibly healthy one."[41]

Wilfried Thürmer's monograph *Zur poetischen Verfahrensweise in der spätesten Lyrik Hölderlin's* [On the Poetic Method of Hölderlin's Last Poems], which appeared in 1970, is especially stimulating for the study of the last poetic sequence. The book concludes with this challenge: "One must recognize the strange and necessarily singular mode of being of the texts themselves in order to value them adequately."[42] The researcher's basic premises are very well suited to the development of this insight: "By closer study [Hölderlin's writing toward the end of his life] is revealed as a process involving profound artistic understanding."[43] "The 'childlike-simple' poem is created by a linguistic sensibility that firmly leaves its mark upon all parts. Signs of apparent helplessness prove to be calculated operations and apparent slips in the flow of language to be a deliberate control of the system."[44] Above all, "the entire literary life of this poetry" is to be investigated "on all levels of linguistic expression" — "even the particles, functional words, syntactic peculiarities, and peculiarities in the choice of words."[45]

To be sure, one has to protest that every attempt to study Scardanelli's verbal patterns attentively leads one to contradict Thürmer's supposition that these poems have no "compact architectonics,"[46] that "extended connecting lines" were "simply not possible in these verses," and that no "architectonic relations" exist between individual stanzas.[47] The total structure of Scardanelli's poems of two, three, or four quatrains exhibits the same degree of sustained development as do their individual stanzas or verses. It will suffice, in addition to peculiarities in the systematic distribution of grammatical categories and their lexical analogues, with which 'Die Aussicht' is interwoven [discussed in depth in the longer essay of which this is part — Trans.], to mention a few other structural characteristics of the poem, especially to determine certain analogues both of sound and meaning within the eight-line poem, whose architectonic cohesiveness proves to be impressive.

DIE AUSSICHT

I₁ Wenn in die Ferne geht   der Menschen wohnend Leben,
₂ Wo in die Ferne sich   erglänzt die Zeit der Reben,
II₁ Ist auch dabei   des Sommers leer Gefilde,
₂ Der Wald erscheint   mit seinem dunklen Bilde.

III$_1$ Daß die Natur   ergänzt das Bild der Zeiten,
  $_2$ Daß die verweilt,   sie schnell vorübergleiten,
IV$_1$ Ist aus Vollkommenheit,   des Himmels Höhe glänzet
  $_2$ Den Menschen dann,   wie Bäume Blüth' umkränzet.

THE PERSPECTIVE

I$_1$ When into the distance fades   the mortal life of human beings,
  $_2$ Where into the distance   gleams the season of the ripening vines,
II$_1$ There too are   the summer's empty fields,
  $_2$ The wood appears   with its dark image.

III$_1$ That Nature   completes the image of the seasons,
  $_2$ That while it lingers,   they pass by quickly,
IV$_1$ Is something of perfection,   the heights of heaven glow
  $_2$ Upon human beings then,   as blossoms wreathe the trees.*

The genitive I$_1$/ *der Menschen* "of human beings" and the dative IV$_2$// *Den Menschen* "to human beings," which is juxtaposed to it (two different cases of the same word), allude first to the passing of human life and then to the grace that is bestowed upon it from above. The interrelation of both [grammatical] forms involves axial symmetry: one case is found at the beginning of the second hemistich and the other at the beginning of the second-to-last hemistich of the entire poem. Of the two nouns I$_2$ *Zeit* "time, season" and IV$_2$ *Vollkommenheit* "perfection," which rhyme with one another and take part in the resolution of a dramatic contrast, the former belongs to the fourth and the latter to the fourth-to-last hemistich of the poem, and both rhyming words are assigned to the same two lines as the two verbs with the same root, I$_2$/ *erglänzt* "gleams" and IV$_1$ *glänzet* "glows"//.

By means of other kinds of symmetry, the components of *Vollkommenheit* "perfection" [literally "to come" (*kommen*) to "full-" (*Voll*) ness" (*heit*) — Trans.] are provided with their antonyms. The beginning of the first line in the last couplet of the poem contains the component IV$_1$ *-kommen-* "to come" and in the first couplet the contrary verb I$_1$ *geht* "goes." The third

---

* The translation is a literal one and makes no attempt to reproduce the poem's rhythm or its complex (and untranslatable) texture of end- and internal rhyme, alliteration, occurrence of verbs having the same root, etc. Some of these devices are discussed later in this article; others are considered in the first part of the larger essay from which this is taken. – Trans.

line of the final stanza contains *Voll-* "full-" in the beginning hemistich in contrast to the third line of the beginning stanza with the adjective II_1 *leer* "empty" in its closing hemistich. The situation is similar for two words that are closely linked lexically and grammatically, II_2 *Wald* "woods" (the only masculine noun in the nominative case), and the corresponding IV_2 *Bäume* "trees" (the only masculine noun in the accusative case): one word belongs to the last verse of the beginning stanza and the other to that of the final stanza.

Of the thirty-three nasals in the text, the overwhelming majority are concentrated in the outer couplets — twelve in each — with the last three manifesting axial symmetry in their relation to the first three lines of the poem: eight nasals each in the first (I_1) and the last line (IV_2); four each in the second (I_2) and the second-to-last (IV_1); one each in the third (II_1) and the third-to-last (III_2) line. The two hemistichs with the greatest number of nasals both emphasize the word *Menschen* "human beings," and each contains — in the closing half of the first line and the beginning half of the last line — four *n's* and one *m*, with the final beginning hemistich generalizing the tonal structure of the word *Menschen* "human beings" and all four syllables of the hemistich ending with an *n*: IV_2 *Den Menschen dann*/"to human beings then."

In the significant linking of two nouns — III_1 *das Bild der Zeiten* "the image of the seasons" — the inclusive *Bild* "image" of the beginning verse of the final stanza responds to the fleeting II_2 *Bilde* "image" of the last verse of the beginning stanza, and the genitive III_1 *der Zeiten* "of the seasons" in the beginning line of the couplet that opens the final stanza has an anticipatory parallel in the last line of the couplet that opens the beginning stanza — I_2 *die Zeit der* "the time of the." The verse that brings the three concepts *Vollkommenheit* "perfection," *Höhe* "heights," and *Glanz* "glow" (IV_1) together is the first that imprints a vertical movement upon the poem (that of sending something from above), before it closes with another vertical image, that of blossoms wreathing the trees.

In the praise of a higher realm, built up vertically verse by verse within the twelve-line poem 'Der Sommer' [Summer] ('Das Erntefeld erscheint') [The harvestfield appears] from the year 1837,[48] the words I_1 *Höhen* "heights," IV_2 *hohes* "high," VI_1 *hoch* "high" run through all three stanzas. The other two decisive word-images (*Glanz* "glow" and *Fülle* "abundance, fullness") occur in the same lines as the earlier ones: IV_2 "Ein hohes Bild, und golden glänzt der Morgen" [A lofty image, and golden glows the morning], VI_2 "und was er hoch vollbringet" [and what he achieves so well].

The texture of the repeated words and of the correspondences they find plays an essential and, at the same time, an extremely varied role in

Scardanelli's poetry. The emphasis lies either upon the multiple repetition of the same words or their complement is developed with special emphasis, where the number of recurring words is slight (cf., e.g., 'Die Aussicht'). In the distribution of the repeated words as well, the different poems of this period show considerable individuality.

The poem 'Höheres Leben' [More Noble Life] from the year 1841 generally repeats within two of its three quatrains a number of words either exactly or with morphological variations: I, III *Mensch* "human being" — III *Menschheit* "humanity"; I, III *Leben* "life" — III (twice) *des Lebens* "of life"; II, III *Sinn* "meaning"; the three degrees of comparison of the same adjective, namely, III *hohen* "high" — II *höhern* "higher" III *höhres* "highest" — III *Das Höchste* "the highest thing"; I *innern* "inner" — II *in seinem Innern* "in his inner being"; I (twice) *sein* — II *seine* — II, III *seinem* ["his" for different genders, cases, and persons — Trans.], etc.

The uniqueness — on several counts — of the last three lines of the 'Aussicht' when compared to the five preceding verses is one of the striking indications of a complex and purposeful design. The *sectio aurea* [golden section], established most clearly since Leonardo da Vinci,[50] emerges distinctly in Hölderlin's last 'Aussicht' [there are three poems with this title — Trans.].[51] The shorter section ("minor") is to the longer one ("major") as the longer one is to the entire, undivided passage. The golden section (8:5=5:3) contrasts two unequal parts of an eight-line whole and divides 'Die Aussicht' into two syntactically symmetrical groups of five *verba finita*, or five clauses each, with the distribution of verbs in the hemistichs of the five-line major (3:2) and the three-line minor (2:3) according to axial symmetry. This demarcation thereby exists in a dynamic and tense contrast to the static symmetry of the two four-line stanzas, with which two parallel complex sentences are correlated. The only transitive verbs of the poem and their direct objects, which conclude the major (III_1 *ergänzt das Bild* "completes the image") and the minor (IV_2 *Bäume . . . umkränzet* "trees . . . wreathe), bring the golden section into prominence.

It should be noted that the last term of the proportion 8:5=5:3, which asserts itself as being marked within the whole, is different due to the marked joining of rounded and palatal vowels in the five-line segment (i.e., in the mean proportion). The divergence between the golden section and the strophic likeness accentuates the fifth verse of the poem, because it simultaneously begins the second stanza and concludes the first, the five-line segment of the "golden row": III_1 "Dass die Natur ergänzt das Bild der Zeiten" [That Nature completes the image of the seasons]. This verse is undoubtedly the semantic centerpiece of the whole, a verse that emphasizes the determinative idea of *Nature* and neutralizes the dialectic opposition between permanence and change.

Viewed syntactically, this line constitutes the only developed clause with a subject (S) in the beginning hemistich and a predicate (P) in the closing hemistich; the other two lines, which distribute the subject and predicate beween the hemistichs, begin the first two couplets and place the predicate before the subject (I_1 *Geht* / ... *Leben* //; II_1 // *Ist* ... *Gefilde* // I_1 Goes / ... life; II_1 // Are ... fields //" [(*Das*) *Gefilde* "(the) fields" is singular in German, hence the verb *ist* "is" – Trans.]. On the other hand, it is the first of four lines where, within the beginning hemistich, the verb is not followed by a nominative (the last three end with a verb). The intermediate position of verse III_1 is evident (cf. the chart).

I_1	geht		Leben
2		erglänzt die Zeit	
II_1	Ist		Gefilde
2	Der Wald	erscheint	
III_1		Natur	ergänzt
2		die verweilt	sie	vorübergleiten
IV_1				Höhe glänzet
2				Blüth' umkränzet

I_1	goes		life
2		gleams the season	
II_1	Are		fields
2	The wood	appears	
III_1		Nature	completes
2		it lingers	they	pass by quickly
IV_1				heights glow
2				blossoms wreathe

I_1		P		S
2			P	S
II_1	P				S
2	S	P		
III_1		S	P	
2	S	P	S		P
IV_1				S	P
2				S	P

Thus every odd-numbered verse of the first five-line segment is character-ized by a division of subject and predicate between the two hemistichs. At the same time, an inverted relationship of the two segments of the "golden row" is maintained: minor + major = 3 + 5, and each of the first three lines is distinguished from all five further lines by the fact that the predicate precedes the subject. Within the poem the boundary line of the five-line major is hinted at in both directions (3 + 5 and 5 + 3) by the presence of the signal word *Bild* "image": compare the fifth verse — III$_1$ *ergänzt das Bild* "completes the image" — with the fifth-to-last — II$_2$ *erscheint mit seinem dunklen Bilde* "appears with its dark image."

The way in which beginning hemistichs with two or three feet are distri-buted within the poem can also be attributed to the golden section. A third variation of the same procedure contrasts the three long verses of the eight-line poem (2 + 1) with its five short verses (4 + 1), whereby the only common rhyme joins the major and minor and thereby crowns the eight-line whole: IV$_1$ *glänzet* "glows" — $_2$ *umkränzet* "wreathes."

For insight into and feeling for Hölderlin's dialectical poetics with its internal conflict between identity and exchange of all parts, the poem 'Der Rhein' [The Rhine],[52] with its five *parthien* of three stanzas each, written in 1801, (i.e., on the threshold of acute psychosis), is especially instructive, including the expert comment of the author in the margin: "The law of this poem is that the first two *parthien*, according to their form, are in opposition through progress and regress, but in content are similar; the two following *parthien* are similar in form, but contrast in content; the last *parthien*, however, through its sustained metaphor, resolves everything."[53]

Hölderlin's final phase of poetic activity is often criticized for its "stereo-types," "sameness," and "dry monotony," but in fact there prevailed in Scardanelli's workshop a tension between the strictest canon and an amazing richness of creative shadings and variations comparable to that in the monu-mental art of the Middle Ages. The established topoi of the elderly Hölderlin appear in boldly renewed forms. Words, for example, that occur in the rhymes of the 'Aussicht,' belong for the most part to the rhyme-repertoire of other poems of the same period as well, yet with a variety of complements: I$_1$ *Leben* "life" rhymes in other instances with *Streben*, — *geben* "striving — to give"; II$_1$ *Gefilde* "fields" with *Milde* "mildness"; III$_1$ *Zeiten* "seasons" with *geleiten, breiten* "to accompany," "to extend"; and only the final rhyme IV$_1$ *glänzet* — $_2$ *umkränzet* "glows — wreathes" persists, at least in a lexical sense: *glänzen* — *kränzen* "to glow — to wreathe."[54]

One has sometimes mistakenly seen in Hölderlin's "latecomers," as Eduard

Mörike called them, a helpless return on the part of the sick old man to the style and form of his youthful poems; but even a cursory overview of all twenty-three poems signed with the name Scardanelli reveals enormous differences in construction and intention when compared with verses from the poet's beginnings. In the youthful poems there are only accidental and isolated parallels to what is typical in the late poems. It is only here that one finds the verses to have consistently femine endings, that there is continuous variation within a poem between five- and six-foot iambs, that there is a decided preference for poems of eight lines divided into two quatrains and a tendency toward plain rhymes. (In fourteen Scardanelli poems they are used throughout and in six others at least for the second quatrain).

THE SPEECH AND VERBAL ART OF SCHIZOPHRENIA

Waiblinger's poem to the "wretched-saintly" Hölderlin was published in 1826 in the *Mitternachtblatt für gebildete Stände* with the editor's comment on the celebrated author of the novel *Hyperion*: "now an intellectually dead man, insane for many years."[55] The "intellectually dead man" continued his literary output for another seventeen years. A question raised often in Hölderlin studies, especially by psychiatrists, concerns the relations between the development of his illness and of his poetry. In order to be useful, an answer demands truly interdisciplinary work in psychiatry, linguistics, and poetics and could, as Jaspers anticipated, "throw light on the nature of the schizophrenic [in any event only on one specific type within this broad category of illness] and make our concept of the schizophrenic more concrete,"[56] as well as further the diagnosis of such mental attacks, just as interdisciplinary efforts in the area of aphasia do already. Yet when, for example, it is the language of the ill Hölderlin that is under discussion, one must warn others firmly against making an attempt to exclude "all interpretative and linguistic-aesthetic points of view" from consideration,[57] for it is precisely to the aesthetic point of view that the poetic texts owe their special treatment in Hölderlin's language-world in relation to the other classes and varieties found within the totality of the *Sprachbotschaften* "verbal messages," to use Bühler's technical term.[58]

Basic to the entire linguistic nature and creative strength of the mentally-ill Hölderlin is the crude contrast between his appalling loss of the gift for conversation with others and his strangely intact and enthusiastic wish and capacity for effortless, spontaneous, and purposeful impromptu poetry. Everything that belongs to conversation — the mutual address, the dialogue with questions and answers, the capability of the speaker and the attentiveness of the listener, the effectiveness of one's own statements and the ability to comprehend those of the other — the entire technique of conversation could be imitated only laboriously and imperfectly; it was confused and virtually lost.

Out of the madman's zeal "to annul the other person immediately" and to make speeches aloud "to himself day and night," there arose, despite the purely subjective character of such utterances, a kind of conversation that had reference to a partner. Within Hölderlin's linguistic activity, it reveals the same symptoms of unhealthy decline as does his verbal contact with every companion.

The genuine and pure monologues, which (in amazing contrast to the debris of Hölderlin's everyday prattle) exhibit an inviolable cohesiveness and completeness in their linguistic structure, are the poems that were written in the last years of the poet's life. As Christoph Theodor Schwab had already noted in this connection, "It was wonderful what magic the poetic form exerted on Hölderlin," whereas in prose he easily became "very bewildered." Schwab documents this difference by comparing two dedications that Hölderlin (in 1841) inscribed in the same book:[59] on the one hand prosaic sentences and on the other "Überzeugung" [Conviction] — an iambic quatrain.[60]

Appropriate to the late poetic form of Scardanelli, which was furthest from a prosaic manner of speech, is a remark by Hölderlin ("exhausted in his confusion") that was written down by Sinclair and repeated by Bettina von Arnim in Die Günderode: "Language forms all thought, for it is greater than the human mind, which is only a slave to language, and the human intellect will be less than complete as long as language alone doesn't evoke it. But the laws of the intellect are metric — one feels that in language, which throws a net over the intellect; while caught within it, the mind must [still] express the divine."[61]

Scardanelli's poems, which have regular meter and one that allows variation only in the length of the lines (either ten or twelve syllables), present a stark contrast to Hölderlin's helpless and unsuccessful transactions with other people.

The schizophrenic person, as Ruth Leodolter has emphasized in her careful observations, "avoids dialogue and confrontation with the environment, whether this be conscious or unconscious"; in such a syndrome, "the ability — or willingness — to communicate," i.e., the "competence for dialogue," of the sick person has been more or less lost, whereas the "competence for monologue" remains.[62] Hölderlin's language presents a classic example of disturbed competence for dialogue, coinciding with a pronounced mastery of monologue, which is intact and even enhanced.

Scardanelli's poems differ from social discourse in their systematic renunciation of basic conversational forms. In contrast to the everyday language practices of the mentally-ill man, these poems possess no deictic linguistic signs and no references to the immediate circumstances. It was Charles Sanders Peirce who gave special emphasis to the essential nature of the different *indices* for our daily speech:

If, for example, a man remarks, "Why, it is raining!" it is only by some such *circumstances* as that he is now standing here looking out at a window as he speaks, which would serve as an Index (not, however, as a Symbol) that he is speaking of this place at this time, whereby we can be assured that he cannot be speaking of the weather on the satellite of Procyon, fifty centuries ago.

On the other hand, as has often been observed and explained in the poems from the end of Hölderlin's life, especially by F. Beissner,[64] direct experience did not stimulate the mind of the poet. Consistent with this is the fact "that he never actually depicts a single occurrence in its particularity ... That is demonstrated by the strange preference for the generalizing conjunction *wenn* 'when, if,' " with which more than a third of the so-called Last Poems begin.[65] According to Beissner, Hölderlin was careful to exclude from his poems of that period everything individual or personal, i.e. everything *accidentelle*, to use the poet's term from an earlier time. When one compares the two poles in the language usage of the schizophrenic poet, it seems appropriate to emphasize, as does Karl Bühler, that "deixis and naming are two acts that should be differentiated, that words of ostension and naming words are categories that should be kept sharply separated," and one should add that in contrast to the "act of pointing that does not name" [literally "is naming-free" — Trans.] of the quasi-dialogic activity of Hölderlin in his social contacts, his late poetry is, instead, focused on "naming" that is divested, is independent of ostension.

The Scardanelli poems, as well as the other "latecomers" of Hölderlin's, dispense with the grammatical category of "shifters," which delineate the reported activity in reference to the speech act and its participants.[66] The absence of this basic category is especially striking in comparison with the earlier works of the poet, which were oriented around dialogue, where shifters asserted themselves firmly and effectively. In contrast to the complete lack of marked classes for both persons of immediate interest (the first and second) in Hölderlin's last works,[67] the Diotima elegy ("Wenn aus der Ferne . . ." [If from the distance . . .]) from the year 1820 includes in its fifty-one lines twenty-six pronouns of the first and second person in different grammatical cases plus six possessives, *mine* and *yours*, and a large number of verbs for the same two persons.[68] In contrast to the strict monopoly exercised by the unmarked present tense in the later poems, there is in the Diotima elegy competition between the present tense and twenty-six examples of the marked past tense. Modal relationships, later reduced to the unmarked indicative, were also represented in the elegy by imperative and subjunctive forms (such as $_{42}$ "Nehme vorlieb und denk / An die . . . ,$_{49}$ Du seiest so allein" [Be satisfied and think / Of the . . . ,$_{49}$ That you are so alone]). Utterances that rest upon dialogue, such as questions ($_{21}$ "Wars Frühling? war es Sommer?" [$_{21}$ Was it in spring? was it summer?]), affirmative answers, forms of address ($_3$ "O du Theilhaber meiner Leiden!" [O you sharer in my sufferings!]), and exclamations ($_{46}$ "Ach! wehe mir!" [$_{46}$ Ah! woe is me!]) no longer occur in Hölderlin's poems of the last period of his life. The cooperation of the *verbum dictionis* and its *dictum*, which place the speech act as such in the foreground, is similarly a characteristic device of the Diotima elegy and one that is abandoned in Hölderlin's later writing: $_5$ "So sage, wie erwartet die Freundin dich? — $_9$ Das muss ich sagen, einiges Gute war // In deinen Bliken — $_{15}$ Ja! Ich gestand es, ich war die deine. — $_{49}$ Du seiest so allein in der schönen Welt // Behauptest du mir immer, Geliebter!" [$_5$ So tell me, how does your lover await you? — $_9$ I must admit, there was something good // In your glances — $_{15}$ Yes! I confessed I was yours. — $_{49}$ That you are so alone in the lovely world // So you always assert to me, loved one!].

Grammatical traits similar to those of the "method" in the elegy discussed permeate Hölderlin's poetry of the 1820s up until the communication "Dem gnädigsten Herrn von Lebret" [To the most gracious Lord of Lebret], apparently from the winter of 1829/1830.[69] The first poem titled 'Aussicht,' which is found on the same manuscript copy ("Wenn Menschen fröhlich sind" [When human beings are happy]) is thought to be from the same period and, together with the preceding poem, have been "written at a student's request, in exchange for a pipe of tobacco."[70] Yet in its construction, this 'Aussicht' approaches the poems about the seasons,[71] which were written later, and especially the Scardanelli cycle.

The very last poetic monologues of this "greatest of schizophrenics" (as F. L. Welles called Hölderlin) are characterized by their suppression of every allusion to the speech act and its date as well as to its actual participants. The taboo name of the sender is resolutely replaced by "Scardanelli";

the recipient of the verses and the fate of the manuscripts, which are provided
with dates as distant in time as possible, remained a matter of indifference
to the author. The grammatical tenses of the text are limited to the unmarked present. This "despotism of the present," as Böschenstein called
it, does away with the sequence of the seasons and reveals "throughout
every season the entirety of the cycle."[72] Hölderlin's treatise, 'Über die
Verfahrensweise des poëtischen Geistes' [On the Method of the Poetic Spirit],
which proved to be instructive for the poet's later development, casts a new
light especially on Scardanelli's symbolism. This essay, written in Homburg,
warns poetry about the empty "infinity of isolated moments (a series of
atoms, so to speak)" and, at the same time, about believing in "a dead and
deadening unity." In the poetic present, "the manifestation of infinity" is
recognized and, in order to elucidate this manifestation, Hölderlin adds
immediately: "That which is opposed and that which is one are indivisible
within it."[73]

There is no evidence in Scardanelli's poems of the futile effort involved in
Hölderlin's attempts to say something abstract to a visitor, as Thürmer
recognized perceptively: "Effortlessness, an utterance that refuses to allow
even the slightest trace of effort — that is at the heart of the matter."[74]
Because deixis is rejected, nouns are liberated from ostension in such poems
as 'Die Aussicht' and are transformed into unified sequences of abstract
terms, and it should be noted that many purely conceptual nouns, which
were foreign to Hölderlin's poems of the first two decades of the nineteenth
century, first appeared in the last poems from "the period of his madness":[75]
Aussicht "perspective, view, outlook," *Erhabenheit* "loftiness, sublimity,"
Erscheinung "appearance," *Geistigkeit* "intellectuality, spirituality,"
Gewogenheit "goodwill," *Innerheit* "inwardness," *Menschheit* "humanity,"
Vergangenheit "the past," *Vertrautheit* "intimacy," etc.

The spatial and temporal perspective ('Aussicht') — revealing title word for
three late poems — lays a trap for the ill man as soon as there are two
participants in a conversation and the coordination of two angles of vision is
involved. When Christoph Theodor Schwab entered Hölderlin's room in
January, 1841, and praised the view ["die Aussicht" — literally "out-look" —
Trans.], the poet looked him over and said quietly to himself: "He is so nicely
dressed."[76] ["Er ist so schön angezogen" = "Er sieht so schön aus," literally
"He sees so good out," i.e., "He looks so good." — Trans.] At the end of July
of the same year, a new visitor, Marie Nathusius, noted in her journal: "I said
to him: 'You have a pleasant view here.' He answered: 'One can look good'
[or "One can have a good lookout." The German, "Man kann gut aussehen,"

literally means "One can look out good/well," i.e., look attractive or have a good view. — Trans.]. The semantic field of the verb stem is apparently condensed and reduced in both instances [*zieh* for *sich anziehen* "to dress" and *seh* for *sehen* "to see" — Trans.], whereas in the elegy "Wenn aus der Ferne . . . " [If from the distance . . .] the double meaning of the etymological configuration — $_{12}$ "mit finstrem // Aussehen" [$_{12}$ of gloomy // appearance] and $_{40}$ "aus hoher Aussicht" [$_{40}$ with a view from on high] becomes apparent.[78]

According to psychiatric statements about Hölderlin's mental disorder, it was in poetic expression that "the character of the final stage [of the disease] showed itself most clearly;" cited here as a typical feature of the "sculpture of schizophrenia" is Hölderlin's "geometrical tendency."[79] This quality is closely related to the progressive decline in referential, deictic activity. Consequently, Scardanelli's verse monologues are dominated by an "introversive semiosis": they become a "communication that carries its meaning within itself." As 'Die Aussicht' and related poems show us, the various components form manifold equivalences; it is precisely in such an interplay of the parts as well as in their integration into a carefully constructed whole that the magic grace of these allegedly naive verses consists.[80]

'Hölderlin and the Essence of Poetry' is the title of the speech that Heidegger gave forty years ago, on April 2, 1936, in Rome.[81] Five themes from the poet's work were chosen and commented upon by the philosopher, among them the ending (one typical of Hölderlin) of the poem 'Andenken' [Remembrance] from the year 1803: "Was bleibet aber, stiften die Dichter" [What is lasting, however, the poets create],[82] and just before it the four lines with which the last draft for the unfinished poem "Versöhnender der du nimmergeglaubt" [Peacemaker, you who never believed] from the year 1801 breaks off.[83] The most important of these lines — $_{50}$ "Seit ein Gespräch wir sind" [Because we are a conversation] — prompted Heidegger to the following comments:

We — human beings — are a conversation. The essence of a human being is rooted in language, which first truly presents itself in *conversation*. This is, however, not only a way in which language is realized, but, rather, it is only as conversation that language is essential. What we otherwise mean by "language," namely an inventory of words and rules governing their combinations, is only the foreground of language. But what then is a "conversation"? Apparently the talking with one another about something. Speaking thereby facilitates the coming together.[84]

Whatever Hölderlin's view of the world and of language had been in the eighteenth century, his later development, in any case, reverses the concept quoted. Not as conversation but only as poetry is language — with its immense supply of words and deeply interesting rules that govern their combinations — essential, whereas this speaking and coming together were rejected by Hölderlin (all the more decisively as he grew older) as the mere anteroom of language: "Was bleibet aber, stiften die Dichter" [What is lasting, however, the poets create]. The reported event excludes reference to the speech act from the purely poetic account.

Harvard University, and
Massachusetts Institute of Technology

NOTES

*From an essay by Roman Jakobson and Grete Lübbe-Grothues, 'Ein Blick auf "Die Aussicht" von Hölderlin' [A Study of 'The Perspective' by Hölderlin], in Roman Jakobson, 1976, *Hölderlin, Klee, Brecht: Zur Wortkunst dreier Gedichte* [Hölderlin, Klee, Brecht: On the Verbal Art of Three Poems], Elmar Holenstein (ed.), Frankfurt am Main: Suhrkamp Verlag, pp. 27–97.
     Translated by Susan Abrams
1 *See*, for example, U. Supprian (1974).
2 Friedrich Hölderlin, *Sämtliche Werke* [Collected Works], ed. Friedrich Beissner (Stuttgart: Verlag W. Kohlhammer, 1974), 7:2 no. 291, p. 262. [All subsequent citations to works by Hölderlin and to documents of his contemporaries are to this edition (the so-called *Grosse Stuttgarter Ausgabe*), listing volume number (and portion of volume for volume 7, which is in two parts), number of document (where applicable), and page. – Trans.].
3 Hölderlin, 7/2: no. 345, p. 262.
4 Hölderlin, 2: 117. [All translations (which are literal rather than poetic) are my own. – Trans.]
5 Hölderlin, 7/3: no. 489, p. 41.
6 Hölderlin, 7/3: no. 499, p. 64.
7 Hölderlin, 7/2: no. 357, p. 371.
8 Hölderlin, 7/2 and 7/3.
9 Nussbächer (1971). [The idealized loved woman, to whom Hölderlin addresses several poems, Diotima is also a central figure in his long epistolary work of poetic prose, *Hyperion* (1797/99). The character was much influenced by his love for Susette Gontard, a married woman at whose home he lived as a tutor. Hölderlin took the name from Plato's *Symposium*: the author's statement of the highest form of love is expressed by Socrates and attributed to his former teacher, the priestess Diotima. The concluding segment of R. Jakobson and G. Lübbe-Grothues's essay from which this article is excerpted is titled "Diotima." – Trans.].
10 Hölderlin, 7/3: no. 551, p. 203.
11 Hölderlin, 7/3: no. 535, p. 156.
12 Hölderlin, 7/3: 158.
13 Hölderlin, 7/3: no. 470, p. 10.

[14] Compare the 'Excursus: Hölderlin's Illness,' in Hölderlin, 7/3: no. 632, p. 341.

[15] Hölderlin, 7/3: no. 499, p. 69. The poet did not, however, sign any of his works with this name; he began to use the name Scardanelli in 1837 or 1838. [Reference given on page 30 of the longer essay from which the current discussion is taken. – Trans.]

[16] Hölderlin, 7/3: no. 608, p. 297.

[17] Hölderlin, 7/3: no. 596, p. 280.

[18] Reference is to page 31 of the longer Jakobson/Lübbe-Grothues article, on which the following appears – Trans.:

> On January 21, 1841, Christoph Theodor Schwab noted in his journal: "Today I was with him again, in order to pick up a few poems that he had written. There were two that had no signature. Zimmer's daughter told me to ask him to write the name H. beneath them. I went in to him and did so. Then he became enraged, ran around the room, picked up the armchair and set it down furiously here and there, screamed words I couldn't understand, although among them the phrase "My name is Scardanelli" was spoken clearly. But finally he sat down and in his rage signed the name Scardanelli to the poems." (Hölderlin, 7/3: no. 551, p. 205.)

[19] U. Supprian (1974).

[20] Hölderlin, 7/3: no. 528, p. 134.

[21] Hölderlin, 7/3: no. 642, pp. 366–7.

[22] Hölderlin, 7/3: no. 608, p. 301.

[23] See E. Trummler (1921).

[24] Hölderlin, 7/3: no. 663, p. 413.

[25] Cf., e.g., Hölderlin, 7/3; no. 470, p. 7.

[26] Hölderlin, 7/3: no. 553, p. 211.

[27] B. von Arnim (1848); cf. Hölderlin, 7/3: 255.

[28] B. von Arnim (1848); cf. Hölderlin, 7/3: 915.

[29] Hölderlin, 7/3: no. 536, p. 172.

[30] Hölderlin, 7/3: no. 644, p. 371.

[31] See W. Häussermann (1961); W. Böhm (1930); W. Rehm (1950); E. Bach (1965); cf. W. Thürmer's summary (1970).

[32] B. Böschenstein (1965/66).

[33] W. Kraft (1959).

[34] W. Lange (1909).

[35] K. Viëtor (1921).

[36] C. Litzmann (1890).

[37] L. von Pigenot (1923); cf. U. Häussermann (1961).

[38] Cf. B. Böschenstein (1964).

[39] See A. Bennholdt-Thomsen (1967); W. Kudszus (1969).

[40] W. Michel (1949).

[41] Z. Żygulski (1964).

[42] W. Thürmer (1970), p. 80.

[43] Ibid. p. 52.

[44] Ibid. p. 53.

[45] Ibid. p. 80.

[46] Ibid. p. 53.

[47] Ibid. pp. 35, 39, and 53.

[48] Hölderlin, 2: 285.

49 Hölderlin, 2: 289.
50 Cf. M. C. Ghyka (1927); H. E. Timerding (1929); O. Hagenmaier (1949); G. V. Cereteli (1973).
51 *See* pp. 43ff. of the longer essay by R. Jakobson and G. Lübbe-Grothues.
52 Hölderlin, 2: 142ff.
53 Hölderlin, 2: 730.
54 Hölderlin, 2: 307.
55 Hölderlin, 7/3: no. 685, p. 483.
56 K. Jaspers (1926).
57 Cf. U. Supprian (1974).
58 K. Bühler (1934).
59 E. Trummler (1921).
60 Cf. Hölderlin, 2: 360, 977.
61 B. von Arnim (1914).
62 R. Leodolter (1975).
63 C. S. Peirce (1933).
64 F. Beissner (1947).
65 Hölderlin, 2: 261–312.
66 Compare R. Jakobson (1974).
67 Compare also U. Supprian (1974).
68 Hölderlin, 2: 262ff.
69 Hölderlin, 2: 282, 908.
70 Hölderlin, 2: 281, 909.
71 Hölderlin, 2: 283–5.
72 B. Böschenstein (1965/66).
73 Hölderlin, 4: 251.
74 W. Thürmer (1970).
75 Cf. B. Böschenstein (1964).
76 Hölderlin, 7/3: no. 551, p. 203.
77 Hölderlin, 7/3: no. 579, p. 253.
78 Hölderlin, 2: 262.
79 *See* R. Treichler (1935).
80 Cf. R. Jakobson (1974).
81 M. Heidegger (1971).
82 Hölderlin, 2: 189.
83 Hölderlin, 2: 137.
84 M. Heidegger (1971).

REFERENCES

Arnim, B. von.: 1914, *Die Günderode*, 2nd ed., 2 vols., Leipzig.
Arnim, B. von.: 1848, *Ilius Pamphilius*, 2 vols., Leipzig.
Bach, E.: 1965, '*Einst* and *Jetzt* in Hölderlin's Works,' *Deutsche Beiträge* 5, 143–56.
Beissner, F.: 1947, 'Zu den Gedichten der letzten Lebenszeit,' *Hölderlin-Jahrbuch* 2, 6–10.
Bennholdt-Thomsen, A.: 1967, *Stern und Blume: Untersuchungen zur Sprachauffassung Hölderlins*, Bonn.

Böhm, W.: 1930, *Hölderlin*, vol. 1, Halle/S.

Böschenstein, B.: 1965/66, 'Hölderlins späteste Gedichte,' *Hölderlin-Jahrbuch* **14**, 35–56.

Bühler, K.: 1934, *Sprachtheorie*, Jena.

Cereteli, G. V.: 1973, 'Metr i ritm v poème Rustaveli i voprosy sravnitel'noj versifikacii,' *Kontekst*, Moscow.

Ghyka, M. C.: 1927, *Esthétique des proportions dans la nature et dans les arts*, 3rd ed., Paris.

Hagenmaier, O.: 1949, *Der Goldene Schnitt. Ein Harmoniegesetz und seine Anwendung*, Ulm/Donau.

Häussermann, U.: 1961, 'Hölderlins späteste Gedichte,' *Germanisch-Romanische Monatsschrift* **42**, n.s. **11**, 99–117.

Heidegger, M.: 1971, *Erläuterungen zu Hölderlins Dichtung*, 4th ed., Frankfurt am Main.

Jakobson, R.: 1974, *Form und Sinn*, Munich.

Jaspers, K.: 1926, *Strindberg und van Gogh: Versuch einer pathographischen Analyse unter vergleichender Heranziehung von Swedenborg und Hölderlin*, 2nd ed., Berlin.

Kraft, W.: 1959, 'Hölderlin,' in Kraft, W., *Wort und Gedanke*, Bern.

Kudszus, W.: 1969, *Sprachverlust und Sinnwandel: Zur späten und spätesten Lyrik Hölderlins*, Stuttgart.

Lange, W.: 1909, *Hölderlin: Eine Pathographie*, Stuttgart.

Leodolter, R.: 1975, 'Gestörte Sprache oder Privatsprache: Kommunikation bei Schizophrenen,' *Wiener Linguistische Gazette* **10–11**, 75–95.

Litzmann, C.: 1890, *Hölderlins Leben in Briefen von und an Hölderlin*, Berlin.

Michel, W.: 1949, *Das Leben Friedrich Hölderlins*, Bremen.

Nussbächer, K.: 1971, *Friedrich Hölderlin – Gedichte: Auswahl und Nachwort* Stuttgart.

Peirce, C. S.: 1933, 'The Simplest Mathematics,' in Peirce, C. S. *Collected Papers*, vol. 4. Cambridge, Mass.

Pigenot, L. von.: 1923, *Hölderlin: Das Wesen und die Schau*, Munich.

Rehm, W.: 1950, *Orpheus. Der Dichter und die Toten: Selbstdeutung und Totenkult bei Novalis, Hölderlin, Rilke*, Düsseldorf.

Supprian, U.: 1974, 'Schizophrenie und Sprache bei Hölderlin,' *Fortschritte der Neurologie/Psychiatrie* **47**, 615–34.

Thürmer, W.: 1970, *Zur poetischen Verfahrensweise in der spätesten Lyrik Hölderlins*, Marburg.

Timerding, H. E.: 1929, *Der goldene Schnitt*, 3rd ed., Leipzig and Berlin.

Treichler, R.: 1935, 'Die seelische Erkrankung Friedrich Hölderlins in ihren Beziehungen zu seinem dichterischen Schaffen,' *Zeitschrift für die gesamte Neurologie und Psychiatrie* **155**, 44–144.

Trummler, E.: 1921, *Der kranke Hölderlin*, Munich.

Viëtor, K.: 1921, *Die Lyrik Hölderlins: Eine analytische Untersuchung*, Frankfurt/M.

Wells, F. L.: 1946, 'Hölderlin: Greatest of "Schizophrenics," ' *Abnormal and Social Psychology* **41**, 199–206.

Żygulski, Z.: 1964, *Fryderyk Hölderlin*, Warsaw.

WENDY LEHNERT

PROBLEMS IN QUESTION ANSWERING

I. INTRODUCTION

Research in computational question answering has always been conducted with respect to specific tasks. Woods' LSNLIS program answers questions about its technical knowledge of moon rocks (see Woods 1972); Winograd's SHRDLU answers questions about the manipulation of blocks on a table (see Winograd 1972); Shortliffe's MYCIN helps physicians diagnose diseases and prescribe drugs by engaging in question answering dialogues (see Shortliffe 1974); Schank's SAM reads stories and answers questions about what it reads (see Schank et al. 1975). While all of these programs are concerned with question answering, each one has perceived the problem from a different angle.

Each of these programs has attacked the problem of question answering for very different reasons. Wood's program was designed to be used by scientists as a reliable retrieval system while Winograd used question answering to demonstrate a computer's understanding in a world of blocks. Shortliffe wanted a program which physicians could query for explanations and Schank was interested in showing how general world knowledge is used in natural language processing. My own research on question answering has been in conjunction with SAM and other story understanding systems which answer questions as a demonstration of comprehension (see Lehnert 1975a; Lehnert 1976; Schank and Abelson 1976).

For example, here is a story which was input to SAM:

INPUT TO SAM: John went to New York by bus. On the bus he talked to an old lady. When he left the bus, he thanked the driver. He took the subway to Leone's. On the subway his pocket was picked. He got off the train and entered Leone's. He had some lasagna. When the check came, he discovered he couldn't pay. The management told him he would have to wash dishes. When he left, he caught a bus to New Haven.

After SAM processed this story, the following dialog was held. The questions were input to SAM and the answers are SAM's actual responses.

Q1: Why did John go to New York?
A1: Because John wanted to go to Leone's.

137

L. Vaina and J. Hintikka (eds.), Cognitive Constraints on Communication, 137–159.
© 1984 by D. Reidel Publishing Company.

Q2: How did John get to Leone's?
A2: John went to New York by bus and then he went to Leone's by subway.
Q3: Did anything unusual happen on the bus?
A3: I don't remember anything.
Q4: Did anything unusual happen on the subway?
A4: A thief picked John's pocket.
Q5: What did John order?
A5: John ordered lasagna.
Q6: Did anything unusual happen at the restaurant?
A6: John discovered that he couldn't pay the check and so he had to wash dishes.
Q7: Why couldn't John pay the check?
A7: Because John did not have any money.
Q8: Why didn't John have any money?
A8: Because a thief picked John's pocket.
Q9: How was John able to take the bus to New Haven?
A9: Probably John had a ticket.

When you try to get a computer to answer questions of the sort that SAM answers, various difficulties arise which reveal the complexities of human question answering (Q/A). This paper will describe some of the problems involved when people understand questions and produce answers. The cognitive processes which underly Q/A span a wide range of human cognition. The most visible processes are involved with social interactions and the verbal behavior of people engaged in conversation. The least visible processes are concerned with the form and organization of information in memory. Some of the processes described in this paper have been implemented in computer programs like SAM. I will indicate which Q/A techniques have been modeled by a computer program. Since my research in computational Q/A has proceeded by modeling human Q/A, there is no need to distinguish between techniques proposed for computers and techniques proposed for people; I adhere to the view that artificial intelligence in machines must be defined in terms of human intelligence and pursued by modeling people.

The overall content of a Q/A dialogue can be viewed on three levels. On the highest level Q/A dialogues are social interactions between or among people. On the next level Q/A entails natural language processing on the part of the participants. By natural language processing I am referring specifically to the ability to understand and generate language, be it spoken or written. Finally, on the lowest level we can view questions and answers in terms of memory retrieval and memory organization. There is much that can be said about the semantic characterization of questions and answers, but only if we approach the phenomenon on all three levels.

The discussion of questions and answers presented here is hierarchically arranged on three levels of analysis. The three levels are described in terms of social interaction, language processing, and memory retrieval.

II. SOCIAL INTERACTIONS

A. *Social contexts*

On the highest level, the semantic description of an utterance in a question answering dialogue is described by social context. There are four classes of social context in which to interpret a question. Corresponding to these four classes of questions are four classes of answers.

(1) INQUIRY/INFORMATIVE
>   Q10: What time is it?
>   A10: 3:25.

An inquiry question is designed to elicit information about something. An informative answer provides information.

(2) REQUEST/PERFORMANCE
>   Q11: Would you pass the salt?
>   A11: (salt is passed)

A request question conveys a desire for someone to perform some action. A performance answer is the actual performance of the act requested.

(3) AMENITY/AMENITY
>   Q12: How are you?
>   A12: Fine, thanks.

An amenity question is a social convention. An amenity answer is some appropriate response consistent with social convention.

(4) STRATEGY/STRATEGY
>   Q13: Who told you you could come in here?
>   A13: Who told you I couldn't?

A strategic exchange is a complicated form of social interaction. A strategic question conveys information and is intended to leave the respondent in a defensive position. A strategic response to a strategic question is an answer intended to acknowledge the strategy posed by the question and offset it with a stronger one. In the example given, the first question should not be interpreted as a serious question. It is really an expression of disapproval which effectively says "I don't want you in here." The strategy set forth places the speaker in a position of implicit authority. The response to this indicates that the person answering understands that a game of strategy is being played (else the question would have been taken 'literally' as an inquiry), and the answer is another pseudo question which says in effect "You have no authority over me."

These classes of social context have important consequences in the semantic interpretation of Q/A dialogues. Pairs of question classes and answer classes can be characterized as being standard or non-standard combinations. When a Q/A exchange occurs in standard combinations of question and answer types, the dialogue makes sense and is understood as a typical and routine exchange. In a non-standard combination, a Q/A interaction is either nonsensical, disturbing, or comical.

The standard combinations are INQUIRY/INFORMATIVE, REQUEST/ PERFORMANCE, AMENITY/AMENITY, and STRATEGIC/STRATEGIC. Examples of these were given above. REQUEST/INFORMATIVE combinations are standard when the answer conveys information pertaining to the action requested. Since requests always ask that an action be performed in the future (Will you pass the salt?) it is perfectly reasonable to answer informatively if the action is going to be delayed (Yes, just a minute) or not performed at all (Sorry, I can't). This is the only time that REQUEST/ INFORMATIVE combinations appear to be standard.

Some non-standard combinations are:

INQUIRY/AMENITY
>   Q14: (to man just hit by a car) How are you?
>   A14: Fine thanks, how are you?

REQUEST/INFORMATIVE
>   Q15: Do you have change for a dollar?
>   A15: Yes. (with no accompanying action)

STRATEGY/INFORMATIVE
>   Q16: How were you able to vote for Nixon?
>   A16: Well first I registered, and then I . . .

AMENITY/INFORMATIVE
>   Q17: How are you?
>   A17: Terrible. Last month my dog got run over, and then . . .

There is something inappropriate about these exchanges. Yet the inappropriateness strikes us as being funny because these exchanges are almost all right. They are not totally nonsensical. They are semi-acceptable because the question could be shifted to another context class for which the response would be standard. "How are you?" could be taken as an amenity question were it not addressed to a man who was just hit by a car. Then the amenity answer would be appropriate. "Do you have change for a dollar?" could be an inquiry if the person asking just wanted to know for future reference. Then the informative response would be standard. In the same way, "How were you able to vote for Nixon?" could conceivably be taken as an inquiry in which case an informative reponse would be all right. And if taken 'literally' as an inquiry, "How are you?" would elicit an informative answer.

The sudden shift from one contextual frame to another has a humorous effect. In processing these dialogues you initially interpret the question in one context class, but when you get to the answer you realize that the answer is not in the class of standard responses. You then go back to the question and try to reinterpret it so that its question class can smoothly combine with the answer class. Since there are reinterpretations for these questions which would render the exchanges standard, there is some sense of resolution. In other words, expectations for a standard exchange result in a garden path betrayal which is then resolved by backtracking. Subjectively, the effect of such processing is experienced as humor.

Some combinations of context classes simply do not seem to occur. Performances can only follow requests since a performance is defined to be the enactment of a requested action. And it is very hard to answer a request, inquiry, or strategic question with an amenity.

Of course some questions and answers do not fall completely within one category or another. For example, "Would you like a cigarette?" Is both an amenity and an inquiry. Since appropriate answers to this question all indicate an acceptance or refusal, appropriate answers to this question are all informative. This suggests that there is a hierarchy of question types. It appears that the hierarchy ranks strategic questions first, then requests, followed by inquiries, with amenities taking lowest precedence. When a given question falls within more than one question class, appropriate answers come from the class with higher precedence. This is why the Q/A exchanges 14–16 were odd. Q14 could have been an inquiry but was answered as an amenity. Q15 could have been a request but was taken as an inquiry. And Q16 was viewed as an inquiry instead of a strategy question. Had these questions been interpreted according to the precedence hierarchy, the misinterpretations would not have occurred. The problem with Q17 occurred because there are situations in which "How are you?" may be a genuine inquiry. But without an overall contextual setting (as in Q14) this question is not given the option of an inquiry interpretation. It is important to realize that in actual dialogues all interpretations are constrained by the overall context of the dialogue. The hierarchy of question classes proposed here is useful only when a contextual setting does not impose interpretive constraints.

B. The Use of Social Context in Understanding

When people understand a Q/A exchange, one level of semantic information is derived from the social context of the dialogue. Each question and answer is interpreted in some contextual class. The class combinations for consecutive questions and answers are checked, and if a non-standard combination occurs, the dialogue may require extra processing.

Some non-standard combinations activate general inference mechanisms. For example, when a strategic response follows a non-strategic question, a mechanism is activated which examines the social status of the participants. If the person answering has lower social status, then the exchange should be interpreted as a challenge. If the two people are on equal footing, the exchange may be taken as jovial. And if the person answering has indisputably higher social status, then the exchange should be interpreted as a show of power. To see these three sets of inferences, consider the exchange "Would you pass the salt?" — "Only if you say please," in three different social contexts: first as a dialogue between older and younger siblings (challenge), then as a dialogue between two adults (joking), and finally as a dialogue between a child and parent (power).

Knowing about social dynamics of this sort is very important in understanding dialogues. Once a social dynamic is identified, it sets up predictions which will be used in understanding subsequent dialogue. For example, in the context of a challenge situation, an ensuing battle makes sense as a fight for status. But if the context is one of a joke, it is difficult to understand why a battle would follow. An extension of our previous dialogue will illustrate this:

A: Would you pass the salt?
B: Only if you say please.
A: I want the salt.
B: No.

While it is easy to imagine this dialogue between two children, or even a child and a parent, it is hard to imagine two adults speaking like this. This is because the conversation only makes sense as a challenge or power exhibition, and it is not likely that two adults would seriously engage in such dynamics over some salt. By some stretching of the imagination it can be pictured, but only with the understanding that the adults are 'acting like children.' It is impossible to understand this dialogue as a joke unless it is interpreted as a parody. Taken as a parody it mimics a challenge or exhibition of power. In the context of a challenge, the dialogue describes the beginning of a good fight where both sides are vying for superiority. In the context of a power display, the dialogue describes a firm ruler and a rebellious underdog.

These three social contexts determine different sets of inferences about the participants. An inference is an assumption that could be wrong, and the ability to make inferences is a crucial part of understanding language (see Schank 1975a). For example, in the context of a challenge, we infer that the challenger is hopeful of success, and the person being challenged is expected to be somewhere on a continuum between being threatened and being annoyed, depending on his perception of the situation. In this particular exchange, the person being challenged has not given any ground, so we infer that he cannot be terribly threatened, and the likely stances span a lesser continuum from being worried to being annoyed. But in the context of a power display, we expect the rebel to be angry and frustrated while the ruler is probably just annoyed. Inferences of this sort have to be drawn according to rules about the contextual interpretation of social dynamics.

There is a tremendous amount of knowledge about social interactions which is needed in order to understand dialogues in general, and Q/A exchanges in particular. But this level of understanding represents a very high order of processing. It is possible to understand a dialogue in some ways and not in others.

A child, for instance, might understand a dialogue on some levels but miss completely the more subtle phenomena which occur on the higher levels of social interaction. The same thing happens when particular dynamics of a relationship are somewhat esoteric, or known only to the participants of the dialogue. For example, dialogues between married couples often have a level of interaction known only to that couple.

There is a hierarchy to the levels of semantic characterization in language. It is possible to have some understanding of a story or dialogue, without complete understanding on the highest level. But it is impossible to have a high level of understanding without comprehension on the lower levels. A lot of the understanding processes which entail knowledge about social interactions could be ignored without suffering a total loss of comprehension.

III. LANGUAGE PROCESSING

The next level of semantic description is concerned with understanding language on a more explicit level. In discussing questions and answers in terms of social context classes, we saw how a question could be 'taken literally' by interpreting it in a lower context than it could assume. For example, "How were you able to vote for Nixon?" should be interpreted in a STRATEGIC context. But if taken literally it is an INQUIRY question. The level of semantic processing which we will consider now is concerned with understanding in a literal sense. We will look at some of the problems which arise in the class of questions and answers which fall into the INQUIRY/INFORMATIVE class of Q/A exchanges.

The INQUIRY/INFORMATIVE class of Q/A dialogues include all testing situations (whether written or oral) where one person is trying to access the knowledge state of another person. Q/A dialogues are often the only way to assess someone's understanding of a subject or problem. For example, if someone reads a story, the ability to answer questions about that story is a strong demonstration of their comprehension. For the remainder of this paper, the examples used to illustrate problems which arise on lower levels of semantic processing will all be presented in the context of answering questions about stories.

A. Semantic Analysis and Context

It is very dangerous to speak of a semantic representation for a question when it is considered in isolation of a natural context. In section II we saw how shifts in context classes affect the meaning of questions. The same sort of thing happens on lower levels of semantic analysis as well. For example, consider the following story:

Context 1

John had just bought a new car. He was so happy with it that he drove it at every possible opportunity. So last night when he decided to go out for dinner, he drove over to Leone's. When he got there he had to wait for a table . . .

Q18: Why did John drive to Leone's?

Appropriate answers to this question will be "Because he just got a new car

and he liked to drive it whenever he could," or "Because he was very happy
with his new car," or "Because he enjoyed driving," etc. The point is that the
question here is interpreted to be asking about driving. Now consider another
story:

Context 2

John had a crush on Mary. But because he was so shy, he was happy to just
be in her proximity. So he was in the habit of following her around a lot.
He knew that she ate at Leone's very often. So last night when he decided to
go out for dinner, he drove over to Leone's. When he got there he had to wait
for a table . . .

Q19: Why did John drive to Leone's?

The question now has a different meaning. Appropriate answers are "Because
he knew that Mary ate there," or "Because he hoped to run into Mary there,"
or "Because he wanted to see Mary," etc. etc. Here the question has been
interpreted to be asking about Leone's.

The semantic representation of a question is dependent on the context
in which that question is asked. There is nothing ambiguous about "Why did
John drive to Leone's?" in context. In fact, from a semantic viewpoint, these
two occurrences of "Why did John drive to Leone's?" are not even the same
question. They just happen to coincide on a lexical level. In the first context,
"Why did John drive to Leone's?" is semantically equivalent to asking "Why
did John drive to dinner?" In the second context, "Why did John drive to
Leone's?" is semantically equivalent to "Why did John go to Leone's?" But
"Why did John drive to dinner?" and "Why did John go to Leone's?" are not
interchangeable across contexts. If asked "Why did John go to Leone's?" in
the first context, the question asks for information which is not there.
Similarly, "Why did John drive to dinner?" cannot be answered in the second
context. In answering a question, determining the semantic content of the
question is a crucial problem. Since semantic content can be determined by
context, it is dangerous to consider examples out of context.

B. Focus in Understanding and Answering Questions

The above examples illustrate the phenomenon of focus. When interpreting
a question semantically, very often context determines a focus for the

question. In the first story, focus fell on the act of driving, while in the second story, focus fell on the choice of restaurants. Sometimes the context of a question determines the focus of the question. But in other cases general world knowledge must be used:

John got up early one morning and was famished. He put on his roller skates and skated to a restaurant for breakfast.

Q20: Why did John skate to the restaurant?"

People do not interpret questions according to what information is available for an answer. People will answer Q20 with "I don't know," indicating that the question focuses on the act of skating. Had the focus been on John's destination, the question could be answered according to explicit information in the story: "Why did John go to a restaurant?" — "Because he was famished." But in the case of Q20 general knowledge about the world establishes the focus. People know that it is not normal for adults to use roller skates as a means of transportation. There is nothing to indicate that John is a child, and the inference that John is an adult is reinforced by his going out alone to a restaurant. Therefore people reading this story feel that John's behavior is strange. When focus needs to be established in a question by general world knowledge, some hierarchy is consulted to determine what is the most interesting thing about the question. If an element of the question refers to something unexpected, or relatively interesting, then that element receives the focus. Since the question here refers to strange behavior, the question is interpreted as being focused on that strange behavior.

The principle of focusing on variations rather than expectations is used in answering questions as well as understanding them. The following technique for finding the focus of a question is used by the SAM system. A21 is the way SAM answers Q21 after reading the following story:

INPUT TO SAM: John went to a restaurant. The hostess gave him a menu and he ordered a hamburger. The waitress served John the hamburger and he ate it.

Q21: Did the waitress give John a menu?
A21: No, the hostess gave John a menu.

It is very natural for people to elaborate when they answer a yes or no question negatively. But where does an elaboration like the one in A21 come from? Elaborations of this sort are actually answers to unspoken questions. This particular elaboration answers the question "Who gave John a menu?" So we've reduced the problem of finding the right elaboration to one of finding the right unspoken question. Suppose we base an elaboration on some other unspoken question: "What did the waitress give John?" The resulting answer from this would be "No, the waitress gave John a hamburger." While this is not an incorrect answer, it seems less natural than the original elaboration.

In order to pick one elaboration over another, we have to use some general world knowledge about restaurants. When you hear a story about someone eating out in a restaurant, you make a lot of inferences about what things must have happened, even if you weren't explicitly told about them in the story. In the above story, you infer that John sat down before he ordered, the waitress gave his order to a cook, and the cook prepared the hamburger. None of this was mentioned in the story. These inferences are made on the basis of general world knowledge about restaurants. This sort of mundane knowledge about restaurants has to be used in finding the best elaboration for our answer.

Once we've answered the question "Did the waitress give John a menu?" with "No," we have contradicted an implicit expectation on the part of the person asking the question. There was some expectation that the waitress might have or should have given John a menu. In elaborating our answer, we wish to address this expectation and explain why it was violated. One act which is strongly expected in the course of eating at a restaurant is that of receiving a menu. We know that the menu may come from a waiter, or waitress, or hostess, or maitre-d', or maybe the patron just picks it up himself; but wherever it comes from, we expect the patron to receive a menu. This expectation is the one which tells us how to elaborate our response. The strong expectation underlying the question "Did the waitress give John a menu?" is that John must have gotten a menu somewhere. So in answering the question, it is most natural to describe where the menu came from.

The problem of focus is important in both questions and answers. The semantic content of a question often relies on the determination of focus. And answers which 'miss the point' are those which have assumed the wrong focus. "Why did John fly to New York?" – "Because it was too far to walk." is a typical example of focus misplacement. For a description of how heuristics involving focus are used in the SAM system, see Lehnert 1975a; Lehnert 1976.

C. Semantic Categories for Questions

In section II we saw that questions and answers can be usefully classified in terms of social context. These classes were meaningful because they could be used to determine inference processes needed in understanding. On lower levels of processing, a classification of questions would be useful only if it determined what kinds of retrieval techniques are needed to answer the question.

In discussing focus, the importance of semantic content was mentioned. If two questions are different on the lexical level, but elicit the same answers, then they are semantically equivalent and require the same processing in terms of memory retrieval. On the other hand, if two questions are identical on the lexical level, but elicit different answers (in different contexts), then they are semantically distinct and require different processing in terms of memory retrieval. So if a question is going to be classified according to the type of processing that is needed to answer it, then the most useful categories are those defined in terms of a semantic representation.

Traditionally, questions are categorized according to lexical features. This approach gives us a set of how-questions, why-questions, when-questions, what-questions, etc. While this is a very easy way to classify questions, it is not terribly meaningful. Consider the various kinds of memory processes that can be invoked by a how-question:

QUANTIFICATION QUESTIONS
    How long is this?
    How much is that?
    How often does this happen?
    How (well) do you like him?
    How (well) is your husband?

ENABLEMENT QUESTIONS
    How were you able to buy this without any money?
    How did you have time for all this?
    How could you hear what he said?

INSTRUMENTALITY QUESTIONS
    How did you get here?
    How did you send word to him?

CAUSAL-ANTECEDENT QUESTIONS
    How did this happen?
    How did the glass break?

PROCEDURAL QUESTIONS

    How did you make this?
    How do I get to your house?
    How do you get any service around here?

The semantic representation for a how-question should determine which of the above categories the question belongs in. Just as context can change the meaning of a question by shifting its focus, context can also change the meaning of a question by shifting its semantic category type. For example, "How did you break the glass?" is a question demanding an ENABLEMENT if the context established the intentionality of the act. But the same question is a CAUSAL-ANTECEDENT question in the context of an accident.

Question categories of this type are useful on two levels of processing. In terms of memory retrieval, they indicate what sorts of memory structures should be examined in order to find an appropriate answer. "How did the glass break?" elicits the same response as "What happened to the glass?" If these two questions are represented identically on the semantic level as a CAUSAL-ANTECEDENT question, then the same memory retrieval processes will be invoked for either question. Hence the same answer will be returned in either case. In our computer programs we use the semantic representation of Conceptual Dependency (see Schank 1975a). When a question is encoded in Conceptual Dependency it is easy to categorize in the desired manner.

The other advantage to these categories is in terms of inferencing. While questions are usually thought of as entities which simply elicit information from another person, a question can convey information as well as simply ask for information. Some of the information conveyed by a question is determined by its semantic question type, and this information manifests itself in the form of inferences. For example, an ENABLEMENT question conveys some degree of surprise on the part of the person asking it. "How did you pay for dinner?" suggests that there was reason to believe you might not have been able to pay for dinner. This inference effect is lost in the artificial context of a test situation, but it is very present in actual conversations. In fact, this inference effect is exploited in a very obvious way when STRATEGIC questions are posed as ENABLEMENT types: "How did you get into Yale?" is really a statement designed to communicate surprise or incredulity on the part of the questioner. The listener realizes that the question is not a straight INQUIRY question, but the inference effect of surprise from the lower level of semantic processing remains to convey the STRATEGIC message.

IV. MEMORY RETRIEVAL

Most of the problems connected with memory retrieval are technical problems related to the representation and organization of memory. Researchers in AI have recently recognized that the representation of world knowledge is a crucial problem for AI in general as well as for natural language processing in particular (see Bobrow & Collins 1975). But a general discussion of these issues would take us far afield from the phenomena particular to Q/A dialogues. So in order to stay as close to Q/A as possible, this section will present a few of the problems which are associated with memory retrieval, but which can be discussed without reference to a particular theory of memory representation.

A. *Answer Selection*

Memory retrieval is mainly guided by the understanding process. But in a question answering dialogue, an answer may be extracted from memory for reasons concerned with generation as well as understanding.

John took a subway to Leone's. But while he was on the subway a thief picked his pocket. When he got to Leone's he had some lasagna. Then when the check came, he discovered he couldn't pay. So John had to wash dishes at Leone's.

Q22: Why did John wash dishes at Leone's?

A22a: Because he couldn't pay the check.
A22b: Because he had no money.
A22c: Because he was pick-pocketed on the subway.

All of these answers are reasonable and correct. Yet A22c is clearly the best answer. A22c is preferable because it conveys more information than the other two. It does this by setting up inferences. The importance of inferencing has been mentioned in discussing the understanding process. But from the viewpoint of generating language, the same principles of inference must come into play.

Given that John washed dishes at a restaurant, people can readily infer that John couldn't pay the check. This is an inference which is made by world knowledge about restaurants. Not being able to pay a check in a restaurant is a classic interference in the normal routine of eating out. Its equally classic resolution is washing dishes. Since there are no other standard interferences in the restaurant routine which normally result in washing dishes, the causal antecedent of washing dishes in a restaurant is easily inferred. The person who asks "Why did John wash dishes?" must know that John washed dishes, so the person asking this question very likely makes the obvious inference that John couldn't pay the check. A basic rule in genera- tion is that you don't say things which are obvious. So A22a would be a poor answer since it doesn't tell the questioner anything he was not liable to know himself on the basis of general world knowledge. The same criticisms hold for A22b. General world knowledge allows people to infer that if you can't pay a check, then you must not have (enough) money.

So finding the best answer to this question is more than finding a causally correct answer. It involves finding an answer which conveys information that is not obvious to the questioner. In this case A22c is the obvious choice because it describes a causality which is not generally inferred on the basis of world knowledge. Information from the story itself is needed to give this answer. A set of heuristics involved in answer selection have been incorporated in a computer program which selects the best answer to a question given a choice of possible answers. When confronted with the three answers discussed for Q22, the program will choose A22c. For a description of this program, see Lehnert 1975b.

Why-questions are particularly prone to these complications of answer selection. In the above example the choice is fairly straightforward, but in most cases it is very difficult to know what information is or is not obvious to the questioner. This is particularly hard in the artificial context of a test situation. The person answering has to make assumptions about what the questioner wants to see. In a real INQUIRY context, one can assume that a question is being asked because the person asking is missing some piece of information and he wants to fill that in. In natural contexts, knowing how to best answer someone involves assessing the other person's knowledge state so that the answer can supply new information. This is very often done by making some default assumptions about the questioner's knowledge and relying on him to indicate when those assumptions are wrong:

A: How do I get to Washington Heights?
B: Well you could take the IND up to . . .
A: The IND?
B: Yeah, that's the Eighth Avenue line which runs . . .

A: Is that a subway?
B: Yeah, you can catch it at Eighth Avenue and 34th Street.
A: Which way is 34th Street?

But in a test situation, it may be very hard to know what knowledge state the questioner wants you to address. Whenever a question is asked about a story you know that some knowledge of the story is present in order for the question to be asked in the first place. Exactly what can and can't be assumed is a difficult problem in artificial contexts.

The problem of answer selection is both a retrieval problem and a generation problem. Retrieval mechanisms must guide a memory search for correct responses. Then generational considerations must guide a selection process in the event that the memory search produces a choice of responses. The rules which must be used in making a selection conform to some theory of effective human communication. Until such a theory is developed which can be described in terms of heuristics, the generational skills of any natural language system will be painfully clumsy in casual dialogue.

B. Questions about Expectations

Any system which claims to understand a story must generate some internal representation for that story. This story representation will then be the basis for all memory retrieval tasks concerning the story. In particular, any questions which are asked about the story must be answered by examining that story representation. But there are questions which require more information than can be found in the story representation alone. In section III we saw how general world knowledge was needed in both understanding questions and elaborating negative responses. Here we will discuss a class of questions which need even more than the story representation and general world knowledge in order to answer them.

The story we will consider here is an actual input story which the SAM system has read. The three questions we will discuss were asked of SAM after it read the story and the answers given here are the answers which SAM generated. The memory retrieval process described is the one which SAM uses when answering why-questions about non-events. For a more detailed account of the processing presented here see Lehnert 1976.

INPUT TO SAM: John went to a restaurant and the hostess gave him a menu. When he ordered a hot dog, the waitress said that they didn't have any. So John ordered a hamburger instead. But when the hamburger came, it was so burnt that John left.

When people talk (or write) they leave out any information which can be readily inferred. So a major part of the understanding process is concerned with filling in this missing information via inferencing. When a person understands a story like the one above, he does more than understand each individual sentence. World knowledge is used to connect up the acts explicitly mentioned in the story. This connecting process is done by filling in the gaps with inferred states and acts. So a memory representation for a story must contain those inferences which connect the input into a coherent whole. The following list of actions represents some of the inferences which must be made when the above story is understood. (SAM makes all of these inferences along with additional inferences about locations, relationships of possession, and other state changes.)

John goes to restaurant
John enters restaurant
hostess sees John
hostess goes to John
hostess takes John to table
John is seated
John gets a menu from the hostess
John looks at menu
waitress sees John
waitress goes to John's table
John orders a hot dog
waitress tells John they don't have any hot dogs
John orders a hamburger
waitress takes order to the cook
cook prepares hamburger
waitress gets hamburger from the cook
waitress brings hamburger to John
waitress serves John the hamburger
John sees that the hamburger is burnt
John gets angry
John gets up
John leaves the restaurant

Notice that all of these inferences are assumptions that any person would make based on mundane knowledge about eating in a restaurant. For the purposes of this paper, we will refer to the above list of conceptualizations as the story representation. This story representation is generated at the time the story is read and it becomes part of the knowledge base used for all subsequent question answering.

Now consider three questions about the story:

Q23: Why didn't the waitress serve John a hot dog?
Q24: Why didn't John eat the hamburger?
Q25: Why didn't John pay the check?

Why-questions demand that a causality be identified. In this case we need to know what caused the waitress to not serve John a hot dog, what caused John to not eat a hamburger, and what caused John to not pay the check. How can a memory retrieval process find information about not serving a hot dog, not eating a hamburger, and not paying a check? The story representation is the sequential chain of events shown above. The problem here lies in the fact that we are asking for the causation behind acts that did not take place. Yet the story representation does not embody information about non-activities.

One approach would be to examine the story representation for events which 'contradict' the acts in question. For example, in trying to answer "Why didn't the waitress serve John a hot dog?" perhaps there is some way of recognizing that serving John a hot dog and serving John a hamburger are in some sense 'mutually exclusive' acts. Therefore serving a hamburger would replace the act of serving a hot dog, and we could answer "Because the waitress served John a hamburger." But is this the best answer? Does it make sense to say that the waitress didn't serve a hot dog because she served a hamburger instead? There is no real causality between these two acts (or act and non-act). More importantly, this approach will often fail to find any answer.

While a retrieval process which looks for 'mutually exclusive' acts might be able to determine that a hamburger was served instead of a hot dog, what will happen when we try to answer the second question this way? (Why didn't John eat the hamburger?) Which act in the story representation is going to contradict this? There is no eating activity to contradict eating a hamburger. While acceptable answers here are "Because he got angry," or "Because it was burnt," we can't identify these acts as being 'contradictory' to the act of eating a hamburger. The same thing happens with the last question, "Why didn't John pay the check?" Getting a burnt hamburger and being angry do not always preclude paying the check.

Sometimes insight about a process is gained by examining what happens when the process breaks down. Consider what happens when we ask "Why didn't John swim across the lake?" The question makes no sense. The only way that this question could make sense is if the story had at some point set up an expectation about swimming in a lake or getting across a lake. In general, it can make sense to ask about something which didn't happen only if there was at some time a possibility (or probability) that it would have happened had things not taken the turn they did. So answering questions of this type requires an examination of the expectations which were aroused during the understanding process.

As people read stories they have a tremendous number of expectations about what is liable to happen next, or what they are going to hear about. While some of these expectations are remembered (so it wasn't the butler after all!) most of them concern information on a very low level (if he orders a hot dog you expect him to eat a hot dog). These low level expectations cannot be built into the memory representation at the time of understanding because there would be a tremendous proliferation of data. When a low level expectation is made on the basis of mundane world knowledge, there is no need to store it in memory. Any expectations which were generated on the basis of world knowledge can be reconstructed when they are needed. When a question asks about a non-event, memory retrieval cannot rely on the story representation for all the information it needs; the expectations which occurred while the story was being read must be reconstructed so that these expectations can be examined.

In order to reconstruct these expectations the story representation is examined for points of interference. That is, the places in the story where something happened which was somewhat unexpected are singled out. These points of interference are places where expectations change. Just prior to an interference point we have one set of expectations, but at the point of interference these are replaced by a revised set of expectations. So we go to the places in the story just prior to the interference points, and reconstruct our expectations by pretending that the story ended right there. We are essentially setting up a new story and processing it. When it ends prematurely we make inferences on basis of mundane world knowledge about what probably happened next. These inferences which close off the unfinished stories effectively recapture the expectations which were made at the time the original story was heard.

In our sample story, there are two points of interference: when the waitress tells John they have no hot dogs, and when John sees that the hamburger is burnt. The act preceding the first interference is John ordering a hot dog. So we use mundane knowledge about eating in a restaurant to 'finish' a story in which John goes to a restaurant, gets a menu from the hostess, and orders a hot dog. We finish this story in the sense of generating a ghost path of events which we expect will occur. The ghost path generated at this point is a chain of events which includes the waitress serving John a hot dog, John eating the hot dog, getting a check, paying, and leaving. Similarly, a ghost path is generated from the point in the story representation where the waitress serves John a hamburger.

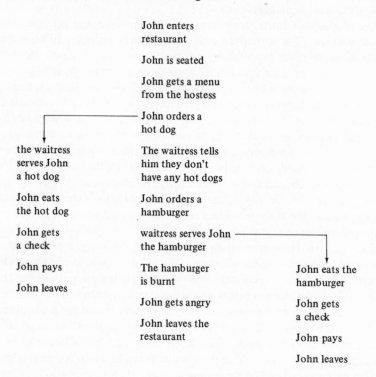

When we examine these ghost paths we find the non-activities in our questions. Once an act in question is found in a ghost path, we can answer the question by tracing the ghost path back up to its branch off the main path and returning the interference or unusual occurrence right after the branch. So we can answer:

Q23: Why didn't the waitress serve John a hot dog?
A23: Because the waitress told John that they didn't have any hot dogs.

Q24: Why didn't John eat the hamburger?
A24: Because the hamburger was burnt.

For the last question, the act of paying a check occurs in both ghost paths. When this happens we trace back the last (most recent) ghost path to find its answer. It is also the case that paying the check had a stronger expectation than being served a hot dog or eating a hamburger. (For an explanation of how this is recognized see Lehnert 1976). Since paying the check was strongly expected, its non-occurrence was highly unexpected. In question answering there is a basic principle which roughly stated says: the more unexpected an occurrence is, the more explanation is needed to satisfactorily account for it. So the memory retrieval process for this question picks up not only the story interference, but also its associated resolution and any negative mental state changes as well:

Q25: Why didn't John pay the check?
A25: John was angry because the hamburger was burnt and so he left.

V. CONCLUSIONS

Question answering dialogues require semantic analysis on a number of levels. We have seen some of the difficulties which arise on the levels of social context, language processing, and memory retrieval. The problems presented here emerged in the course of building a computer system which can understand stories and demonstrate its comprehension by answering questions. The human ability to respond to different kinds of questions in a variety of contexts is generally taken for granted as a trivial human phenomenon. But when you try to get a computer to do something comparable, you begin to appreciate just how non-trivial the phenomenon really is.

One of the goals in natural language processing is to someday have a computer which will be able to converse with people in a natural human manner. In moving toward this goal, two major problems have been encountered:

(1) A tremendous amount of mundane knowledge about the world must be organized in memory so that relevant information can be found easily when needed. In order for a computer to understand and generate language, the computer must have some knowledge about what is being said.

(2) A theory of human conversation must be present in the system. Before a computer can participate in a conversation, it must know what a conversation is.

The first problem has become a critical issue for artificial intelligence in general. Consequently, a number of researchers are currently working on the representation and organization of world knowledge (see Bobrow and Collins 1975; Norman and Rumelhart 1975; Schank and Abelson 1976). The second problem is less pressing since a great deal needs to be accomplished before this becomes a central issue. It is also the case that a very general system (say a general story understander) can be built without incorporating a full theory of conversation. A general story understanding system which knew only to answer all questions as INQUIRY questions demanding INFORMATIVE answers in the context of knowledge demonstration, would be a very impressive achievement in natural language processing.

Question answering in the context of a story understanding system is a very useful base for studying the wide range of semantic processing which must be present in human conversation. By studying general stories without restrictions on the knowledge domain, the problem of organizing world knowledge is readily attacked. In considering the set of all questions which could be asked of a story, a wide range of INQUIRY questions must be dealt with on the levels of language processing and memory retrieval. Since so much generality is covered by such a story understander, the principles which are found to be successful in this task will be extendible to larger task domains.

Yale University

REFERENCES

Bobrow, D. G., and Collins, A. M.: 1975, *Representation and Understanding*, Academic Press, New York.
Lehnert, W.: 1975a, 'What Makes SAM Run? Script-Based Techniques for Question Answering,' *Proceedings for Theoretical Issues in Natural Language Processing*, Cambridge, Ma.
Lehnert, W.: 1975b, 'Question Answering in a Story Understanding System,' Department of Computer Science Research Report #57, Yale University Press, New Haven, Ct.
Lehnert, W.: 1976, 'Human and Computational Question Answering,' *Cognitive Science* 1.
Norman, D. A., Rumelhart, D. E., and the LNR Research Group: 1975, *Explorations in Cognition*, W. H. Freeman, San Francisco.
Schank, R. C.: 1975a, *Conceptual Information Processing*, American Elsevier, New York.
Schank, R. C.: 1975b, 'The Structure of Episodes in Memory,' D. G. Bobrow and A. M. Collins (eds.), *Representation and Understanding*, Academic Press, New York.
Schank, R. C., and Abelson, R. P.: (forthcoming), *Knowledge Structures*, Erlbaum Associates, Hillsdale, New Jersey.
Schank, R. C., et al.: 1975, 'SAM – A Story Understander,' Department of Computer Science Research Report #43, Yale University Press, New Haven, Ct.

Shortliffe, E. H.: 1974, 'MYCIN: A Rule-Based Computer Program for Advising Physicians Regarding Antimicrobial Therapy Selection,' Stanford Artificial Intelligence Laboratory Memo-AIM251 Stanford University, Stanford, Calf.

Winograd, T.: 1972, *Understanding Natural Language*, Academic Press, New York.

Woods, W. A., Kaplan, R. M., and Nash-Webber, B.: 1972, 'The Lunar Sciences Natural Language Information System: Final Report,' BBN Report No. 2378, Bolt Beranek and Newman, Inc. Cambridge, Mass.

ROGER C. SCHANK

LOOKING FOR A PROCESS MODEL OF DIALOGUE:

Speculations from the Perspective of Artificial Intelligence

My aim here is to attempt to determine some of the rules that may legitimately be used for the process of response creation in a conversational setting. My assumption is that people bring a great deal of background information and rules about how to interpret what someone really means to the conversational setting. The process of communication is extremely complex, hence it is possible to make many different responses to a sentence. Also, sometimes the very act of not taking one of these options can be a statement in itself. Thus a large part of the conversational process takes place under the surface of the actual conversation. Our task, then, in trying to spell out the rules that people use in conversing, is to respond to all of what is going on, rather than solely to what is going on at the surface.

Perhaps the best vehicle for examining what goes on under the surface of a conversation is to look at a conversation between emotionally related people who share a great deal of background information. We have chosen, therefore, a hypothetical argument between a husband and a wife. When we begin to discuss our conversation, bear in mind that all we shall be trying to do is to help determine what can legitimately be said next. The "topic" of a sentence in a conversation is very much dependent on responses that are normally considered to be reasonable to that sentence. The speaker of the sentence in question usually has the best idea of what kind of response he expects or that he would find acceptable. The speaker himself knows what aspect of his sentence he considers to be most important, or the crux of what he is saying. A participant in a conversation must determine what the speaker expects from him in the way of a response and decide for himself how much he will conform to the speaker's expectations. These are the kinds of notions that we will be attempting to deal with here.

With this in mind let's look at the following conversation:

A1: Why were you out so late last night?
B1: I went bowling with the boys.

A2: I thought you hated bowling.
B2: It's ok when I have some company.

L. Vaina and J. Hintikka (eds.), Cognitive Constraints on Communication, 161–173.
© 1984 *by D. Reidel Publishing Company.*

A3: Aren't I company?
B3: It's not the same.

A4: Sure, because you can't pick up women at home.
B4: I don't pick up women at the bowling alley.

A5: Well, who says you go to the bowling alley?
B5: If I told you that's where I was, that's where I was.

A6: Then how come you smelled of perfume last night?
B6: What perfume? That was smoke.

A7: It sure was a funny kind of smoke.
B7: Well maybe it was.

A8: You'll get arrested if you do that in a bowling alley.
B8: We didn't do it in a bowling alley.

A9: Then where were you last night?
B9: All right. I was at Joe's house. We had a few beers and smoked some
    dope. I didn't want to tell you because I know you can't stand Joe.

A10: Liar! And hanging around with that creep. I want a divorce.

Now let's consider what is happening in this conversation. The first sentence is:

  (A1)   Why were you out so late last night?

If we ask ourselves what the topic of this sentence is, we find that we have a
difficult time defining it. Is the topic here B's lateness, or his whereabouts
last night, or the reasons for both of those or what? A simpler question to ask
is what the expected response to A1 is. That is, what does A expect to hear
back? This is the major determinant in B's response, so from a process model
point of view it is a much more germane question than that of determining
the topic of A1. In a sense then, since A1 is a very specific question, its topic
is exactly equal to its expected response. As we have said, the key element in
creating a response is the attempt to ascertain what the speaker had in mind
for a response. When the speaker indicates directly what response he had in
mind, then the rules for responding can work from there. Temporarily we can
call the topic of a sentence the expected response.

Topic of A1: = REASON for C1   where C1 is the event
                                      C1: B WAS OUT LATE LAST NIGHT

The problem here is with the idea of REASON. Clearly there are a great many reasons for a given event. The range of possible responses to A1 depends on the particular concept or concepts in C1 for which REASONS are being requested. In fact, appropriate responses depend crucially on the interpretation of the underlying meaning of A1 as determined by the hearer.

For example, any of these seven possible responses to A1 would be all right in the right context:

1.   I was out bowling.
2.   Listen, I was home early the last seven nights in a row!
3.   Come on, I still love you.
4.   I just didn't have a chance to call you.
5.   It is not necessary to spend every night with your wife.
6.   I didn't know that you cared to go with me.
7.   It was for business reasons.

If, as we have assumed, these seven sentences can be appropriate responses in the right context, then it is incumbent on a theory of dialogue to explain this phenomenon. Notice that the notion of topic as expected response will not work here. The expected response may well be the reasons for C1 (B's lateness), but this will not explain why response 3 could ever be uttered and taken as relevant to the conversation. The reason that it is relevant has to do with the context of the conversation. To make this more explicit, we will define context for our purposes as the extant themes in any situation. (A theme is defined in Schank and Abelson, 1977 as a kind of goal generator for interpersonal relationships, societal relationships, and certain character traits.)

The themes that are relevant here are the HUSBAND role theme and the LOVE theme, both of which help to establish the prior context of the situation. Basically the HUSBAND role theme which is used in A1 implicitly deals with the expectations that a wife can reasonably make on a husband in our society. The LOVE theme deals with what lovers expect from each other. The relevant pieces of these are given below:

LOVE THEME	HUSBAND ROLE THEME
X LOVE Y	X HUSBAND OF Y

1 if X has free time then X will want to	1 X goes to work 2 X comes home

spend it with Y

2 if X goes to some
   social event, Y will
   ordinarily go along.

3 if X is out alone then
   X does not get involved
   with members of the
   opposite sex

3 X spends evening with Y choices:
   (A) X&Y spend evening at home
   (B) X&Y go to MOVIES, RESTAURANT
        BOWLING, DANCING etc

4 if X goes out at night
   X tells Y where and
   comes home on time
5 X tells the truth to Y

Also relevant here is the MARRIAGE theme which encompasses the
HUSBAND theme as a subpart. In addition certain societal rules are necessary.
These are given below:

THE MARRIAGE THEME X MARRIED TO Y	SOME SOCIAL RULES
1 X loves Y	1 You may only love one person at a time
2 X marries Y	2 If you avoid doing something it's because
3 then either:	you dislike it
X&Y are unhappy	3 People avoid people they dislike
or X&Y are happy	4 People do what they like to do
IF X&Y are unhappy, then:	
X&Y fight	
X may go out alone	
X may find other woman	
this causes:	
Y becomes unhappy	
X&Y fight more	
X&Y may get divorced	

The use of the above thematic information, plus some standard rules of
inference can help to explain why the above possible responses can actually
make sense. They make sense because the initial question (A1) has been
reconstructed by the hearer (B) into a new question or statement that he has
decided to respond to. This process of reconstruction is a crucial part of the
conversational situation. We will now attempt to outline this process in each
of these seven instances:

The original questional was:

A1:   Why were you out so late last night?

The first response above is actually a response to a reconstructed question of
the form:

1 :   Where were you last night?

This question is obtained by straightforward inference procedures of the following sort: A1 is examined and answered internally. In order to express an answer of the sort 'because the bowling lasted a long time' it is necessary for B to assess the knowledge of A to find if she knew that 'bowling' was where he had been. When the answer to this is discovered to be negative, the question is internally reconstructed to be 'where were you last night' using the conversational rule that all logically prior questions must be answered first.

2 :   Why weren't you with me last night?

This question is obtained by first doing the reconstruction necessary for (1) and then checking the HUSBAND role theme to see if there is any relevant rule there that might be the source of the reconstructed question. Rule 3 from the husband role theme is found (Husbands are supposed to spend the evening with their wives). This rule transforms A1 into (2).

3 :   You don't love me anymore.

Two rules that match the reconstructed (1) are also found in the LOVE theme. LOVE rules 1 and 2 both speak to the issue of what someone who loves someone is supposed to do in the evening. Since C1 violates this rule the underlying LOVE theme itself is open to question. (Notice that this does not happen with role themes such as husband. We would not expect that his actual status as husband can be questioned. But LOVE is an interpersonal theme and interpersonal themes change more easily and thus can be called into question, producing (3)).

4 :   Why don't you tell me what you do?

Rule 4 from the HUSBAND theme is used here. This works the same way that rule 3 was used for (2) above.

5 :   Our relationship is in trouble.

The MARRIAGE theme has a kind of script for good and bad marriages. The "unhappy" path in the MARRIAGE theme outlines some characteristics of a bad marriage. When one of these is matched (B going out alone) it can be the source of a question. Thus the reconstruction process comes up with (5).

6 :   Don't you like spending time with me?

Sometimes themes can combine to produce a question. To reconstruct (6) both rule 1 from the LOVE theme and rule 3 from the HUSBAND theme are used.

7:            Husbands are supposed to be home with their wives at night.

There are many ways to actually reconstruct a question using the same rules. (7) is an example of Husband role theme rule 3 applied slightly differently. The question has been reconstructed into a statement that is a reiteration of the thematic rule itself. In this case an answer can be a discussion of the validity of the rule or of conditions on the rule that allow for exceptions. In a sense then, what we would have here is a discussion of the rule itself. A says that husbands should be home, and B says 'well, not every night'.

What we can see from all this is that conversations can take place on a variety of different levels. There is a sense where when a question is being responded to on one level, it is being explicitly not answered on the other levels. Another way of saying this is that there are a variety of different conversations going on at once.

We have isolated twelve different levels that a conversation can take place on. These are:

1. Direct Q-A: This is the standard surface level of responding to precisely what was asked.

2. Knowledge State: Statements here fill in the gaps in the knowledge of the hearer or attempt to subtly elicit what the hearer really knows about a situation.

3. Dominance Games: At this level a statement tries to get the upper hand in an adversary type conversation. A speaker will try to put his hearer on the defensive, blunt an attack with an accusation, and so on.

4. Emotions of A: Many statements can be interpreted to be expressing how the speaker is feeling at the moment. The conversation can surface to talk about these things explicitly.

5. Emotions of B: This is the same as the one above, except it is about the emotions of the other participant.

6. Relationship of A and B: This is the level at which implicit or explicit statements are made about the relationship between the participants. This goes on all the time (mostly implicitly) even in formal discussions.

7. Argument strategy: Here we have the level at which an argument itself can become the topic for discussion within an argument.

8. Import: The overall significance of information being discussed implicitly or explicitly can often be discussed (implicitly or explicitly).

9. Implicit Beliefs: The beliefs used as presuppositions for a statement

are constantly being accepted (by not discussing them) or explicitly rejected.

10. Points: The ultimate point of a conversation can often be about something other than what it seems to be about. (Discussions between un-attached men and women frequently have this flavor.) This level keeps track of the actual point of the discussion and is responsible for coding information in terms of that point.

11. Topic Shifts: Statements such as 'Don't change the topic' are surface realizations of this level. Topics themselves are tracked and can be discussed.

12. Truth and trust: The truth, believability, or trust of the other parti-cipant are constantly monitored and sometimes surface.

These twelve levels of conversation each carry with them a set of informa-tion appropriate to responding at that level. We shall now consider what the rules are like for a few of the levels. In doing so, we shall use as our example sentence A1: "Why were you out so late last night?" We shall consider what that statement looks like at each level we discuss. To begin we will look at the simplest level, level 1:

CATEGORY: level 1: Direct Q–A
INPUT ANALYSIS: why question
HOW WE KNOW: rules for analyzing English are used
RESPONSE REQUIREMENTS: Requires fact
WHERE FROM: The needed fact will be found in episodic event memory.
HOW WE KNOW WHAT TO SELECT: assessment of knowledge state of A establishes
     what fact is missing and selects it
HOW WE KNOW TO DO THAT: rules about answering why questions provide
     algorithm

The above information must be available for every level of response. Sentence A1, if it is to be answered at level 1 must be analyzed as being a "Why Question". This is sufficient for beginning to create a response at level 1. This information is obtainable from the input English itself, which is where you look if you want to respond literally to a sentence.

Once this information is determined, the response requirements must be obtained. In this case we need a fact. Its availability must be obtained; here the fact should be in episodic memory. A choice algorithm must be given as well. Here the choice is based on the assessment of the knowledge state of A.

To better see how this works we will examine some of the other levels in the same way. Level 3, dominance games, is responsible for tracking the power relationships in the conversation itself. That is, a conversation is some-times a battlefield on which subtle tactics are being used. Conversations may address this level of conversation both implicitly and explicitly.

CATEGORY: level 3: Dominance Games
INPUT ANALYSIS: "You are going to be on the defensive now!"
HOW WE KNOW: 'Why questions' are candidates for level 3 analysis. If the reason
    being asked for bears on a role theme violation (or other potential inadequacy
    on the part of the hearer), then the above analysis applies.
WHY WE LOOKED THERE: A level 3 analysis is performed whenever an inadequacy
    or failure to conform to expectations occurs as an inference from a remark.
RESPONSE REQUIREMENTS: Level 3 responses are almost always under the surface.
    When one is put on the defensive, one has the choice to either return the fire or
    accept the defensive. The decision is based on the emotional relationship and
    power relationship of the participants. Once the choice has been made it affects
    the form of the content of the response.
HOW WE KNOW WHAT TO SELECT: This is based on whether there is a reason to be
    defensive or offensive. Thus, we need to check the facts as they exist in memory.

What we are saying here is that there are many different kinds of information exchanges going on at one time. Our sample conversation can be viewed
in many possible ways, one of which is as a kind of battle. Certain sentences
overtly address the power gaming issue but nearly every sentence in an
argument addresses this issue in some way. In this conversation A is attacking
B. B is on the defensive initially, but B fires back in B2 by saying 'It's
(bowling) okay when I have company'. Now this statement says many things,
but on the level of dominance games, it is a covert attack on A's value as
company. A responds explicitly to the attack but not to the dominance game.
An explicit response to the dominance game here might be "Don't attack me
just when I've got you!".

A retakes the offensive in A4 by averring that B is picking up women at
the bowling alley which is presumably an agreed upon bad thing. This puts B
back on the defensive again in B4. This kind of jockeying for position in an
argument is quite common. It is necessary, then, for a participant in such a
conversation to be aware of what strategies are being pursued by his partner
and to respond to them. Understanding what argument strategies are being
employed by your conversational partner, and using such information in the
creation of your response, is thus an integral part of the conversational process.

Another conversational level is level 4, which can be construed to be a
conversation about the emotional state of one of the participants in the
conversation:

CATEGORY: level 4: emotions of A
INPUT ANALYSIS: "You don't love me anymore"
HOW WE KNOW: Violations of themes are always checked. When some are violated
    they imply that their preconditions are no longer valid. Here, HUSBAND rule 3
    applies and we can infer the above analysis from its violation.

RESPONSE REQUIREMENTS: Assurance, Agreement, or Ignore if under surface.
WHERE FROM: What to do is decided by the hearers desires to reassure the speaker in his response.
HOW WE KNOW WHAT TO SELECT: It is necessary to check the truth of implicit assertions such as this. The appropriateness of an explicit response on this level is dependent on the current emotional relationship and the desires of the speaker in this argument.

Here again, although the conversation may never explicitly be about how A is feeling, implicitly it may be about that. In fact, in this conversation, as in many conversations between emotionally related people, the conversation might be construed to be almost exclusively about that issue. This is of importance to the people in the conversation because they may be expected to respond on level 4 at any given time.

In our sample conversation A3 ("Aren't I company?") can be considered to be a statement at level 4 meaning 'You don't love me, do you?' B's response to that ("It's not the same") can be understood as explicitly ignoring the issue, thus, in a sense saying a qualified 'yes you're right'. This analysis can be seen as part of the reason for the escalation of matters by A in A4. At this point she goes directly on the attack, stating her suspicions overtly. Part of the explanation for this can be gotten from the refusal to discuss the level 4 aspect of the conversation. That is, B has rejected A by not reassuring her here. To see how level 4 can actually appear on the surface, we need only change response B3 to 'I still love you'. Such a response makes no sense at any analysis of conversational topics or other rules of continuity. It is not an inappropriate response however. It is appropriate because level 4 has been implicitly brought up by A and thus can be responded to explicitly by B if he so chooses. This can only be done if this level is being tracked continuously throughout the conversation.

People can also talk about their relationship in a conversation. Here again, this conversational level is usually implicit but it can be frequently brought to the surface. The rules here are as follows:

CATEGORY: level 6: relationship of A and B
INPUT ANALYSIS: "Our relationship is in trouble"
HOW WE KNOW: We look at the marriage theme and find that rule 1 has been violated.
WHY WE LOOKED THERE: In talking to someone, we evaluate the implications of what they say on our relationship with them. The input sentence violates one of the rules for marriage. A violation of a thematic rule implies that the theme may not hold.
RESPONSE REQUIREMENTS: Assurance, Agreement, Ignoring (if under surface)

WHERE FROM: To respond here, we must check to see how we feel about the
    relationship and decide if it is worth pursuing that line of discussion directly.
    Indirect reassurance can be made by arguing that a theme violation has not
    actually occured. This is what B does here. A's analysis of B's response would
    have to take it as a kind of level 6 reassurance ("no our relationship is not in
    trouble, you do not know the facts").

The relationship between the individuals in a conversation is liable to
become an explicit topic of conversation in exactly the same way that the
emotions of A were. In A10 were see an explicit statement about the relationship of A and B ('I want a divorce'). In a sense this entire conversation is
about the relationship of A and B. We can imagine that the rules for deciding
what to say for both A and B used information about what the other was
saying about their relationship continually throughout the conversation.

In addition to rules about A and B themselves, an important part of the
implicit conversation taking place are the thematic rules (discussed above)
themselves. When these rules are invoked the hearer either implicitly acknow-
ledges their validity by answering what was stated directly or else discusses
them explicitly:

CATEGORY: level 9: beliefs
INPUT ANALYSIS: "Husbands are supposed to be home with their wives at night"
    "Husbands should tell wives what they do"
HOW WE KNOW: Checking the husband role theme, brings up a violation of rules 3
    and 4. Statements that implicitly refer to role theme violations can be taken to be
    statements asserting one's belief in that role theme.
WHY WE LOOKED THERE: Beliefs about husband's behavior are relevant when a
    wife is talking to a husband. The husband role theme thus constitutes a back-
    ground against which inputs are checked.
RESPONSE REQUIREMENTS: Ignoring implies acceptance. Belief must be countered
    if it is disagreed with.
WHERE FROM: To do this, one must consult one's own beliefs.
HOW WE KNOW WHAT TO SELECT: Contradictory beliefs are selected to be ex-
    plicitly output if they exist. Thus if B does not share A's belief he can say some-
    thing like "Being married doesn't mean you are in jail you know."

According to the level of beliefs, many implicit beliefs are being discussed in
this conversation. A belief oriented interpretation of the beginning of this
conversation might be as follows:

A1: Husbands should tell wives what they do.
B1: That's true

A2: People don't do things they don't enjoy

B2: True, but good company helps make dull things interesting

A3: Yes, but a wife should be a good companion
B3: Friends are more interesting companions than wives

So, another aspect of conversation has to do with the implicit agreement or explicit disagreement about the presuppositions inherent in a given statement. The same is true about underlying accusations or assertions about the truth or falsity of each statement and thus the general level of trust in a conversation. In this conversation trust is a key (but implicit) point for A1:

CATEGORY: level 12: truth and trust
INPUT ANALYSIS: "Why don't you tell me where you go? Its causing me to not trust you."
HOW WE KNOW: After finding the violations of rules 3 and 4 in the husband theme, trust is inferred to be low. B can respond to the relationship problem or belief problem (above) or to the issue of trust.
RESPONSE REQUIREMENTS: Giving required information (if it is safe) helps foster trust. The trust issue can be responded to directly also. This has the advantage of also changing the dominance game. Thus "Why don't you trust me?" is legitimate here and it also puts A on the defensive.

A trust oriented interpretation of the beginning of this conversation might look as follows:

A1: Why don't you tell me where you go?
    It's causing me not to trust you.

B1: I'll tell you. There is no reason not to trust me.

A2: No reason? You are lying right now.
B2: No I'm not.

Using the rules we have developed so far, we can now look at some of the other sentences in this conversation with an eye towards how they respond on the various levels we have proposed:

B1:   I went bowling with the boys.

B1 responds to A1 only at the direct Q-A level. The other seven questions we proposed remain unanswered.

A2:   I thought you hated bowling.

Here are some possible interpretations of A2 using the thematic and social rules mentioned above, together with the levels they address (L=love, S=social, M=marriage, H=husband):

1: You wouldn't go bowling if you loved me.	L2,S2,S3 levels 4,6,9
2: You must be trying to avoid me.	S3 levels 4,6,9
3: I still don't understand why you won't spend time with me.	H3,L2 levels 4,6,9
4: People don't do things they hate- I don't believe you.	S4 levels 9,12
5: What were you really doing?	H5 levels 3,12

The actual response of B to A2 addresses some of these levels explicitly (E) and some implicitly (I):

  B2:   It's ok when I have some company.

1: I went with other people.   2E (updates knowledge state)
2: I didn't go with you you'll notice.   L2,H3
                7I (takes offensive here)
                9E (modifies her belief about his belief)
                4I (implicitly says that her emotions do not matter)
                6I (yes the relationship is in trouble)
3: I had fun without you.
                9E (wives are not the only company for husbands)
                6I (you do not satisfy my companionship needs)

A's response ("Aren't I company?") addresses levels 4,6 and 9. A3 can be seen as a response to the implicit statements made above.

The rest of the conversation can be analyzed in this way, but to do so here would be pointless. The major point here is that this multifaceted approach to conversational analysis is necessary in order to build a program that is capable of sensible human reponses. People do not speak at only one level and therefore a program ought not to either. The twelve levels of analysis are at this point rather arbitrarily defined. We will be able to determine a correct set of them by attempting to actually write the program to analyze sentences and come up with appropriate responses. Clearly such a program will need a data base of world knowledge, episodic knowledge, goals and emotional relationships in order to converse effectively. We are currently working on specifying exactly how it will all work.

By way of conclusion, and just as a method of pointing out how hard this all is, we can examine A10. Here, A can actually respond to B on nearly every single level explicitly. The last statement of B was:

  B9:   All right. I was at Joe's house. We had a few beers and smoked
          some dope. I didn't want to tell you because I know you can't
          stand Joe.

This can be responded to on each level as follows:

1. Direct Q–A: How can you stand Joe?
2. Knowledge State: Why didn't you tell me that in the first place? I really like Joe, I just never told you about my change of heart about him.
3. Dominance Games: Well I've got news for you. I've been seeing Joe when you actually do go bowling.
4. Emotions of A: I can't love a person who lies to me like that.
5. Emotions of B: You couldn't love me and be friends with him.
6. Relationship of A and B: I want a divorce.
7. Argument strategy: You mean you created this giant argument out of just that little thing?
8. Import: That's what you were worried about? I don't care about that.
9. Implicit Beliefs: You were smoking dope? That's immoral. I won't stand for it.
10. Points: That's my point exactly. You are a liar.
11. Topic Shifts: (The topic has not been shifted so this is also inappropriate.)
12. Truth and trust: How can I trust you after you lied to me like that?

In addition to what we have listed above, it is also possible to combine many of the levels in one response. (Indeed it was quite difficult to avoid doing that in what was written above.)

To effectively model conversation then, it is necessary to find the levels at which we people operate, the rules people use to relate inputs to these levels, the methods of response generation appropriate at each of these levels, and the rules people use to select from alternative responses. When we have understood how to do all this, we will have made a start at analyzing the process of conversation and will then be ready to attempt to build an automated conversationalist.

Yale University

ACKNOWLEDGEMENTS

The research described here was done at the Yale Artificial Intelligence Project and is funded in part by the Advanced Research Projects Agency of the Department of Defense and monitored under the Office of Naval Research under contract N00014–75–C–1111.

The author would like to thank Wendy Lehnert, who helped formulate some of the ideas brought forth in this paper, and Chris Riesbeck, who read the rough draft and made useful suggestions.

REFERENCE

Schank, R. C. and Abelson, R. P.: 1977, *Scripts, Plans, Goals and Understanding: An Inquiry Into Human Knowledge Structures*, Lawrence Erlbaum Associates, Hillsdale, New Jersey.

MARVIN MINSKY

JOKES AND THE LOGIC OF THE COGNITIVE UNCONSCIOUS

ABSTRACT. Freud's theory of jokes explains how they overcome the mental "censors" that make it hard for us to think "forbidden" thoughts. But his theory did not work so well for humorous nonsense as for other comical subjects. In this essay I argue that the different forms of humor can be seen as much more similar, once we recognize the importance of *knowledge about knowledge* and, particularly, aspects of thinking concerned with recognizing and suppressing *bugs* – ineffective or destructive thought processes. When seen in this light, much humor that at first seems pointless, or mysterious, becomes more understandable.

INTRODUCTION

A gentleman entered a pastry-cook's shop and ordered a cake; but he soon brought it back and asked for a glass of liqueur instead. He drank it and began to leave without having paid. The proprietor detained him. "You've not paid for the liqueur." "But I gave you the cake in exchange for it." "You didn't pay for that either." "But I hadn't eaten it".

– from Freud (1905). [0]

In trying to classify humorous phenomena, Sigmund Freud asks whether this should be called a joke, *"for the fact is we do not yet know in what the characteristic of being a joke resides."* Let us agree that some of the cake-joke's humor is related to a logical absurdity – leaving aside whether it is in the logic itself, or in keeping track of it. Later Freud goes on to ask what is the status of a "knife without a blade which has no handle?" This absurdity has a different quality; some representation is being misused – like a frame without a picture.

Freud, who never returned to the subject after writing his 1905 book on the theory of jokes {0}, suggested that "censors" in the mind form powerful, unconscious barriers that make it difficult to think "forbidden" thoughts. But jokes can elude these censors – to create the pleasure of unearned release of psychic energy, which is discharged in the form of laughter. He explains why jokes tend to be compact and condensed, with double meanings: this is to fool the childishly simple-minded censors, who see only innocent surface meanings and fail to penetrate the disguise of the forbidden wishes.

But Freud's theories do not work as well for humorous nonsense as for

L. Vaina and J. Hintikka (eds.), Cognitive Constraints on Communication, 175–200.
©1980 *by Marvin Minsky.*

humorous aggression and sexuality.[0] In this essay I try to show how these different forms of humor can be seen as much more similar, once we make certain observations about the nature of commonsense reasoning. Here is our thesis:

1. *Common sense logic is too unreliable for practical use.* It cannot be repaired, so we must learn to avoid its most common malfunctions. Humor plays a special role in learning and communicating about such matters.

2. *It is not enough to detect errors in reasoning; one must anticipate and prevent them.* We embody much of our knowledge about how to do this in the form of "censors" that suppress unproductive mental states. This is why humor is so concerned with the prohibited.

3. *Productive thinking depends on knowing how to use Analogy and Metaphor.* But analogies are often false, and metaphors misleading. So the "cognitive unconscious" must suppress inappropriate comparisons. This is why humor is so concerned with the nonsensical.

4. *The consequences of intellectual failure are manifest in one's own head, while social failures involve other people.* Intellect and Affect seem less different once we theorize that the *"cognitive unconscious"* considers faulty reasoning to be just as "naughty" as the usual "Freudian" wishes.

5. *Humor evolved in a social context.* Its forms include graciously disarming ways to instruct others about inappropriate behavior and faulty reasoning. This deviousness makes the subject more confusing.

Our theory emphasizes the importance of *knowledge about knowledge* and, particularly, aspects of thinking concerned with recognizing and suppressing *bugs* — ineffective of destructive thought processes. When seen in this light, much humor that at first seems pointless, or mysterious, becomes more understandable.[1]

I. PROBLEMS OF COMMON SENSE REASONING

When you tell a young child *"I am telling a lie"* then, if he is old enough to reason so, he will think: *"If that is false, then he's not telling a lie. But, then it must be true. But then, it must be a lie, for it says so. But then — "*. And so on, back and forth.

A child might find this situation disagreeable for several reasons. It challenges the belief that propositions are always either true or false. It threatens to propagate through his knowledge-structure, creating other inconsistencies. And he can make no progress when his mind returns again and again to the same state.[2] Common sense can go awry in endless ways.

Beliefs can be wrong from the start, one can make mistakes from each step to the next, and one can wander aimlessly, getting nowhere. But before we discuss these, we should observe what actually happens when you say things like *"this statement is false."* Often the listener first seems puzzled, then troubled, and finally laughs. *"That's funny,"* he says. *"Tell me another liar joke"*.

The Problem of Truth: How do we know where to begin? The conclusions of even the best reasoning can be no better than its premises. In mathematics, this is of little concern (because one cares more where premises lead than where they come from). But in real life, few propositions are perfectly trustworthy. What does one do when an accepted "fact" turns out false? One of my children was once entranced by an ornamental fish-shaped bowl with four short legs. After a while she announced, somewhat uncertainly: *"Some fish don't have legs."*

We never know anything for certain. What should one do upon reaching a conclusion that appears false — erase all the assumptions? When a long held belief turns false, should one erase all that has been deduced from it? When an acquaintance once tells a lie, should one reject everything else he ever said? There is no simple, single rule: each person must find his own ways to maintain his knowledge about his knowledge. [1]

Whence the Rules of Inference? How do we know how to infer? Most people believe that *if most A's are B's, and if most B's are C's, then most A's are C's.* Though false, this has great heuristic value, especially for children who encounter few exceptions. *Psychologically*, I see no great difference between heuristic and logical reasoning; deduction is "just another" kind of evidence. We firmly believe a deduced conclusion only when it seems plausible on other grounds as well. At one time, many philosophers held that faultless "laws of thought" were somehow inherent, a priori, in the very nature of mind. This belief was twice shaken in the past century; first when Russell and his successors showed how the logic men employ can be defective, and later when Freud and Piaget started to reveal the tortuous ways in which our minds actually develop.

After Russell observed that the seemingly frivolous *"Who shaves the Barber, who shaves everyone who does not shave himself?"* was a truly serious obstacle to formalizing common sense logic, he and others tried to develop new formalisms that avoided such problems — by preventing the fatal self-references. But the proposed substitutes were much too complicated to serve for everyday use.

I am inclined to doubt that anything very resembling formal logic could be a good model for human reasoning. (The paper by Hewitt and Kornfeld might suggest a possible avenue of compromise [2].) In particular, I doubt that any logic that prohibits self-reference can be adequate for psychology: no mind can have enough power — without the power to think about Thinking itself. Without Self-Reference it would seem immeasurably harder to achieve Self-Consciousness — which, so far as I can see, requires at least some capacity to reflect on what it does.[3]

If Russell shattered our hopes for making a completely reliable version of commonsense reasoning, still we can try to find the islands of "local consistency," in which naive reasoning remains correct. It seems that only certain kinds of expressions lead to paradoxes and inconsistencies, and it seems worth taking some risks, gambling for greater power — provided we can learn, over time, to avoid the most common disasters. We all know the legend of the great mathematician who, warned that his proof would lead to a paradox if he took one more step. He replied *"Ah, but I shall not take that step."*[4] One would miss the point to treat this as a "mere" joke. What it means, really, is that we build into our minds two complementary functions:

We work to discover "islands of power" within which commonsense reasoning seems safe.

We work also to find and mark the unsafe boundaries of those islands.

In civilized communities, guardians display warnings to tell drivers about sharp turns, skaters about thin ice. Similarly, our philosophers and mathematicians display paradigms — like the Barber, the Tortoise, and the Liar — to tell us where to stop — and laugh. I suggest that when such paradigms are incorporated into the mind, they form intellectual counterparts to Freud's emotional censors. This would help explain why purely logical nonsense so often has the same humorous quality as do jokes about injury and discomfort — the problem that bothered Freud. The cake-joke reminds us, somewhat obscurely, to avoid a certain kind of logical absurdity — lest we do ourselves some vaguely understood cognitive harm. Hence our thesis: since we have no systematic way to avoid all the inconsistencies of commonsense logic, each person must find his own way by building a private collection of "cognitive censors" to suppress the kinds of mistakes he has discovered in the past.

Heuristic Control of Logic: How do we know what next to do? I once tutored a student having trouble with middle-school geometry. I began to explain the axioms, and how proofs were structured. *"I understand all that,"* he said, *"only I was sick the day the teacher explained how to find the proofs."*

It is not enough just to know the principles of reasoning; one must know also when to apply them. We each know millions of facts, and perhaps millions of rules of inference. But which to apply to what and when? There is a basic problem of direction, of not meandering, lest one aimlessly derive billions of inferences, all perfectly logical but none relevant to any goal. First, some "plan" is required. Next, one must avoid circling — returning to the same place again and again. Finally, to avoid confusion, one needs an administrative structure to keep track of what one is doing, and why.

The new science called Artificial Intelligence is concerned with just such issues of the efficiency and effectiveness of Reason — matters rarely discussed in Logic or Philosophy, which focus on verifying that proofs are valid, or that arguments are sound, rather than on how proofs are discovered. Much has been learned, in "AI", about how to avoid excessive meandering and confusion, by using goal-structures and plans — techniques for insuring progress. Using such methods, some modern computer programs can thread their ways through some quite complicated situations.

Nevertheless, the problem of meandering is certain to re-emerge once we learn how to make machines that examine themselves to formulate their own new problems. Questioning one's own "top-level" goals always reveals the paradox-oscillation of ultimate purpose. How could one decide that a goal is worthwhile — unless one already knew what it is that is worthwhile? How could one decide when a question is properly answered — unless one knows how to answer that question itself? Parents dread such problems and enjoin kids to *not take them seriously.* We learn to suppress those lines of thought, to "not even think about them" and to dismiss the most important of all as nonsensical, *viz.* the joke *"Life is like a bridge." "In what way?"* *"How should I know?"* Such questions lie beyond the shores of sense and in the end it is Evolution, not Reason, that decides who remains to ask them.

II. CENSORSHIP

Just like taboos in human societies, certain things must not be thought inside the Mind. The best way for a child to learn not to do a certain bad thing would be to learn *not to even to think of it.* But isn't that like trying "not to think of a monkey"? Constrast two ways: (i) suppress an idea already in the mind or (ii) prevent it from being thought in the first place:

(i)   Stop thinking that!
(ii) Don't even (or ever) think that!

It is easy to begin to make a type (i) censor: wait for the specified "bad" event to happen, and then suppress it. But how does one prevent it from recurring? It seems harder to begin to make a type (ii) censor, because it must be able to recognize the repressed thought's Precursors – but it is easier to see what to do next, since each Precursor usually leads to several options, and suppressing one still leaves the others. So we shall discuss only the second censor-type.

So, our censor-builder has to learn to recognize Precursors – mind-brain states that precede a recognizable (and, here, to be prohibited) activity. To do this, it will need a short term memory (to remember what *just* happened) and a long term memory (to store the result of learning). The latter may eventually become quite large, because a prohibited event may have many different precursors. In any case, an experienced type (ii) censor can recognize its joke by the situation and need not wait for the punch line. A type (i) censor makes you wait till the comedian finishes: only then can you complain *"Oh, I've heard that one before!"*

To place these in a larger framework, let's consider a simple "two-brain" theory. An "A-brain" has sensory inputs from the world, and motor outputs to the world. The B-brain's inputs come from the interior of A – so B can perceive "A-states" – and its outputs go into A, so B can affect activities in A. Thus, B can "see" what is happening inside A, and act to influence it, just as A can "see" and affect what happens in the world. B need not – and probably cannot – know what A-events "mean," vis-a-vis the world, but B is in a position to recognize such metapsychological conditions such as A being "meandering, circling, or confused."[5]

When a B-censor acts, it must disturb the A-brain so as to suppress the undesired activity. (It would be even better for B to remember, from past events, which is a *good* way to go, but that is outside this essay's concern.) In any case, the point is that precursor-sensitive censors can do their work *before* the problems that they evade actually arise. Probably, also, they can do this so quickly and gently as to produce no noticeable mental pheno-menology. This would explain why censors are (in the) unconscious.

The censorship theory explains why a joke is not so funny if you've heard it before; this is because a new censor has been constructed, or an old one extended. Freud touches on "novelty" as a component of humor, but never dwells on why old jokes get few laughs. I presume that he simply considered it too obvious to mention, that censors are learners.

How big must the censor memory be, to protect us from naive reasoning mistakes? Probably not so large for formal logic, considering how rarely we discover a new paradox. But for avoiding nonsense in general, we might accumulate millions of censors. For all we know, this "negative meta-knowledge" — about patterns of thought and inference that have been found defective or harmful — may be a large portion of all we know.

Consider the activities called *play* and *practice*. The insensitive learning theories of behavioristic psychology regard *play* not at all, and see practice as reinforcing something repetitive. But *practice* (I conjecture) is often far from mere repetition and refinement of the same thing; often it is exploratory, testing out a skill's minute variations and perturbations — and learning which of them to enhance or suppress. Similarly *play*, (commonly seen as "mere") is often also an exploration of variations on a larger scale. Many other everyday activities can so be seen as ways to learn to avoid bugs and mistakes.

I know a young child whose sense of humor tends toward jokes like "*what if the spoon were rubber*," apparently observing that a flexible spoon would be absurd because the food would fall out of it. Is he enforcing a "must-be-rigid" property of some spoon-frame, or is he censoring the use of some spoon-frame that lacks the property? The humor-behavior of children also needs more study.

III. MEANING AND METAPHOR

Two villagers decided to go bird-hunting. They packed their guns and set out, with their dog, into the fields. Near evening, with no success at all, one said to the other, "We must be doing something wrong". "Yes", agreed his friend. "Perhaps we're not throwing the dog high enough."

When you want to fasten a screw and therefore reach for a certain screwdriver, your mind has chosen to see that screwdriver as a screw-driver; you could have seen it as a kind of dull knife, or as a hammer without a head. When we see something only in its "intended" aspect, we are "confusing the thing with itself." As Korzybski [3] intoned, "*whatever a thing is, it is not*".[6,7]

Frames: I suggested in [4] that perceptions are ordinarily interpreted by the mind in terms of previously acquired description-structures called *Frames*. A frame is a way to represent a stereotyped situation, like being in a certain kind of room, or going to a certain kind of party. Attached to each frame are several kinds of information; some about how to use the frame, some about what one might expect to happen next, some about what to do if those expectations are not confirmed, and so forth. This theory was proposed to explain the speed and virtual absence of noticeable phenomenology in perceiving and thinking, and here I propose to sketch just enough of it to explain some features, and some "bugs," of reasoning. Then we can return to unconscious censorship and error-correction.

Each frame includes, among other things, a variety of *terminals* to which other frames are attached. Thus a chair-frame specifies that a (certain kind of) chair has a *seat*, a *back*, and four *legs*. The details of these would be described, not in the chair-frame itself, but in other frames attached to its terminals. Each frame includes also a set of features which, if enough of them are present, may activate the Frame. So, when you see enough parts of a chair, these will activate one of your chair-frames which, in turn, will activate the sub-frames attached to its terminals. These, then, will "look for" other chair-parts that were not recognized at first — because of being unusual, or partially hidden from view, or whatever. Finally, if some elements required by the frame are not seen at all — one rarely sees all the legs of a chair, and *never* all the sides of a box — the missing elements are supplied by *default*. This is easy because most terminals of most frames have certain sub-frames already attached as *default assignments*. When one reads in a story about some shoe or some chair, these cause one, "by default" to assume a certain kind of shoe or chair.

The concept of default goes much further. When one sees a person in a sitting posture then, even if every part of his chair is hidden from view, one will pseudo-see a chair under him. Unless your attention is drawn to the fact, you never notice that no chair was actually seen. This is because the "sitting" frame includes a "must-be-supported-by" sub-frame terminal, and this is attached to some "typical" chair-frame, for its *default assignment*.[8]

The chair-frame that is selected can depend, however, on the context for default assignments are weak and easy to "displace". If there are other chairs around, the invisible chair will be assumed to be like one of them. If the scene is set in a park, then a park-bench frame might be activated to serve as default. If one then noticed an arm-chair arm, the system would replace the weakly-attached bench-frame by one that better suits what was seen — and one now "sees" an armchair.

According to the theory in [4] this is done very swiftly because the "corresponding" terminals of related frames are already pre-connected to one another. This makes it easy to change a faltering interpretation or a frustrated expectation. Shifting from one related frame to another should be so fast and efficient as to be imperceptible to introspection. This is why one so easily recognizes any chair as "a chair", even though particular chairs are so different from one another. I do not suggest that all this happens by magic; *the interconnecting network is constructed over a lifetime of experience.* In [5] I discuss how new frames arise usually as revised versions of older ones, bringing those "common terminals" along with them. In [6] are more details, but one must read between the lines of that paper because it does not use the terminology of frames.

Frames and frame-systems are used at conceptual as well as perceptual levels, and there we find other kinds of *frame-systems* — families of inter-connected frames — that are not transformed so easily, hence more effort is noticed. Consider, for example, Wittgenstein's paradigmatic question about defining "game." [7] The problem is that *there is no property common to all games*, so that the most usual kinds of definition fail. Not every game has a ball, nor two competing teams; even, sometimes, there is no notion of "winning." In my view, the explanation is that a word like "game" points to a somewhat diffuse "system" of prototype frames, among which some frame-shifts are easy, but others involve more strain. The analogy between football and chess is strained only a little, more with solitaire, and so on. Shifting from one familiar kind of kitchen-chair to another is imperceptible, but changing a park-bench to an arm-chair would be strain enough to "surprise".

Now I propose that much of commonsense logic itself is based on learning to make shifts between frames that have terminals in common. For example, if a situation fits a frame like *A implies B, and B implies C*, a simple frame-shift re-represents it as *A implies C.* Seen in this light, Freud's cake story appears to display some sort of incorrect-logic script in which each consecutive pair of sentences matches some such tried-and-true kind of reasoning step.

I presume that when we "understand" this sort of story, we represent it in our minds as a series of pairs of overlapping assignments of things to terminals of such frames. And somewhere along the way, in the cake story, there is an improper assignment-change. Is it the payment moving from the cake to the drink? Is it a pivot between "owns" and "possesses?" Each listener must make his own theory of what is wrong — and devise his own way to avoid this confusion in the future. Some people will do better at this than others.

Metaphor: All intelligent persons also possess some larger-scale frame-systems whose members seemed at first impossibly different — like water with electricity, or poetry with music. Yet many such analogies — along with the knowledge of how to apply them — are among our most powerful tools of thought. They explain our ability sometimes to see one thing — or idea — as though it were another, and thus to apply knowledge and experience gathered in one domain to solve problems in another. It is thus that we transfer knowledge via the paradigms of Science. We learn to see gases and fluids as particles, particles as waves, and waves as envelopes of growing spheres.

How are these powerful connections discovered? For the simple ones, there is no great problem: some frames are easily recognized as similar because their terminals accept the same sorts of entities; these could be located and classified by simple algorithms, e.g., searches for best match. As for those most subtle, once-in-a-lifetime insights, whose analogical powers are hidden deep in the procedural structures that operate on them, we hardly need a general theory to account for them since — like favorable evolutionary mutations — few are ever discovered by any single individual, and those can be thereafter transmitted through the culture. In any case, putting aside the origins of those rare, greatest insights, each individual must have his own ways to build new connections amongst his frames. I will contrast particular methods against general methods, arguing that the two have problems that seem somewhat opposite in character — that the errors of "particular" methods can be managed additively, while bugs in the "general" methods must be repaired subtractively. This last point will eventually bring us back to censors.

Particular Analogies: In the course of thinking, we use different frames from one moment to the next. But frequently one of the active frames will fail — "that's not a door, only a big window." Winston, in [8] suggests that whenever such an error is (somehow) detected, described, and corrected, we can attach to the failing frame a "pointer" to some other frame that has been found to work in this circumstance. The pointer must contain, of course, a description of the failure circumstance. A family of frames connected in such a way is called a *difference network*.[9] We can explain [4] the definition difficulty (e.g., that of defining "game") by supposing that such words point not to any single frame, but into such a network.

Any such link between two frames implies a generalization of the form "*A's are like B's, except for D*". Thus, such a link is a fragment of an analogy.

Of course, like any generalization, it will likely soon fail again and need refinement. Winston's thesis [8] suggests ways to do this. The important point here is that, particular analogies discovered in the course of experience, can be remembered by adding *positive*, active links between frames.

General Analogy Methods: What if one is confronted with a novel situation that does *not* arouse any particular frame? Then, it makes sense to try some "general" method, e.g., to compare the situation to some large class of frames, and select the one that "best fits." Such a method can do much better than chance, but what if it yields a result that does more harm than good? I will argue that one now must build a censor, and that there is a general principle here that learning theorists have not appreciated: *positive general principles need always to be supplemented by negative, anecdotal censors.*

For, it hardly ever pays to alter a general mechanism to correct a particular bug. Almost every instance-specific modification of a best-match mechanism would reduce its general usefulness. So when the general mechanism yields a bad result, one can only remember to suppress its subsequent appearances — that is, to build a censor. If a child wants his sibling's toy, he will first try seizing it — the most general way to get things one wants. Once the parents see to it that this is censored, then he can find other ways. But he must *not* learn *in general* not to take things he wants, lest he become helpless.

Some forms of humor, notably puns, turn on changing the meaning-sense of a word. (Besides the easily distinguished dictionary senses, most words have also many others that would never be separated in a dictionary. "Lift," for example, has different implications when an object weighs one gram, or a thousand,[7] and really to understand lifting requires a network for making appropriate shifts among such different micro-senses.) While verbal sense-shifting can be funny, and even useful, it is dangerous, and especially hazardous to be subject to the fortuitous, meaningless sense-shifts that depend on superficial word-sound similarities. In a fragment of a schizophrenic's transcript, the patient sees a penny in the street, says "copper, that's a conductor," then must run to a street car to speak to the conductor. Perhaps this disorder is one of frame-shift control, either disabling the bad-analogy suppressors or irresponsibly enhancing the general analogy-finder.

The element that seems to me most common to all the different kinds of humor is that of unexpected frame-substitution, in which a scene is first described from one viewpoint and then suddenly — typically by a single word — one is made to view all the scene-elements in another, quite different

way. Some such shifts are insightful, of course, while others are mere
meaningless accidents. Next we turn to a kind that could be turning points in
each individual's personal evolution.

IV. TRAUMATIC COGNITIVE EXPERIENCES

> *"Yields truth when appended to its own quotation"*
> yields truth when appended to its own quotation.
> — W. V. Quine

In the popular psychology of our day, Intellect is seen as straightforward,
deliberate, conscious, and emotionally neutral; but in regard to emotional
matters, the public has come generally to accept the psychoanalytic view that
Affect is dominated by unknown terrors and traumas, lurking in the unconscious since childhood. Now I want to challenge this affect-intellect
"dumbbell". I certainly do not mean to suggest that there are no differences
of kinds in mental affairs — only that this particularly popular distinction,
however useful in everyday life, does more harm than good in psychology.[6]

In any case, the Affect-Intellect distinction would lose much of its force if
Reason, too, employed a powerful "cognitive unconscious" — and that is
exactly what I shall argue: that Intellect, too, has its own buried secrets. In
Freud's scenario, the ego develops largely in contexts of fear of deprivation,
punishment or mutilation; of anxiety about uncertainty and insecurity; terror
of losing the esteem or person of parent or attachment-figure. New families
of censors — new domains of repression — are created when wishes conflict
enough with reality to justify attempting to keep them from becoming
conscious.

Does anything like that happen in the intellectual sphere? One might
suppose not, because a necessary element is missing — that of a beloved — or
punitive — authority figure. However, while Freudian taboos originate from
outside, the child needs no external authority-figure to point out his gross
cognitive failures; he needs no parent to scold him, when an encounter with
paradox throws his mind into a frightening cyclone. The momentary loss of
mental control should provoke anxiety in its own right.

But, one might ask, if we bear the scars of frightening cognitive
experiences, why do they not reveal themselves (like the affect-laden ones) in
nightmares, compulsions, phobias, and the like? Perhaps they do; it would
not show in the interpretations of present-day psychiatry. But every teacher
knows (and fears) the rigid inhibition of children's cognitive phobias: *"I don't*

want to learn this; I couldn't possibly do that". Let us speculate on how such fears might originate. Consider the paradox of *Nearness*: Every child must once have said to himself:

Hmmm. Ten is almost Eleven. And Eleven is nearly Twelve. And so on; Ninety-Nine is nearly a Hundred. But then Ten must be almost a Hundred!

To an adult, this is not even a stupid joke. But we each must once have thought something like: "there is obviously something wrong here. Is it in my premises or in my logic? Well, what's my premise? Obviously, that *"if A is near B, and if B is near C, then A must be near C."* Nothing wrong with that. So there must be something wrong with my logic. But I'm only using something like: *"If A implies B, and if B implies C, then A implies C."* "How could *that* be wrong? No way!"

To be sure, not everyone remembers such experiences as frightening. In fact, *ad hominem*, readers of essays like this one would more likely complain that they *like* such problems and cannot see them as "traumatic." No matter, such readers are just the ones who have found ways to transform — what did Freud call it? — to *sublimate* such problems into constructive thinking about thinking. In any case, in one private manner or another, everyone somehow comes to deal with such problems, and I see only one practical way: we must each grow for ourselves some structure, of large complexity and little elegance, to tell us when — and when not — to trust each such pattern of inference. For example, we each learn never to repeat a *near* deduction more than a few times in any one argument. Furthermore, the accumulation of such experiences leads us eventually to realize that this is not peculiar to "near" alone: perhaps one shouldn't use *any* inference method too many times. What is "too many?" There is, I fear, no elegant answer. We each have to learn and master large bodies of knowledge about the limitations of each species of reasoning.

It might be useful to try to catalog the kinds of cognitive incidents that must have so baffled each of us in early life. Each reader must recall the distress of being made to discern the arbitrary boundaries between one ocean and another, or at trying to answer *"which came first, the chicken or the egg?"* Every child must have wondered about his origin and from whence came the *first* person. Only the dullest child never found for himself some sort of Zeno paradox, or Achilles and Tortoise problem. I remember being especially disturbed to discover that there were questions that adults had *no* way to answer.

Mystical Experience: Another family of disturbances arise when we question our own purposes. *"Why should I do this,"* — whatever it is — one asks, and proposes some answer. But then one is impelled to continue, "why should I want *that*," and so forth. There is a not uncommon phenomenon — sometimes called mystical experience — from which a person emerges with the conviction that some unsolvable problem (like the purpose of existence) has been completely explained; one can't remember quite how, only that it was answered so well as to leave no doubt at all. This, I venture, reflects some mental mechanism (perhaps one of last resort) that, in a state of particularly severe turmoil or stress, can short-circuit the entire intellectual process — *by creating the illusion that the problem has been settled.* Powerful but dangerous, such a mechanism short-cuts the canons of normal confirmation. One kind of confusion-cycle is thereby broken, but this may damage other ways in which sane minds confront beliefs with evidence. Then, anything can happen.[10]

V. HUMOR AND EVOLUTION

> If you wish to study a granfalloon
> just remove the skin of a toy balloon.
> — Kurt Vonnegut, in *Cat's Cradle*

In the 1912 edition Freud, still perplexed about the purpose of nonsense, recounts a joke of this form:[11]

A man at the dinner table dipped his hands in the mayonnaise and then ran them through his hair. When his neighbor looked astonished, the man apologized: "I'm so sorry. I thought it was spinach."

We have argued that learning about bugs is central to the growth of reason. But reason itself grows in no vacuum; most of our ideas — *and our ideas about ideas* — come via our families and cultures, and this poses some special communication problems. For one, it is risky to point out the mistakes of a person one wants to please. So this must be done in some "conciliatory" manner — and humor seems involved in this. For another, if learning about bugs involves a special kind of memory, then this communication must somehow engage that memory. In this section we propose that humor — and more specifically, *laughter* — is innately enabled to do this, too.

But first we digress to discuss an important methodological problem: *Why is it so hard to explain why jokes are funny?* Why, for that matter, is it so hard to say precisely what is a joke? We have already mentioned Wittgenstein's problem of defining "game": one can find no single quality common to all the different kinds of examples — and one finds a similar problem in attempting to define "humor." *But we did not stop to ask why this is so.* One might suppose it a mere surface difficulty, and hope that we may yet find a single underlying structure from which all funny things spring — some basic "grammar of humor," or "comical deep structure." Not so, I fear; when we look deeper for that underlying structure of humor we shall still find a vexing lack of unity. I argue that this is a consequence of the way things usually evolve in biology.

In mechanisms designed by plan, it is reasonable to ask about purpose or cause. What is the purpose of that beam in this house? Simple: to hold up this roof — and, perhaps, to hold those walls apart. But, when we ask questions about structures created by evolution, we find that only rarely does one evolutionary increment serve a single purpose — and rarely is one alone in serving any particular purpose. Behavior emerges from a network of inter-dependent mechanisms, and one cannot expect any compactly circumscribed theory (or mechanism) completely to "explain" any single surface component of behavior. What a theory *can* do, though, is to describe some fragment of that larger network of interacting subsystems.

Humor, like games, serves and exploits many different needs and mechanisms. It lacks sharp, natural boundaries because those underlying things themselves overlap and exploit one another. When we employ a *word* like "humor," one has the illusion of designating something sharper than this kind of complex web of relations among laughter, faulty reasoning, taboos and prohibitions, and unconscious suppressor mechanisms. But, I think the very clarity of words is itself a related illusion; as — mentioned in Note 7, language itself works only because oversimplification is more useful than realistic confusion — that is, in real life, if not for thinking about psychology.

Roles of Laughter: Consider what happens when a thought-situation comes to be perceived as funny or absurd: further reasoning is drowned in a flood of activity — furious motions of thorax, abdomen, head, limbs and face, accom-panied by loud barking, wheezing, and choking noises. To a Martian, an epileptic seizure would be less alarming. Adults, of course, can train them-selves to suppress this, but that is another matter.

Laughter disrupts reasoning: The laughter reaction is so distracting as to keep the mind from proceeding further along the prohibited or ridiculous path it has started. Whatever that line of thought, the disruption prevents you from "taking it seriously," from acting upon it or considering its further logical consequences.

At the same time, laughter exercises another, complementary function.

Laughter focusses attention: While disrupting further reasoning, laughter takes a firm grip on the thought itself, holding up the absurdity in sharp focus. Perhaps the joke-thought is given full attention, holding the incongruity in some "short term memory" — so that "censor-learning" agency can absorb it.

Thus "humor" might serve to mediate the process in which the censors learn, much as "pleasure" is often supposed to mediate ordinary learning.[12]

Evolution of Humor: How might all this have evolved? We conjecture that it happened while our evolving minds passed through stages of increasing ability to reflect — to think not merely about the physical problems at hand, but about how we should apply our mental resources to them; in a word, when we were learning to *plan. In order to make realistic plans, we had to learn to take account of what we could make our minds do.*

This ability could not have emerged all at once. There must have been intermediate steps — such as the appearance of multi-level schemes like the one suggested above, in which an A-mind is monitored by a B-mind. Eventually we became able to symbolize and manipulate *representations* of plans, and this allowed the first direct references to our own mental activities. Now, suddenly, we could do such tricks as to relate statements to their own quotations, and make propositions that (for better or for worse) could discuss their own truth — as in Quine's *"yields truth"* tour de force.[13]

In any case, once able to accomplish intricate chains of reasoning, we became vulnerable to new kinds of bugs: faulty variable bindings, subtle changes of sense, and more obscurely circular logic. This same epoch probably saw also the emergence of Language for social communication, which also converged toward using more concise and manipulable symbolic representations. And, because we could not weaken the expressiveness of symbol-manipulation without losing its power, we had to evolve those censor memories. Of course, what actually happened was surely not this simple, but we had better return again to our speculations about laughter.

Laughter's facial component suggests that it evolved in connection with social communication. It appears to be derived (ethologically) in part from a "conciliatory" expression, but it includes also a baring of teeth that suggests a defensive-aggressive mixture.[14]

Laughter's bizarre vocal component also suggests social functions that combine ancestral "releasers" for both conciliation and aggression. Perhaps it came somehow to serve as a signal to induce another person to stop whatever he was doing: whether because dangerous, pointless, objectionable, ridiculous, or otherwise forbidden.

Later, this function became internalized. If a person could feel and hear himself laugh, grimace, and shake, why not exploit these side-effects also to make one's own self to stop doing something ridiculous or prohibited? Perhaps, literally, men first learned to laugh at their own mistakes, and later learned to censure themselves in silence.

I make no plea for this particular scenario, only that something of this general sort must have happened, in which several pre-existing complexes grew together. They each brought along a variety of older interactions with other systems and purposes — that were exploited to produce the puzzling combinations of conciliation, aggression, sexuality, and nonsense that are now mixed together in humor. If other mental structures also share this kind of tangled ethological ancestry, then a mind grown this way must now resemble a great spider-web, in which many threads of different biological purpose intersect in many nodes of different multi-purpose mechanisms. If so, the goals of psychological theories must be to describe different fragments of that web — each to make a map of some few of those threads and nodes.

By a curious coincidence, our *theories* of how minds work must probably have themselves this same peculiar, web-like character — albeit for a different reason. For (I think) the only way a person can understand anything very complicated is to understand it at each moment only locally — like the spider itself, seeing but a few threads and crossings from each viewpoint. Strand by strand, we build within our minds these webs of theory, from hard-earned locally intelligible fragments. The mind-spider's theory is correct to the extent that the model in his head corresponds to the mechanism in his head.[15]

Finally it is probably futile to ask *precisely* what humor is. Korzybski's injunction applies here especially: the word "humor" points to no real thing. Instead, in each different person's mind it points to a slightly different web-model. We each use — and mean — the word a little differently — just as we each laugh at different jokes. Now I do not mean to hint that the problem is unreal, or even that it is especially incomprehensible. I only want to suggest that "humor" may be less a Thing-Part *of* the mind, and more a Thing-Theory *in* the mind. This makes it no less worthy of study, but one must be clear about what one is doing. If we get confused between making theories about theories and making theories about things, we may spin forever.[16]

Time Constants: According to our thesis, familiar types of jokes should seem less funny, because the censors have learned more about them. Why, then, do some kinds of jokes remain so persistently funny? People tire of old nonsense jokes, but not of jokes about forbidden aspects of sex. Does this falsify our theory? Not necessarily; it may mean only that the censors for this particular subject are much slower to learn and to change. Is that plausible?

Most psychological theories of our day — both popular and professional — seem to suppose that all memories are made of the same stuff, stored in the same huge container. (I argue otherwise in [6].) But, on reflection, we see that some memories *ought* to be less changeable than others. Contemplate, for example, the plight of a mother with a new infant, that will demand her time and attention for several years. Why doesn't she wonder *"Why am I doing this,"* or *"what could this baby do for me to justify such a sacrifice."* One might argue *"To preserve the race,"* or *"because you will love it,"* or *"because it will repay you some day,"* but these would hardly convince any rational person; raising a child is not, let's face it, a notably sensible enterprise.

Conventional wisdom recognizes that love is far from rational, and holds that an "instinctive" attachment is somehow created and somehow protected from casual alteration. Clearly so, but we must know more about those "somehow"s. This maternal self-questioning doesn't usually go too far, perhaps because we are protected by the web of personal pleasure and social compulsion surrounding child-rearing. But the problem is real, and there are occasional (and invariably concealed) tragedies in which a young mother's frustration overwhelms her attachment.

The simplest way might be to build attachment into a special kind of memory that, once established, tends to persist for several years. After all, long time-constants characterize other aspects of attachment. Some persons always choose different partners of similar appearance; as though unable to alter a fixed stereotype. Others find themselves in the grip of undesired infatuations, that reason declares inappropriate. And most familiar is the seemingly inexorable time-span of mourning — the year or two it takes to adjust to separation or loss. All these could be by-products of adaptations of older mechanisms whose slowness was/is of value in our sociobiological evolution.[17]

Perhaps one can also interpret in this light the prolonged, mourning-like depression associated with sexual assault, presuming that the momentary association of violence with sexuality somehow impairs the entire attachment machinery. The large time-constant make recovery slow, from a profound disturbance of normal social attachments. No matter if the victim manages to view the incident "rationally;" this does not automatically restore those sluggish mechanisms to their normal state, and one must suffer the prolonged functional deprivation of an important mind-part.

All this suggests that the curious robustness of sexual humor may reflect only that the associated censors are among the "slow learners" of the mind, like retarded children. Perhaps they indeed *are* retarded children — the nearly static remnants of our own early selves. They change only slowly, and our tireless enjoyment of certain censured subjects may be a side-effect of that circumstance.

So, we finally conclude: jokes are not really funny at all, but reflect the most serious of concerns; the pursuit of sobriety through the suppression of the absurd.

MIT Artificial Intelligence Laboratory

ACKNOWLEDGMENTS

I thank Howard Cannon, Danny Hillis, William Kornfeld, David Levitt, Gloria Rudisch, and Richard Stallman for suggestions. Gordon Oro provided the dog-joke.

This report describes research done at the Artificial Intelligence Laboratory of the Massachusetts Institute of Technology. Support for the laboratory's artificial intelligence research is provided in part by the Office of Naval Research under Office of Naval Research contract NOOO14–79–C–0260.

NOTES

0 Freud seemed somewhat puzzled by "nonsense jokes" and suggested, to explain the worst of them, that they "give the teller the pleasure of misleading and annoying, by rousing the expectation of a joke and then frustrating the listener" – who in turn – "damps down his annoyance by determining to tell them himself later on." The enjoyment of nonsense, he goes on, might also reflect a wish to return to a childhood of relaxed, careless thought in which one *"puts words together without regard to the condition that they should make sense, in order to obtain from them the pleasurable effect of rhythm or rhyme. Little by little he is forbidden this enjoyment, till all that remains to him are significant combinations of words. But when he is older attempts still emerge at disregarding the restrictions that have been learned."* [0, p.125] In connection with alcoholic cheerfulness, Freud recounts a pun: "It is most instructive to observe how standards of joking sink as spirits rise" – and later – *"the grown man becomes a child, who finds pleasure in having the course of his thoughts freely at his disposal without paying regard to the compulsion of logic"* [0, p.127)]

Freud's later image of childhood was different, with more emphasis on fears, frustrations, and the oppression of a growing self-image that emerges from internal models of authority and attachment figures. In the present essay's conception of the growth of logic in the child, I suggest a comparable self-image of Rationality – only here with less need for an external human model, because confusion automatically imposes its own sanctions.

It was not quite accurate to say that Freud never returned to the subject, for in 1927 [9] he published a brief essay in which, still regarding jokes as a source of pleasure, he now portrays humor (in contrast) as a way to ward off suffering. The super-ego, like a parent, comforts the frightened childlike ego, repudiating reality by suggesting that however dangerous the world may seem, it is nothing but a game for children. Freud is troubled, though, that this seems out of character for the superego; perhaps the thesis of this essay resolves that. In any case, all this impinges on the area of "adult theory" that I hesitate to discuss here, for the reasons given in Note 16.

¹ *The Society of Mind.* Some of the ideas in this essay originated in my earlier work with Seymour Papert, especially the ideas about the construction of the mind through exploitation of different agencies by one another. The present paper, along with [4], [5], [6] and [12] are all related, but I have yet to attempt a single, comprehensive account. The key idea is to reject the conventional view of the mind as a Single Agent that either thinks of something or doesn't; rather, the mind is composed of many smaller minds, themselves composed of yet smaller ones. It would mean little to talk about what these separately "think", for each becomes specialized to perform functions meaningful only vis-a-vis those few others that it has connections with. The phenomenological observations that a "person" makes about himself emerge in a very indirect way from those interactions.

One (of many) reasons to consider decentralized psychological theories is that they seem potentially better able to provide for mechanisms that exploit *knowledge about knowledge* than do the control structures that have become traditional in the literatures of AI and of Cognitive Psychology. It is perfectly understandable that the early years of the "Information Processing Approach" should have focussed on the astonishing power of the newly-invented single-process serial computer. But "meta-knowledge" is not easily accommodated by such machines, and I see the strain showing in attempts to realize more ambitious ideas about intelligent learning – *viz*, in [10] and [11].

² *Partial Mental state.* I don't mean to suggest that the *entire* brain ever repeats the same global state. One could say but little about "mental states" if one imagined the Mind to be a single, unitary thing. But if we envision a mind (or brain) as composed of many partially autonomous "agents", then we can talk of repeating a "partial mental state" – that is, a *subset of the states of those agents.* This is discussed more precisely in [6]. The notion of partial mental state allows one to speak of entertaining *several partial states at once* – to the extent they are compatible – that is, they do not assign different states to the same individual agents. And even when they conflict, the concept still has meaning if such conflicts can be settled within the Society. In [6] I argue that such local mechanisms for conflict resolution could be the antecedents of what we know later as *reasoning* – useful ways to combine different fragments of knowledge.

³ *Consciousness.* As I see it, "consciousness" phenomena can emerge from the operation of a "self-referent" mechanism when it tries to account for some of what it itself is doing. I doubt we possess any especially direct and powerful ways to do this, so we probably do it much as we understand anything else – that is, by making and refining models that may never be particularly accurate. Technically, discussing such matters is messy because of the web of different meanings for "self-reference" itself. Should we call a system self-referent just because it operates on data derived from its own operation?

It might be considered so if it can be seen as trying to describe itself. The self-reference of planning – as when one says *"I shall do X"* – is different from simply expecting to to do X, because it entails (usually) subsidiary plans like *"I shall remain firm and not allow Y to cause me to 'change my mind' "*. Should we call a system self-referent when, only by accident, a structure inside it happens to resemble (in an outside observer's opinion) a larger-scale description of itself? In any case it seems quite clear that our psychological self-models are far from technically accurate – yet serve a variety of social-heuristic-survival needs. In [12] I discussed how models that are technically quite wrong can still be useful; in particular it suggests an explanation of the illusion of free will.

In general, I see little reason to suppose that the "conscious" parts of our minds have any direct access to our own "top-level goals" – or even to suppose that any such "top level" exists, i.e., that the mental society has a strict hierarchy. Even if there were, Evolution probably would have found a way to block the rest of the mind from being able to examine it too closely – if only to keep the logical bull out of the teleological china shop.[10] In any case I suspect that if there *is* a top-level it consists of agencies access to which would reveal nothing intelligible (for reasons described in[12]). In [5] I discuss some possible mechanisms that might be "central" in thinking, because their use would be as limited, scarce resources. These might indeed play roles in our articulate, self-model formulations but, again, those models could be very unrealistic.

4 *Non-monotonic logic.* I discussed these problems with logic very briefly in [4]). Doyle's 1980 thesis [11] has a very imaginative discussion of such matters. One might ask whether the safe regions are like separate islands, or is logic generally safe if we avoid scattered pitfalls.

5 *Confusion.* When a person can say "I'm confused," he is a large step beyond merely being confused because, presumably, he has gone on enough to have recognized a somewhat specific metapsychological condition.

6 *Familiar.* Schank [13] points out that it is only when one doesn't quite recognize something that one thinks *"that looks familiar"*. When something is decisively recognized there is no such phenomenology; one notices the matching process only when the match is imperfect and strained.

7 *Ambiguity.* All but the most childish jokes have two or more meanings "condensed" into one expression or situation. It is commonplace to wonder about non-humorous ambiguities of words and phrases, and how the mind decides which thought is intended. It is not so often realized that *thoughts themselves can be ambiguous* – because a (partial) mental state can be a precursor of many others, depending on the computational context within the mind. [5]

8 *Excuses.* This is oversimplified in many ways. Defaults are not mere conveniences; they are perhaps our most powerful means for making generalizations, because they activate whatever is "typical" of some class by activating the memory of a typical individual of that class. And even when they are not useful, such assumptions are usually innocuous – provided that they are weakly enough attached so that they are easily displaced by "reality". However, this hypothetical default mechanism has many potential bugs of its own. In particular, one must not make mistakes about "supported-by" for all sorts of personal safety reasons. If there is no visible support *and* no intervening object then this is a levitation absurdity.

I suspect that *ethnic humor* exemplifies a larger-scale sociobiological bug that emerges from the frame mechanism. Why are nonsense jokes so often used also to deride alien social groups? A popular theory is that it provides an opportunity to display aggression, and no doubt this is true. But there may also be a more technical reason. I argue in [4] that *it is hard to understand a story about a person unless one is provided with a specific person-frame – it does not matter how stereotyped.* Communication is simplified when the listener does not have to choose a frame for himself. Thus bigotry may emerge spontaneously as a side-effect of this circumstance of representation; when, for example one makes a joke about stupidity, it is psycho-computationally convenient to project it onto some stereotype – preferably alien to avoid conflict with known reality. Obviously, this may become a runaway process, as that stereotype accumulates undeserved absurdities. Sooner or later one loses track of the humorous origin of that structure. It will be hard to eradicate prejudice without understanding the importance (and value) of stereotypes in ordinary thinking.

9 Many of the ideas about the importance of discerning differences came as early as [14] and [15], but [8] had the first clear idea of a difference-network. More recently, in [16] Winston has considered using frames for more complex analogies. The serious study of "bugs" was perhaps first considered in the work of Papert on early education [17] and then in the doctoral theses of Sussman [18] and Goldstein [19].

10 Defense. Lewis Thomas remarks in [20] that philosophers and linguists *"are compelled to use as their sole research instrument the very apparatus they wish to study."* He recounts that, while listening to a proof of Gödel's theorem: "just as I was taking it all in, I suddenly felt something like the flicking of a mercury wall switch and it all turned to nonsense in my head" and suggests – presuming one can tell when this scientist-poet is serious – that *there is a "scrambler in the brain, a protective device preserving the delicate center of the mechanism of language against tinkering and meddling, shielding the mind against information with which it has no intention of getting involved."* Perhaps he's right.

11 *Spinach.* A reader mentioned that she heard this joke about *broccoli*, not mayonnaise. This is funnier, because it transfers a plausible mistake into an implausible context. In Freud's version the mistake is already too silly: one *could* mistake spinach for broccoli, but not for mayonnaise. I suspect that Freud *transposed the wrong absurdity* when he determined to tell it himself later on. Indeed, he (p.139) seems particularly annoyed at this joke – and well he might be if, indeed, he himself damaged it by spoiling the elegance of the frame-shift. I would not mention this were it not for the established tradition of advancing psychiatry by analyzing Freud's own writings.

12 *Enjoyment.* As Freud demanded, we have to explain why humor is pleasant, yet is so often about unpleasant – painful, disgusting, or forbidden matters. There is nothing really funny about most good jokes – except perhaps in the skill with which the content is disguised. Now, there is no shortage of explanations of how this reversal of sign might come about: the censor-energy theory, the "I'm glad it didn't happen to me" theory, the minimizing the importance of reality theory, and so forth. Yet the question remains all the more important and difficult because, everyone supposing the matter to be obvious, no one seems to have proposed any sophisticated theories of *pleasure* itself – so all those commonsense "mini-theories" seem built on sand.

What is pleasure, and why do we like it? It is not a tautology. Clearly pleasure involves a complex web concerned with: learning and goals; with activities one wants to continue and/or repeat; and with anticipations and rehearsals of such. What makes the issue elusive, I think, is that we "sense" pleasure only through an elaborately constructed illusion – typical of our tendency to represent things to ourselves as though they were more coherent than they really are.

We indulge in such illusions even when we say the seemingly simplest things of the form "*I feel xxx*". These exemplify a "single agent" concept of mind, an illusion of coherency that denies that within the mind different agencies play different roles at the same moment. For example, one part may be rewarded for disciplining another. Yet if, as I suppose, the pleasure phenomenon does indeed involve a complex web of different activities, we still need to explain why they seem phenomenologically to have so much in common.

Here is one conjecture: what was initially common to all those activities was only a metapsychological feature – *they were just the ones most subject to being disturbed by the "noise" of other members of the Society of Mind.* This would create an ecological niche, within that Society, for the emergence of a special brain center that, when activated by any of them, tends to depress all the others. (One does not so welcome the offer of one kind of pleasure, while involved with another.) Once such a center comes into existence, that very fact would facilitate the formation, in a growing mind, of a concept or belief in the commonality of the mechanisms associated with it.

A second conjecture: such a centralization would better enable each member of the mental society to be able to tell when it has done something to satisfy a need of another – without having to understand which one, or any of the what or why of it. But note how my use of the word "satisfy" betrays my intention by intimating that same unintended uniformity. It is perhaps this betrayal that fools us all into thinking it a tautology, unworthy of study, to ask "*why do we like pleasure*".

Seymour Papert has suggested to me yet another, more sociobiological conjecture about how evolution might have gathered these ingredients together and provided them with a single, common, output. It would make it easier for a mother to tell when she has satisfied her child's need of the moment, without having to learn specific signs for each such need. Similarly, this would help one person tell when he is convincing another, and so forth. All that is accomplished by attaching a suitable collection of different internal processes to one single "consummatory act" – to use Tinbergen's term.

13 My daughter Julie watched "yields truth" for a while and then said, "*well, it's not exactly a paradox, but it does keep saying that it's true, back and forth.*"

14 *Displacement.* Lorenz [21] and Tinbergen [22] frequently observed peculiar, seemingly pointless behaviors when an animal is poised between fight and flight. What better time to consider negotiating? So, one might *a priori* expect to find ambiguities in the primordial germs of social sign-systems.

15 I don't mean all this to seem pessimistic. It is not necessary, in understanding something, to have all one knows about it active in the mind at one time. One *does* need to have access to fragments of maps, at various levels of detail, of what one knows. The thesis of Kuipers [23], which proposes a theory of how a person's knowledge of a city might be represented in computational terms, might be re-interpreted as a metaphor for how minds might deal with their own knowledge.

16 *Theories.* There is, I think, a special problem in making theories about the psychology of adults, in whom cultural evolution has had its full interaction with individual and organic evolution. Consider that complex of laughing, smiling, good-natured interactions called "good humor", in which we as often enjoy engaging and surprising frame-shifts of high quality as we enjoy nonsense worthy only of being

suppressed. The joking ambiance is used as much to develop analogies as to restrict them – and my distinction between positive and negative seems to fall apart. If anything remains uniform in the different varieties of humor, it is perhaps only that highlighting of manipulating unexpected frame-shifts – but in a bewildering variety of ways. Does this mean the theory is refuted? I think not, but to explain why I must digress to discuss "adult development."

No, a baby theory is not necessarily refuted by an adult counterexample. Most psychologists have not sufficiently appreciated the full power of an adult intellect to re-construct itself – to exploit and rearrange its earlier components. Stage after stage of intricate developments are superimposed, in which both internal and cultural influences modify earlier ones. This process would be complicated enough if it were spontaneous – that is, if only internal factors were involved. But much of it is also socially institution-alized; everyone in the culture "knows" which concerns, and which manners of behavior, are "appropriate" for four-year-olds, nine-year-olds, college students, or professors of philosophy.

The most powerful theoreticians of developmental psychology have struggled to untangle the different principles and forms of these influences; still only the surface has been touched. We yet know far too little to confidently declare that such-and-such a behavioral exhibition either illustrates or refutes a given psychogenetic hypothesis. In my view, the most profitable activity in the present era is to experiment, not on people to see if an hypothesis about the mind is true or false, but on computers to see if a proposed theory-fragment can be made part of a system that shows mind-like activity. To be sure, this can never show, by itself, that the theory in question then must resemble a human mechanism – but it seems hardly worth trying to verify *that* until a theory shows signs of meeting a first condition – that it be capable of contributing to life-like activity. In short, we are unlikely to discover much of that which is, until we discover more of that which could be.

[17] *Attachment.* Of course, the sociobiology of reproduction is far more complicated than suggested here. Provisions for child-raising conflict in many ways with provisions for gene-dissemination. Many different sociobiological islands of stability exist, both potentially and actually.

An *"acquisition envelope" hypothesis:* Here is a different example of how both individual and social development might be influenced by a genetic control of a learning-rate. It is a commonplace observation that persons who learn second languages after adolescence rarely acquire the phonetic competence of native speakers; they rarely come to speak the new language "without an accent". When told to pronounce something "like *this*, not like *that*," they seem to sense too little difference to know what changes to make. I conjecture that this reflects a post-pubertal change in a brain mechanism – and may illustrate an important way for genetic control to affect cognitive development.

More precisely, the conjecture is that (i) phonetic learning occurs in some particular brain structure whose capacity to learn new discriminations is (ii) shut off by a genetic mechanism linked to pubertal changes. *It is linked to puberty because that is the biological moment when one's role shifts from learning to teaching.* Its "evolutionary purpose" is to prevent the parent from learning the child's language; this makes the child learn the adult language.

After all, a young parent's principal goal is not language instruction – it is communi-cation. If it were easy for the parent to adopt the child's idiosyncratic phonology, that's what would happen! But then the parent would learn the child's language – and the child would have less drive, or opportunity, to learn the adult's. And, over the span of generations, it would be hard for any common social language to develop at all!

When we talk of innate vs. acquired aspects of development, we must face the problem of encoding for structures whose acquisition cannot be genetically anticipated – e.g., details of cognitive or linguistic structure. Our idea is first to look instead for ways for genetics to affect directly the "acquisition envelopes" – *the control structures that mediate how things are learned.* The foregoing hypothesis illustrates, I think, one way that brain genetics might circumvent the complexity of devising direct constraints on the representations of not-yet-acquired cognitive structures.

Artificial Intelligence Laboratory, M.I.T.

REFERENCES

[0] Freud, Sigmund: *Jokes and Their Relation to the Unconscious*, 1905, (transl. Strachey) Standard Edition, vol. 8, Hogarth Press, 1957.

[1] Doyle, Jon: *Truth Maintenance Systems for Problem Solving*, M.I.T., Artificial Intelligence Laboratory, AI/TR–419, January 1978.

[2] Kornfeld, William A.: *Using Parallel Processes for Problem Solving*, M.I.T., Artificial Intelligence Laboratory, AI Memo 561, Cambridge, Ma., December 1979.

[3] Korzybski, Alfred: *Science and Sanity*, Science Press, Lancaster, Pa., 1941.

[4a] Minsky, Marvin: *A Framework for Representing Knowledge*, M.I.T., Artificial Intelligence Laboratory, AI Memo 306, Cambridge, Ma., June 1974.

[4b] Minsky, Marvin: 'A Framework for Representing Knowledge' (condensed version), *The Psychology of Computer Vision*, Edited by P. H. Winston, McGraw-Hill, New York, 1975.

[5] Minsky, Marvin: 'Plain Talk About Neurodevelopmental Epistemology,' *Proceedings of the Fifth International Joint Conference on Artificial Intelligence*, Cambridge, Ma., August 1977. Condensed version in *Artificial Intelligence*, edited by Winston and Brown, Vol. 1, MIT Press, 1979.

[6] Minsky, Marvin: 'K-lines: A Theory of Memory,' *Cognitive Science* 4 (1980), 117–133.

[7] Wittgenstein, L.: *Philosophical Investigations*, Blackwell, Oxford, 1953.

[8] Winston, P. H.: 'Learning Structural Descriptions by Examples,' *Psychology of Computer Vision*, Edited by P. H. Winston, McGraw-Hill, New York, 1975.

[9] Freud, Sigmund: *Humour*, 1927, (transl. Strachey) Standard Edition, Vol. 21, Hogarth Press, 1957, 161–166.

[10] Davis, Randall: 'Meta-rules: Reasoning about Control,' to appear in *Artificial Intelligence* 0000.

[11] Doyle, Jon: *A Model for Deliberation, Action and Introspection*, Ph.D Thesis, M.I.T., Artificial Intelligence Laboratory, Cambridge, Ma., August 1980.

[12] Minsky, Marvin: 'Matter, Mind and Models,'.*Proceedings of IFIP Congress 1965*, May, 1965, 45–49. Reprinted in *Semantic Information Processing*, MIT Press, 1968.

[13] Schank, Roger: 'Language and Memory,' *Cognitive Science* 4 (1980), 243–284.

[14] Newell, A, Shaw, J. C., and Simon, H. A.: *Preliminary Description of General Problem Solving Program*, (GPS-1), CIP Working Paper No. 7, December 1957.

[15] Minsky, Marvin: *Heuristic Aspects of the Artificial Intelligence Problem*, Lincoln Laboratory, M.I.T., Lexington, Mass. Group Report No. 34–55. ASTIA Doc. No. AS236885, December 1956.

[16] Winston, Patrick H.: *Learning by Understanding Analogies*, M.I.T., Artificial Intelligence Laboratory, AI memo 520. Cambridge, Ma., June 1979.

[17] Papert, Seymour: *Mindstorms: Children, Computers and Powerful Ideas*, Basic Books, New York, 1980.

[18] Sussman, Gerald J.: *A Computational Model of Skill Acquisition*, Ph.D. Thesis, M.I.T., Artificial Intelligence Laboratory, IA/TR–297, Cambridge, Ma., August 1973.

[19] Goldstein, Ira P.: *Understanding Simple Picture Programs*, Ph.D. Thesis, M.I.T., Artificial Intelligence Laboratory, IA/TR–294, Cambridge, Ma., April 1974.

[20] Thomas, Lewis: 'The Scrambler in the Mind,' *The Medusa and the Snail*, Bantam Books, New York, 1980.

[21] Lorenz, Konrad: *King Solomon's Ring*, Thomas J. Crowell, New York, 1961.

[22] Tinbergen, Niko: *The Study of Instinct*, Oxford University Press, London, 1951.

[23] Kuipers, Benjamin: *Representing Knowledge of Large-Scale Space*, Ph.D. Thesis, M.I.T., Artificial Intelligence Laboratory, IA/TR–418, Cambridge, Ma., July 1978.

WILLIAM A. MARTIN†

A LOGICAL FORM BASED ON THE STRUCTURAL DESCRIPTIONS OF EVENTS*

1. INTRODUCTION

Facilitating the precise interpretation of statements first made in natural language — this has been the role of mathematical notations like predicate calculus and lambda calculus. Their use has been for the clarification of argument. They were faulted for inadequate precision or the introduction of paradox, never for forcing too much precision. Formal languages are precise, but selective in what can be easily expressed. It has always been understood that quantifiers like ∀ and ∃ only modeled some aspects of a system of natural language quantifiers. However, they captured the most useful properties very neatly.

When one turns from the refinement of argument to the modeling of human behavior in processing natural language, or to the creation of computer programs which respond appropriately to natural language inputs, then the requirements for a notation also change. It is desirable to have the option of leaving some traditional distinctions unmade, and at the same time to make other distinctions.

Here I will present some ideas about an alternative notation which arise from work in computational linguistics and artificial intelligence. Space does not permit me to address a wide spectrum of issues, but I have tried to cover some distinctions which are traditionally of interest to linguists and philosophers. My goal is to make the traditional distinctions, but in a way better suited to language processing.

It is widely understood that computer scientists deal more with issues of process than do mathematicians, linguists, and philosophers. Thus it is thought that computer science might have something to say about difficulties of parsing and the like. It is less well recognized that computer science also deals with representation. Indeed, the key to successful processing is often thought to lie in having the correct representation of the problem. Thus, I begin by developing some ideas about the description of structures.

2. ROLES

The concept of a *role* has been introduced frequently by designers of know-

201

L. Vaina and J. Hintikka (eds.), Cognitive Constraints on Communication, 201–228.
© 1984 *by D. Reidel Publishing Company.*

ledge representation languages taking the form of a semantic network (e.g. Martin 1979, Fahlman 1979, Brachman 1978). The notion of role is illustrated by the simplified semantic network in Figure 1.

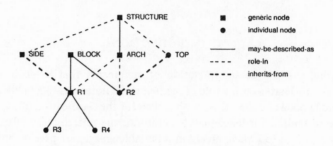

Fig. 1. Simplified structural description of an arch.

This network has two kinds of nodes and three kinds of links. Hollow circles represent *generic nodes*, solid circles represent *individual nodes*. A generic node is the locus of a generic description of some type of entity and serves the function of what others have termed a frame, unit, or concept. An individual node differs from a generic node only in that while there may be any number of entities of the type described by a generic node, there is *at most* one entity which meets the description of an individual node. We say "at most one", because the network may contain information that an individual meeting that node's description doesn't exist.

The description of a node is inferred from the rest of the network by tracing out the links. Nodes in the *structural description* of a given node, e.g. R1 in ARCH, are linked to the given node by *role-in* links. These nodes are termed *roles* in the description of the given node. As illustrated in Figure 1, a role may be either generic or individual.

One node, e.g. ARCH, *may be described as* another node, e.g. STRUCTURE, if for any individual which would meet the description of the first node we are willing to describe it by the second node. We are willing to describe a SQUARE as a RECTANGLE because a SQUARE is defined as a RECTANGLE with four equal sides. The relation holds by definition. SQUARE and RECTANGLE are said to be related on the basis of *analytic* knowledge. More commonly our willingness to describe one node as another is based on assumptions about the world, e.g. that COW may be described as DOMESTIC-ANIMAL requires us to know that the world doesn't contain wild cows (at least not enough of them to affect our description of the generic cow). Such knowledge of the world is termed *synthetic* knowledge. Our willingness to describe one node as another is generally based on a combination of analytic and synthetic knowledge. The analytic/synthetic distinction is not a basic distinction in our network.

The *may-be-described-as* relation models the subset relation. Instead of saying that a square may be described as a rectangle, we could have introduced notation to say that the set of all squares is a subset of the set of all rectangles. However, we prefer not to introduce, as a fundamental construct, the notion of the set of all entities meeting a certain description. We will work instead with generic nodes (as intensions) and individual nodes (as extensions). Quine (1970) points out that a system like ours still allows reasoning of the form done with the Boolean operations of set theory, without introducing Russell's paradox. It also lets us side-step problems arising in the discussion of non-existent entities.

Using these conventions we may interpret Figure 1 as saying that an ARCH may be described as a STRUCTURE. Its structural description consists of an individual node, R2, which may be described as a BLOCK and inherits the description of a TOP, a generic, R1, which may be described as a BLOCK and inherits the description of a SIDE, and two individual nodes, R3 and R4, which may be described as the generic R1.

We make the convention that since R3 and R4 may be described as R1, and R1 is a role in ARCH, then R3 and R4 are also roles in ARCH.

Note that the roles of a node correspond to the slots of a frame in a theory like Minsky's (1975), as implemented in FRL by Goldstein and Roberts (1977). However, there is a significant difference. Since slots are not frames themselves, slots and frames are not described by the same conventions. But since roles are nodes, they may be described by applying the node description conventions recursively. The ideas in this paper could also be formulated representing frames with modes and slots with links. (1)

2.1 Structure and Context

A second point to note is that this network does not deal with contextual problems by assuming a set of objects called contexts or partitions and then somehow stipulating for each node and link what contexts or partitions it is present in. Instead, the position is taken that roles actually allow a more natural modeling of the phenomena partitions were designed to model. For example, Figure 2 shows how Hendrix (1978) would represent the fact that

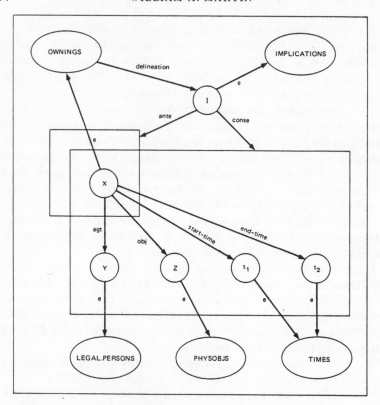

Fig. 2. The delineation theorem of ownings.

legal persons can own physical objects. In this figure rectangles (including the square) represent partitions, ovals represent sets, and circles represent individuals. An individual or set is in a partition if its representing circle or oval is in the rectangle representing that partition. In this figure the individual, I, is an implication that any individual owning, X, has an individual agent, Y, which is a legal person, an individual object, Z, which is a physical object, an individual start-time, t_1, which is a time, and an individual end-time, t_2, which is also a time.

This same information is shown in Figure 3, using the notation presented here. The key differences between the representations in Figures 2 and 3 are:

(a)(i) Figure 2 shows the set of ownings. To indicate properties which much be true of every member of this set, an individual implication I is created. I is related to OWNINGS by the link, *delineation*. The antecedent of

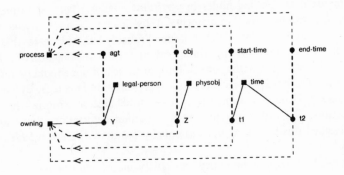

Fig. 3.

I is a partition containing an individual, X. By convention this individual, X, in the antecedent of I is the typical member of ownings. The individuals in the structural description of X are in the partition which is the consequent of I.

(ii) In Figure 3, the node, owning, represents the typical member. As a generic representing the typical owning it does not need to be contextually constrained. Thus, it is not taken to be a role in any other node. Part of the complexity of Figure 2 is avoided by making the typical member a primitive notion (generic node) rather than constructing it as an individual which exists only in an abstract space (the antecedent and consequent of an implication).

(b)(i) In Figure 2 the individuals Y, Z, t_1, and t_2 which are in the structural description of X are given context by being placed in the partition which is the consequent of I.

(ii) In Figure 3 the individuals Y, Z, t_1, and t_2 which are in the structural description of X are given context by being made roles in X itself. Thus a typical member serves as the context of its own structural description.

(c) In Figure 2, the individuals X, Z, t_1 and t_2 are related to X by links labeled with "case relation names" of "slot names". Thus, as mentioned above, a distinction is made between nodes and slots. By contrast in Figure 3, agt, obj, start-time, and end-time are themselves nodes and can be described just like any other node. It is perhaps worth pointing out that the logical organization of Figure 3 does not prevent memory from being physically organized so that given *owning* and *agt* one can retrieve node Y at least as quickly as it can be done with the organization of Figure 2.

In summary, Figure 2 takes as primary the notion of *context* and implements it by placing nodes in *partitions*. Figure 3 takes as primary the notion of *structure* and implements it by making a node a *role* in the structural description of another node. Probably all will agree that both structure and context are important notions for the organization of information. The question is whether one or both of these notions should be reflected by the most primitive constructs of a representation language. By choosing just context, Hendrix is forced to go to a formal abstract notion – he picked implication – in order to represent a structural description. Some authors have avoided this by taking both as equally primitive (Fahlman 1979, Hayes 1977).

Figure 4 shows how an entity can satisfy more than one individual node

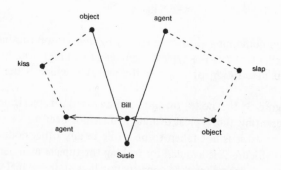

Fig. 4. Bill kisses Susie and Susie slaps Bill.

at the same time. This figure specifies that whatever is described as Bill is also described as the agent of kiss and the object of slap. This entity is the individual agent in the kiss at the same time that it is the individual object in the slap. (In this figure I have left out the links to generic nodes and the role-in links of Bill and Susie. I will continue to leave out links which are not the focus of discussion in order to simplify the figures.)

2.2 Inheritance

Fahlman (1979) has pointed out an interesting question which arises in the interpretation of structures like that shown in Figure 1, the structural description of an arch. If this figure is a description of the structure of the generic arch, then it should be possible to put this description into correspondence with the description of an individual arch, say ARCH-1. Figure 5

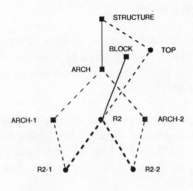

Fig. 5.

shows a fragment of Figure 1 extended to include the corresponding fragments of two individual arches, ARCH-1 and ARCH-2.

The dotted links from R2-1 to R2 and R2-2 to R2 specify inheritance. In
this case R2-1 and R2-2 inherit all the description of R2 except the role-in
link from R2 to ARCH. This role-in link is overridden by their own role-in
links.

Inheritance links specify the inheritance of all description which is not
explicitly overridden. *May-be-described-as* links indicate an alternative
description. One might think that the inheritance links are not needed in
Figure 5, that they could be replaced with may-be-described-as links. However, this leads to a problem pointed out by Fahlman.

Suppose we were to say that since R2-1 is the top of an individual arch,
ARCH-1, it may be described as R2, the top of an arch. That is, when one
node is described as another, its roles are described as the corresponding roles
of the other. Doing this gets one into difficulty. To see this note that we may
ask "which individual block in the generic arch is the top", and the answer is
R2. R2 is taken as an individual node and clearly it represents a single one of
the three blocks comprising an arch. But now suppose that nodes ARCH-1
and ARCH-2 describe arches in the real world. Then R2-1 and R2-2 describe
the tops of these arches, and since R2-1 and R2-2 may be described as R2,
R2 describes the tops of these arches. Thus, it would seem that R2 does not,
in fact, describe a single individual. The reader will no doubt be able to
articulate to his satisfaction what is going on in this example. We hope to
capture this by expressing and invoking a rather far-reaching principle of
interpretation.

Accordingly, we will stipulate:

Every individual node, R, must be a role in some other node, N. Any entity, r, described by the node, R, is only taken to be an individual with respect to the entity, n, described by N. The only exception is that the real world is not in the structure of anything.

One effect of this stipulation is to make the role-in link an essential part of any description of an individual. Now by using inheritance links instead of may-be-described-as links from R2-1 to R2 and from R2-2 to R2, we can override the role-in link from R2 to ARCH and thus preserve R2 from describing these individuals.

The essential difference between inheritance and alternative description is that an inheriting node can override a criterial part of an inherited description, so that the inherited description no longer picks out the same individuals. By contrast, alternative description preserves the integrity of individuals. It lets one get a different description of the same individual.

2.3 Making Every Individual Node a Role

This section will touch briefly on the philosophical ramifications of making every individual node a role. In the Tarskian (1944) view of English semantics correspondence between descriptions and the world is described in terms of propositions. A proposition is true if it corresponds to the world and false otherwise. Propositions are either atomic or compound — formed by conjunction, etc. The truth or falsity of atomic propositions must be given. The truth or falsity of compound propositions is then determined from the truth or falsity of their components by applying rules of composition associated with their connectives.

In the theory proposed here, discussion of correspondence between descriptions and the world is not limited to propositions. We can discuss correspondence for any individual, proposition or not (2). However, the key difference is that since every description of an individual must include a description of the structure containing it, it doesn't make sense to ask for the truth or falsity of atomic propositions independently of the truth or falsity of the structures containing them. The view presented here shifts away from *composition* to a system which places more weight on *decomposition*. One starts with a node representing the world and structurally decomposes it in various ways. The parts of these decompositions are then further decomposed in turn to any desired depth. This produces a structural hierarchy of descriptions. This structural hierarchy is complemented by the abstraction hierarchy of descriptions produced by the may-be-described-as links.

The importance of this approach comes out if one believes that there are, in fact, individuals which have no description which does not depend criterially on their being part of a structure. This realization has caused some philosophers to deny that such individuals are entities at all. This view is put forward by Benacerraf (1965) in debating the existence of numbers:

> Therefore, numbers are not objects at all, because in giving the properties (that is, necessary and sufficient) of numbers you merely characterize an *abstract structure* – and the distinction lies in the fact that the "elements" of the structure have no properties other than those relating them to other "elements" of the same structure. If we identify an abstract structure with a system of relations (in intension, of course, or else with the set of all relations in extension isomorphic to a given system of relations), we get arithmetic elaborating the properties of the "less-than" relation, or of all systems of objects (that is, *concrete* structures) exhibiting that abstract structure. That a system of objects exhibits the structure of the integers implies that the elements of that system have some properties not dependent on structure. It must be possible to individuate those objects independently of the role they play in that structure. But this is precisely what cannot be done with the numbers. To *be* the number 3 is no more or less than to be preceded by 2, 1, and possibly 0, and to be followed by 4, 5, and so forth. And to *be* the number 4 is no more and no less than to be preceded by 3, 2, 1, and possibly 0, and to be followed by . . . *Any* object can *play the role of* 3; that is, any object can be the third element in some progression. What is peculiar to 3 is that it defines that role – not by being a paradigm of any object which plays it, but by representing the relation that any third member of a progression bears to the rest of the progression.
>
> Arithmetic is therefore the science that elaborates the abstract structure that all progressions have in common merely in virtue of being progressions. It is not a science concerned with particular objects – the numbers. The search for which independently identifiable particular objects the numbers really are (sets? Julius Caesars?) is a misguided one.
>
> On this view many things that puzzled us in this paper seem to fall into place. Why so many interpretations of number theory are possible without any being uniquely singled out becomes obvious. There is no unique set of objects that are the numbers. Number theory is the elaboration of the properties of *all* structures of the order type of the numbers. The number words do not have single referents. Furthermore, the reason identification of numbers with objects works wholesale but fails utterly object by object is the fact that the theory is elaborating an abstract structure and not the properties of independent individuals, any one of which could be characterized without reference to its relations to the rest. Only when we are considering a particular sequence as being, not the numbers, but *of the structure of the numbers* does the question of which element is, or rather *corresponds to*, 3 begin to make any sense. (Reprinted with permission from Paul Benacerraf, 'What Numbers Could Not Be', *The Philosophical Review* 74 (1965), 47–73.)

While I agree with Benacerraf's analysis of numbers, I am unwilling to therefore deny that numbers are entities. In a semantic network it is simplest to have nodes represent entities and one needs nodes for anything which will be described, including numbers. (3) Rather than deny that numbers are entities I prefer to put all entities on the same footing as numbers — to require the description of any individual to describe the structure in which it is used. For some individuals, like numbers, the structure in which they are used will dominate their description. Other entities will have a complex structural description of their own.

3. REFERENCE AND DEFINITE DESCRIPTIONS

The above quote by Benacerraf deals with numbers in part because the philosophy of mathematics has historically been the main proving ground for formal representation systems. Our concern here, however, is with the logical structure of English sentences, and enough constructs have now been presented to permit a treatment of some well known phenomena. We begin with a discussion of definite descriptions.

3.1 Co-Referent Descriptions

Russell's (1905) analysis of a singular definite description required that there be a unique object satisfying the description in order for the expression to denote anything, and hence it fails to account for the successful reference of a noun phrase like "the clock" in

> Did you wind the clock?

The problem is that "the clock" only picks out an individual clock given the context of a particular use of the expression. Thus the expression picks out an individual only when paired with a description of the context of use. It is widely recognized that some method of describing this context has to be made available.

The general importance of context in forming descriptions of individuals may be seen in Strawson's essay, *Individuals* (1959). Strawson begins with a discussion relevant to the above difficulty with definite descriptions:

When shall we say that a hearer knows what particular is being referred to by a speaker? Consider first the following case. A speaker tells a story which he claims to be factual. It begins, 'A man and a boy were standing by a fountain,' and it continues: 'The man had a drink.' Shall we say that the hearer knows which or what particular is being referred to by the subject expression in the second sentence? We might say so. For, of a certain range of two particulars the words 'the man' serves to distinguish the one being referred to, by means of a description which applies only to him. But though this is, in a weak sense, a case of identification, I shall call it only a *story-relative* or, for short, a *relative* identification. For it is identification only relative to a range of particulars (a range of two members) which is itself identified only as the range of particulars being talked about by the speaker. That is to say, the hearer, hearing the second sentence, knows *which* particular creature is being referred to *of the two particular creatures being talked about by the speaker*; but he does not, without this qualification, know what particular creature is being referred to. The identification is within a certain story told by a certain speaker. It is identification within his story but not identification with history.

We need a requirement stringent enough to eliminate relative identification. The hearer, in the example, is able to place the particular referred to within the picture painted by the speaker. This means that in a sense he can place the particular in his own general picture of the world. For he can place the speaker, and hence the speaker's picture, in that general picture of his own. But he cannot place the figures, without the frame of the speaker's picture in his own general picture of the world. For this reason the full requirement of hearer's identification is not satisfied. (Reprinted from *Individuals* by P. F. Strawson (Methuen 1959).)

In the above passage every description is in some context; the hearer has a description of the speaker in his (the hearer's) general picture of the world. To this description of the speaker is tied the speaker's story. To the speaker's story are tied the descriptions of the individuals. What the hearer lacks are other descriptions of the same individuals which are tied directly to his general picture of the world.

Following this line of thought, the sentence "did you wind the clock" might cause a machine to create a structure which would look in part like Figure 6. The nodes *clock-1* and *the-clock-1* will be termed *co-descriptors*, because they both describe the same individual. The term co-description is chosen over co-reference or co-denotation because no implication of speaker intentions or existence of the individual described is intended.

In presenting Figure 6 we assume that the sentence "did you wind the clock" undergoes some sort of lexical and structural analysis. This analysis

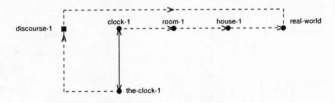

Fig. 6. Co-description between clock-1 and the-clock-1

results in a description which will be termed a *sentence structure*. The node *the-clock-1* in Figure 6 is a sentence structure co-descriptor of the words "the clock" in the sentence "did you wind the clock". It is during the listener's process of analysis that he decides to "understand" the description *the-clock-1* by making it a co-descriptor of *clock-1*. Had the phrase "a clock" been used, the listener might well have chosen not to find a co-descriptor of the corresponding node, *a-clock-1* (particularly if he didn't wind any clocks).

In Figure 6 the relationship between *clock-1* and *the-clock-1* is shown to be absolutely symmetrical. Yet one intuitively feels that clock-1 is somehow more fundamental than *the-clock-1*. That, for example, *clock-1* should be the "value" of *the-clock-1*. Indeed, it should be, if we view the purpose of evaluation to be the discovery or creation of more useful descriptions of entities – e.g. 2 + 2 being for most purposes a less useful description than 4. It is the description *clock-1* which is already tied through sense data to the world. *Clock-1* is the most useful description for most purposes (but not, for example, for understanding the anaphoric references discussed by Webber (1978)). The difference between *clock-1* and *the-clock-1* is captured in Figure 6 not by the links between them but by the structures in which they occur. Procedures which operate on such data structures must have the goal of finding co-referent descriptions which meet certain criteria, such as being a single number, or being a role in a certain structure. It is assumed that data structures like the one in Figure 6 will be operated on by procedures which are either implicitly or explicitly so goal directed.

3.2 Nodes in Sentence Structure

To establish the network in Figure 6 the hearer must be able to make the inference that in *discourse-1, the-clock* would refer to *clock-1*. But surely not every occurrence of *the-clock* in discourse-1 will refer to clock-1. Rather, it is the only occurrence in an instance of the sentence "did you wind the clock". Figure 6 needs to be amended. One way to amend in it is shown in Figure 7.

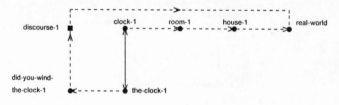

Fig. 7.

(The sections to follow will argue that a slightly more complex solution is needed.) Here *the-clock-1* is an instance of *the-clock* which occurs in an instance of *did-you-wind-the-clock* which occurs in discourse-1.

In her study of anaphora, Webber also points out the importance of recording the sentence in which an expression was used. Consider the sentences:

(3.1)   Wendy bought a yellow T-shirt that Bruce had liked.
(3.2)   It cost twenty dollars.

Webber points out that an appropriate description of the entity referred to by "it" in the second sentence is not "the yellow T-shirt that Bruce had liked" since sentence 3.1 is true even if Bruce had liked several T-shirts (and both the speaker and the listener were aware of the fact). Nor is it "the yellow T-shirt that Bruce had liked and Wendy bought", since sentence 3.2 can be true even if Wendy had bought several such T-shirts. What is an appropriate description for this entity is something like "the yellow T-shirt that Bruce had liked and that Wendy bought and that was mentioned in sentence 3.1." This interpretation is achieved by a structure like that in Figure 7.

3.3 *Referential and Attributive Use of Definite Descriptions*

Donnellan (1966) has suggested that definite descriptions like "the clock" have two uses, referential and attributive. What we have done above captures Donnellan's referential use. Fortunately, the distinction which Donnellan wants to make is one which our development can easily be expanded to handle.

Explaining his distinction, Donnellan says

I will call the two uses of definite descriptions I have in mind the attributive use and the referential use. A speaker who uses a definite description attributively in an assertion states something about whoever or whatever is the so-and-so. A speaker who uses a definite description referentially in an assertion, on the other hand, uses the description to enable his audience to pick out whom or what he is talking about and states something about that person or thing. In the first case the definite description might be said to occur essentially, for the speaker wishes to assert something about whatever or whoever fits that description; but in the referential use the definite description is merely one tool for doing a certain job — calling attention to a person or thing — and in general any other device for doing the same job, another description or a name, would so as well. In the attributive use, the attribute of being the so-and-so is all important, while it is not in the referential use.

To recapitualate, attributive use asserts something about whoever or whatever is the so-and-so. Referential use enables the user to pick out whom or what is being talked about. The distinction is brought out nicely by two sentences used by Moore (1973).

(3.3)   The President has been married since 1945.   (*referential*)
(3.4)   The President has lived in the White House since 1800. (*attributive*)

Sentence 3.3 refers to the person who is currently President, while sentence 3.4 says that since 1800 it has been true of whoever was President that he lived in the White House. Both of these sentences have both attributive and referential readings, but in each case the listener can reject one reading as counterfactual.

3.4 Procedural Interpretation of Descriptions

In Figures 8 and 9 our representation has been expanded to capture the distinction between attributive and referential use (4). The structural difference between these two figures is that in the referential use, (Figure 8) *the-President-1* is a role in discourse-1 and is co-descriptive with a role, *President-1*, in the discourse, while in the attributive use, (Figure 9), it is a role in The-President-lives-in-the-White-House. Computationally the decision for referential over attributive interpretation amounts to the decision of what to make a substructure a role in. In order for this structural difference to produce the difference in interpretation noted by Donnellan, it is necessary to introduce a specific procedure for determining the truth of descriptions.

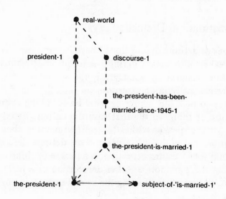

Fig. 8.   Referential use of *the President.*

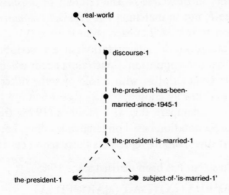

Fig. 9. Attributive use of *the President*.

We will refer to an individual node as *true* if it can be put into correspondence with exactly one individual in the world; otherwise it is false. This
notion of truth as correspondence with reality is an old one (see Eaton 1924)
although it has long been eclipsed by the school of thought which restricts
truth to propositions. We stipulate as a part of our theory that *the semantic
interpretation of a description proceeds top down, as a structural decomposition*. This will produce the desired interpretation of Figures 8 and 9.

Ignoring issues of tense not crucial to the current argument, we interpret
"the President has lived in the White House since 1800" to mean "between
1800 and now x is true" where x is "the President lives in the White House".
Now comes the key point. This is true if we can pick any time between 1800
and now and "the President lives in the White House" is true at that time. For
this to be true it must be possible to pick referents for *the-President-1* and
the-White-House-1 which have the right relationship at that time. The central
fact to note is that the truth of the higher statement is not dependent on the
behavior of any one individual. Rather the behavior of several individuals is
such that at any time the statement is true. This is the whole point of
Donnellan's remarks. So far as this statement is concerned it doesn't really
matter who is filling the role of President. In fact, we can go even farther. In
the past the President has been killed and it takes a while to swear in the new
President. During this time there is no President, yet 3.4 is still true. It seems
that 3.4 is true if there usually is a President, and when there is, he lives in
the White House.

In contrast to the attributive case just covered, in the referential case, *the president-1* is a role in *discourse-1*. The referent of *president-1* is picked in matching *discourse-1*, not in matching *The-President-is-married-1*. Therefore, we are not at liberty to re-pick it at each point in time (5).

In summary, the semantic interpretation of a description proceeds top down, as a structural decomposition. Constraints occur when one of the roles of a description is co-descriptive with a role of some other description and thus not free to be arbitrarily chosen.

It is instructive to compare this with Moore's (1975) treatment of these two sentences using a notation based on lambda binding. Letting *T-A-T* name a predicate "true at time" Moore represents these sentences as

(3.5)   The President has been married since 1945.

(3.6) $\ll$LAMBDA (?X) (T-A-T (MARRIED ?X)
          $<$EVERY (?T) (AFTER ?T 1945)$>$)$>$
          $<$THE (?Y) (PRES ?Y)$>\gg$

(3.7)   The President has lived in the White House since 1800.

(3.8) $<$T-A-T
          (LIVE-IN $<$THE (?X) (PRES ?X)$>$ W-H)
          $<$EVERY (?T) (AFTER ?T 1800)$>\gg$

Expression 3.8 says that for every time in the set specified by $<$EVERY (?T) (AFTER ?T 1800)$>$ the expression $<$THE (?X) (PRES ?X)$>$ *has a unique value, say* X, such that (LIVE-IN X W-H) is true at that time.

Now in the case of 3.5 we want to pick the President at the current time and then use this value in an expression like 3.8. That is, in 3.8 we pick the time first, but in 3.6 we want to pick *the President* first. Since this notation, like LISP, is evaluated outside in, *the President* is picked first by lambda abstracting it to an outer expression.

We achieve by a pointer to a co-descriptive expression what Moore achieves by lambda abstraction. Is there a significant difference? We claim that our notation should be more effective in minimizing the difference in the representation and interpretation of the two cases. In our notation one need not worry about the referential/attributive distinction until the *the-President* node is reached. Also in our notation the referential/attributive decision can be delayed by just not making the role link. This is important because in most sentences, e.g. "The president has owned a terrier since 1977" the listener will not be able to distinguish between the two readings. If a later sentence requires the listener to make a distinction, all he has to do is add the role link. Also, the degree of semantic distinction between the two readings depends on how much is known about the discourse co-descriptor. This addresses an issue mentioned in Partee (1972)

having a particular individual in mind (the 'referential' case) and knowing nothing about an individual other than some descriptive phrase (the 'attributive' case) may be just two extremes on a continuum of 'vividness'. One may consider, for instance, the case of a detective tracking down a criminal and obtaining more and more clues, including finger-prints, voice recordings, photographs of varying clarity, etc. It is not at all clear at what point the detective, who may be described as 'looking for the man who did so-and-so' stops looking for 'whoever it is that did so-and-so' and starts looking for a particular individual.

3.5 Subject Co-Descriptors

Both Figures 8 and 9 employ co-description between a *the-President* node and a *subject-of-x* node in order to indicate the role played by the noun phrase in the verb. More evidence for this structure can be supplied in the form of an ambiguity brought out by verb phrase deletion.

Sag (1976) gives a number of examples to argue that verb phrase deletion occurs under identity of structure. For example, the following sentences are two, not four ways ambiguous.

(3.9)   John likes flying planes, and Bill does too.

(3.10)   The chickens are ready to eat, and the children are too.

Now consider the following sentence (Partee 1978)

(3.11)   *The prosecutor* believed that he would win the case, and so did *the defense attorney.*

The missing verb phrase can be understood in two ways. Either the defense attorney believed that he, the defense attorney, would win, or the defense attorney believed that the prosecutor would win. Assuming some version of deletion under identical structure to be operative, and assuming referential interpretation, these two readings argue that the phrase "the prosecutor believed that he would win" can have either of the structures shown in Figures 10 and 11. In Figure 10, *he-1* is co-descriptive with the subject role, so when the defense attorney replaces the prosecutor as a co-descriptor of the subject, the co-descriptor of *he-1* changes. This structure has been expressed with lambda calculus as

$$\lambda(x) \ (x \text{ believed that } x \text{ would win}).$$

In Figure 11, on the other hand, *he-1* is co-descriptive with *the-prosecutor-1*,

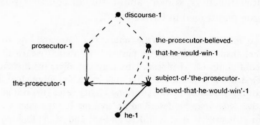

Fig. 10. Structure of "the prosecutor believed that he would win" leading to "the defense attorney believed that the defense attorney would win".

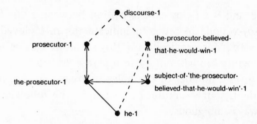

Fig. 11. Structure of "the prosecutor believed that he would win" leading to "the defense attorney believed that the prosecutor would win".

and can stay so even when *the-defense-attorney-1* replaces *the-prosecutor-1* as co-descriptor of the subject. Partee (1978) has termed this *pragmatic anaphora*, that in Figure 10, *bound variable anaphora*.

It is fair to ask whether, in Figure 11, *he-1* shouldn't be co-descriptive with the discourse role *prosecutor-1* instead of the sentence role *the-prosecutor-1*. The trouble with this is that the ambiguity also occurs with attributive interpretations where there is no discourse role. Consider, for example:

(3.12)   Since 1800, the President has believed that he was the top government figure and so has the Chief Justice of the Supreme Court.

Another, more attractive, possibility would be to claim that

(3.13)   The prosecutor believed that he would win.

has the single structure shown in Figure 11, and that verb phrase deletion would optionally copy the co-description with *he-1* to the new co-descriptor of the subject role, thus producing two readings. Perhaps further evidence can be found to choose between these possibilities.

3.6 Restrictive and Non-Restrictive Modifiers

Another opposition which structural descriptions can help to capture is the distinction between restrictive and non-restrictive modifiers. The sentence

(3.14)   My uncle, who is 70, is bald.

has a non-restrictive relative clause, "who is 70", modifying, "my uncle". That is "who is 70" is not used to pick out the uncle who is bald, but just gives extra information about him. This sentence is equivalent to the two sentences

(3.15)   My uncle is 70.
(3.16)   My uncle is bald.

By contrast, in the restrictive reading of

(3.17)   My uncle who is 70 is bald.

"who is 70" is used to pick out a particular uncle.

The distinction between 3.14 and 3.17 can be captured as shown in Figures 12 and 13, if we assume that a discourse is ongoing in time, with its roles matched sequentially.

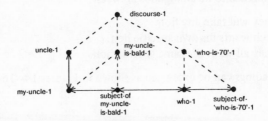

Fig. 12. My uncle, who is 70, is bald.

Note that the head of the relative clause must be either attributive or referential for both main and relative clauses. It is not possible to have, for example,

(3.18)   The President, who has been married since 1945, has lived in the White House since 1800.

This argues that the relative pronoun, here "who", is a co-descriptor of a sentence role of the main clause, not a discourse role.

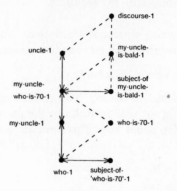

Fig. 13. My uncle who is 70 is bald.

4. DISCOURSE ITERATION

Consider the sentence

(4.1)   Every boy wants a lion.

We take this sentence to be ambiguous between

(i)   They will take any lion.
(ii)   Each wants his own specific lion.
(iii)   They all want the same specific lion.

These three readings can be expressed as shown in Figures 14–16.

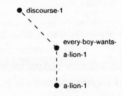

Fig. 14. They will take any lion.

Figures 14–16 can be interpreted as follows: In each case *want-a-lion* must be true for each boy. In Figure 14, *a-lion-1* is attributive. It can be picked as needed for each *wanting*. Figure 15 uses a new construct. Here *a-lion-1* is

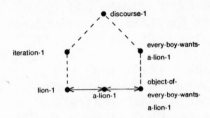

Fig. 15. Each wants his own specific lion.

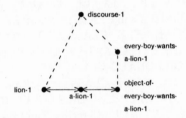

Fig. 16. Each boy wants the same specific lion.

referential, but it refers to a role, *lion-1*, in the iteration, *iteration-1*, of *want* at the discourse level. It's not surprising, given our account, that this is a difficult reading for people to construct. Finally, Figure 16 gives the by now familiar referential case where every boy is constrained to wanting the same lion. (6) We turn now to a discussion of the new construct used in Figure 15, discourse iteration.

4.1 Procedural Representation of Knowledge

It may be helpful to distinguish between procedural representation of knowledge and representation of knowledge about procedures. By *procedural representation of knowledge* we will mean casting that knowledge in the form of knowledge about the results of a procedure. For example, the knowledge that every boy wants a lion could be cast in the form "if you check every boy and count those who want lions, then the count of those who want lions will be equal to the count of the boys checked."

Woods (1977) introduced a *FOR* iteration construct for representing knowledge of quantified propositions procedurally (7). Examples of the use of this construct are:

(FOR EVERY X / CLASS : $(P\,X)$; $(Q\,X)$)
　　"Every X in CLASS that satisfies P also satisfies Q."
(FOR SOME X / CLASS : $(P\,X)$; $(Q\,X)$)
　　"Some X in CLASS that satisfies P also satisfies Q."
(FOR GEN X / CLASS : $(P\,X)$; $(Q\,X)$)
　　"A generic X in CLASS that satisfies P will also satisfy Q."
(FOR THE X / CLASS : $(P\,X)$; $(Q\,X)$)
　　"The single X in CLASS that satisfies P also satisfies Q."
(FOR (ORDINAL 3) X / CLASS : $(P\,X)$; $(Q\,X)$)
　　"The third X in CLASS that satisfies P also satisfies Q."
(FOR (GREATER 3 E) X / CLASS : $(P\,X)$; $(Q\,X)$)
　　"More than 3 X's in CLASS that satisfy P also satisfy Q."
(FOR (EQUAL 3 E) X / CLASS : $(P\,X)$; $(Q\,X)$)
　　"At least 3 X's in CLASS that satisfy P also satisfy Q."
(NOTE (FOR EQUAL 3 E) X / CLASS : $(P\,X)$; $(Q\,X)$)
　　"Fewer than 3 X's in CLASS satisfy P and also satisfy Q."
(EQUAL 3 (NUMBER X / CLASS : $(P\,X)$: $(Q\,X)$))
　　"Exactly 3 X's in CLASS satisfy P and also satisfy Q."

Woods assumes that for each CLASS there exists an enumeration function which will produce all the members of the CLASS. The FOR statement specifies that the predicate $P(x)$ be applied in turn to each element aduced by the enumeration function. The predicate $Q(x)$ is then applied to those for which $P(x)$ is true.

The first argument of the FOR divides the statements into those (EVERY, THE EQUAL GEN) which exhaust the enumeration function and those (SOME, ORDINAL, GREATER) which enumerate either until exhaustion or until a termination criterion is satisfied. The description of the termination conditions and the resulting states assumes that, in general, three counts are maintained.

(i)　　　a count, C, of the elements enumerated so far.
(ii)　　a count, CP, of the elements passing $P(x)$ so far.
(iii)　　a count, CPQ, of the elements passing $P(x)$ and $Q(x)$ so far.

For example, the (FOR EVERY ...) statement says that in the situation resulting from its execution $CP = CPQ$.

By converting Wood's FOR construct to our notation, the difference between the two referential readings of "every boy wants a lion" can be spelled out in more detail as shown in Figures 17 and 18. Figure 17 shows the

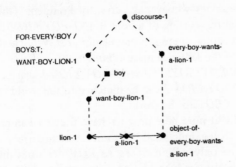

Fig. 17. Each boy wants a different lion.

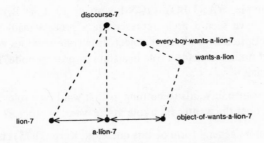

Fig. 18. Each boy wants the same specific lion.

situation where each boy wants a different lion. On our account, to understand this reading it is necessary to construct a structure in the discourse in
which lions are, in effect, individuated by the boys who want them. In doing
this, there are two ways that "every boy wants a lion" could be understood.

(i)   If you pick any boy, he wants a lion. This is the GEN option of
        the FOR iteration.
(ii)   If you iterate through the boys and check each, each will want a
        lion. This is the EVERY option of the FOR iteration.

In this example, either option could be picked. The use of the quantifier
"every" (as contrasted with, for example, "any boy wants a lion") suggests,
but does not force the EVERY option. (8) In Figure 17, a FOR iteration with
the EVERY option has been chosen. This iteration is represented by the node
FOR-EVERY-BOY/BOYS:T;WANT-BOY-LION-1. This node has a generic
role *BOY* which always describes the boy for the current iteration, just as

the-President describes whoever is currently President. Given *BOY* there is always an individual wanting of a lion, *WANT-BOY-LION-1*, unique to *BOY*, and given this wanting, there is a unique lion, *LION-1*. This last node is made a co-descriptor of the sentence node *a-lion-1*.

FOR-EVERY-BOY/BOYS:T;WANT-BOY-LION-1 can be matched to the world if *WANT-BOY-LION-1* can be matched to the world uniquely for every possible match of *BOY* to the world.

The reader might note here how we have utilized Fahlman's notion of an individual only being individual to some structure (refer to Section 2.2). *LION-1* is unique only within *BOY*. As *BOY* describes different boys, the properties of LION-1 are inherited to different lions. (9). Note also that this formulation allows the same lion to be wanted by more than one boy, the standard understanding of such a quantified expression.

In this example, WANT-BOY-LION-1 is made a role in BOY. This is the first time we have seen a node representing a process made a role in the structural description of a physical object. In all the previous examples, any physical object node was made a role in a state or process node. The following question is raised:

(i)   If someone wants something, is that wanting a role of the wanter, or does the wanter fill a role in the wanting process?

Addressing a more general form of this question, Karp (1975) claims that it is all a matter of viewpoint. The same state of affairs can be described two ways: A an attribute of B, or B a role in state A. Since the lion is to be individuated by the boy, we here choose to view the wanting of the lion as a role of the boy.

In contrast to Figure 17, Figure 18 contains no iteration at all. Figure 18 represents the case where all the boys want the same lion. Since in this case nothing is individuated to individual boys, there is nothing to be gained by expanding the sentence structure into an iteration in discourse structure. On this reading, "every boy wants a lion" can be conceptualized just like "a boy wants a lion".

4.2 Constructing an Iteration

It is not always obvious how an iteration should be constructed. When someone hears

(4.2)   A requirement for the course is the carving of a block of wood into each of the 12 designs.

his reasoning might be as follows: "Well, let's see. We take the wood and carve the first design. (Pursuing the distributive referential reading with one block) Oh! Oh! Now how do we carve a second design, the block is used up. Well, maybe we could fit the twelve designs on one block, or we could cut the block into twelve pieces. Or maybe I should abandon the referential reading and use twelve blocks." Here there is a real issue of how this carving can be done.

There can be no doubt that world knowledge is required to choose between readings. Consider

(4.3)   Everybody at MIT knows a dialect of LISP.

(4.4)   Everybody at IJCAI knows a dialect of LISP.

Everyone at a university knows the same specific dialect while everyone at a world conference knows different specific dialects.

4.3 Pushing Decisions into Pragmatics

The notation introduced here makes it easier to cast a decision between readings as a further elaboration of a structure. For example, the difference between the sentence structures in Figure 17 and Figure 18 is that (a) in Figure 18 wants-a-lion-1 has been made an individual node and (b) a different discourse co-descriptor has been chosen for a-lion-1.

One advantage of this ability to defer decisions is that it opens the possibility of a more accurate model of human behavior in interpreting quantified expressions. Van Lehn (1978) found that given a sentence like

(4.5)   A quick test confirmed that every drug was psychoactive.

people claim they understand it, but are then unable to state whether there was one test per drug, or one test for all. Given a sentence like

(4.6)   A beaver bit a representative of the manager of each dam.

people often feel that it is not worth the effort to estimate how many bitings there might have been. The notation introduced here will allow models of how people can think about these sentences without fully understanding their logical form.

The ambiguities in the above sentences are traditionally modeled as ambiguities of operator scope. The notation introduced here handles them in an analogous way, but it doesn't force an immediate decision on the scopes of operators in sentence structure. Instead, the scoping structures are meant to fall out of a data structures created in the process of building a model of the situation described. Ejerhed (1980) points out other ambiguities for which this modeling process seems quite natural, while the scoping of sentence structure runs into problems. For example, the sentence

(4.7)   All the soldiers who fought in World War II are to be awarded a medal on Christmas Day, 1980.

could mean all the soldiers existing on Christmas Day, 1980, or all the soldiers existing at the time of World War II. Using a representation based on quantifier scope, one might be persuaded to try representing this ambiguity as one involving the scopes of temporal operators and quantifiers in the sentence structure. Ejerhed points out, though, that a representation for the second reading such as

(4.8) $P((\forall x)[\text{fight-in-WWII}(x)) \supset \text{be-awarded-a-medal}(x)]$

involves an overlapping, not a nesting of scopes. But is the meaning of "all" in 4.7) really a question of the scope of a temporal operator? There are many questions about what soldiers should be included — surely not those who fought for Germany in World War II. Probably not those who subsequently became Russian spies. In the case of soldiers, dying is probably less of a deterent to being awarded a medal than defecting to the enemy. It is not clear that time is more important than other considerations.

It has always been recognized that every ambiguity or vagueness in English is not a question of logical form. What has been attempted here is to reformulate the insights traditionally expressed by quantifier scope ambiguities in a way which leads naturally to handling other ambiguities as well. At the same time that the notation handles more ambiguities, it also provides a way to let even the traditional scope ambiguities go unresolved.

MIT Laboratory for Computer Science

NOTES

* Ken Church, Lowell Hawkinson, Mitchell Marcus, Peter Szolovits, and Lucia Vaina read an earlier version of this manuscript and made many helpful comments. Ellen Lewis and Anne Schmitt did an excellent job of preparing the manuscript and figures. This research was supported by the Defense Advance Research Projects Agency and monitored by the Office of Naval Research under contract no. N00014—75—C—0661.
[1] A formulation with only three kinds of links allows the network to be self-defining to a larger extent, and thus one would expect the corresponding network interpreter to

have less "compiled in" knowledge, thereby being both more flexible and less efficient. Also, a formulation with fewer links requires less epistomological commitment, whether for better or worse.

2 Since I believe in the use of meta-description, the correspondence of, say, FIDO to the world could be taken as equivalent to the correspondence of the proposition FIDO-EXISTS to the world. This would reduce all correspondence to the correspondence of propositions, but I do not care to operate at the meta-level as this trick requires.

3 We are lead here into the center of the realism/nominalism debate. I embrace the position of Carnap (1950).

4 There has been discussion of whether the referential/attributive ambiguity is a semantic or pragmatic one (e.g. Cole 1978). If we take a semantic distinction to involve two different data structures in the sentence representation and a pragmatic one to involve two different data structures in the discourse, then our solution is a pragmatic one.

5 A method for the sequential binding of quantified variables in determining the truth of an expression was introduced by Hintikka (1976). Although he was working with predicate calculus, he obviously had in mind the same general strategy proposed here.

6 Partee (1972) points out that this type of sentence and those of the previous section pose a problem for the analysis of the indefinite article in terms of the features $\pm$ specific. (Fillmore 1967) Something more is needed to produce all the readings.

7 Readers familiar with iteration macros and programming languages will see that Wood's FOR is quite limited, e.g. iteration is limited to a single variable. I use it here because it is simple, is well explained by Woods, and will facilitate comparison of my suggestions with Wood's earlier work.

8 Further on I will discuss both i) the influence of quantifiers in choosing an option and ii) examples with side effects which require consideration of how an iteration could be done.

9 To carry out the iteration the generic BOY would be individuated by a counter and each of these individuals would inherit the description of BOY.

REFERENCES

Benacerraf, P.: 1965, 'What Numbers Could Not Be', *The Philosophical Review* **74**, 47–73.

Brachman, R. J.: 1978, 'On the Epistemological Status of Semantic Networks', in N. V. Findler (ed.), *Associative Networks – The Representation and Use of Knowledge in Computers*, Academic Press, New York.

Carnap, R.: 1950, 'Empiricism, Semantics, and Ontology', *Revue Internationale de Philosophie* **11** reprinted in L. Linsky (ed.), *Semantics and the Philosophy of Language*, Univ. of Illinois Press, Urbana, Ill.

Cole, P.: 1978, 'On the Origins of Referential Opacity', in *Syntax and Semantics: Pragmatics*, Vol. 9, P. Cole (ed.), Academic Press, New York.

Donnellan, K.: 1966, 'Reference and Definite Descriptions', *The Philosophical Review* **75**, 281–304.

Eaton, R. M.: 1924, *Symbolism and Truth, An Introduction to the Theory of Knowledge*, Harvard Univ. Press, Cambridge.

Ejerhed, Eva I.: 1980, 'Tense as a Source of Intensional Ambiguity', in Frank Heny (ed.), *Ambiguities in Intensional Contexts*, Reidel, Dordrecht, The Netherlands.

Fahlman, S. E.: 1979, 'A System for Representing and Using Real World Knowledge', MIT Computer Science PhD thesis, to be published by MIT Press, Cambridge, Mass.

Goldstein, I. P. and Roberts, B. R.: 1977, 'NUDGE – A Knowledge Based Scheduling Program', *Proceedings of 5th IJCAI*, available from Dept. of Computer Science, Carnegie-Mellon Univ., Pittsburg, Pa.

Hayes, P. J.: 1977, 'On Semantic Nets, Frames and Associations', *Proceedings of 5th IJCAI*, available from Dept. of Computer Science, Carnegie-Mellon Univ., Pittsburgh, PA.

Hendrix, G.: 1978, 'Encoding Knowledge in Partitioned Networks', N. V. Findler (ed.), *Associative Networks – The Representation and Use of Knowledge in Computers*, Academic Press, New York.

Hintikka, K. J. J.: 1976, 'Quantifiers in Logic and Quantifiers in Natural Languages', in S. Korner (ed.), *Philosophy of Logic*, Basil Blackwell, Oxford, pp. 208–232.

Karp, D. J.: 1975, 'General Ontology', MIT Philosophy PhD. Thesis.

Martin, W. A.: 1979, 'Descriptions and the Specialization of Concepts', in P. Winston (ed.), *Artificial Intelligence, An MIT Perspective*, MIT Press, Cambridge, Mass.

Minsky, M.: 1975, 'A Framework for Representing Knowledge', in *The Psychology of Computer Vision*, P. H. Winston (ed.), McGraw-Hill, New York.

Moore, R. C.: 1973, 'D-SCRIPT: A Computational Theory of Descriptions', *Advance Papers of the Third International Joint Conference on Artificial Intelligence*, pp. 223–229.

Moore, R. C.: 1975, 'Reasoning About Knowledge and Action', MIT Computer Science PhD thesis.

Partee, B. H.: 1972, 'Opacity, Co-Reference, and Pronouns' in *Semantics of Natural Language*, D. Davidson and G. Harman (eds.), D. Reidel, Dordrecht, Holland.

Partee, B. H.: 1978, 'Bound Variables and Other Anaphors' in *Proceedings of Theoretical Issues in Natural Language Processing – 2*, available from ACM.

Quine, W. V. O.: 1970, *Philosophy of Logic*, Prentice-Hall, Englewood Cliffs, New Jersey.

Russell, B.: 1905, 'On Denoting' in H. Feigl and W. Sellars (eds.), *Readings in Philosophical Analysis*, pp. 85–102, Appleton-Century-Crofts, New York, 1949.

Sag, I.: 1976, 'Deletion and Logical Form', MIT Linguistics PhD Thesis, available through Indiana University Linguistics Club.

Strawson, P. F.: 1959, *Individuals: An Essay in Descriptive Metaphysics*, Anchor Books Edition (1963).

Tarski, A.: 1944, 'The Semantic Conception of Truth', *Philosophical and Phenomenological Research* **4**, reprinted in L. Linsky (ed.), *Semantics and the Philosophy of Language*, Univ. of Illinois Press, Urbana, Ill.

VanLehn, K. A.: 1978, 'Determining the Scope of English Quantifiers', MIT Artificial Intelligence Laboratory Report AI-TR-483.

Webber, B. L.: 1978, 'A Formal Approach to Discourse Anaphora', Bolt Beranek and Newman, Inc. Research Report No. 3761.

Woods, W.: 1977, 'Semantics and Quantification in Natural Language Question Answering', Bolt Beranek and Newman Report 3687.

GRETCHEN P. BROWN

LINGUISTIC AND SITUATIONAL CONTEXT IN A MODEL OF TASK-ORIENTED DIALOGUE

1. INTRODUCTION[1]

In recent years, it has come to be widely accepted that linguistic and situational context must be used in understanding an utterance. It is not at all clear, however, how to represent such contextual information or what its precise role in the understanding process is. In fact, even the very nature of context remains problematic. In this paper, we look at task-oriented dialogue[2] and propose some initial answers to these questions. Our answers take the form of several distinctions and structures, from which we draw some broad implications. The reader is cautioned that we intend our observations to be suggestive rather than in any way exhaustive. (See, for example, Grosz [4] for a different, but complementary, perspective on this problem.)

The basic approach taken has been to model natural language dialogue as a process. Knowledge of how to carry out a dialogue is represented explicitly in the model, primarily in the form of structures called *methods*. Methods provide a high level, hence relatively declarative, representation for procedural knowledge, and they are used to represent both linguistic and non-linguistic activities. In addition, they are used to represent both knowledge about particular tasks (such as writing a computer program for someone else) and more general knowledge about dialogue (for example, the sequences of activity involved in asking and answering a question, asking for and giving a description, and so forth). The similar treatment of task knowledge and general dialogue knowledge stems from the conviction that although the two areas differ in some respects, activities from both areas contribute directly to dialogue production. To model particular dialogues, the relevant methods are "evaluated" step by step (i.e. variables in the methods are bound to appropriate pieces of representation), so that at any given point significant aspects of the linguistic and situational context are represented by the evaluated model.

This research has been based on typewritten task-oriented dialogue in computer console session environment. In particular, we were interested in developing a computational model that could serve as a basis for English dialogue between computer users and expert systems. Examination of dialogue transcripts from other environments suggests to us, however, that

229

L. Vaina and J. Hintikka (eds.), Cognitive Constraints on Communication, 229–240.
© 1984 *by D. Reidel Publishing Company.*

the ideas presented here have more general applicability. In the next section, we introduce a structure called a conversational exchange and then distinguish four basic types of utterance. In Section 3 we describe methods, and Section 4 relates methods to the four basic utterance types. Finally, Section 5 contains remarks on the role of context in the modelling of particular dialogues.

2. CONVERSATIONAL EXCHANGES

To start, we distinguish a structure at the interpersonal level of social interaction called the *conversational exchange* (henceforth *CE*). Informally, CEs are underlying structures realized by groups of utterances that "go together" to form a completed event. A simple example of a CE would be a question plus its answer; one of the more complex exchanges would be formal debate.[3] Although many CEs are uninterrupted over time, occur in a single physical setting, and are clearly goal-oriented (see Moore et al. [7]), neither temporal unity, spatial unity, nor goal orientation is a necessary characteristic of the range of behavior that we wish to categorize. We say instead that a CE is a set of conventions about communication, where the realization of each CE either performs a recognizable function (e.g., getting information) or is seen as a unit in some other way. The utterances realizing CEs may be either oral or written, but one necessary condition is that each CE permits at least one instance of turn-taking behavior.

One useful test for whether a set of utterances can be considered to realize a CE is whether there is a special name (in some language), e.g., interview, console session, or cross-examination. The existence of a name guarantees that the set of utterances is viewed as a conceptual unit. Absence of a name does not, however, disqualify a set of utterances as the realization of an exchange, as long as the set is perceived as a unit. The question-answer example we used above has no special name in English. Note that even where no name exists, there is often general agreement about when a CE is incompletely realized or when its conventions have been violated. For example, we talk about refusal to answer a question, indicating an unsatisfactory end to a question-answer exchange. Note that our notion of a CE is similar in spirit to the ideas of sequence and adjacency pair formulated by Schegloff and Sacks [9]. In both cases the concern is to establish a structural unit with associated expectations, so that it is possible, among other things, to account for a situation where some conversational event does *not* occur.

Although we intend CEs to play an important role in modelling dialogue, we do not mean to imply that dialogues can only proceed by relentlessly completing exchanges. Many dialogues are much less orderly, their structure influenced by a set of competing goals. The notion of a CE should not be rigidly applied in modelling a particular dialogue. Instead, the exchange structure is to be viewed as a set of expectations about the way that a dialogue will proceed, unless there is reason that it should proceed in some other way. Exchanges provide a sense of what is "normal" for a dialogue, even though most dialogues probably violate one or more expectations set up by the exchange structure.

3. BASIC UTTERANCE TYPES IN TASK-ORIENTED DIALOGUE

The discussion so far has been at the level of blocks of utterances. In this section we move to a lower level of aggregation and distinguish four basic utterance types: *initiator, standard path successor step, recovery discussion,* and *metadiscussion.*[4]

3.1 Initiators

To introduce initiators we first need the notion of a *main task* in a task-oriented environment. Main tasks are the largest independent procedural units. For example, in an office environment, main tasks might include telephone answering, typing a letter, scheduling a meeting, etc. Note that the definition of a particular task is largely a matter of point of view. Scheduling a meeting, for example, might involve extensive telephone answering, but in this context the calls would be considered subtasks rather than main tasks. The important concept here is *independence.* Tasks must begin in some way, and we call the class of substantive utterances that may start off a main task *initiators.*[5]

What is the justification for viewing initiators as a separate class? First there are some types of utterances that may not act as initiators, e.g., speech acts that are inherently responses. Examples of these are the acknowledgements "O.K.", "Sure," "I understand," etc. and responses such as "Why not?" or "I agree." Such utterances could not normally act as initiators, irrespective of the dialogue environment. Second, and most important for processing, the initiator is typically understood in a weaker semantic environment than other utterances. Because we have defined tasks as independent, the expectations about what will come next in a task-oriented dialogue tend to be less constrained when switching between tasks than when a task is already underway. Once a task is initiated, it brings with it a whole group of expectations as to what will come next. These may, of course, be violated in the course of the dialogue, but the fact remains that they have been evoked.

3.2 Standard Path Successors

The next utterance type is the standard path successor: an utterance may correspond to a step in a task that is already underway. Examples are the answer to a question or the acknowledgement of a statement. Standard paths are the normally expected sequences of events for an activity. They embody the relatively small number of ways that an activity can be concluded success-fully, i.e. can be concluded such that any associated goals are met. When an English description of an activity is given, it is the standard path steps that are included. If deviations from the standard path(s) are described at all, it is only the most important ones that are given. This indicates that the standard paths of an activity embody the minimum of necessary information about it. For example, when giving someone directions for getting somewhere we normally describe only the successful routes. In the normal case, we do not discuss all the many ways someone could get back on the route again after having made a wrong turn. Even when a particular mistake is very common or particularly costly, we usually describe how to avoid it (e.g., "Don't follow the signs") rather than how to recover from it.

To decide which steps belong to standard paths, we can ask whether it would normally be necessary to describe a step when describing the activity, or whether it would be necessary to describe some step of which it is a substep. (This second case applies to low-level detail left out because it is either obvious or unnecessary.) Another useful criterion is whether the *absence* of a step is seen as an event. (This criterion is similar to the one used in [9] to determine what should go in a sequence.) For example, if someone asks a question and does not get an answer, this is generally worthy of note. If one asks a question and the hearer does not ask for clarification, this absence of discussion is not, in most cases, considered remarkable. Standard path steps, then, are the normally expected sequences of events for an activity, those whose non-occurrence is normally considered an event.

3.3 Recovery Discussion

A third basic utterance type is *recovery discussion.* We said that the possible standard path steps of a dialogue constitute the relatively small number of ways that an exchange can be concluded successfully. This is fine as long as the dialogue does as intended and no expectations are violated. In practice this will probably not be long, and a failure, with its attendant recovery discussion, will result.[6] A familiar example of recovery discussion is a clarifying utterance such as "Do you mean X?" where X stands for one possible interpretation of the previous utterance.

We justify recovery discussion as a separate category by appealing to the opposite of those criteria used for standard path successors: recovery steps are those not usually included in descriptions (in this case, descriptions of conversational processes) and the absence of recovery discussion is not normally an event of note in a dialogue.

3.4 Metadiscussion

Turning from recovery discussion, the fourth basic utterance type is *metadiscussion*, which deals with the conversational situation itself. Metadiscussion is used to change the flow of activity in a dialogue or clarify the current flow of activity when no expectations have been violated. Based on dialogue transcripts we have looked at, it appears that true metadiscussion involves a relatively narrow range of utterances. Many utterances that one would initially class as metadiscussion because they deal with the conditions of conversation turn out, on closer examination, to be better classified as recovery discussion, because they occur in response to the violation of an expectation. Common examples of metadiscussion include a participant suspending a CE (e.g., "Let's stop this for now."), reopening a suspended or closed one (e.g., "I want to go back to what we were talking about yesterday."), specifying what he or she is going to do next (e.g., "Now I'll describe the format."), or smoothing the transition to a new task (e.g., "While we're on the subject . . . ").

4. THE OWL-I METHOD: A STRUCTURE FOR
REPRESENTING PROCEDURES

The last two sections contained observations about the nature of task-oriented dialogues; in this section we consider how these phenomena are to be modelled. To this purpose, we turn to a knowledge representation formalism called OWL-I and describe a structure called a *method*.[7] Methods are the major construct in OWL-I for representing procedural knowledge, and as such they are also used for activities other than language. This use of a uniform structure for both verbal and nonverbal activities is a central feature of our approach. One result of this uniformity is that nonverbal aspects of communicative behavior, such as a glance in the direction of the topic of the conversation, can be easily integrated in with verbal ones. In addition to uniform treatment of verbal and nonverbal activities, OWL-I methods have the property that they are a high level representation. Their relatively declarative nature means that the methods themselves can be easily inspected or used as the basis of an explanation facility. (See Swartout [10].) Our discussion of methods will avoid issues of notation; the reader interested in a more detailed account is referred to Hawkinson [5] and Brown [1].

Before describing the structure of methods, we briefly compare them to related work. OWL-I methods represent chunks of knowledge in the tradition of Minsky's frames [6] and Schank and Abelson's scripts [8], and as such they should be familiar types of structures. The use of such structures for the purpose of representing dialogue activities is similar to work by Bruce (social action paradigms [2]) as well as Moore, Levin, and Mann (dialogue games [7]). The most important contrast between methods on the one hand and social action paradigms and dialogue games on the other is the distinction between standard path method steps and recovery path steps. Note that while the static representations are similar in all of these different schemes, the mechanisms by which the representations are related to particular dialogues are either unspecified or quite different from the approach that we have taken.

Turning now to structural description, OWL-I methods have three main parts: a header, argument specifications, and procedure steps. The header is the method's unique name. Argument specifications, organized by semantic cases (see below), are used to check the type of inputs to the method (*input cases*) or to specify the form of results (*output cases*). Procedure steps, along with their associated input case assignments, form the body of the method. The steps come in two varieties, *standard path* and *recovery path*, corresponding to basic utterance types 2 and 3 described in the last section. (Actually, recovery discussion is modelled by two structures; the second will be discussed below.) An important point is that the OWL-I methods used for dialogue contain the parts played by both speakers, a property we call *speaker independence*. Methods can therefore be used either from the point of view of a non-participant to model both parts of the dialogue or from the point of view of a participant, to generate some utterances and understand others.

Since the question-answer exchange is a relatively simple one, we use it to illustrate a discussion of methods in more detail. An English translation of the OWL-I method for the question-answer exchange is given in Figure 1. Here, "ask-and-answer" corresponds to the header of the actual method. Ask-and-answer takes three input cases — object, agent and co-agent — and one output case, principal-result. Agent and co-agent are the two participants in the method; by convention, the agent of an entire dialogue method is the agent of the first step, so that we can identify the agent of the method with the participant who starts it off. The object of ask-and-answer is the question to be asked. Looking at the object case specification in Figure 1, we see that ask-and-answer handles all questions except how- and why-questions.[8] Note that input cases are associated with methods, not surface English verbs. They act as variables for binding the method's inputs and outputs, and input case specifications also give us a site to attach entry conditions.

We turn now to procedure steps. The standard path steps for the question-answer exchange are steps 1 through 6 in Figure 1. The ask-and-answer method also has simplified versions of recovery paths. (Many more, of course,

ask-and-answer

> object: the question to be asked
> > (not a how- or why- question)
> agent: a person or computer system
> co-agent: a person or computer system

> steps:

> > 1. The agent asks the question.
> > 2. The co-agent now knows what the question is.
> > 3. The co-agent checks to see whether he is willing to answer.
> > 4. The co-agent finds the answer.
> > 5. The co-agent gives the answer and the agent gives an (optional) acknowledgement.
> > 6. The agent should know the answer to the question.

> recovery path 1: if a stipulation is found along with the answer
> > R1.1 The co-agent states the stipulation.
> > R1.2 The agent agrees to it.

> recovery path 2: if the answer is unknown
> > R2.1 The co-agent says that he doesn't know the answer.

Fig. 1. An English representation of a method for asking a question and getting an answer.

actually exist.) The first handles the situation where an answer can only be given if there is an associated qualification, e.g.,

P1:   Will the shipment fit in the van?
P2:   Yes, *if nothing else is going that day.*

The second recovery path handles the case where no answer can be found. Both of these failures occur in the process of finding the answer, step 4, but the recovery path is associated with the ask-and-answer method. A different recovery path would be used if the find-answer method were called in another context, e.g., reasoning.

When methods are used to model particular dialogues, they are evaluated with respect to the dialogue environment, that is, method steps are thought of as being executed, and variables in their input case specifications are bound to representations of the participants, etc. One use of this process is to produce evaluated representations of expected next steps (either standard or recovery path). We refer to these method steps as *evaluated structural expectations.* Evaluated structural expectations can play an important role in constructing an understanding process; we expand on this in Section 6.

5. METHODS AND THE BASIC UTTERANCE TYPES

In this section, we briefly relate OWL-I methods to the four basic utterance types described in Section 3. In general, the first three categories of utterance — initiator, standard path successor, and recovery discussion — correspond to types of method steps. The fourth category, metadiscussion, contains utterances that specify how other utterances relate to method steps. Looking first at initiators, note that they are not necessarily produced by the first steps of methods. Instead, they are produced by the first speech act steps. A mental process step, for example planning a way to meet a goal, might be the first step in a method but would not customarily produce any verbal output. In this case, the initiator would correspond to some subsequent step of the method for the main task.

Of the structures needed to model recovery discussion, one, the recovery path, has already been introduced. Recovery paths can probably be used to model most recovery discussion that occurs in dialogue, due to dialogue's heavy reliance on conventions. Recovery paths are, however, a very local way to model recovery discussion, and consequently they are not expected to be useful for all cases where expectations are violated. A more general mechanism is also necessary, and for this we look to autonomous methods for handling particular failures. The more general mechanism appears to be necessary for recovery discussion related to the overall conditions of the dialogue, such as the conversational channel (e.g., "We have noise on the line.") or the participants or their relationship to each other (e.g., "You don't have to be so rude.").

Finally, utterances classified as metadiscussion are not represented by corresponding method steps. Instead, they specify ways that other utterances relate to method steps. The method step referred to may either occur prior to the metadiscussion (e.g., "While we're on the subject . . . " refers to the steps that developed "the subject") or subsequent to it (e.g., "Now I'm going to . . . " refers to the participant's immediate successor turn).

6. IMPLICATIONS FOR MODELLING CONTEXT

So far we have identified one discourse phenomenon — the conversational exchange, distinguished four basic utterance types, and described a structure to represent CEs. In this section we apply what has been developed to the three questions from Section 1: what is context, how can it be represented, and what is its role in the understanding process within task-oriented dialogue. (Recall our earlier cautionary note that, while we propose answers, we do not consider these questions to be "answered.")

With respect to the first question, the CE can be viewed as one of the fundamental structures that constitute "context"; we suggest it as a direct, although of course only partial, explication of the nature of context.[9] Our answer to how this particular facet of context is to be represented (question 2) centers on the OWL-I method described in Section 4. (Some of the necessary supplemental structures and mechanisms are discussed in Brown [1]). This brings us to the third question, the role of context in understanding, which we discuss at greater length.

To start, recall that methods can be used to model a task-oriented dialogue from the point of view of one of the participants (P1) so that some method steps correspond to all or part of the underlying form of generated utterances and some provide underlying forms for utterances that are understood. Once P1 uses a method step to generate an utterance we can identify a set of patterns that are highly likely as underlying forms of the response by the other participant (P2), given that the dialogue continues along the same lines. This set of patterns, which we have called structural expectations, includes the possible active successor steps[10] to the generated step, the lead-ins to recovery paths related to the generated step, or lead-ins to recovery paths related to its successor steps. Since P2 need not respond only to P1's goals, we must also include initiator and metadiscussion patterns in the set of structural expectations. P2's utterance can then be matched against this set of structural expectations, evaluated with respect to the current dialogue environment.

Since methods are a relatively abstract structure, however, we have the problem of relating the set of structural expectations to the language actually used in the utterance. This is a computationally difficult problem due on the one hand to the ambiguity inherent in any utterance and on the other to the large number of utterances that could occur at any given point in a dialogue. The four basic utterance types distinguished in Section 3 suggest a strategy for attacking this problem. In determining whether an utterance matches a known pattern, we can use different approaches depending on the type of the pattern being matched. Recognition procedures for initiators, metadiscussion, and the more general variety of recovery discussion which tend, particularly in task-oriented dialogue, to be only weakly determined by context, can depend heavily on the utterance itself. Recognition procedures for standard path successor steps and that recovery discussion which is closely tied to the structure of the dialogue can be driven by the evaluated structural expectations, since in this case the expectations will tend to embody the better information. Using such a mixed recognition strategy, the understanding process can take advantage of the context supplied by the method representation and use different, more utterance-centered strategies when strong contextual information is not available.

In this paper we have made two observations about task-oriented dialogue: the existence of conversational exchanges and the existence of four basic utterance types. In addition, we have described a structure for modelling CEs, the OWL-I method, and related it to the basic utterance types. Finally, we have applied these structures and distinctions to major questions related to context.

MIT Laboratory for Computer Science

NOTES

[1] This paper reflects research carried out from 1974 through 1977, which was support-by the advanced Research Projects Agency of the Department of Defence and was monitored by the Office of Naval Research under Contract Number N00014-75-C-0661.

Many of the ideas presented here grew out of discussions with William A. Martin and with the L.C.S. Knowledge Based Systems Group. The notion of a method and the OWL-I representation formalism described here were the result of their efforts.

2 *Task-oriented dialogue* was defined by Grosz as "one in which two (or more) people communicate for the sole purpose of completing some task" [3]. We extend this definition beyond people to include communicating systems (i.e. computers).

3 Note that CEs are not limited to two participants, although this is the only case that will be considered in this paper: Sample multi-person exchanges are classroom instruction and role calls.

4 We leave the scope of an utterance deliberately unspecified. The language chunks that fit into these categories vary in surface form from lexical or sub-lexical (e.g. *uh, mm, er*) to multi-sentential.

5 *Substantive* is used here to exclude greetings and other such formalized openers, although we do not wish to imply that such openers are totally without substance.

6 We define *failure* as the violation of an expectation. This is slightly broader than its normal usage, and we do not intend for the usual negative connotations to accompany it.

7 OWL methods were initially defined by William A. Martin, OWL-I is the version of OWL that was used in the dialogue project; for a general description of OWL-I, see Szolovits et al. [11].

8 These other two varieties of question are handled by methods called ask-and-describe and ask-and-explain; one motivation for the split is the relative complexity of many answers to how- and why-questions as compared to other sorts of questions.

9 We are not alone in this approach. It seems fair to say that the wish to represent salient aspects of context motivates all of the work cited in Section 4. The major difference among these approaches lies in their answers to the second and third questions.

10 Here, *active* is used to rule out strictly conceptual steps such as thinking of an answer (step 4, Figure 1).

REFERENCES

[1] Brown, G.P.: 'A framework for processing dialogue,' LCS TR-182 (June 1977), Laboratory for Computer Science, MIT, Cambridge, Mass.

[2] Bruce, B.C.: 'Belief systems and language understanding,' BBN Report No. 2973 (January 1975), Bolt, Baranek and Newman, Inc., Cambridge, Mass.

[3] Deutsch, B.G.: 'The structure of task oriented dialogs,' *Proceedings IEEE Speech Symposium*, Carnegie-Mellon University, Pittsburgh, Pa. (April 1974).

[4] Grosz, B.: 'The representation and use of focus in a system for understanding dialogs,' *Proceedings of the Fifth International Joint Conference on Artificial Intelligence*, Cambridge, Mass. (August 1977).

[5] Hawkinson, L.: 'The representation of concepts in OWL,' *Advance Papers of the Fourth International Joint Conference on Artificial Intelligence*, Tbilisi, Georgia, USSR (September 1975).

[6] Minsky, M.: 'A framework for representing knowledge,' in: Winston (ed.), *Visual Information Processing*, MIT Press, Cambridge, Mass. 1975.

[7] Moore, J.A., Levin, J.A., and Mann, W.C.: 'A goal-oriented model of human dialogue,' *American Journal of Computational Linguistics*, Microfiche 67 (1977).

[8] Schank, R. and Abelson, R.: *Scripts, Plans, Goals, and Understanding*, Lawrence Erlbaum Associates, Hillsdale, N.J. 1977.

[9] Schegloff, E. and Sacks, H.: 'Opening up closing,' *Semiotica* 8 (1973).

[10] Swartout, W.: 'A digitalis therapy advisor with explanations,' *Proceedings of the Fifth International Joint Conference on Artificial Intelligence*, Cambridge, Mass. (August 1977).

[11] Szolovits, P., Hawkinson, L., and Martin, W.A.: 'An overview of OWL, a language for knowledge representation,' *Proceedings of the Workshop on Natural Language for Interaction with Data Bases*, International Institute for Applied Systems Analysis, Laxenburg, Austria; also available as LCS TM-86 (June 1977), MIT, Cambridge, Mass.

ARNOLD GÜNTHER

SOME WAYS OF REPRESENTING DIALOGUES*

The object of this paper is to introduce some *types* of formal objects which may serve the dual purpose of representing natural dialogues as well as being models of a mathematical theory of dialogues. When trying to develop a mathematical theory one way to proceed is by characterizing its set-theoretical models and this can be initiated by characterizing their basic structure. Lacking a definite proposal as to the form the theory should have the best strategy seems to be to define and compare objects with different (basic) structures which may serve as models of the theory. This is the strategy I use. To put it roughly: What I attempt to do here is to *reduce* the notion of dialogue, not to *define* it.[1]

Let me first fix my terminology. By a *dialogue* I understand a complex action which is performed by two people using (expressions of) a language. This is not intended to be a definition but only to be a rough indication of the sort of entities a theory of dialogues has to deal with. By a *natural dialogue* I understand an individual event, locatable in space and time, which is a dialogue. Natural dialogues are the empirical phenomena a theory of dialogues has to characterize. By a *formal dialogue* I understand a formal object which is a dialogue. Formal dialogues are formal models, e.g. set-theoretical models, of a theory of dialogues. By a *representation of a dialogue* I understand an object (in a very general sense) which is structurally similar to the dialogue, i.e. each essential property[2] of the dialogue has a counterpart in its representation. Usually representations of dialogues are formal dialogues. Of course an object is a representation of a dialogue only according to a theory of dialogues, because it is in such a theory that essential and non-essential properties of dialogues are distinguished. By a *form of representation for dialogues* I understand the basic structure (or type) of objects which are representations of dialogues (according to a theory of dialogues). Objects are said to *belong* to a form of representation when they have the appropriate basic structure. By definition representations of dialogues as well as dialogues themselves belong to a form of representation — but not only these: Those objects which are neither dialogues nor representations of them but have the same basic structure do also belong to a form of representation. By a *possible dialogue* I understand any object belonging to a form of representation for

241

L. Vaina and J. Hintikka (eds.), Cognitive Constraints on Communication, 241–250.
© 1984 by D. Reidel Publishing Company.

dialogues.[3] A dialogue, then, is a possible dialogue which fulfills certain — dialogue-specific — conditions.

With these concepts at hand let us return to the problem of developing a mathematical theory of dialogues. Any theory of dialogues has at least one form of representation associated with it, furthermore for any form of representation there is a class of theories of dialogues compatible with it. Thus a class of theories of dialogues is singled out and choice between theories is constrained by characterizing forms of representation when they are based on representations of natural dialogues. This is the plan I follow.

I shall now introduce various forms of representation for dialogues starting with an elaboration of the concept of natural dialogue. A natural dialogue is a complex action — or interaction — in which two persons, to be called dialogue-partners in the following, participate by performing actions according to rules. The dialogue-partners use, i.e. utter expressions of, a language and thereby perform speech acts. By performing speech acts they try to reach various goals and thus perform higher-level actions. Natural dialogues take place during a certain stretch of time. Forms of representation, which should present the basic structure of at least these natural dialogues, are now introduced by defining the objects belonging to them — possible dialogues.

A very simple and fundamental form of representation is given by

$\mathcal{R}1$:   A possible dialogue is a finite sequence of well-formed expressions.

Interpretation:

(a) The well-formed expressions represent the expressions used by the dialogue-partners.[4]

(b) The sequence represents the temporal order in which these expressions are used.

(c) The occurrence of a well-formed expression in the sequence represents the use of the expression represented.

More formally: D is a possible dialogue according to $\mathcal{R}1$ iff

there is a language L and a natural number n such that for every i, $1 \leqslant i \leqslant n$, there is a well-formed expression φ_i of L and $D = (\varphi_1, \ldots \varphi_n)$.

Ill-formed expressions will be excluded in my discussion although in natural dialogues ill-formed expressions are common enough to merit representation. Eventually this restriction will have to be given up, but here I take a competencist stand. i.e. dialogue-partners are thought to be ideal speaker-listeners and therefore to use only well-formed expressions. It should be noted, however, that I do not exclude nonsignificant expressions by the well-formedness condition.[5] $\mathcal{R}1$ is certainly deficient as a form of representation for dialogues, its deficiencies being at least:

$\mathcal{R}1$ does not represent

(1) speaker/listener alternation,

(2) the speech acts performed,

(3) the higher-level actions performed,

(4) goals of actions,

(5) causes of actions, and

(6) the rules according to which actions are performed.

It is to remedy these deficiencies that we look for other forms of representation.

$\mathcal{R}2$:   A possible dialogue is a finite sequence of pairs each of which consists of a name and a well-formed expression.

Interpretation:

(a) The names are the names of the dialogue-partners.

(b) The well-formed expressions represent the expressions used by the dialogue-partners.

(c) A pair of name and well-formed expression represents the named dialogue-partners' utterance of the expression represented.

(d) The sequence represents the temporal order in which expressions are used.

$\mathcal{R}2$ thus represents speaker/listener alternation.

More formally: D is a possible dialogue according to $\mathcal{R}2$ iff

there is a language L, a two-element set $\mathcal{N}$ of names and a natural number n such that for each $i, 1 \leqslant i \leqslant n$, there is a well-formed expression φ_i of L and a name $N_i \in \mathcal{N}$ such that $D = ((N_1, \varphi_1), \ldots, (N_n, \varphi_n))$.

$\mathcal{R}2$ avoids deficiency (1) of $\mathcal{R}1$; deficiencies (2)–(6) of $\mathcal{R}1$, however, are deficiencies of $\mathcal{R}2$ as well.

As an aside I sketch another possibility of representing speaker/listener alternation over and above temporal order.

$\mathcal{R}2'$:   A possible dialogue is a finite sequence of sequences of well-formed expressions.

Interpretation: Each sequence of well-formed expressions represents a "contribution" of one dialogue-partner uninterrupted by the other.

A more formal version can be easily supplied by the reader. Deficiencies (2)–(6) of $\mathcal{R}1$ are deficiencies of $\mathcal{R}2'$ as well.

There are various possibilities to develop a form of representation avoiding the deficiencies mentioned and although I eventually introduce a certain type of representation as nearly complete I now consider some inferior forms of representation – for the sake of illustration of how to proceed.

For motivation let us consider the forms of representation introduced from another point of view. If someone is to "understand" a representation of a dialogue of type $\mathscr{R}1$ or $\mathscr{R}2$ he must make various assumptions in order to make head or tail of it. Take an example: If an interrogative sentence occurs in a representation of a dialogue, it will be understood as the representation of the use of the interrogative sentence but there is no indication whether the sentence was used to ask a question or e.g. to give an order. In order to make representations of dialogues less dependent on interpretational assumptions we may e.g. introduce indicators. Let us follow this train of thought for a while.

$\mathscr{R}3$:   A possible dialogue is a finite sequence of triples each of which consists of a name, a well-formed expression, and a performative verb.

Interpretation:

(a) The names are the names of the dialogue-partners.

(b) The well-formed expressions represent the expressions used by the dialogue-partners.

(c) The performative verbs indicate the type of speech act performed by the use of the expression.

(d) A triple of name, well-formed expression, and performative verb represents the use of the represented expression by the person named, indicating the type of speech act.

(e) The sequence represents the temporal order in which expressions are used.

More formally: D is a possible dialogue according to $\mathscr{R}3$ iff
there is a language L, a two-element set $\mathscr{N}$ of names, a set G of performative verbs and a natural number n such that for each i, $1 \leqslant i \leqslant n$, there is a name $N_i \in \mathscr{N}$, a well-formed expression φ_i of L and a performative verb g_i such that $D = ((N_1, \varphi_1, g_1), \ldots, (N_n, \varphi_n, g_n))$.[6]

Here I take performative verbs as indicators of speech act type, in principle I could have taken other objects to do the same job. An analogous remark applies to other indicators to be introduced hereafter. $\mathscr{R}3$ represents the types of speech acts performed by a dialogue-partner, but all the same it does not represent the speech acts performed, as it does not represent the products of the speech acts. To remedy this deficiency we may introduce a further form of representation.

   $\mathcal{R}$ 4:   A possible dialogue is a finite sequence of 4-tuples each of which consists of a name, a well-formed expression, a performative verb, and a designatory phrase.

Interpretation:

(a) The names are names of the dialogue-partners.

(b) The well-formed expressions represent the expressions used by the dialogue-partners.

(c) The performative verbs indicate the type of speech act performed by the use of an expression.

(d) The designatory phrase identifies the speech act product of the speech act performed.

(e) The 4-tuple of name, well-formed expression, performative verb, and designatory phrase represents the speech act performed.

(f) The sequence represents the temporal order of the speech acts.

More formally: D is a possible dialogue according to $\mathcal{R}4$ iff

there is a language L, a two-element set $\mathcal{N}$ of names, a set G of performative verbs and a set P of designatory phrases and a natural number n such that for each i, $1 \leqslant i \leqslant n$, there is a name $N_i \in \mathcal{N}$, a well-formed expression φ_i of L, a performative verb $g_i \in G$ and a designatory phrase $p_i \in P$ such that $D = ((N_1, \varphi_1, g_1, p_1), \ldots, (N_n, \varphi_n, g_n, p_n))$.[7]

Representations of type $\mathcal{R}$ 4 are at least immune to criticisms based on deficiencies (1) and (2) of $\mathcal{R}$ 1 but considering the remaining deficiencies (3)–(6) of $\mathcal{R}$ 1 one may well feel some doubt whether it is a good strategy to add element after element into a sequence, especially as it seems that there are differences between the elements of the sequence and that these are slighted over.

In order to motivate a completely different type of representation let us concentrate on the use of expressions. Although expressions taken by themselves are often ambiguous as far as their meaning and their role are concerned, they are usually not ambiguous when being used: they are disambiguated by their context.[8] It seems possible to locate the context "in" the user of the expression, for the attitudes of the user of an expression determine

(a) which speech act is performed (or at least intended) by using the expression,

(b) which higher-level action is initiated, continued or completed by using the expression,

(c) what is the goal of an action,

(d) what is the cause of an action, and

(e) what are the rules according to which actions are performed.

It seems natural to add the representation of attitudes of dialogue-partners in order to get a rather complete representation of a dialogue. This of course can be done in various ways.[9]

That a person has a certain attitude may be described by a sentence in which the person is identified by his (or her) name, the type of attitude by a verb of propositional attitude and the object of the attitude by a that-phrase, as e.g. 'John believes that Venus is a goddess.', where 'John' is the name of the person having the attitude, 'believes' characterizes the types of the attitude he has, and 'that Venus is a goddess' identifies the object of his attitude. A possible representation of an occurrence of such an attitude may be by a triple which consists of the person's name, a verb of propositional attitude, and a designatory phrase (usually a that-phrase). Thus a relevant attitude of a dialogue-partner at some point of the dialogue may be represented by a triple of the kind just described.[10]

$\mathcal{R}$ 5:   A possible dialogue is a finite sequence of triples each of which consists of a name, a well-formed expression, and a set of triples such that each of them consists of a name, a verb of propositional attitude and a designatory phrase.

Interpretation:

(a) The names are names of the dialogue-partners.

(b) The well-formed expressions represent the expressions used by the dialogue-partners.

(c) A triple of name, verb of propositional attitude and designatory phrase represents an occurrence of a propositional attitude (see the description above).

(d) A set of triples representing (occurrences of) propositional attitudes represents those propositional attitudes of the dialogue-partners which are relevant for the dialogue.

(e) A triple of name, well-formed expression, and set of triples represents both the speech act the person named performs and the propositional attitudes connected with this speech act.

(f) The sequence represents the temporal order of the speech acts and of the emergence, change and disappearance of propositional attitudes connected with the dialogue.

More formally: D is a possible dialogue according to $\mathcal{R}$ 5 iff there is a language L, a two-element set $\mathcal{N}$ of names, a set V of verbs of propositional attitude, a set P of designatory phrases, and a natural number n such that for each i, $1 \leqslant i \leqslant n$, there is a name $N_i \in \mathcal{N}$, an expression φ_i of L, and a set E_i of triples of the form (N, v, p), $N \in \mathcal{N}$, $v \in V$, $p \in P$, such that $D = ((N_1, \varphi_1, E_1), \ldots, (N_n, \varphi_n, E_n))$.[11]

This form of representation may be elaborated upon a little in two respects.

(a) We may introduce some kind of further structure into the set of attitudes, e.g. by replacing the set E of attitudes at some point of the dialogue, in which attitudes of both dialogue-partners are pooled together, by a pair of sets of attitudes, where each set contains only attitudes of one person. Another possibility of introducing some structure — which seems to be called for, as attitudes form systems and not just sets, as one may put it roughly — consists in grouping attitudes according to their type. So one may replace the set of attitudes by a sequence of sets of attitudes where one set represents the belief system of a person, another his system of intentions, and another again his system of rules etc.

(b) We may give some prominence to the use of expressions by making explicit that speech acts performed by the use of expressions are those basic acts into which any dialogue may ultimately be analyzed. Actions change their context, so in order to make this explicit for the basic acts we may represent the attitudes of persons before and after the use of an expression. This idea leads to the following kind of representation.

$\mathcal{R}$ 6: A possible dialogue is a finite sequence of triples each of which has as first and third element a set of triples, each consisting of a name, a verb of propositional attitude, and a designatory phrase, and as the second element a pair consisting of a name and a well-formed expression.

Interpretation:

(a) The names are names of the dialogue-partners.

(b) The well-formed expressions represent the expressions used by the dialogue-partners.

(c) A pair of name and well-formed expression represents the use of the expression represented by the person named.

(d) A triple of name, verb of propositional attitude, and designatory phrase represents an occurrence of a propositional attitude.

(e) A set of triples representing propositional attitudes which occurs before (after) a pair of name and well-formed expression represents the propositional attitudes of the dialogue-partners before (after) the speech act performed by the use of the expression.

(f) A triple of a set of triples representing propositional attitudes, a pair representing a use of an expression and again a set of triples representing propositional attitudes represents a dialogue step, i.e. a speech act together with relevant attitudes of both dialogue-partners.

(g) The sequence represents the temporal order of dialogue steps.

More formally: D is a dialogue according to $\mathscr{R}$ 6 iff

there is a language L, a two-element set $\mathscr{N}$ of names, a set V of verbs of propositional attitude, a set P of designatory phrases and a natural number n such that $D = (d_1, \ldots, d_n)$ and for each i, $1 \leqslant i \leqslant n, d_i = (A_i, s_i, E_i)$ where A_i and E_i are sets of triples of the form (N, v, p), $N \in \mathscr{N}, v \in V, p \in P$, and $s_i = (N_i, \varphi_i), N_i \in \mathscr{N}$ and φ_i is a well-formed expression of L.[12]

One may continue to refine $\mathscr{R}$ 6 along the lines indicated above but I will stop here and will just point out some peculiarities of the forms of representation proposed.

A first peculiarity is *atomism*: Dialogues consist of (are analyzed into) dialogue steps. Dialogue steps are those basic actions from which to (re)construct dialogues. Atomistic analyses contrast with holistic analyses, according to which dialogues are analyzed into dialogue phases and these are understood to be longer stretches of dialogical interaction. A second peculiarity is *linearity*: Dialogue steps are linearly ordered. This aspect is closely connected with atomism. A hierarchical or dependency order of dialogue steps would be more in line with holistic analyses. A third peculiarity is *functional time*: I neglect "real" time, the flow of time being represented by the sequence of dialogue steps. Pauses e.g. are not represented at all. If it turns out that consideration of functional time does not lead to adequate results, one may introduce a chronology and define a function from the set of dialogue steps into that chronology in order to date the dialogue steps.

By way of conclusion let me indicate some topics which have to be dealt with when one has forms of representation for dialogues at one's disposal. If appropriate sets are fixed each form of representation has a class of possible dialogues (as set-theoretical objects) associated with it. If e.g. a language L is fixed together with its set of well-formed expressions, the class of finite sequences of well-formed expressions of L is the class of possible dialogues according to $\mathscr{R}$ 1. If a language L is fixed together with its set of well-formed expressions and a two-element set $\mathscr{N}$ of names as well then the class of all finite sequences of pairs consisting of a name from $\mathscr{N}$ and a well-formed expression of L is the class of all possible dialogues according to $\mathcal{R}2$ etc.

Now one problem is to characterize the set of formal dialogues. It is not yet clear how this can be done, but some ways of proceeding look promising. We may characterize the set — or at least subsets of it — by induction, i.e. defining first a class of elementary dialogues and then a class of functions which construct dialogues from dialogues.[13] Or we may use a set of entities which are motivated from a different point of view and define a function which assigns a dialogue to every entity of this set.[14] Another problem is to characterize the relations between dialogues belonging to different forms of representation. This is especially important as different forms of representation may be used and useful in different contexts.

Technical University of Berlin

NOTES

* None of my friends and colleagues was given a chance to correct mistakes or suggest improvements in this paper. Nonetheless I want to thank M. Böttner and C.H. Heidrich as both kept discussing my ideas about dialogues with me. If it turns out that this paper contains more errors than can possibly made by *one* person they will serve as my (choice of) culprits.
[1] The distinction between reduction and definition I owe to Montague (1969). See Heidrich (1977) for a discussion of the concept of reduction. Reducing a concept is related to specifying its genus proximum in the traditional theory of definition.
[2] I use a concept of property here which includes relations.
[3] 'Possible' is used here not in contrast to 'actual'. A possible dialogue may *possibly* be a dialogue — if it has certain properties.
[4] Thus a method of representation (in the linguist's sense) is presupposed, as expressions are uttered. Compare e.g. the concept of a linguistic level as a method of representation of utterances, Chomsky (1957).
[5] For a detailed discussion of nonsignificance and ill-formedness and for a statement of the view I adhere to see Goddard and Routley (1973).
[6] '*G*' and '*g*' from 'Gebrauch' or 'Gebrauchsweise'.
[7] '*P*' and '*p*' from 'Sprechhandlungsprodukt'.
[8] See again Goddard and Routley (1973).
[9] Without Hintikka (1962), which laid the foundations for an exact treatment of propositional attitudes, the whole enterprise of studies of dialogues as they were conducted by (ordered alphabetically) A. Günther, M. Lutz-Hensel, and C. Rodewald-Roever in a DFG-research project supervised by C.H. Heidrich would not even have been planned. For more details on these studies see Günther (1977) and Heidrich (1977).
[10] Of course one might use sentences describing (or expressing) propositional attitudes as well. I beg the reader's pardon for my habit of sequencing or "tuplizing".

[11] *'P'* and *'p'* now from 'Proposition' (they are usually designated). *'V'* and *'v'* from 'Verb' (very helpful, isn't it?).

[12] *'A'* from 'Anfang(ssituation)', *'E'* from 'End(situation)', *'s'* from (a little misleading here) 'Sprechhandlung'.

[13] Some interesting recent work on question-answer dialogues by M. Böttner was based on this idea, see Böttner (1979).

[14] This idea was used in recent work on argumentative dialogues where "the entities motivated from a different point of view" were derivations in a system of natural deduction, see Günther (1977).

REFERENCES

M. Böttner: 1979, 'Frage-Antwort Dialoge' in W. Heindrichs and G.C. Rump (eds.) *Dialoge. Beiträge zur Interaktions- und Diskursanalyse*, Gerstenberg, Hildesheim.

N. Chomsky: 1957, *Syntactic Structures*, Mouton, The Hague.

L. Goddard and R. Routley: 1973, *The Logic of Significance and Context*, Scottish Academic Press, Edinburgh.

A. Günther: 1977, *Dialogkonstruktionen auf der Basis logischer Ableitungen*, H. Buske, Hamburg.

C.H. Heidrich: 1977, *Intensionale Analysen von Sprechhandlungen*, H. Buske, Hamburg.

J. Hintikka: 1962, *Knowledge and Belief. An Introduction to the Logic of the Two Notions*, Cornell University Press, Ithaca.

R. Montague: 1969, 'On the Nature of Certain Philosophical Entities' *The Monist* 53, 159–94.

ANCA RUNCAN

TOWARDS A LOGICAL MODEL OF DIALOGUE*

0.1 Research devoted to dialogue, conversation, or communication in general aims to describe the communicative competence which allows the users of a language to produce, by means of a finite number of elements, an infinite number of texts, appropriate to the communicative situations in which they were produced.

The concepts of *communication*, *conversation*, and *dialogue* need to be specified: the term *communication* will be used to designate any exchange of messages between human beings, whatever the number of persons participating in the communication, whatever the code used or the type of situation in which this exchange takes place; *dialogue* is a kind of communication, characterized by two types of constraints: (1) *pragmatic constraints* – every individual who participates in the communication of a sender (D) must in turn become a recipient (D^e). The sender is that participant in the communication who executes a verbal action with the intent of modifying the attitude of the recipient, namely the participant to whom the message is addressed by the sender; this criterion distinguishes dialogue from *monologue*, which is a type of communication in which one or more senders do not in turn become recipients; (2) *semantic constraints* – dialogue is concerned with a specific topic of discussion, so that the statements made by the senders result in the production of a text. This semantic restriction distinguishes dialogue from conversation.

We define a *text* as a set of propositions (the coherence of this set will be assured by the relation of compatibility among the propositions). By *discourse*, we mean the set of utterances that produce a text. The structure of this set is described by a grammar of discourse, which defines the communicative competence of the speakers. Text and discourse are abstract concepts; both are distinct from message which is the concrete manifestation of a text/discourse occurrence, produced by an individual in a particular communicative situation.

Remarks: In accordance with the above specifications, (1) an exchange of messages between two or several participants does not constitute a dialogue unless it results in a text; (2) any change in the topic of discussion marks the end of a dialogue.

L. Vaina and J. Hintikka (eds.), Cognitive Constraints on Communication, 251–266.
© 1984 *by D. Reidel Publishing Company.*

Thus, we consider the dialogue to be an ordered sequence of verbal actions performed by at least two participants, in a given situation, such that all actions aim at modifying the attitudes of the participants with respect to the state of the world.

0.2 Communication may be considered a dynamic system (characterized by its evolution in time), described by means of:

(i)   a set of discrete moments in time;
(ii)   a set of inputs (Commands);
(iii)   a set of outputs (Results);
(iv)   a set of internal states of the system, considered as the set of propositions that the participants know, believe, consider as being obligatory, etc.

Commands and *Results* represent the communicative actions performed by the senders, by means of some natural language or by some other code (non-linguistic).

At every moment in time, the system receives a signal (the utterance produced by a sender); this signal, as a function of the internal state of the system at the moment, will produce the modification of the state, the new state thus obtained will generate a response-utterance by the receiver who has in turn become a sender. The system can be described either by the external relation: entry-exit (external description), or by the relation: entry-internal state-exit (internal description) (Kalman, et al., 1969).

0.3 Research in the domain of speech acts and postulates of conversation might be considered as being the study of the commands or responses by a sender, on the ground of his knowledge of the internal state of the system (represented by the state of the receiver). This research does not yet allow us to study what may be called the communicative competence of discourse of the users of a language, i.e., the processes which produce not isolated utterances but a sequence of coherent statements. With such a goal in mind, it is necessary to study how such speech acts can be linked, based on the changes which these acts produce in the internal state of the system; in other words, we have to study the relation that defines an utterance e_{n+1} as the *answer* to an utterance e_n. The dialogue thus appears as a sequence of ordered pairs of speech acts which represent the minimal units of communication (of dialogue); based on the discovery of these minimal pairs of speech acts, it seems possible to move ahead in the study of communication from the propositional to the textural level.

In what follows, we propose to apply to the study of dialogue a logical model based on von Wright's logic of actions (1968). With this purpose in mind, we will first outline the model of an *external description* of dialogue (Section 1.1) which underlies much of the work which has been done in this domain. Section 1.2 is devoted to the definition of the concepts used in the model that is presented in Section 1.3. Some concepts needed for the application of the model will be discussed in Section 1.4. By way of conclusion, we will suggest some problems that need attention so as to complete and further develop the ideas which are only presented as a first draft in the present study.

0.4 The choice of method used is based on the definition of a language L as the set of couples $<e, L(e)>$ where e represents an utterance and $L(e)$ the meaning of e in the language L. The set of meanings of all possible utterances in a language L represents a set of *possible worlds* (Lewis, 1973). We shall use *possible world* in the sense of Vaina (1976) and Vaina (1977). She considers three definitions of possible world, each constituting a different way of looking at the same Universe of discourse given as an input. We shall recall briefly just as much of Vaina's theory as it is needed for our present purpose.

Thus, based on Chisholm's (1970) affirmation that there are not two types of entries: proposition and state of affairs, but propositions *are* states of affairs, we define a possible world as:

MP-1: A set of propositions $W = \{p, q, r\}$ is a CP-World if

(1) W is maximal: $p \in W$ or $\bar{p} \notin W$
(2) W is consistent: $p \in W$ or $\bar{p} \notin W$
(3) W is a filtre: p or $q \in W \leftrightarrow p \in W$ or $q \in W$

Thus, for representing the text by logical means, Vaina proposes a set of definitions to be applied successively to the text. We know from Carnap, that a possible world is a state of affairs which is maximal and complete. Thus, we have:

MP-1: A set of propositions $W = \{p, q, r, \ldots\}$ is a CP-world if

(1) W is maximal;
(2) W is consistent

(3) W is closed under modus-ponens
(4) $CP^* \subseteq W.$, where $CP^* = \Sigma p: p$ can be verified by propositional calculus)

Definition. A textualized world WT_e is an ordered set $\{w_1 T_e, w_2 T_e, w_n T_e\}$, where $w_i T_e \ i \in (1, n)$ are finite and ordered sets of propositions of the text.
Remarks: Each $w_i T_e$ is a CP-world. Thus, a text is represented as an ordered set of CP-worlds.
Definition. An event is a change (transformation) of a state of affairs initial in a final state of affairs at a certain moment in time. Thus

MP-3: A possible world is a possible course of events.
With this purpose in mind, we will first outline the model of an *external description* of dialogue (Section 1.1) which underlies much of the work which has been done in this domain. Section 1.2 is devoted to the definition of the concepts used in the model that is presented in Section 1.3. Some concepts needed for the application of the model will be discussed in Section 1.4. By way of conclusion, we will suggest some problems that need attention so as to complete and further develop the ideas which are only presented as a first draft in the present study.

1.1 In the study of communication, a certain number of parameters are used which can be regrouped by means of the concepts of *communicative situation* and *communicative act*.
Let:

PART = the set of participants
PART = { $part_0, \ldots, part_n$ }

where each participant, $part_p$ is defined as an ordered and directed couple of roles filled by the individuals who participate in the communication:

$$part_i = <D_i, D^e{}_i>$$

where D = sender, D^e = receiver. To the extent that D and D^e are participants in a social act (communication) they can be considered a set of psycho-social traits: age, sex, social class, etc. and a set of intentions which determine their communicative actions. Based on these traits, there exists a set $\mathcal{R}$ of possible relations established between D and D^e. $\mathcal{R}$ is a set of binary relations. Thus, each R from $\mathcal{R}$ can be reflexive, symmetric or asymmetric, transitive or not. Each relation constitutes an essential pragmatic constraint which acts on the syntactic-semantic structure of every utterance produced in the course of communication. Thus, let us consider the following sets:

> $T = \{t_1 \ldots t_m\}$ is a set of discrete moments in time, ordered by the relation of temporal succession $t_{i-1} < t_i$ where $t_i \in T$ and where $< = precedes$.

> $\mathscr{L} = \{l_0, \ldots, l_n\}$ is a set of disjoint locations where the communication takes place.

It may be considered that when a dialogue occurs between two co-present participants, then the set $\mathscr{L}$ contains a single element.

> $\mathscr{E} = \{e_1, \ldots, e_m\}$ is the set of utterances produced in the course of the communication.

The communicative situation (C) can be defined by the relation

(1) $C = \{\mathrm{PART}, T, \mathscr{L}, \mathscr{R}\}$

which describes the state of the world where the communication takes place.
    Let:

> $P =$ the set of propositions produced in the course of a communication
> $P = \{p_1, \ldots, p_n\}$.

A *proposition* is defined as the content asserted in an utterance, represented in a simple logical form. There exists a set of functions $\mathscr{F}$ (rules of grammar of a language) which allow us to assign one or more utterances to each p, and inversely, to order to each utterance one or more propositions p.
    Let $\mathscr{P}(\mathscr{F})$ be the set of the subsets of $\mathscr{F}$.
    A communicative act (F_p) designates the complex action of a collective agent part_i which can be described by:
    (i) a relationship between a proposition p and an utterance e (in conformance with the rules of a language L);
    (ii) the utterance e with an intention which is entertained by D in connection with this action (this intention is determined in particular by the type of relation which D plans to establish between himself and D^e);
    (iii) the inverse operation of (i), undertaken by D^e, which establishes a relation between the utterance e and a proposition p' (in conformance with the rules of a grammer of L);
    (iv) the establishment of a relation R between D and D^e.

We represent a *communicative act* by

(2) $Fp \subseteq \{T \cdot P \cdot E \cdot \mathscr{P}(\mathscr{F}) \cdot \text{PART} \cdot \mathscr{R}\}.$

A *dialogue* (*D*) is defined as the sequence of communicative acts of length n produced by an agent, defined as part$_i$ (regardless of the physical identity of D and D^e); the dialogue can be described by indicating, for each moment of time, the action that is produced by the agent. Thus:

(3) $\mathscr{D} = \overset{n}{\underset{i=1}{\cup}} F_p \subseteq \{T \cdot P \cdot E \cdot \mathscr{P}(\mathscr{F}) \cdot \text{PART} \cdot \mathscr{R}\}.$

The relation (3) gives an external description of the dialogue which characterizes the external relation (input-output); the internal state of the system, however, remains a *black box* unrevealed by this analysis. In what follows, we propose a model which is centered on the internal states of the system, and establishes a relation between items like participant, situation, communicative act, etc.

Remarks: The concept of *communicative act* used here is not identical with *speech act* defined by Austin (1962) and Searle (1969). We will make a few comments on this so as to clarify the differences, drawing on the theory of action of von Wright. A speech act is defined as the accomplishment of three types of acts:

(1)   a locutionary act;
(2)   an illocutionary act;
(3)   a perlocutionary act.

In our view, only the illocutionary act deserves the name of *speech act* because (a) the locutionary act should rather be considered to be the activity presupposed by the illocutionary act (von Wright distinguishes between *activity* which assures the unfolding of a process, and *action* that produces an event (1963: 41); (b) the perlocutionary act can be defined at times as *effect* or as *consequence* of the illocutionary act, when the agent does not have the *intention* of producing a particular change in the state of the world (in the universe of the discourse of the recipient) (Austin: 118), at other times, as an *indirect speech act* (Austin, 1962; Searle, 1975; Davison), when it is the intention of the sender to produce modification in the state of the universe of discourse of the recipient, based on what he knows about his universe of discourse. Thus, the same state of the universe of discourse of the recipient can be either the result of the communicative act, or a consequence of this act, depending on the conformity or non-conformity with the intention of the agent (von Wright, 1963: 41). The concept of communicative act brings out this distinction; it includes not only the act of the agent, but also the modification that this act produces in the universe of discourse of the recipient. With respect to the relation (2), the formula defining a speech act would be:

(2') $\quad F_p' \subseteq (T \times P \times E \times \mathscr{P}(\mathscr{F}))$.

1.2 In order to be able to describe the changes which a communicative act produces in the internal state of the dialogue-system, it is necessary first to define the concept of *internal state*, in the case of the particular system concerned in our study.

The fundamental concept of this study is that of the *proposition*. A proposition describes a state of elementary facts and represents the assertional content of an utterance, regardless of the type of communicative act by which it was produced. This double status of element of a set of propositions which constitute a possible world, and object of a communicative act justifies the central place of the proposition in this approach (Stalnaker).

Let $\mathscr{T}$ be the text produced by the participants in a dialogue. We will call the set of propositions independent of $\mathscr{T}$ the *textual universe* (U). It is possible to give 2^n different descriptions of U which constitute the possible worlds contained in the textual universe, and which give a total description $(\mathscr{U}_T)$ of it. $\mathscr{T}$ represents a possible description of $\mathscr{U}$ — a possible world, or a set of related possible worlds — realized in the course of the dialogue, and shared by all the participants.

$$\mathscr{T} \subset \mathscr{U}_T$$

From the propositions of $\mathscr{T}$, a set of individuals can be derived about whom something has been stated in the course of the dialogue. This set of individuals will be called the *domain of discussion* (this insures the semantic coherence of the text produced by the dialogue, see Section 0.1). In the course of a dialogue, one cannot introduce or eliminate an individual belonging to the field of discussion without interrupting the dialogue by an act of explanation.

We will designate by $\mathscr{T}_1$ the text formed by all the propositions uttered in the course of the dialogue, without stipulating the condition of consistency.

$$\mathscr{T} \subseteq \mathscr{T}_1.$$

Every communicative act belonging to the dialogue aims at modifying $\mathscr{T}_1$, so that $\mathcal{T}_1$ passes through successive states, the final state being $\mathcal{T}$ (i.e., a constituent set of propositions).

In what follows, we propose a model which describes the successive modifications of the text $\mathcal{T}_1$ that result in a coherent text. The participants in a communication must be characterized by their *universe of thought*; formally speaking, the universe of thought of an individual represents the set of possible worlds that this individual can describe by means of his mother tongue; this set is theoretically infinite, and practically non-denumerable; it can therefore not be analyzed. In analyzing the dialogue, we can reduce the universe of thought of the participants to a set of possible worlds, included in $\mathcal{U}_T$. We will call this set: universe of discourse U_p, where $p = (i, j, k, \ldots)$, designates any participant.

$$U_p \subset \mathcal{U}_\rho$$

In the course of the dialogue, as new propositions are uttered, U_p undergoes successive modifications which represent the respective successive descriptions of the world (or worlds) described by $\mathcal{T}$.

Let:

$U_p = \{w_1, \ldots, w_n\}$ where by $w_i \ i \in [1, n]$ we denote a possible world.

$T = \{t_1, \ldots, t_m\}$ where $t_j, j \in (1, m)$ is a moment of time.

We can associate to each possible world w_i a moment in time t_i. The couple $\langle w_p, t_i \rangle$ represents the state of $\mathcal{T}_1$ at the moment t_i.

In order to initiate a dialogue, it is necessary that, whenever the proposition $p_i \in \mathcal{T}_1$, there exists a $w_i, w_i \in U_p$, such that $p_i \in w_i$. Every participant assigns to the propositions of $\mathcal{T}_1$ a propositional attitude which expresses his attitude with respect to the state of affairs described by the respective proposition. To assign a propositional attitude to a proposition means to select among the possible worlds of U_p a set of possible worlds that is compatible with this propositional attitude. Thus, a propositional attitude appears to be a function whose domain of definition is the cartesian product of a set of propositions P and a set of possible worlds W. The domain of value in the closed interval $[0, 1]$.

$$f : P \cdot W \to [0, 1].$$

An expression such as *Bap* (*a* believes that *p*) expresses the fact that the individual *a* considers the state of facts *p* with respect to several possible descriptions of the world, to be compatible with the beliefs of *a*, and that the state of affairs that p is true in at least one of these descriptions (Hintikka, 1969; 1972). The universe of the discourse U_p is thus formed by a set of propositions and by the propositional attitudes assigned to these propositions by the participant. Let q be an arbitrary proposition, such that $q \vee \bar{q} \in w_p, w_1 \in \mathscr{U}_T$. There exists for every q one or more propositions p such that:

$$q \supset p, \bar{q} \supset p.$$

This is, as a matter of fact, the basic requirement for a necessary proposition, thus:

(4) $\quad ((q \supset p) \cdot (\bar{q} \supset p)) = Lp$

(theorem of the modal system $S4$ (Hughes and Cresswell, 1972).

The relation (4) defines the concepts of *semantic presupposition*, such a proposition has the pragmatic property to be accepted as true by all the participants of the dialogue.

$$(\forall)p_i, (\forall)w_i \in U_p, (Lp_i, w_i) = 1.$$

We may consider that every proposition q that is uttered (*asserted*) can be defined as a logically possible proposition.

$$(\forall)q_i, (\exists)w_i \in U_p, (Mq_i, w_i) = 1$$

where Mq is a logically possible proposition.

If all the participants assume that this proposition is true, it takes on the status of *pragmatic presupposition*. When it is considered as a proposition of the text, it is integrated into the set of propositions of the text in the same sense as the semantic presupposition.

Thus, let us consider two propositions q_i and q_j, where q_i and q_j are two propositions uttered at moments t_i and t_j $(t_i, t_j \in T, j > i)$. If $q_i \supset p_i, \bar{q}_i \supset p_i$ then $q_j \supset p_i, \bar{q}_j \supset p_i$ where p_i is a proposition presupposed by the proposition q_i.

We will call *subject of discussion* (S) the set of propositions $\mathscr{T}_1$ considered semantic and/or pragmatic presuppositions. At every movement of the dialogue t_m; $(t_m \in T)$, S^m constitutes the set of semantic and/or pragmatic presuppositions of all the propositions uttered up to the moment t_m; $\mathscr{T}_1^m$ consists of the set of propositions presupposed and uttered up to the moment t_m. Consider:

(5) $\quad S = \{p_1, \ldots, p_n\}$

(6) $\quad \mathscr{T}_1 = \{p_1, \ldots, p_w, q_1, \ldots, q_m\}$

where pi = the set of propositions presupposed by an uttered propisition q.

(7) $S \subseteq \mathcal{T}_1$.

(8) $S \subseteq \mathcal{T}$.

The ideal limit of the dialogue would be the moment when $S = T$, when the discourse of the participants has resulted in the constitution of a text; at this moment all the participants have selected the same possible description of the textual universe (they have assigned the same propositional attitude to each of the propositions of $\mathcal{T}_1$).

Remarks: The above defined concepts allow to express the external elements of communication (communicative situation, communicative act) by means of semantic concepts. The participants are replaced by their universe of discourse. The place (or places) of communication are represented by propositions which describe the physical circumstances of communication; propositions are presupposed by propositions uttered in the course of dialogue (in fact, these propositions reflect the way each participant perceives and is influenced by these circumstances); the concept of utterance is not pertinent at the level of our analysis, where we use only the concept of proposition.

When we consider the successive states of $\mathcal{T}_1$, it does not matter whether we speak of $\mathcal{T}_1$ at moment t_m ($\mathcal{T}^m_1$) or of U_p at the same moment (U^m_p). A communicative act can be studied via the concept of *communicative event* ($\mathcal{E}$). This concept designates the change produced in the universe of discourse of a participant D^e by means of a communicative act. We represent a communicative event by:

(9) $\mathcal{E} = U_p^{n-1} \, T \, (U^n_p I U_p^{(n)})$

where U^n_p represents the state of the universe of discourse of a participant at a moment in time. The communicative act modifies the state of the universe of discourse U^{n-1}_p of the recipient at the moment $n-1$, and at the next moment n, we obtain the state U^n_p instead of $U_p^{(n)}$ (state of U_p if D had not spoken).

The dialogue can be described as a sequence of communicative events, using the reiteration of the operator T:

(10) $\mathcal{D} = U_p^0 T \, ((U_p^1 I U_p^{(1)}) \, T \, (U_p^2 I U_p^{(2)})) \cdots).$

In order to facilitate comprehension of this approach to dialogue, we will represent the evolution of dialogue intuitively by means of the schematic representation (11):

Let us assume a_i and a_j are two participants who become in turn D and D^e; assume a_i = initial agent; let U_i and U_j be the universe of discourse of a_i and a_j respectively:

(11)

initial state

final state

We have to stipulate the following restrictions:

(i)   the recipient cannot receive information from any other source than the sender;

(ii)   during the time interval $\langle t_{n-1}, t_n \rangle$ no modification occurs in the universe of discourse of the sender.

Since the universe of discourse of the sender is not modified by the performance of a communicative act, we can describe the dialogue by indicating, for each moment of time, the state of the universe of discourse of the recipient.

Remarks: The choice of a model which considers the action of a single agent is based on this same hypothesis; we see the dialogue as a sequence of actions performed by an agent $part_p$, regardless of his physical identity; at every moment the virtual senders who occupy the place of recipients are included in the world of D in the same sense as other individuals or objects of this world are included; thus, for the sake of simplicity, we can reduce $part_i$ to D.

1.3 If we consider the dialogue to be a sequence of actions performed by an agent (D) so as to modify a set of propositions which constitute the universe of discourse of the recipient (D^e), then we can give an overall description of the dialogue as a complex action by indicating the initial state, the final state and the hypothetical final state of the universe of discourse. Thus, by simplifying we can determine the type of dialogue.

$$(10) \qquad \mathcal{D} = \mathcal{U}^I T(\mathcal{U}^F I \mathcal{U}^H),$$

where

$\mathcal{U}^I$ = initial state of the textual universe,
$\mathcal{U}^F$ = final state of the textual universe,
$\mathcal{U}^H$ = hypothetical final state of the textual universe.

The *initial state* $(\mathcal{U}^I)$ of the textual universe is given by the relation which can be established between U^I_i and U^I_j, this relation concerns (a) the propositions contained by U_i and by U_j and (b) the propositional attitudes which each participant assigns to these propositions.

The initial state can be characterized by:

$$(1^0) \qquad U^I_i = U^I_j,$$

$$\text{for } w^1_i \in U_i \qquad (\forall) \, p_i, p_i \in w^1_i$$

$$(\exists) \, w^1_j \in U_j, p_i \in w^1_j$$

$$\text{and } (f_{A_i}, p_i, w^1_i) = (f_{A_j}, p_i, w^1_j)$$

where f_A designates a propositional attitude.

The universe of discourse of two participants are made up of the same propositions, and the same propositional attitude is assigned by all the participants to each proposition p_i.

This theoretically impossible situation defines the relation that exists between two perfect *insiders* (Golopentia-Ereteschu, 1974). In such a situation, a dialogue becomes tautological; communication is reduced to verification of the situation by means of linguistic explanation.

(2^0) $U^I_i \cap U^I_j = 0; (\forall)\, p_i, p_i \in w_i \in U_i$

        $(\nexists)\, w'_j \in U_j, p_i \in w_j$

No proposition belonging to the universe of discourse of a participant belongs to the universe of discourse of any other participant. In such a situation, no dialogue can take place for lack of subject of discussion (U_i and U_j) and not alternative possible worlds to the world described by the propositions of ($\mathcal{U}$): one can say that in this case the subject of discussion cannot be formed.

(3^0) $U^I_i \cap U^I_j \neq 0, w^1_i \in U_i,$

        $(\exists)\, p_i, p_i \in w_i\, (\exists)\, w^1_j \in U_j, p_i \in w^1_j$

        $(f_{A_i}, p_i, w^1_i) = (f_{A_j}, p_i, w^1_j)$

(i)   there exists a sub-set of propositions which constitute the non-empty intersection of U^I_i and U^I_j; this sub-set represents the initial subject of discussion, and can contain a single proposition;[12]

(ii) a_i and a_j attach the same propositional attitute to every proposition $p_i \in w_i, w_i \in\, ^I_i \cap U^I_j$.

The final state of a dialogue is characterized by the relation:

$$U^F_i \equiv U^F_i \equiv S \equiv T$$

Theoretically, a dialogue ends at a moment n where $(\exists)\, w^n_i \in U_i,$

        $(\exists)\, w^n_j \in U_j$ and $(\forall)\, p_i \in w^n_i, p_i \in w^n_j$ and $(f_{A_i}, p_i,\ w^n_i)$

        $= (f_{A_j}, p_i, w^n_j)$

This situation represents in fact the initial state (1^0) which thus characterizes the initial limit of a dialogue.

Final Hypothetical State. In the model proposed by von Wright this situation is defined as the state of the world if the agent had not intervened. In the case of dialogue, given the restrictions which we imposed by our definition of dialogue, the final hypothetical state should always be identical to the initial situation. We will define the final hypothetical state as the state of the universe of discourse of the recipient, as it is imagined by the sender, at the moment when he performed the communicative act.

Remarks: The concepts, *initial state, final state, hypothetical final state* have a purely theoretical character: the relation which exists between the universe of discourse of the participants at every moment of the dialogue is established on the basis of the *a posteriori* reconstitution of the subject of discussion and of the analysis of the communicative acts performed by the participants. With this purpose in mind, the theories.of speech acts and of postulates of conversation offer us a point of departure.

1.4 The relationship between the initial state and the hypothetical final state permits evaluating the *opportunity* of the dialogue: the dialogue will be opportune if

(i)   the sender makes a proper assessment of the initial situation,
(ii)   the sender performs a linguistic action appropriate to the situation of the action.

The *nature* (type) of dialogue can be determined on the basis of the relation between the opportunity of the dialogue and its result. When the intention of the sender coincides with the type of dialogue — and this happens when the dialogue is opportune — then we can speak of a *successful dialogue*.

1.5 One can also define the concepts of *minimal dialogue, maximal dialogue, sub-dialogue* and *monologue*.

(1) A *minimal dialogue* takes place when the initial state presents itself as:

$$U^I_i = \{w'_i\}, U^I_j = \{w'_j\};$$
$$w'_i \cap w'_j \neq 0;$$
$$w'_i - w'_j = q, q \in w'_i, q \notin w'_j,$$

This dialogue is made up of pairs of communicative acts, one of which can remain implicit and can reach the final state: $w_i = w_j$.

(2) An initial state of the form:

$$U^I_j = w'_i = \{p_1, \ldots, p_n\};$$
$$U^I_j = w_j = \{p_1, \ldots, p_m\};$$
$$(\forall) p_i, p_i \in w_i, p_i \in w'_j;$$
$$w'_i - w'_j = \{p_1, \ldots, p_{i-1}, p_{i+1}, \ldots, p_k\};$$
$$w'_j - w_i = \{p_1, \ldots, p_{i-1}, p_{i+1}, \ldots, p_k\}.$$

(There exits a single proposition which is common to the two universes of discourse) theoretically produces a *maximal dialogue*.

(3) A *sub-dialogue* can be defined by the relation (12): let

$$\mathscr{D} = \{w^1, \ldots, w^{2n}\}.$$

(The total state of the universe, formed by all possible descriptions of the world, composed of n elementary states).

The dialogue results in the constitution of a text $\mathcal{T} \subset \mathcal{U}_T$. (The text produced by the dialogue represents a sub-set of possible descriptions of the world.)

A sub-dialogue can be seen as a possible description of the world, so that:

$$(12) \quad {}_s\mathcal{D} = x, ((\exists)\, w^i \in U_p)\, (x \cap w^i = 0, x \cup w^i \subset \mathcal{D})$$

The limit of a sub-dialogue is probably set by the change of a propositional attitude.

(4) If the sub-dialogue represents a semantic concept, attached to the internal description of the dialogue, then the *monologue* defined above (Section 0.1) represents a pragmatic concept: a monologue can be considered a limit case of the dialogue, which the transformation D^e to D remains implicit: inversely, each response in a dialogue can be seen as a monologue.

2. We undertook to introduce the concepts necessary for a logical approach to dialogue. Even though present day linguistics are beginning to take into consideration the pragmatic aspects of communication, the fact remains that it has gone little beyond the phrase level. In order to reach the level of text, it is necessary to be able to study the semantic and/or pragmatic relations established between the propositions of the text. Thus, in the case of the dialogue-text, it is necessary to begin by discovering the minimal pairs of communicative acts (such as question-request-response, etc) by defining an essential concept, that of "response" (conditions under which an utterance produces, by a communicative act, at moment n, a response to a communicative act which occurred at moment $n - 1$).

Based on the discovery of these minimal pairs, it will later be possible to study more complex relations established between pairs of communicative acts, or between sub-dialogues.

We intend to take as our point of departure not the communicative act, but the system of propositions which constitute the text, and to study the transformation of a subject of discussion in the course of a dialogue. With this purpose, it is possible to construct a model, with the help of a system of modal logic, which takes account of propositions independently from the individuals who participate in the communication, and allows us to interpret the significance of each proposition by introducing propositional attitudes, considered as functions which assign to each proposition a value, according to their state of the universe of discourse of each participant. We believe that such an approach to dialogue, which sets aside purely linguistic aspects at the phrase level has the advantage of allowing us to refine a theory of speech acts, and especially, to connect to it a semantic theory. Another advantage of this model would be to include linguistic behavior with other significant types of human behavior.

University of Bucharest

NOTE

* Translated by Magda Tiswa.

REFERENCES

Austin, J. L.: 1962, *How to Do Things with Words*, Oxford University Press, Oxford.

Cole, P. and Morgan, L. (eds.): 1975, 'Syntax and Semantics', Vol. 3, *Speech Acts*, Acad. Press, N.Y.

Golopentia-Ereteschu, S.: 1974, 'Towards a Contrastive Analysis of Conversation Strategy', *Further Developments in Contrastive Studies*, Presses Universitaires, Bucharest.

Hintikka, J.: 1969, 'Semantics for Propositional Attitudes', in *Models for Modalities*, D. Reidel, Dordrecht.

Hintikka, J.: 1972, 'The Semantics of Modal Notions and Indeterminacy of Ontology' in Davidson and Harman (eds.), *Semantics of Natural Language*, D. Reidel, Dordrecht.

Hintikka, J.: 1970, 'Knowing that One Knows', *Synthese* 21, 141–162.

Lewis, D. K.: 1973, 'Lingue e lingue', *VS* 4, 19–25.

Lewis, D. K.: 1974, 'Radical Interpretation', *Synthese* 27.

Runcan, A.: 1979, 'Dialogue', Ph.D. thesis, Univ. de Bucharest.

Searle, J. R.: 1969, *Speech Acts*, Cambridge Univ. Press, Cambridge.

Searle, J. R.: 1975, 'Indirect Speech Acts', in Cole and Morgan (eds.).

Vaina, L.: 1977, 'Lecture logico-mathematique de la narration', Ph.D. Thesis, E.P.H.E., Sorbonne, Paris.

Vaina, L. 'La theorie de mondes possibles dans l'etude des textes', *Revue roumaine de linguistique* 1.

Vaina, L.: 1977, Introduction: les mondes possible du textes,', *VS* 17, 3–13.

von Wright, G. H.: 1963, *Norm and Action*, Routledge and Kegan Paul, London.

von Wright, G. H.: 1968, 'An Essay in Deontic Logic and the General Theory of Action', *Acta Philosophica Fennica* XXI.

DAVID HARRAH

MESSAGE THEORY AND THE SEMANTICS OF DIALOGUE

I

Message theory is concerned with directed messages, the messages that are the units of rational communication. In this paper we present an introductory sketch of message theory and show to what extent it can provide a semantics for dialogue. At first glance it might appear from the description given below that message theory provides only for the semantics, and indeed only for a few of the extensional aspects of the semantics. It should become clear, however, that the message-theoretic framework provides for many possibilities beyond those explicitly mentioned in this paper — possibilities for both the semantics and the pragmatics of dialogue.

The prime examples of directed messages are the formal messages that are standard in large organizations. Typically a formal organizational letter specifies *from* whom it comes, *to* whom it is directed, the *subject* it deals with, the *reference* (if any) to previous messages, the special *assumptions* (if any) being made by the sender, the *body* (i.e., the "message proper"), and just enough *semantic correlation* (perhaps pictures or other attachments, but in any case the signature, which correlates the sender's name with the sender considered as a physical object).

Besides formal organizational letters there are many other kinds of discourse that are best construed as expressing directed messages. Examples: Informal letters and speeches, newspaper editorials, much "non-fiction" literature, and many utterances of "ordinary" (more or less informal) conversation, such as "John, as senior person here, will you please talk to the Chancellor?" Message theory is designed to apply to both the case of the formal, explicitly directed messages of large organizations, and the case of the implicitly directed messages of other areas.

Message theory is designed to apply to the most general case, the case in which n communicants (where n may be indefinitely large) send messages to each other over an indefinitely long period of time. Any message may be sent by a group of communicants, as in the case of a committee or a jury, and any message may be addressed to a group of receivers, as in the case of an

267

L. Vaina and J. Hintikka (eds.), Cognitive Constraints on Communication, 267–276.

organizational directive or a last will and testament. Thus message theory is designed to apply to dialogue conceived in the most general sense.

Now let us make these ideas somewhat more precise. What is described below is one way of developing message theory. We may think of it as leading to one particular semantics for dialogue, or one particular model of the semantics of dialogue.

II

The central item in our model is a formal language L^*. The d-part of L^* is a standard description calculus with individual constants, variables, predicates, functors, identity, and descriptive phrases. The notions of term and d-wff (for "well-formed formula") are defined as usual. For its semantics the d-part has the usual kind of extensional model-theoretic semantics. An *interpretation* consists of a non-empty universe J and an interpretive correlation K that assigns to the constants of the d-part the usual kinds of extensional meanings or denotata. Closed terms (having no free variables) act like denoting phrases. Open d-wffs (with free variables) have extensions, and are true of the things in their extensions. Every closed descriptive phrase denotes something (a null entity, if need be), and every d-sentence (i.e., closed d-wff) is either true or false.

An *interpretation intention* consists of a set A of d-sentences (the axioms or assumptions) and a function K that assigns denotata to some of the constants of the d-part. Given an interpretation intention H (= AK) and an interpretation I (= JK'), we say that H and I *conform to* each other just in case every d-sentence in A is true under I, and the function K is included in the function K'. (Note: In the preceding sentence, and elsewhere in the exposition below, we refer to n-tuples by a notation that omits the customary commas and brackets. With this notation we understand, e.g., that XY is the pair $\langle X, Y \rangle$.)

The d-part of L^* has a logic of the usual sort, complete in the usual sense. Specifically, a d-wff is a d-theorem just in case it is valid.

To provide for communicative applications, we define a particular kind of interpretation as normal. A particular interpretive correlation K^* interprets one individual constant as denoting the empty set, and certain other individual constants as denoting the letters of the alphabet of L^*. There is a set A^* of d-sentences serving as axioms for general set theory, Tarski's theory of syntax, and what may be called communication theory. The latter must include a theory of times and statuses, but this can be simplified if we identify times with tallies (special expressions that behave like numerals but don't denote), and identify statuses with one-place d-wffs (d-wffs with one free variable). There are axioms for a three-place predicate *Com* such that "Com(x, y, z)" means that x is a communicant in status y at time z. There must also be axioms for a four-place predicate *Sig* such that "Sig(w, x, y, z)" means that the communicant w at time x sends the token y to express the type z. One of these axioms, e.g., says that a communicant can sign and send no more than one token at any one time.

Let H^* be the ordered pair A^*K^*. Then an interpretation I ($= JK$) is *normal* iff I conforms to H^*, and certain further conditions hold. (E.g., K must interpret the 'ϵ' predicate as expressing the member-set relation over the universe J.) Where H is an interpretation intention, we say that a set S *normally H-implies* a d-wff F iff (roughly) S implies F in every normal interpretation that conforms to H. Also, a term X *normally H-denotes* Y iff X denotes Y in every normal interpretation that conforms to H.

III

The e-part of L^* ('e' for 'erotetic') is an extension of the d-part. To construct it we add to the d-part an infinite stock of erotetic operators, including various kinds of question mark, imperative sign, and the like. *Atomic erotetic wffs*, or *ae-wiffs*, are formed by applying *ae*-operators to combinations of terms and d-wffs. *Erotetic wffs*, or *e-wffs*, include all the *ae*-wffs and d-wffs, and certain compounds (conjunctions, disjunctions, universal generalizations, existential generalizations, and conditionals in which the antecedent is a d-wff). To each *ae*-wff and d-wff certain erotetic content is assigned, including a set of indicated replies and a set of wanted replies. Every e-wff has an *assertive core*, which is a d-wff. (Example: "Which x's have property P?" has "Some x's have property P" as assertive core.) For *ae*-wffs and d-wffs the *corrective reply* is the negation of the assertive core. A *full reply* is a d-wff that normally implies an indicated reply or the corrective reply. A *partial reply* is a d-wff that is normally implied by either an indicated reply or the corrective reply. The *relevant replies* are the full replies plus the partial replies.

For communicative purposes it is necessary to have a system for determining, from a compound e-wff F, what replies to F are called for. One possibility is to use a derivation system similar to the standard deduction systems applicable to d-wffs. Such a system will contain all of the rules of derivation that are applicable to d-wffs, and some analogues that are applicable to *e*-wffs in general (e.g., a Simplification rule allowing detachment of a conjunct from a conjunction). There will also be special rules peculiar to *e*-logic. E.g., from a given *e*-wff *F*, the *A*-rule allows the derivation of the assertive core of *F*. Roughly, an *e-derivation from* a set *S* is a finite sequence *Z* of *e*-wffs each of which either is a member of *S*, or is an axiom of *d*-logic, or is an axiom in *A**, or comes from preceding members of *Z* by some rule of *e*-logic. The *assertive content* of a set *S* is the set of all *d*-wffs that are *e*-derivable from *S*.

Let *S* and *S'* be any sets. (Intuitively: Think of *S* as what the sender sends, and *S'* as the receiver's background beliefs.) Then:

(1) *S''* is a *framework for reply to S on the basis of S' via Z* if and only if *Z* is an *e*-derivation from the union of *S* and *S'*, and *S''* is a set consisting of *d*- and *ae*-sentences that are members of *Z*.

(2) The *erotetic content of S on the basis of S'* is the set of all sets *S''* such that, for some *Z*, *S''* is a framework for reply to *S* on the basis of *S'* via *Z*.

(3) *S'''* is a *reply set for S on the basis of S'* if and only if there are *S''* and *Z* such that *S''* is a framework for reply to *S* on the basis of *S'* via *Z*, and *S'''* is a set of pairs *XY* such that *X* is in *S''*, and *Y* is a relevant reply to *X*.

(4) *S'''* is a *full reply set for S on the basis of S'* if and only if *S'''* is a reply set for *S* on the basis of *S'*, and, for every pair *XY* in *S'''*, *Y* is a full reply to *X*.

(The notions of *indicated, wanted, partial,* and *corrective* reply set for *S* on the basis of *S'* can be defined similarly.)

Some *e*-derivations are more complete than others, in the sense that they extract more of the content of *S* and *S'*, and thus some reply sets are more complete than others. Is there such a thing as an absolutely complete reply set? Yes, if we don't insist that complete reply sets be effectively recognizable as such. Roughly, we may define an *e*-derivation *Z* as complete just in case (1) all of the rules of *e*-derivation that can be applied in *Z* have in fact been applied, and (2) certain further conditions hold. E.g., we must require that, if a conditional $(F \supset G)$ is in *Z*, and *F* is *e*-derivable from the union of *S* and *S'*, then *F* is in *Z* — the point being that the modus ponens rule will then be applied by condition (1), thus forcing *G* to be in *Z*. Because we can't effectively recognize all cases of *e*-derivability, we can't effectively recognize all cases of complete *e*-derivation. Anyway, given a definition of complete *e*-derivation, we may then define complete framework for reply, complete reply set, complete full reply set, complete partial reply set, and so on.

Problem for research: define the notions of raising and suppressing. A necessary condition for a set *S* to raise a question, for example, is that the assertive content of S contain the assertive core of the question. But what are the sufficient conditions?[1]

IV

Message theory is intended to provide a semantics for utterances. The utterances may be physical, disjointed, and fragmentary; but the messages are "perfect" set-theoretic entities. Our theory of messages is developed in stages as follows. Roughly:[2]

A *communicant specifier*, or *com-spec*, is a triple NFT such that (1) N is either a closed term or a one-place d-wff, (2) F is a one-place d-wff, and (3) T is a tally. Thus a com-spec NFT indicates (1) a communicant (if N is a term) or a set of communicants (if N is a d-wff), (2) a status, and (3) a time. The *assertive counterpart* of a com-spec NFT is a d-wff that says in effect that the communicants N have the status F at time T.

A *message origin specifier* is a non-empty set S of com-specs NFT such that N is an individual constant (a simple name), and, for some com-spec X in S, no com-spec in S has a tally longer than the tally in X (so S has a latest or definitive time).

A *message distribution specifier* is a non-empty set of com-specs.

A *subject list* is a sequence every member of which is either a closed term or an open d-wff.

A *message reference* is a set of pairs PQ such that P is a set of message origin specifiers, and Q is a set of e-sentences.

An *assumption set* is a set of d-sentences.

A *message body* is a set of e-sentences.

A *standard message* is a seven-tuple $ODLRABK$ such that

(1) O is a message origin specifier.
(2) D is a message distribution specifier.
(3) L is a subject list.
(4) R is a message reference.
(5) A is an assumption set.
(6) B is a message body.
(7) K is an interpretive correlation whose domain consists of individual constants and contains every N in the com-specs in O.
(8) For each NFT in O and $N'F'T'$ in D, it is not the case that T' precedes T.

The *time* of a standard message M is the definitive time in O. One message M *precedes* another M' just in case the time of M precedes the earliest time in the O' in M'.

In a *purely formal* message the domain of K consists of just the N's in the com-specs in O; i.e., the message has no attachments except the signatures of the senders.

Let M and M' be standard messages, with R the message reference in M. Then M *refers to* M' *via* R if and only if the origin specifier of M' is in the P in some pair PQ in R.

Let M (= *ODLRABK*) be a standard message, and let I be a normal interpretation. Then:

(1) C is a *sender of* M *under* I if and only if there is an *NFT* in O such that either N is a term, and $I(N) = C$, or N is a d-wff, and C is in the extension of N under I.

(2) M is *coherent under* I if and only if AK is an interpretation intention conforming to I, the set of senders of M under I is finite, and each of O, D, L, R, A, B, K is denotable under I.

An *m-set* is a set of standard messages. Where S is an *m*-set, S' is an *initial segment of* S *up to* T just in case S' is the subset of S consisting of all the messages in S whose times precede T.

An *m*-set S is *coherent under* a normal interpretation I if and only if (roughly):

(1) Every M in S is coherent under I.

(2) Any sender who signs two different messages in S signs them at different times.

(3) If any M in S refers to a message M' via the R in M, then M' is in S, and M' precedes M.

An *m*-set S is *realizable under* a normal interpretation I just in case S is finite and coherent under I.

Given a message M in an *m*-set S, and a normal interpretation I, the *standard context of* M *in* S *under* I is the initial segment of S up to the initial time of M (i.e., up to the earliest time in the O in M). Standard contexts are well behaved. In particular, every initial segment of a coherent *m*-set is itself a coherent *m*-set.

Because the language L^* contains set theory and syntax theory, self-reference is possible in several senses. It is possible for an *m*-set S to contain a message M whose body B contains d-sentences that refer to themselves, and d-sentences that refer to M, and d-sentences that refer to the context of M in S.

A standard message has, or conveys, content of various kinds. In general the content of a standard message M depends not simply on the sentences in the body B but on other parts of M and (via recursion) the messages that precede M in the given *m*-set. Very roughly:

The *presumption set* of M in S under I is the smallest set that (1) includes (a) the assertive counterparts of the com-specs in O and D, and (b) certain sentences connected with the messages that are referred to by M via R; and (2) is closed under normal H-implication, where H is the interpretation intention AK.

The *implication set* of M in S under I is the smallest set that (1) includes the presumption set, B, and the set of assertive cores of members of B, and (2) is closed under normal H-implication.

The *erotetic set* of M in S under I is the set of all e-derivations from the implication set. (This set determines the ways of replying to M.)

The *communicative force* of M in S under I is the set of all triples XYZ such that X is a com-spec in O, Z is a com-spec in D, and Y is an e-derivation in the erotetic set of M.

V

Messages are related to utterances in the following way. There is a process that goes downward, so to speak, from messages to the concrete tokens that express them. Conversely there is a process that starts with utterance tokens and goes upward to messages; the utterance tokens are construed as expressing the messages. More generally we start with a set of tokens and construe it as expressing a set of messages.

Theoretically there are many possible systems for expressing and construing. A simple and natural one is the six-level model:[3] At Level 1 there is the *language L** with its semantics. At Level 2 there are the standard *messages* and *m*-sets. At Level 3 there are *message expressers.* These are pairs XY, where X is an expression of L^* that denotes or displays various components of the given message M according to a well specified system of coding, and Y is part of the K in M. At Level 4 there are *pronominal codings.* These are like message expressers except that they may contain pronouns and indexicals according to well specified rules. At Level 5 there are *utterance types.* These are either pronominal codings or truncated or fragmentary versions of those codings. At Level 6 there are *utterance tokens.* These are physical objects that conventionally express utterance types.

To send a message, one chooses an appropriate message expresser, inserts pronouns and indexicals, deletes items that are redundant (or need not be made explicit), and then chooses a suitable utterance token. To construe a set S of utterance tokens one proceeds in the opposite direction. One first finds the utterance types corresponding to the utterance tokens, de-truncates them (by guessing), replaces pronouns and indexicals, and then decodes the resulting message expressers, thereby arriving at a set S' of standard messages. Now it might be that S' does not satisfy all the coherence conditions required for it to be an m-set. In that case one might have to form an m-set S'' by adding to S' some additional messages that were not represented by any utterance tokens in S.

Utterance tokens may be assigned semantic properties as a function of the semantics of the messages they express. In the other direction, some pragmatic properties may be assigned to messages as a function of the pragmatics of the corresponding utterance tokens.

Exactly how message theory applies to a given dialogue, exactly which utterances are to be construed as expressing messages, may require some judgment and decision. While the dialogue-as-event is occurring, the successive utterances of Speaker 1 might be construed by Speaker 2 as expressing successive messages. Later, however, the various utterances of Speaker 1 might be grouped together and construed as expressing just a few or even just one single message. Example: "Yesterday George was telling me, as a friend, that . . . He was referring to . . . , and his point was that . . . " What are rational criteria for grouping utterances in this process? That is one of the many problems we leave to the future.

VI

Compared with other sorts of model of dialogue, what are the advantages of the message-theoretic model described here? Not enough research has been done yet to develop these models to the point where this question can be answered in detail. Nevertheless we offer three general conjectures.

First, the message-theoretic approach provides a framework for precise study of certain aspects of the semantics of communication. In particular, it provides means for the precise study of the notions of the *content* of a message, the *commitments* made by a sender, and the *consistency* of the sender over a period of time. Indeed, the primary motivation for starting with the formal language L^* and incorporating the set-theoretic and other axioms in A^* is to make possible a precise logical analysis of these notions.

Second, the message-theoretic approach makes possible precise study of some of the pragmatic aspects of communication. Some theorists, notably H. P. Grice,[4] have discussed various rules or maxims of communication. Up to now this discussion has been relatively informal; the message-theoretic approach suggests some means of formalization. Consider, e.g., the maxim "Be relevant." In a standard message M as analyzed above the component L

can act as a filter when applied to the implication set: we define the *relevant implications* as those sentences F in the implication set such that every non-logical constant in F is contained in the subject list L. Then the *relevant erotetic set* is the set of e-derivations from the relevant implication set. On this basis we may study the effect of various kinds of L, especially in relation to the relevant erotetic sets of preceding messages.

For a second example, consider the maxim "Be clear." By putting more and more content into the assumption set A and the interpretive correlation K, the sender puts more and more constraints on the interpretations I that the receiver can use for interpreting M. Thus one thing we can and should study is how, given the relevant erotetic sets of preceding messages, the sender can best choose A and K for the degree of clarity that is wanted in the subsequent message.

Third, as indicated at the end of the previous section, a dialogue may be construed in one way during the course of the dialogue, and in a more or less different way after the dialogue has been completed. Typically the post-dialogue construction is a more condensed and better organized one. Now suppose that a group of communicants wants to keep permanent records of the dialogues they engage in. One kind of record they can keep is the literal one, as in the tape-recording of a conversation. Another kind is suggested by our message-theoretic model. The dialogue is construed in terms of standard messages and m-sets, and the record consists of descriptions of these messages. Our conjecture is that, for information storage and retrieval purposes, the best candidate for the "normal form" of dialogue report is description in terms of our standard messages.

University of California, Riverside

NOTES

[1] For more details on the e-part of L^* see David Harrah, 'A System For Erotetic Sentences,' in Alan Ross Anderson, et al (eds.), *The Logical Enterprise* (New Haven: Yale University Press, 1975), pp. 235–245. Several improvements on the system presented in that paper were suggested in an appendix to the abstract of that paper published in *Zentralblatt für Mathematik und ihre Grenzgebiete* 357 (1978), 30 [02025]. Further development of the improved system is presented in David Harrah, 'The Semantics of Question Sets' (forthcoming).

[2] Early versions of this theory of messages were presented in David Harrah, 'Formal Message Theory,' in Yehoshua Bar-Hillel (ed.), *Pragmatics of Natural Languages* (Dordrecht: D. Reidel, 1971), pp. 69–83; and David Harrah, 'Formal Message Theory and Non-formal Discourse,' in T. A. van Dijk, (ed.), *Pragmatics of Language and*

Literature (Amsterdam: North-Holland, 1976), pp. 59–76. What is given in the present paper is a rough sketch of an improved version of the theory.

In the 1971 and 1976 papers, messages consisted of the components V, W, O, D, A, B. In the improved version the component A (the "aim") has been replaced by the two new components L and R. The component A in the improved version corresponds to W in the old, and the K in the improved corresponds to V in the old.

[3] For more details, and more precise discussion, see the papers cited in Note 2, especially the 1976 paper.

[4] See, e.g., H. P. Grice, 'Logic and Conversation,' in Donald Davidson and Gilbert Harman (eds.), *The Logic of Grammar* (Encino, California: Dickenson, 1975), pp. 64–75.

JAAKKO HINTIKKA

RULES, UTILITIES, AND STRATEGIES IN DIALOGICAL GAMES

In an earlier paper, I have defined certain dialogical games consisting mostly of questions and answers.[1] They are games in what is intended to be the sense employed in the mathematical theory of games. From this vantage point, the definitions so far offered are incomplete, however, in several respects, especially in that the payoffs are left partly undetermined. It is my purpose in this paper to show how the payoffs can be determined somewhat more fully and indicate what theoretical considerations the determination of the payoffs depends on.

I shall also try to do certain other things. Basically, I want to modify somewhat the original definition of dialogical games. Even though the resulting changes are relatively small and the discussion of payoffs purely qualitative, the wide applicability of questioning games lends them considerable general interest. Furthermore, since it is the payoffs that largely govern which strategies are better than others in our dialogical games, the discussion of payoffs also serves as a basis of further discussions of strategy choice in dialogical games.

My dialogical games are essentially question-answer dialogues. They can be defined (partly) by means of the following specifications:

(I) The players: There are two players, here called White and Black.
(II) The moves: There can be moves of the following kinds:

- (a)   Initial moves
- (b)   Deductive moves
- (c)   Interrogative moves
- (d)   Assertoric moves
- (e)   Definitory moves

As a bookkeeping convention, we shall assume that each player has what is essentially like a semantical *tableau* in the sense of E. W. Beth.[2] I shall use in this paper the usual concepts and the usual terminology associated with semantical *tableaux*. They include such concepts as column, *subtableau*, closure, etc.

(a) In the initial move, each player puts forward a thesis. It is put into the

277

L. Vaina and J. Hintikka (eds.), Cognitive Constraints on Communication, 277–294.
© 1984 *by D. Reidel Publishing Company.*

left column of the *tableau* of one's opponent and into the right column of
one's own *tableau*.

After the initial move, the players move alternatively, beginning with
White, until one of the players has reached his or her objective. What this
objective is, is specified partly below in (III). At each stage, the player whose
turn it is may decide what kind of move (see (b)–(e) above) he or she will
make.

(b) In a deductive move, the player in question carries out one step of
tableau construction in accordance with some suitable set of rules for this
purpose. I shall return to the question of the choice of the *tableau* rules
below. The main stipulation needed here for the time being is that all such
tableau rules that don't satisfy the sub-formula principle, e.g. the *tableau*
counterparts to *modus ponens*, to the cut rule, etc., are not admitted to my
games without further explanation.

At each stage of the *tableau* construction, certain *subtableaux* of one of
the players are correlated with certain *subtableaux* of the other one. Originally, the two initial *tableaux* (as they were after the initial move) are correlated
with each other. Whenever a *subtableau* of one of the players is split into two,
both are correlated with the same *subtableaux* of the other one as the old
undivided *subtableau* was. At each move, the players are faced with a pair of
correlated *subtableaux*, in a sense which will be spelled out in connection
with the several types of rules below. Such a pair of correlated *subtableaux*
may be thought of as one line of reasoning the two players are trying out.

(c) In an interrogative move, the player in question addresses a question
to the other one. The latter will give it a conclusive answer, if one is available
(i.e. in so far as the questioner's knowledge and the restrictions on answers
make one possible). If no full answer to a wh-question is possible, any true
substitution-instance of the matrix of the question (with respect to a proper
name) will constitute an answer.

Each question-answer pair is relative to a pair of correlated *subtableaux*
s_1, s_2 of the two players. The answer is written into the left column of the
subtableau s_1 of the questioner and is conjoined with each expression in the
right column of the *subtableau* s_2 of the answerer.

If the presupposition of the question does not occur in the left column of
s_1, the answerer may, instead of answering the question, deny its presupposition. Then the negation of the presupposition is written into the
left column of s_1 and conjoined with each expression in the right column
of s_2.

These definitions presuppose my analysis of questions.[3] I have in earlier publications defined all the requisite concepts, including desideratum, full answer, presupposition, etc.

(d) An assertoric move is likewise relative to a pair of correlated *subtableaux* s_1, s_2 of the two players. In such a move, the player in question puts forward a new thesis, say T. It is conjoined with each sentence in the right column of the relevant *subtableaux* (say s_1) of the asserter.

The other player has a choice of either agreeing or disagreeing with the opponent's assertion. If he (she) agrees, T is written into the left column of the correlated *subtableaux* s_2 of his (or hers). If he (she) disagrees, the negation of T is written into the same column.

(e) A definitory move is similarly relative to a pair of correlated *subtableaux* s_1, s_2 of the players. If the presuppositions of an explicit definition D occur in the left columns of the *subtableaux* s_1 of the player who is putting forth the definition. The player in question may insert D into the left column of s_1. It is also inserted into the left column of s_2.

The presuppositions of different kinds of explicit definitions are as follows:

(i) Definition of a predicate, e.g. a one-place predicate:

$$(x) [P (x) \Leftrightarrow \text{Df} [x]].$$

Here Df (x) is a complex formula (the *definiens*) with "x" as its only free variable.

Presuppositions: none

(ii) Definition of an individual, e.g.

$$(x) [x = a \Leftrightarrow \text{Df} [x]].$$

Presuppositions:

$$(\exists x) \text{ Df} [x];$$
$$(x) (y) [(\text{Df} [x] \& \text{Df} [y]) \supset x = y].$$

(iii) Definition of a function, e.g.

$$(x) (y) [f (x) = y \Leftrightarrow \text{Df} [x, y]].$$

Presuppositions:

$$(x) (\exists y) \text{ Df} [x, y];$$
$$(x) (y) (u) [(\text{Df} [x, y] \& \text{Df} [x, u]) \supset y = u].$$

(III) The aim of the game: in a tentative heuristic sense, the aim of each player α is to deduce the sentences in the right column of α's *tableau* from those in the left column of α 's *tableau* in the sense of bringing about the closure of α 's *tableau*.

After one of the players has reached his or her objective, the other player is allowed to continue to make moves until he or she has also reached his (her) aim. Indeed, some of the moves he (she) makes may re-open the *tableau* of the opponent who for a while had seemed to have nothing further to do, viz. by addressing questions to the opponent. The opponent's answers become further conclusions he (she) has to prove.

These definitions of moves in a dialogue game presuppose certain further explanations.

(i) Language: It is assumed that we are given some finite first-order language with the help of which the theses, answers, and the desiderata of questions (except for the epistemic operators) are to be formulated. What other non-logical concepts we might want to admit into theses, answers, and questions (and if so, on what conditions) will have to be discussed separately. As a first and simplest case, we shall in this paper restrict our attention to questions which contain only non-logical constants from the given first-order language. In other words, the desiderata of questions must not contain any intensional operators except for the initial operators "K_I", and all the non-intensional concepts must belong to the given language.

An important part of the specification of the underlying language is a sharp separation of actual *names* that stand for individuals in the domains of our models (worlds) introduced in (2) below and *dummy names* introduced by the rules of *tableau* construction, more specifically those dealing with existential sentences in the left column or universal sentences in the right column.

(ii) Models: In order to make sense of the notion of full answer and also in order to be able to discuss certain other problems, we need a few model-theoretical notions.

What is assumed to be given is the following:

(1) A set Σ of models ("worlds").

(2) One of them is a designated model ("actual world").

At each stage S of each subtableau of either player, that subtableau picks out two subsets σ_1, σ_2 of Σ. Here σ_1 is the set of all those worlds w in which all the sentences in the left column are true but none of those in the right column is true. Likewise, σ_2 is the set of all worlds in which all the members of the left column of S are true. We shall say that σ_1 is *determined by* S and that σ_2 is *positively* determined by S.

When dummy names occur in the columns of S, a world w belongs to σ_1

iff all the formulas of the left column are true in w and all the formulas of the right column are not true in w *for at least evaluation of all the dummy names*. (Likewise for σ_2.)

(3) A set of world lines connecting the members of Σ is also assumed to be given. For reasons explained more fully elsewhere, we cannot assume that each world line spans all the worlds of Σ. To summarize these reasons briefly, suppose that a world line connects all the worlds in a subset σ (determined by a stage s of some tableau). Such a world line specifies an individual whose identity is known to the player in question at s. If the world line of no individual ever breaks down, the identity of every individual is known to each player. This assumption is not realistic in general.

Then a sentence of the form $(\exists x) K_\alpha (b = x)$ (where α = White or Black) is considered true at some stage s of some subtableau of α's if and only if there is a world line connecting all the worlds in the set σ associated with s such that its nodes are the individuals picked out by "b" in the several worlds in question.

Dummy names introduced by instantiation rules of *tableau* construction are supposed to go together with a world line connecting the relevant worlds. (For a discussion of what those worlds are and how they are to be captured, see Jaakko Hintikka, 'New Foundations for a Theory of Questions and Answers'.)[4]

This suffices to specify what the moves in the dialogical games look like. What we have seen enables us to make some interesting observations.

DEDUCTIONS VS. QUESTIONS AND ANSWERS

Consider first a deductive move which turns on a disjunction $X \vee Y$ occurring in the left column of some subtableau σ of one of the players, say σ. Then this subtableau is divided into two, σ_1 and σ_2. In both, the right column stays the same while in σ_1 we add to the left column X and in σ_2 we add Y.

Now $(X \vee Y)$ is the presupposition of the propositional question "Is it the case that X or that Y?". Hence α can ask this question and receive an answer. The full answer to this question (on its existential reading) is either X or Y. Whichever it is, α needs to consider only one of the two *subtableaux* which ensued from an application of the deductive rule for disjunctions. This will never hurt α, and normally it facilitates α's game.

Likewise, a deductive rule applied to $(\exists x) S(x)$ in the left column of *subtableau* σ of α's yields $S(d)$, where "d" is a new dummy name. But $(\exists x) S(x)$ is the presupposition of the question: "Who (what), say x, is such that $S(x)$? on its existential reading. Suppose that there is nothing in the additional restraints on interrogative moves we might want to introduce that would be an impediment to asking this question, and suppose that α in fact asks it. Suppose further that there is a conclusive answer to this question, say "c", where α knows who or what c is. Then α can continue his (her) game with $S(c)$ in his (her) left column instead of the expression $S(d)$ which would have been then if he (she) had made a deductive move applied to $(\exists x) S(x)$. Now "c"'s not being a dummy name can only help α to reach his (her) goal, never hurt this enterprise. Hence, again, a deductive move can be replaced by an interrogative one, provided this time that there is a full answer available to the relevant wh-question.

Hence certain deductive moves can be profitably replaced (in favorable circumstances) by interrogative ones. Moreover, the applications of a *tableau* rule to $(\exists x) S(x)$ in the left column are not normally trivial moves as one's deductive strategies go. On the contrary, we know from studies in deductive strategies (e.g. strategies of mechanical theorem-proving) that the choice of the optimal instantiations is typically the crucial factor for the success of attempted deduction. Hence we can see how certain important *deductions* (deductive moves) are often replaceable by *questions* (interrogative moves). Hence there is an extremely close conceptual connection between successful questioning and successful deduction. Questions can occasionally do the same job as deductions, only better. The search for powerful deductive strategies is closely related to looking for the right questioning strategies. No wonder, therefore, that I have been able to interpret the "deductions" of a Sherlock Holmes as so many series of well-chosen questions (with answers).[5]

Likewise, definitory moves can all be replaced by suitable interrogative ones if the latter ones are interpreted universally. I shall leave the details to the reader. Once again it turns out that questioning can be used to replace a purely "logical" step.

DIAGRAMMATIC EXPOSITION OF GAMES

The model-theoretical situation in our semantical games can be depicted by means of the usual Venn diagram.

Here the rectangle represents the totality of relevant alternatives ("possible worlds") each being represented by a point. W is the range admitted by White's thesis or theses, and B the range admitted by Black's thesis or theses.

In the rest of this paper I shall for simplicity refer to the theses W, B, and to the Venn diagram areas they determine, in the same way.

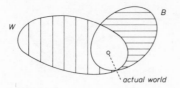

Fig. 1

Figure 1 can represent the situation after the initial move. The W and B are specified by the initial theses of the two players.

Alternatively, Figure 1 may represent the situation determined by a pair of correlated *subtableaux* s_1, s_2 (the former White's, the latter Black's). Then W and B are the sets of worlds positively determined by s_1 and s_2, respectively.

In either case, the task that remains for White to try to do is to eliminate the worlds in the horizontally shaded area, and the task for Black is to eliminate the worlds in the vertically shaded area.

FURTHER RESTRICTIONS ON ANSWERS

In specifying our dialogical games, we may want to introduce restrictions on the way in which answers to questions are determined. By introducing different restrictions, we can in fact use dialogical games to model several different processes. Here are some possibilities:

(i) One of the players (say Black which we can think of as "Nature") knows what the actual state of affairs is and always gives true answers accordingly.

(ii) The players answer according to the best of their belief. The situation is then as depicted in one of the following versions of Fig. 1:

In Figure 2 (a)–(b) w is the set of worlds compatible with everything that White believes, and b the set of worlds likewise determined by what Black believes. It has been assumed in 2 (a)–(b) that each player believes in his (her) theses and that one's beliefs are compatible with one's opponent's theses. It is easy to see what situations become possible when these assumptions are given up.

In 2 (b) these sets of beliefs are compatible with each other, in 2 (a) they are incompatible. Whenever possible, White will give an answer which includes all of w, and analogously for Black. White's successive answers thus typically converge to an area which is w or a subset of w, and *mutatis mutandis* for Black.

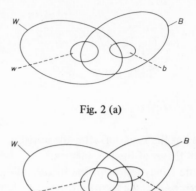

Fig. 2 (a)

Fig. 2 (b)

An important assumption which it is natural to make in this situation is that neither of the players knows what the opponent believes. Obviously, the success of a player's strategy may then depend heavily on that player's finding out what the opponent believes.

STRATEGIC CONSIDERATIONS

These simple observations, and others like it, enable us to analyse some aspects of the strategic situation in dialogical games. The following points can be made here as examples of what can be done in this direction:

(i) The aims of the two players are not entirely contrary to each other. (Dialogical games are not zero-sum games.) Indeed, the game (or a line of play, as codified by a pair of correlated *tableaux*) can result in the elimination of both the shaded areas of Figure 1, i.e. result in a situation in which the total theses W and B coincide. Then both players have reached their aim, and no further continuation of this line of play is possible.[6]

This common end thesis of the players need not be represented by the intersection of the initial W and B. It may be represented by a subset of $W \cap B$.

This can happen only when the initial theses are compatible, i.e. only if $W \cap B \neq \phi$ in Figure 1. If $W \cap B = \phi$, the game is reduced to a much clearer conflict situation than what it is when $W \cap B \neq \phi$. For then White is trying to prove $\sim B$ and Black is trying to prove $\sim W$, i.e., each is trying to disprove his or her opponent's thesis. In such a situation we shall say, the dialogue becomes a *dispute*.

A dispute does not have to obtain from the beginning, but can come about as a result of the moves made in the course of the play. For instances, if W denies the presupposition of one of B's questions, it is easily seen that the game degenerates into a dispute. (This illustrates further the force of our notion of presupposition).

Likewise, denying one's opponent's assertion turns the game into a dispute.

(ii) If it is assumed that Black answers questions truthfully, that Black knows which alternative is true, and that Black's assertions are true, then White's questions (and Black's assertions) may be expected eventually to reduce Black's thesis B (see Figure 1) to some area B' close to the actual world.

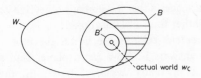

Fig. 3

It is assumed here that $W \cap B \neq \phi$ and that both W and B are true, i.e. that for the actual world w_0 we have $w_0 \in W$, $w_0 \in B$.

Then we can see what the best strategy one of the players, say W, has in answering his/her opponent's questions. This is shown by the following figure.

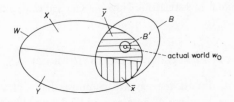

Fig. 4

It is assumed here that W is being asked the propositional question, X or Y?

Then the vertically shaded area $\bar{x}$ represents the additional possibilities W has to eliminate if (s)he answers "X" and the horizontally shaded area $\bar{y}$ represents the extra possibilities W has to eliminate if (s)he answers "Y". It is seen at once that, on the assumption of B's omniscience and especially truthfulness, W's best bet is to answer X. What makes the difference here is of course that $w_0 \in X$, $w_0 \notin Y$, In other words, it is seen that against a truthful opponent defending a true thesis, honesty is one's best policy.

On the same assumptions concerning the way in which Black answers questions, it likewise can be seen that White's best strategy (*ceteris paribus*) is to agree with Black's assertions when they are true (and disagree with them when they are false).

In spite of the obviousness of these observations, they are not devoid of philosophical suggestions. For instance, let us think of White as a scientist playing a game of information-seeking against nature (= Black). It is often said that truthfulness (objectivity) is an ethical requirement for scientists. Our simple observation suggests that a scientist's objectivity may be a prudent (strategic) imperative rather than an ethical one.[7]

(iii) A question is *ceteris paribus* the better the more informative each of its several possible answers is. How can a player find such questions to ask? Now in the case of many types of questions, the information of each of the answers is (at least roughly) proportional to the information (improbability) of the presupposition of the question. An obvious case in point is a yes-or-no question, but some wh-questions, e.g. why-questions, are also cases in point. For such questions, we thus have a rule of thumb for finding strategically promising questions: look out for unusual (unlikely) features of the situation, and ask questions about them − the unlikelier the better.

Again we are dealing with a familiar phenomenon. Focusing on the anomalous features of a problem situation is a long-established tactic of both scientists and criminal investigators. Now we can see one sound rationale for their procedure.[8]

PAYOFFS: GENERAL CONSIDERATIONS

The next task is to discuss the payoffs. Suppose that a play of a dialogical game runs its course. How are we to assess it? Who won? What is the winner's payoff, and what is the loser's?

The first point to note here is that we cannot determine the payoffs on the sole basis of the end state. Our dialogues are information-seeking ones. What counts in them is not who "has the last word". Rather, the whole series of moves that constitute the dialogue has to be kept in mind.

One way in which the different moves can be thought of as affecting the payoffs is to think of certain kinds of moves as involving a profit or a cost to the player who makes the move. The way in which we want to think of such a cost is this: the cost is the higher the greater contribution this move may be expected to make to the achieving of the goals of the player in question in the dialogue.

PAYOFFS: THE EFFECT OF DEDUCTIVE MOVES

This applies especially clearly to deductive moves. What are the characteristics of such deductive steps as are likely to facilitate the overall aims of the deduction? This is essentially a proof-theoretical question. Now it is known from proof theory that the crucial parameter in deductive first-order proofs is the number of existential instantiations of new dummy names introduced in the course of a deduction). Somewhat more accurately, we can use as the measure of this parameter the depth (in the sense I have defined elsewhere) of the existential closure of

$$(s) \qquad (A_1 \ \& \ A_2 \ \& \ \ldots \ \& \ A_k) \supset (B_1 \ v \ B_2 \ v \ldots B_m)$$

(with respect to all the dummy names), where A_i ($i = 1, 2, \ldots, k$) are the sentences in the left column and B_j ($j = 1, 2, \ldots, m$) those in the right column of a *subtableau*. Whenever a deductive move increases this parameter by n units, the player making the move incurs a "cost" proportional to n.

This idea can be applied in two different ways. Given some usual set of rules of *tableau* construction, this convention regulates the cost of deductive moves made by means of such "natural" *tableau* rules. However, if someone should use such *derived* rules of *tableau* construction as *modus ponens* or the cut rule, their use will also be regulated by the same cost convention. Indeed, it seems to us that the measure of deductive costs just introduced is in certain ways the natural one. We venture the conjecture that on the basis of our cost convention alone the use of *modus ponens* or the cut rule never gives a player an advantage.[10] To put it in other terms, the only advantage that such rules as *modus ponens* possess in our games is to increase the depth of the deduction in the sense of the depth of the intended existential closure of (s).

Notice that this cost convention does not eliminate the strategic element even from the deductive moves of the game. For, even though increasing the depth of a deduction is a *necessary* condition for deductive success, as can be shown in many different ways, it is not a *sufficient* condition. Indeed, there is no recursive method of telling to what depths one must carry an attempted deduction before it can succeed.[11]

INTUITIVE MEANING OF THE COST OF DEDUCTIVE MOVES

Intuitively, increasing the degree of a deduction i.e. (of a game *tableau*) means considering more individuals in their relation to each other. Even though hard facts are difficult to come by in this area, it seems to us that such increase is characteristic of non-trivial reasoning both in the purely deductive case and also when other kinds of moves are admitted in our dialogical games. For instance, the gist of Sherlock Holmes' observation about "the curious incident of the dog in the nigh-time" which I have analysed elsewhere seems to be a case in point.[12] Sherlock's observation makes his audience consider for the first time also the watch-dog in its relation to the principals in the case, and thus he increases the complexity of the configuration of individuals considered.

More systematically speaking, the introduction of a new individual into one's reasoning is what geometers used to call a *construction*. What the use of the depth of the closure of (s) as an index of the difficulty of a deduction amounts to is therefore a generalization of the old idea that the difficulty of a geometrical demonstration is due to the constructions it presupposes. As Leibniz once put it, we still [sic] do not have a way of always determining what the best constructions are in geometry.

THE COST OF DEFINITIONS AND QUESTIONS

The parallelism between deductive, definitory, and interrogative moves suggests imposing similar payments on all these different moves. Thus the cost of the definition (II) (c) (i) above is directly proportional to the depth of 'Df' with the same proportionality constant as in the deductive case; and likewise for definitions of the other types.

Furthermore, the cost of asking a question will be proportional to the depth of the desideratum of the question. This time, some considerately greater proportionality constant will be used than in the earlier cases.

Here we are beginning to see the role of definitions in dialogical games a little bit more clearly. Why are definitions useful in information seeking, anyway? Because by means of suitably chosen definitions we can reduce the depth of the questions that have to be asked in order to obtain the desired information, and hence the cost of these questions. It is in general an advantage of dialogical games as a model of various kinds of pursuits of knowledge, especially of the scientific method, that it assigns a role to definitions. Their theory has in fact been neglected recently by most serious philosophers.

WAYS OF REDUCING THE COST OF MOVES

Doesn't this trivialize the game in that it makes all the different ways of trying to reach a player's aims equally expensive? It does not, because a player α can increase the degree of (s) (for some *subtableau* of α's) by asking a wh-question. Even though the cost of the question is assessed in accordance with its degree, the introduction of the name of the individual which *is* the answer (properly speaking, the value of the free variable of the matrix which yields the answer) can increase the depth of the intended existential closure of (s) without any corresponding extra cost. This presupposes that the answer to a wh-question always has the form of a proper name even when this proper name does not occur in our original language. We shall make this assumption in what follows.

"BEGGING THE QUESTION" AND ITS ANALOGUES

These stipulations also enable us to meet an objection that naturally occurs to a reader here. Why isn't it always possible for a player to trivialize our dialogical games by asking at the first opportunity: Is my thesis T true or not? The answer to this criticism is that in most nontrivial cases T has a considerable depth. Hence the potentially trivializing question is prohibitively expensive for the player in question to ask.

We are moving here in the vincinity of classical philosophical concepts. Asking the trivializing question is precisely (as Richard Robinson has shown) what Aristotle meant by the fallacy of "begging the question".[13] (The literal meaning of the original Greek term is "asking for the question", where "question" means the overall problem of deriving one's own thesis from one's opponent's admissions.) We can now see why such a move is bad, not because it involves a fallacy in the sense of a wrong deductive step but because it represents a bad strategy in our dialogical games. Aristotle never explains himself in a satisfactory manner why begging the question is a no-no. Hence our model dialogues offer the first real diagnosis of this so-called fallacy.

There is an intriguing similarity between "begging the question" and introducing trivial extra premises of the form $(X \lor \sim X)$ in a deduction (or in the deductive part of a dialogical game. In both cases, such steps are made ill-advised by the indiscriminate increase of depth.

Now the extra force of *modus ponens* and the cut rules lies in effect just in the introduction of such apparently trivial extra premises. The so-called natural deduction rules of deduction are characterized precisely by the absence of such extra premises.[14] Their replaceability by suitable additional natural deduction steps is what Gentzen's first *Hauptsatz* establishes. Hence there is a partial but nevertheless interesting analogy between Aristotle and Gentzen. Both want to get along without extra premises whose real function (as we can now see) is merely to increase the depth of the attempted deduction. Aristotle's injunction against begging the question is analogous to cut elimination in Gentzen.

THE COST OF NEW CONCEPTS

One main problem which remains to be discussed is what concepts (non-logical constants) the questions which the players ask are allowed to contain. Here I do not want to be categorical. Clearly some "fee" is to be levied sometimes on the player who introduces new concepts into the game. However, the proper way of assessing these fees will depend on what kind of dialogical game we want to consider, which in turn depends on the purpose of considering a game in the first place.

One possibility might be to disallow new concepts altogether in the answers to questions and make questions of more than a minimal depth prohibitively expensive. Then much of the power of interrogative moves will be lost unless we allow the questions themselves to contain new concepts. If we keep everything else intact, we can then raise the question: How much is it worth to a player to be allowed to introduce some particular new non-logical constant, e.g. the name of an object in the domain of the actual world. This gives us a way of discussing the value of new concepts in reasoning.

Another possibility might be to make the introduction of new names for individuals free for one of the players, say White. What this means is to make it possible for White to look for and ideally to find suitable individuals to ask questions about. In other words, this way of setting up the payoffs makes our dialogical games into something like the semantical games of game-theoretical semantics. The latter can in this way be considered a special variant of our dialogical games.

More generally, by weighting the cost of the introduction of new names of individuals in a question differently we can codify into our payoff structure different assumptions as to how "expensive" it is to seek and find individuals in the players' domain.

MOTIVATING ASSERTIONS

A definition of the payoffs must explain why it is rational for the players to make the kinds of moves they are allowed to make. There is no problem in this respect about interrogative, deductive, or definitory moves. But what about assertoric moves (and the initial move, which can be considered a special case of the assertoric move)? Why doesn't a player trivialize the game by choosing a tautology as his or her sole thesis?

The question is closely related to Popper's criticism of all approaches to the scientific method in terms of confirmation or safety of some other kind. Our solution to the problem is also somewhat reminiscent of Popper's. We can "motivate" the players to make assertoric moves by making the payoff to a payer α resulting from a play of the game dependent on the informativeness of the conjunction of α's theses. This will "motivate" a player to put forward logically strong theses in the initial move and in assertoric moves. Admittedly, they will make it more difficult for α to reach the desired goal, but at the same time they will make reaching it more valuable to α. It is the role of information and the value of highly informative (and hence *a priori* improbable) theses that reminds us here of Popper.

Several comments are in order here. The notion of semantical information and the ways of measuring it have been discussed at length in my earlier publications. I shall not now try to specify any one detailed measure. On the contrary, one of the most striking features of the philosophical situation in this connection is that there are many different varieties of information several of which can legitimately be thought of as (partly) determining the payoffs of dialogical games. It would in fact be interesting to discuss what the different choices here mean intuitively.

In one respect the reasonable choice of a measure of information is fairly clear, however. Since what we are studying is the interplay of deduction and questioning, it is eminently appropriate to use a measure of information such that deduction can increase one's information.

I have shown in earlier publications how such measures of information can be defined for languages of the kind we are considering here.[15] Recently, it has been shown how such measures can be given a model-theoretical backing by means of the so-called urn models of Veikko Rantala.[16]

Once again it is advisable not to try to specify completely the payoffs once and for all, not only because we may be interested in different kinds of information for different purposes but also because it may be interesting to study the influence of the value of information on the optimal strategies of inquiry. When is it rational to go out of one's way and to "put questions to Nature" — and when is it the best strategy to sit back and make the most of the information one already has, merely trying to deduce more and more consequences therefrom, presumably in conjunction with particular data? When is it advisable for a scientist to put forward strong "theories" (in our terms, to make strong assertions) and then try to prove them, and when is it prudent to be content with poorer but more easily provable generalizations? Even if we cannot answer these questions now, it looks as if they can be profitably studied by means of our framework, which admits of more sophisticated problems than most of the conventional models of scientific inquiry.

INTERIM PAYOFFS: THE LENGTH OF GAMES

The value of information comes into play primarily when a player has reached his (her) goal. However, this is not necessary for the purpose of bringing the concept of information to bear on our dialogical games. The value of what one of the players, say α, has achieved up to a point can be measured by considering which *subtableaux* α has managed to close. Moreover, I have shown how one can measure the amount of deductive information an incomplete proof yields. Hence we can think of the game as being stopped at any stage whatsoever, and still be able to assess (in principle) the payoffs of the two players.

So far we have not used at all in determining the payoffs what to some philosophers apparently seems to be the most obvious measures of deductive success: the shortness of a completed deduction. It is indeed clear that this is a factor which can be taken into account in determining the payoffs. However, whether a deduction can be short or long depends often on considerations which have nothing to do with the real ease or difficulty of the deduction. Hence not much weight ought in any case to be put on the length of a play of the game or the number of moves one of the players makes in determining the payoffs. The same goes for the question as to which player achieves his or her aim first.

THE INFLUENCE OF THE EPISTEMIC ELEMENT ON TABLEAU RULES

One aspect of the game rules that also requires further attention are the rules for *tableau* construction. Now why can we not be happy with the usual rules? Don't they go hand in hand with the normal intended semantics for our language?

The answer is yes, but that does not close the issue. For there is, or can be assumed to be, a tacit epistemic element in the moves of my dialogical games and hence in the sentences codifying them. Instead of using the extensional formulations we have been using, a knowledge operator should perhaps be prefaced to all of them. Even if we don't do so explicitly, as I prefer not to do in this paper, we must formulate the *tableau* construction rules as if these epistemic operators were present. What the resulting rules are like is shown in a joint paper by Jaakko Hintikka and Esa Saarinen.[17] It turns out that the logic they define is neither classical nor intuitionistic.

Florida State University

NOTES

[1] See 'On the Logic of Information-Seeking Dialogues: A Model' in W. Becker and W. Essler (eds.), *Konzepte der Dialektik*, Vittorio Klostermann, Frankfurt am Main, 1980, and cf. Jaakko Hintikka and Merrill B. Hintikka, 'Sherlock Holmes Confronts Modern Logic: Toward a Theory of Information-Seeking Through Questioning' in Else Barth (ed.) *Theory of Argumentation*, Benjamins, Amsterdam, 1981.

[2] E. W. Beth's original exposition of the *tableau* method is still the freshest. See his 'Semantic Entailment and Formal Derivability', *Mededelingen der Koninklijke Nederlandse Akademie van Wetenschappen, Afd Letterkunde*, N. R., vol. 18, no. 13.

[3] See Jaakko Hintikka, *The Semantics of Questions and the Questions of Semantics* (Acta Philosophica Fennica, vol. 28, no. 4), North-Holland, Amsterdam, 1976, and "New Foundations for a Theory of Questions', forthcoming in the proceedings of the 1980 symposium on questions and answers, Visegrad, Hungary.

[4] Note 3 above.

[5] See my joint paper with Merrill B. Hintikka (note 1 above) and my paper also 'Sherlock Holmes Formalized' forthcoming in a *Festschrift* for Alwin Diemer.

[6] Here we can see some of the many features of my dialogical games which make them a promising model of a dialectical process. On this application of dialogical games, see the paper of mine mentioned in note 1.

[7] For other applications to the philosophy of science, see my paper 'On the Logic of an Interrogative Model of Scientific Inquiry', *Synthese* 47 (1981) 69–83.

[8] We have here a partial explanation of the importance of the role which anomalies have played in scientific discovery.

[9] Jaakko Hintikka, *Logic, Language-Games, and Information*, Clarendon Press, Oxford, 1973, pp. 141–142 (especially note 33).

[10] This conjecture is apparently proved by the results of Jaakko Hintikka and Ilkka

Niiniluoto in 'On the Surface Semantics of Quantificational Proof Procedures', *Ajatus* 35 (1973), 197–215.

[11] The role of depth in logical reasoning is one of the main themes of my book, *Logic, Language-Games, and Information* (note 9 above).

[12] See 'Sherlock Holmes Formalized' (note 5 above).

[13] See Richard Robinson, 'Begging the Question', 1971, *Analysis* 31 (1971), 113–117. Robinson refers to the relevant passages in Aristotle. (I owe this reference to Russell Dancy.)

[14] For the whole problematic in this direction, see e.g. Dag Prawitz, *Natural Deduction*, Almqvist & Wiksell, Stockholm, 1965, or Gais: Takeuti, *Proof Theory*, North-Holland, Amsterdam, 1975.

[15] See e.g. Jaakko Hintikka, 'Surface Information and Depth Information' in Jaakko Hintikka and Patrick Suppes (eds.), *Information and Inference*, D. Reidel, Dordrecht, 1970, pp. 263–297; and cf. 'Knowledge, Belief, and Logical Consequence' in Jaakko Hintikka, *The Intentions of Intentionality*, D. Reidel, Dordrecht, 1975, pp. 179–191.

[16] Veikko Rantala, 'Urn Models: A New Kind of Non-Standard Model for First-Order Logic', *Journal of Philosophical Logic* 4 (1975), 455–474. Cf. Jaakko Hintikka, 'Impossible Possible Worlds Vindicated'; *ibid.*

[17] Jaakko Hintikka and Esa Saarinen, 'Information-Seeking Dialogues: Some of Their Logical Properties', *Studia Logica* 32, 355–363.

LAURI CARLSON

FOCUS AND DIALOGUE GAMES

A Game-Theoretical Approach to the Interpretation of Intonational Focusing

TABLE OF CONTENTS

L. Vaina and J. Hintikka (eds.), Cognitive Constraints on Communication, 295–333.
© 1984 *by D. Reidel Publishing Company.*

PREAMBLE

The present paper, long as it is, is an excerpt of a monograph manuscript entitled *Dialogue Games — A Game-Theoretical Approach to Text Linguistics.* As the name indicates, the more comprehensive work develops the intonational ideas presented here in the wider perspective of a game-theoretical theory of textual concepts (such as *theme, rheme, topic, old vs. new information, textual connectedness*).*

As a consequence of its character as an excerpt, the present paper exhibits conspicuous lacunae. Perhaps the most embarrassing one is the patent inadequacy of the basic rule (D.emphasis) in most actual dialogue situations. Very rarely is one able to match a new sentence word by word with any actual earlier sentences in a dialogue. There are two main reasons for this. First, it is usually the meaning of sentences that is involved in such matching, not (or not exclusively) their form. Second, there is a lot of suppressed reasoning going on in a dialogue. No model where assumptions are given as static, unorganized lists can represent the situation adequately.

These shortcomings are met in the monograph by enriching the simple dialogue game model with game rules of explanation and inference (these rules allow one to interpolate missing steps in reasoning) and by replacing the simple assumption lists of the present model with internalized dialogues (this allows the players to think on their feet, i.e. to enrich their assumptions between their explicit moves, to plan ahead in the dialogue, and so on).

Another conspicuous gap is the absence of any mention of multiply focused sentences. I have decided to leave out my treatment of multiply focused sentences for the reason that it would bring in much of the text linguistic apparatus that could otherwise be left out (the concept of *topic* of a dialogue in particular).

Third, the examples of focused sentences in this paper are all declarative sentences. Of course, sentences of other sentential moods are focused too, with functional consequences closely analogous to those witnessed in declarative sentences. In the longer work, it is claimed that (D.emphasis) is applicable to focusing irrespective of mood, i.e. that no new modifications are occasioned to the framework presented here in order to accommodate the whole variety of examples. For the present, this finding must be left to be made by the reader, or else to be taken on faith.[1]

Last but not least, the length of the paper prohibits a discussion relating the present approach to the competing ones.[2] Though the work presented here started rather from scratch, inspired mainly by Hintikka (1979), its further developments have brought it closer to the main streams of text linguistics. The at times unnecessarily provocative tone of the present excerpt is largely due to a beginner's zeal.

I. DIALOGUE GAMES DEFINED

1. Discourse as a Game

The topic of the present paper is *intonational focusing*. Intonational focusing is involved when parts of a sentence — phrases, individual words, or even parts of words — are specially emphasized by intonational means: intensity, pitch, duration. The conventional graphic counterpart of such intonational emphasis is underlining, italics or capital letters.

What interests me in this paper is the *meaning* of intonational focusing. Surely there is some quite striking difference in meaning between various italicizations of a sentence, say, the immediately preceding one. I certainly had something specific in mind in italicizing *meaning*. The point of my sentence would have seemed to be elsewhere had I italicized *this* or *intonational*.

Whatever the difference in meaning, it is hard to describe in terms of truth conditions. My sentence would not have turned into a false one under any of the alternative emphases. Rather, what changes are the implicit presuppositions that the sentence seems to be predicated on. My emphasis on *meaning* contrasts my interest in interpreting focusing to structural linguists' preoccupation with the phonology of focusing. Italicizing *intonational* would have presupposed that there are other sorts of focusing besides intonational.

My conclusion, and the starting point of this paper, is that intonational focusing is a discourse phenomenon. This means among other things that the concept of presupposition complementary to the concept of focus is not the concept of logical presupposition. A sentence is a logical presupposition of another sentence if the former is true whenever the latter is true or false. In classical logic, all logical presuppositions are tautologies. In a logic with truth value gaps, a sentence may have contingent presuppositions. For instance, many maintain that a sentence whose subject is a definite noun phrase presupposes that one and only one individual satisfies the subject phrase; if this presupposition fails, the sentence is neither true nor false.

In contrast, the failure of the so-called presupposition of a focussed sentence does not create a truth value gap. The sentence preserves whatever truth value its unfocussed variant has. Rather, whatever presuppositions may be involved in focus interpretation concern propositions *asserted, believed,* or just *entertained* by participants of a dialogue in which the focussed sentence is appropriately used. In terms of Morris' classical definition, these presuppositions are *pragmatic* in nature.[3]

A pictorial way of representing use of language is in terms of a *language game.* The idea is originally Wittgenstein's, but it has been applied since by several writers, in particular Stenius (1967) and Hintikka (1973, 1975, 1976a, 1976b, 1977, 1979).

What I propose to do in this essay is to develop a new type of language game, called *dialogue games.* They are a generalization of the semantic language games of Hintikka's game theoretical semantics. Hintikka's semantical games serve to connect declarative sentences of a given language with the models they speak about so as to yield a definition of truth and falsity of sentences of the language with respect to its intended models.

The dialogue games are games of *using* sentences of different moods to convey information, to debate, and for other conversational purposes. Moves in such games include in the first place complete sentences put forward by the dialogue members but possibly other types of moves. The successive sentences put forward in a dialogue game need not be related to each other structurally or lexically. Nothing like a subformula principle (implicit in the semantical games) need therefore hold.

Another thing that distinguishes dialogue games from semantic games is increased explicitness about the respective *aims* and (propositional) *attitudes* of the players; such considerations are part and parcel of pragmatics.

The difference between the semantical games of verification and dialogue games is not absolute. Members of a dialogue game have at their disposal any moves of the semantical games connected with sentences put forward in the dialogue game; but in addition, they can use rules of different kinds.

Typical rules of dialogue games regulate the use of sentences of different sentential *moods*: declarative, interrogative, or imperative sentences, exclamations, and so on. These rules together with the dialogue framework they are embedded in (the other rules and the aims of dialogue games) can be seen as constituting a *theory of meaning* for those sentential moods.

The leading idea here of course originates from Wittgenstein; it has been developed in Stenius (1967) and Carlson (1976). The idea is that dialogue games can in themselves be taken as so many definitions of meaning of sentential moods. To define what, e.g., the declarative mood means, one has to specify the language games in which it is characteristically used.

This specification includes not only the admissible moves by the players, but their (conventionalized) aims. Thus much of the meaning of the declarative mood is captured by the declarative dialogue moves (D.say), (D.reply), (D.answer) and others together with the rest of the dialogue game construction.

Now my idea concerning the interpretation of intonational focusing is to add to the repertoire of dialogue games a number of rules of intonation interpretation. By these rules, it will turn out, a member of a dialogue may point out *connections* and *contrasts* between different moves of a dialogue. My thesis is that making such connections and contrasts is exactly what intonational focusing is all about.

2. What's in a Game?

The game theoretical point of view immediately suggests a number of parameters which can be expected to be operative in the interpretation of intonational focusing.

First there is the number of players. With no loss of generality of the subsequent account of intonational focussing we can restrict the membership of a dialogue to two players.

Next comes the question of the *aim* of the game. One has to distinguish clearly between the *internal* aim of a game (represented in the mathematical theory of games by the payoff function of the game) and whatever *external* motives a number of actual individuals may act on when they decide to enter a given game. Clearly these are different concepts. Two people may play a highly competitive game of chess from fully cooperative motives: they just want to have a good time together. Nevertheless, white does his best to defeat black and vice versa. If one wishes, one can view the zero-sum game of chess as a subgame of a more extensive cooperative game of entertainment.

What is relevant for the present concern is the aims internal to a dialogue, as defined by the roles of the players in the dialogue game. Two extremities may be distinguished, which may be described respectively as a cooperative activity of information sharing and an all-out competitive debate. In the former game, the payoff of both players increases as the inverse of the sum of their ignorance: a maximum is attained when no move by either player can narrow the range of states of affairs compatible with what either player knows (or believes).

In the latter game, a player increases his payoff by replacing the opponent's assertions by his own: the more beliefs my opponent has to give up, the better for me. Both types will be relevant for the interpretation of intonational focusing.

A third typical consideration in the game theoretical description of any game concerns the players' knowledge of the game situation at each stage of the game. If each player knows how the situation looks like in full detail at each stage of the game, we have a game of *perfect information*; else the game is one of imperfect information.

The dialogue games obviously are games with imperfect information *par excellence*. One of their main functions is precisely to make the players' information about each others' assumptions less imperfect.

Game theory describes lack of perfect information by means of information sets, a special technical device with restricted expressive power. In Carlson (1976) I suggested generalizing this notion with the help of possible worlds semantics for epistemic logic. In that generalization, imperfect information is represented simply as underdetermination of the actual game situation by the set of epistemic states of affairs compatible with each player's knowledge of the game. Instead of a unique game tree, each player has to cope with a set of equally possible game trees.

Such a generalization would give a more realistic description of a dialogue. For instance, in such a description a representation can be given automatically not only to what each player believes about the game situation, but also what each player takes each other participant to believe, and so on *ad libitum*.

3. A Simplified Model

For the present purposes, however, I propose a drastically reduced and simplified representation. Despite its simplicity, it is sufficient to bring out the essential logic of intonational focusing.

In this reconstruction, the dialogue is represented by a *board*: a two column list of sentences, each side listing sentences successively uttered or written down by one of the dialogue participants. This is the list of the explicit dialogue moves made in the game. In addition, each player keeps a private list, not seen by the other player. In this list, again on one side, are entered the player's own assumptions at each stage of the game. On the opposite side, the player enters assumptions that he takes the other player to make or have made in the game.

Each player, then, can work on two lists: the common board and his own list of assumptions. He can read from both sides of the board and his own assumption list, but not from the other player's private record; and he can write on his side of the board as well as write and delete on either side of his own record. The game quite resembles the children's game at sea war, played by two players on separate sheets of paper.

This simplified description allows us to make the aims of the players in each extreme type of game (cooperative information sharing and competitive debate) more precise. The initial situation in each game includes a (possibly empty) set of assumptions on the private lists of each player, and an empty board.

The aim of the players in the cooperative game is to make their private lists match each other: to impart their own privileged information to the opposite side and to enrich their own assumptions by means of items on the list of their interlocutor. Straightforward pooling together of the two sides of his private record by each player on his own is generally not a good strategy, since typically a player's description of the other's assumptions is poor and inaccurate. The two sides of a player's private record may also contain conflicting items. But the board can be used to pass assumptions from one player to another. (This is of course a primitive but graphical description of what communication is all about.)

The aim of each player in the competitive game is optimally satisfied if the opponent is forced to unilaterally give up his conflicting assumptions and accept the other's view. It may be noted that the optimal end points in each type of game are the same, although the methods of arriving at them differ. Whether by cooperative information sharing or by competitive debate, the players attempt to make their sets of assumptions coincide.

Here, the aim of (matter of fact) dialogue is defined in terms of consistency only: the aim of a dialogue is attained when players agree, however false the consensus may be. Often, however, one does not want to maximize one's set of beliefs at the cost of their trustworthiness. Facts usually decide when one has to deal with a contradiction between one's own assumptions and those of the interlocutors: the assumptions that go by the board should be the false ones.

This further aspect can be built into the aims of a dialogue when desirable. As a result, one can distinguish between *agreement-seeking* and *truth-seeking* dialogues, whether cooperative or competitive. Technically, there is no obstacle to construing Hintikka's semantical games as a restricted sort of truth-seeking debate. Thus moves defined in the semantical games can freely occur as moves in a dialogue game, interspersed with genuine dialogue moves. We shall see examples of such rule interaction in the sequel.[4]

In order not to trivialize the task of the players, some logical constraints should be put on the players' assumption lists. (Otherwise anything can be accepted and denied.) A strong but natural suggestion is that all assumption lists must be internally consistent at each point of the game. Although this is not the most realistic representation of a real life dialogue, it will do for the moment. What this restriction means is that the players must be required not only to add new assumptions on their lists but to delete or modify a sufficient number of earlier ones so as to preserve logical consistency. The exact manner in which the lists are modified can (and ought to) be left to the individual player's discretion.

A related complication due to our decision to represent the players' beliefs in syntactic rather than semantic terms concerns redundancy. There is nothing so far to stop excessive redundancy in the players' assumption lists: an assumption may be entered which in fact is a consequence of an assumption already made. I shall assume at this point that redundancy in the players' assumption sets is immediately eliminated. For example, as soon as a substitution instance of an existential sentence is introduced on a list, the existential sentence itself will disappear.

4. Rationality

The characteristic moves in a cooperative dialogue and in a debate differ. This is not due to special further rules of dialogue, but a function of the *aims* of the two types of game. A rational debater tries to challenge the assertions of his opponent, in order to approach his goal of refuting the opponent and vindicating his own theses. In contrast, it is in the interests of the members of an information-sharing dialogue to accommodate as many of the assertions of the interlocutors as possible in order to approach the goal of shared beliefs.

In a conventional activity like a game there is often a certain give-and-take between the concepts of rule and strategy. Rules are motivated ultimately by the fact that they fix a good strategy of bringing about the external aim of the game. Communication being conventional behavior with clear external aims, there is often a descriptive choice whether some feature of linguistic behavior should be treated as a conventional rule of language games or as a likely (because effective) choice of communication strategy.

This is particularly true in a cooperative game of information sharing, where the internal aim of the game agrees with its external purpose. For instance, is it a rule of language, or just a good move, to answer a question if one can? Is it a linguistic convention that one does not ask what one already knows?

As a rule, one would of course prefer to leave as much as possible to be systematically explained by considerations of the players' aims and strategies. For instance, surely it is no slip of tongue to ask what one already knows: it is just a foolish thing to do if one is out to learn something new. In a dialogue with different aims, it is quite all right, e.g. at school or in court. The rules of dialogue ought to fix only what is really conventional in the game. Rules state what cannot be explained.

The concept of rational game strategy inherent in the dialogue game idea promises interesting insights into the Gricean *maxims of conversation*. As Asa Kasher has pointed out,[5] it is not likely that the Gricean maxims represent any independent linguistically motivated principles at all. They ought to fall out from a general characterization of the *aims* and *means* of linguistic exchanges together with obvious assumptions of *rationality* of the participants. One important advantage of such a more general approach is its systematic character. One can for instance vary the aims of a linguistic exchange and obtain systematic predictions as to what conversational maxims emerge in each case. And it is clear that conversational maxims do vary from case to case in intuitively reasonable ways. Brevity may be at a premium in a fire but not in story-telling.

The concept of a dialogue game might offer a way to register such variations systematically. With all its limitations, game and decision theory is still the best theory of rationality available. Rationality is the very concept the theory of games tries to characterize: different proposed solutions for different classes of games yield so many partial definitions of rationality. In the two-person zero-sum games, a satisfactory definition of rationality has been obtained in von Neumann's minimax theorem. A general definition is hard to give even in 2-person variable sum games. There are several competing theories, none of them quite satisfactory or general enough.

Whatever the definition of rationality, it can be used to define conversational maxims. An example of a Gricean maxim is the maxim of *relevance*. It implies among other things that one should not waste breath with sentences that are obvious to everyone. By construing dialogue games as *recursive* games so that the payoff is a decreasing function of the length of the game, this maxim can be made to follow from any reasonable assumptions of rationality. What is significant, this construction does not just register the maxim, but *explains* it as a consequence of the aims of the exchange.

More detailed definitions of relevance are forthcoming when textual concepts like the *topic* of a dialogue (the *dialogue specific* aims of the players) are available. A dialogue move is relevant to the topic of a dialogue if it shortens the way to attaining the specific aims of the dialogue (e.g. resolving some particular issue).

5. Rules of Dialogue

The remaining essential parameter in the description of any game concerns the *strategies* of the players: what moves each player has at his disposal at each stage of the game. In this section, I shall propose some elementary rules of dialogue. The proposals are somewhat tentative, but they will do for my purposes, and at any rate they should be on the right track.

I start with rules associated with declarative sentences. Naturally enough, a dialogue may start with one player making known an assumption of his. This gives us the first dialogue-initiating rule:

(D.say)   A player may assert an assumption of his.

Assume player *A* has asserted a sentence, which is duly inscribed on the board. The other player *B* now has a number of alternative responses. He can *accept* the assertion. He then adds the sentence (or some abbreviation of it, such as 'yes') on his side of the board, and enters it on his assumption list if it was not there already; he also knows to enter it on his list of *A*'s assumptions.

Or *B* may *deny* the assertion. In the dialogue game, this means that the negation of *A*'s assertion (or some abbreviation of it, e.g. 'no') is put on *B*'s side of the board, and on *B*'s private list, if it is not there already. (*A*'s opposite view will of course be entered on *B*'s record of *A*'s beliefs anyway.)

A common reply is to *question* the other player's assertion. What this logically amounts to is a request for the other player to prove his point or clarify it: to make the questioner able to understand the assertion or to support it by further arguments. The questioner may question the whole assertion (put forward a polarity question) or just formulate search questions (wh-questions) designed to fill in gaps in his understanding of the assertion.

Questioning is one way to acknowledge a claim while suspending judgment. Alternatively, one may just vaguely encourage one's interlocutor to go on and make his point clearer. The expression of such encouragement in English is typically a sustained 'yes' — i.e. a 'yes' which has a continuation contour overlaid on it. Compare this to the final intonation of a 'yes' of acceptance. The choice of intonation is predictable, for an acceptance makes further defense unnecessary.

Let me now formulate a game rule for such responses:

(D.reply)   When a player has put forward an assertion, the other player(s) may choose to accept it, deny it, or (just) to acknowledge it (e.g. by prompting the interlocutor to continue).

Now a move by (G.say) is a typical *initial move* of a dialogue game, while (D.reply) is not. Its proper application is conditional on a preceding assertive move, to which it acts as a response. It is an example of a *countermove*. The distinction between initial moves and countermoves will be important in focus interpretation.

In order to allow A to follow B's encouragement to continue, we may recognize an addition to an assertive move as a subtype of an assertive move. The addition is made by the same player who makes the move it is an addition to. This characterization also covers cases where the addition is actually made by another person, for such an addition implies acceptance of the preceding assertion — in effect a repetition of that assertion by the person who makes the addition. We thus have

(D.add)   A player may add another assertion to an assertion he has already asserted (or accepted).

Additions are of course often marked by conjunctions 'and', 'but', 'yet' and others. By definition, additions are not initial moves in a dialogue.

Question-answer dialogues are particularly well suited for focus determination just because questions are a systematic way of actualizing presuppositions. By seeing which questions given focussed sentences are appropriate answers to we can determine which presumptions they can be predicated on. Hintikka's game theoretical semantics for questions combined with the dialogue games for emphasis promise to sharpen these analytic tools and make their application more mechanical.

One concept of Hintikka's semantics of questions is important for the present purposes. That is the *presupposition* of a question. (For the definition, see Hintikka, 1976b.) In the connection of asking a question (either as a precondition of it or as a consequence), the presupposition of the question will appear among the assumptions of the dialogue. Actually, this is a consequence of the *aim* of a question-answer dialogue. As Hintikka points out, the aim of a questioner in an honest information-seeking dialogue is for the addressee to make true the *desideratum* of the question, a sentence systematically related to the question describing the questioner as informed of the (or a) correct answer to the question. A condition for this state of affairs to obtain, hence a condition for the addressee to comply with the questioner's request, is that there *be* an answer to the question. The appearance of the presupposition of the question in the assumptions of the questioner is hence no peculiarity of a 'logic of questions' but an instance of the Kantian principle of rational demands that 'ought' implies 'can'. This is another case where an apparent linguistic regularity falls out from the aims of dialogue games together with obvious requirements of rationality of its participants.

Another inference valid on the same grounds is available for the addressee of the question: that the desideratum of the question is not yet true, i.e. that the questioner does not already know the answer. The reflection of this inference in the dialogue game is that no (or not all) substitution instance(s) of the question appear(s) among the assumptions of the questioner.

Since these inferences follow from a consideration of the aims of a question-answer dialogue, they need not be registered in a game rule for questioning. Besides, requiring that these felicity conditions be satisfied before a question is well-formed would make it impossible for players to know when a dialogue rule is applicable or not: the game being one of imperfect information, the players are not always in a position to know if the above conditions of a successful question are satisfied. And although the choice of best *strategy* may be impaired by imperfect information, we do not want the *rules* of the game to be sensitive to it.

Therefore the rule for asking a question will be as simple as

(D.ask)   A player can ask a player a question.

As Stenius (1967) observed, the meaning of a question is actually revealed in the game rule for *answering*. The game rule for answering relies on a prior explication of the semantics of (indirect) questions and the concept of an *answer* to a question. Such an explication is already available in Hintikka (1976b). What the dialogue game rule adds to it is only an explication of the meaning of the "optative operator" in Hintikka's analysis. The dialogue game construction explicates the fact that a questioner succeeds, by uttering a direct question, to put his interlocutor under a commitment to provide an answer to that question. The point of that explication is that the interlocutor has agreed to play a dialogue game of asking and answering with the questioner, following the rules of the game and accepting the aims set for him by his role in it.

Another choice concerning the logic of questions is whether answering a question is required by a linguistic convention, or whether answering is a strategic option. I shall assume here that at least some response to a question is a linguistic duty. I propose the rule

> (G.answer) When a player has asked another player a question, the addressee has the choice whether to put forward a (partial or full) answer to the question, to deny the presupposition of the question, or to present some other excuse for failing to answer the question.

The most common excuse of course is 'I don't know'. It is fair to call all other responses except answering excuses, for the *aim* of the questioner in a question-answer dialogue is that the addressee make true the desideratum of the question. A *bona fide* question-answer dialogue being a cooperative dialogue of information sharing, it is assumed that the addressee shares the preferences of the questioner.

Note that the language game explication of the meaning of the interrogative mood confirms Wittgenstein's insights about the difference in meaning between questions and assertions. A question is not a disguised assertion: it is not a move in an assertion-reply dialogue. It is not accepted or denied, but answered or not. Although it conveys the questioner's desire for an answer, it does not *assert* that desire. The desire can only be *inferred* from the assumption that the questioner is playing the game of asking and answering according to rules.

II. INTONATION RULES INTRODUCED

1. The Logic of Intonational Focusing. (D.emphasis)

It has been a consensus among recent writers on the topic of intonational focusing that the 'logical form' of a focused sentence is represented in the form of some quantificational expansion of the logical form of the intonationally unmarked variant of that sentence (either in terms of standard quantification theory or some other formal language, e.g. lambda calculus).[6]

I shall depart from this tradition. However, in a later section, I shall try to give an explanation why such a procedure has a great deal of initial appeal, and indeed does reflect certain facets of the logic of focusing.

In contrast to the consensus, I take the logical form of, say, the sentence

(1)   *Bradley* lives here.

to be simply (that of)

(2)   Bradley lives here.

That is, as far as logical force, or semantic interpretation, is concerned, (1) is just a variant of (2). The added information of the emphasis will only appear when (1) is used as a move of a dialogue game.

Now what is the use of (1) as contrasted with (2)? One natural situation in which (1) might be uttered instead of (2) is when the dialogue partner has just asked a question, namely

(3)   Who lives here?

It is obvious what the intent of the emphasis on *Bradley* is given (3): it construes (1) as an *answer* to the question (3), deaccenting the part shared by the answer with the question and emphasizing the news in it.

This insight, I claim, can be generalized. The function of an emphasis is nothing else than to relate a dialogue move as a *countermove* to an explicit move or an implicit assumption entered in the dialogue. The focusing intonation thus serves as a *pointer* to an earlier step in a dialogue.

The focusing emphasis indicates the respect in which the countermove differs from the move(s) it is a response to, while the backgrounded stretch is recoverable from earlier context.

Turned into a dialogue game rule, this insight gives us as a first approximation

(D.emphasis)   When a player has put forward a sentence of the form
               (i) $X - A - Y$
               where A receives special emphasis, the listener may look for a sentence of the form
               (ii) $X - B - Y$
               among the sentences entered on the board or on his private record. If such a sentence (ii) is found, the listener may construe (i) as a countermove by some noninitial dialogue rule to (ii).

What (D.emphasis) says is that a sentence with special emphasis will always be construed as a *response* to some related move, either explicit or assumed. This seems to be the right generalization intuitively. Focussed sentences are curious discussion openers; they indicate that some implicit assumptions were entertained by the speaker which motivate the emphasis.

A condition on the appropriateness of intonational focusing is now obvious: no uninterpretable emphases should occur on sentences put forward in a dialogue game. This can be expressed by the following prediction about well-formedness:

(4)   No sentence with focusing emphasis can be an initial move of a well-formed dialogue.

In the example at hand, the listener is able to apply (D.emphasis) appropriately. He finds on the board A's antecedent question (3), which has the appropriate form specified in (D.emphasis) with respect to (1). He can then construe (1) as a countermove, by (D.answer), to (3), and go on with the dialogue.

So although (1) can be understood perfectly well without the accompanying background assumptions which make an application of (D.emphasis) possible, its *textual intent* remains unclear in their absence. Something is at fault; yet the fault does not concern the *content* of the information, but rather its *flow* between the speakers.

Turning the tables, a listener hearing (7) and failing to apply (D.emphasis) properly may assume that the *speaker can* do so and infer that his representation of the speaker's hidden assumptions is inadequate. In that case, he first enriches his representation of the speaker's assumptions by adding some sentence of the appropriate form and is now able to apply (D.emphasis). In this way, unexpected intonations give inferential knowledge of the assumptions of one's interlocutor.

This possibility gives the necessary insight why a representation of focused sentences in terms of quantificational expansions such as

(5)   Someone lives here and it is Bradley

has so much initial appeal. When no context is provided, the minimum conversational implication (in the specific sense of the preceding paragraph) of (1) is roughly expressed by (5). The existentially quantified sentence (5) abstracts over the various sentences of form (ii) that might be found in the speaker's assumptions motivating the emphasis, and the identificational part of (5) renders the assertory force (2) of (1).

2. *Against Quantificational Expansions*

There are a number of arguments against the approach of complicating the semantic representations of focussed sentences in the manner exemplified by (5). First and foremost, such representations do not capture the essential point of focusing. Logically, (5) says nothing more or less than (2) alone. Unless the expansion is given some further interpretation which forces a difference between (5) and (2), nothing is gained by the expansion. Such additional principles of interpretation are likely to end up saying precisely what is said by the dialogue game setup and the rule (D.emphasis).

What is perhaps more persuasive, I shall present evidence that the *range* of interpretations of focussed sentences can be systematically predicted from the pragmatic context provided in the dialogue games, especially from the character of the preceding moves and the aims of the dialogue. Such predictions are missed in a context-free representation of focussed sentences in terms of logically equivalent quantificational expansions.

Furthermore, an ontological problem concerns the domains of quantification presupposed by quantificational expansions such as (5). Contrastive focus can be laid on almost any imaginable domain, from sentence polarity through major phrases, words, and morphemes down to meaningless syllables and individual sounds. Context-free representations of the sort (5) can hardly be more than suggestive in some of the more exotic domains. Quantification over concrete objects is clear enough, but what about propositions or abstract objects in general. In the other extreme, what is the range of quantification in a sentence like

(6)   I said six*teen.*

In order for quantifiers to make sense in such cases, their range must be contextually restricted. Such a restriction is built into the game rule (D.emphasis): the listener of a focussed sentence does a limited search among a contextually circumscribed set of assumptions asserted or entertained by participants of the same dialogue. The formulation of (D.emphasis) is equally applicable in cases like (6). A sufficient condition of appropriateness of the emphasis in (6) is the presence of another sentence, e.g.

(7)   Did you say sixty?

in the dialogue in which (6) is a move. To make the received approach do some actual work one has to develop a way to restrict the interpretation of presuppositional quantifiers to discourse context in a way which would essentially recapture the effect of (D.emphasis). This more fundamental task has been neglected in structuralist studies of focusing.

The neglect reminds one of the neglect of structuralist semanticists to provide interpretations of their formalism in terms of a nonlinguistic universe of discourse.

The structuralist theory of focusing so far falls short of explaining data for the same reason why a syntactic treatment of semantic concepts is insufficient: there is a number of essential variables which are not recognized. In structuralist semantics, what is missed is the systematic variability of domains of interpretation. In structural pragmatics, what is missed is the variability of the uses and users of language. Only a theory which explicitly recognizes these as essential parameters can hope to give a satisfactory account of pragmatic phenomena.

If focusing is indeed essentially a pragmatic device, the above considerations are a challenge to the received view. One might even argue that the pragmatic point of view alone gives a clear answer to what it is that one *has to explain* in intonational focusing. The question remains unclear if only syntactic and semantic concepts are allowed: there seems to be "some difference in meaning", but what is it? There is no satisfactory concept of syntax or semantics which could give the answer. But as soon as the pragmatic variables which define a game are made explicit, the right questions can be asked: what is the influence of intonational focusing on the flow of the language games people play.

3. Nonfinal Accent. (D.nonfinal)

The second major claim about focusing intonation I want to make is that there is a significant intonational opposition between the most likely pronunciation of (1) in the context (3) and the following variant:

(8)   *Brádley* lives here.

The acute accent marks what is in the Appendix described as a nonfinal focusing accent. It places a low-rise accent on the intonation center of the focused phrase and (in declarative sentences) adds a terminal rise to the whole utterance.

What are the characteristic contexts for (8)? If the present approach is right, there are two natural dialogue contexts for (8).

First, (8) can be used to *contradict* and *correct* an assumption of a dialogue partner roughly to the following effect:

(9)   It is Bradley who lives here, not someone else.

Secondly, (8) can have an 'at least' interpretation: I am asked who might be the inhabitants here, and I start the list by putting forward (8) as a partial answer: the implication is that there may be others, as far as I know.

How do these subtle intuitions come about? Now one invariant about both uses of (8) is that they *suggest a continuation:* in the case of a correction or contradiction, there is an expectation that the correction will be either expanded on by the speaker or reacted to by the listener with an acknowledgement or a denial. It would be odd to say (8), with its nonfinal emphasis, as the last line of a debate and leave without looking back to see whether the point sank in. Compare for instance

(9)   *Bràdley* lives here and that's that.
(10)   *Bràdley* lives here, and that's that.

While (9) can form a close intonational phrase, (10) is not pronounceable except perhaps by construing the second sentence as an afterthought, separated by a pause from the first one.

The partial list use of (8) likewise strongly suggests that the list is not meant to be complete: It might be continued, perhaps by the speaker himself or by someone else. Again, (8) would be out of place as a final note to a discussion, as the only unqualified response to a question.

Let us compare the contrastive and list implications of the nonfinal accent in a revealing minimal pairs of examples.

As Wittgenstein points out, sincere questions are not disguised assertions. Therefore one does not expect that a nonfinal intonation on a direct answer to a question (as distinguished from a denial of its presupposition) can be interpreted as corrective. And so it seems to be: I don't think that the nonfinal intonation of the answer (12) to an *honest offer* made by (11) can possibly be understood as a correction:

(11)   − Who wants tea?
(12)   − *Í* want tea.

Rather, it is the polite answer to (11) in a situation in which (11) is jointly addressed to a number of people. It is felt to be more polite than the same answer with a final intonation, because it suggests that others may have their say, too.

The situation is different if (11) is understood not as an offer but as a rhetorical question. A rhetorical question *is* a disguised assertion. It is a characteristic of sincere questions that one questions what one does not already know or believe. If one thinks one already knows what there is to know, one may pose a *rhetorical* question: that is, a question that one thinks no one has an answer to because there is none. In Hintikka's semantics, rhetorical questions can be represented as questions whose presupposition is the *negation* of their *bona fide* presupposition. Clearly, then, the aim of a rhetorical question cannot be that the *bona fide desideratum* of the question be made true. Rather, it just conveys the questioner's belief that the addressee has no other reply than denying the *bona fide* presupposition.

For example, (11) as a rhetorical question does not imply its *bona fide* presupposition

(13)   Somebody wants tea,

rather, it invites the denial of (13), i.e.

(14)   Nobody wants tea.

As the actual aim of the rhetorical questioner is to wring from his addressee the reply (14), in effect an assent to his own opinion, the dialogue (11)–(12) is actually an assertion-reply dialogue disguised as a question-answer exchange.

Correspondingly, the nonfinal intonation of (12) is on this interpretation less likely to suggest that the speaker does not constitute the only exception to the questioner's supposition; rather, it is a challenge for the questioner to respond.

The corrective implications of the nonfinal intonation are perceptually more salient than the suggestion of incompleteness, when sentences are considered out of context. However, contexts like (11) show that the 'at least' interpretation is just as possible and often the by far more likely one. Now what is the context variable that decides which of the two interpretations is more likely in each particular case?

The answer seems obvious from the foregoing example. The preferred interpretation depends on the *aims* of the players, whether they are opposed or compatible. When an assertive move is construed as an impartial or amiable exchange of information, the 'at least' interpretation prevails; when it is a move in an ongoing dispute, it is more likely to be understood as a corrective.

But this difference now proves to be an automatic corollary of the setup of the dialogue game. For we saw that the optimal strategy of a participant of a debate is to contradict his opponent's assumptions whenever feasible, while it furthers the common goals of the participants of an information sharing dialogue to add to the other player's assumptions if consistently possible.

These considerations serve to explain the different implications of nonfinal emphasis in different dialogue contexts. They leave as the invariant contribution of the nonfinal intonation contour in (8) into the game as distinguished from (1) the simple message that the exchange connected with the current move is not complete.

What could be the theoretical reconstruction of this in the theory of dialogue games? A simple proposal is that a sentence with nonfinal intonation *cannot constitute the last move, or end point of a well-formed dialogue game.*

I think this is just about all one needs to say about the meaning of nonfinal emphasis over and above what is already said in (D.emphasis). The back-referential function of the added prominence seems to remain invariant between final and nonfinal focus. This allows us to factor out the suggestion of nonfinality from the function of the emphasis.

The conceptual analysis of the nonfinal emphasis in (8) turns out, then, to be quite simple. The added emphasis on some given constituent of a sentence is interpreted just as it is in the previous cases. In addition, nonfinality constitutes the equally general and invariant interpretation of the nonfinal intonation contour. No new rule of focusing is needed for the emphasis. A rule for nonfinal intonation interpretation is enough:

(D.nonfinal)   A sentence with nonfinal intonation cannot constitute an end point of a well-formed dialogue game.

As already explained, what further moves are expected to follow is a function of the language game in which the inconclusive sentence is a move. If it is an answer to a question, it may be followed by a completion of the answer or else it may elicit a further comment from the questioner, more likely perhaps the former.

In the corrective cases, similarly, either the contradiction is in need of some expansion by the speaker, or it expects a further response from the opponent. Generalizing from these examples, incompleteness of the dialogue game may involve either that the speaker's move is incomplete or that the language game it is in needs completion by another player.

Note that the characterization in (D.nonfinal) squares well with other nonfinal contours (terminal rise or at least absence of terminal fall). A polarity question with its terminal rise clearly cannot be intended as a discussion stopper either. Another clear case is the continuation rise in a sustained sequence of coordinated constituents. No other meaning but the organizational message: this is not the end of my move – can be discerned here.

Observe the direction of implication here: I am not suggesting that e.g. all questions should have rising intonation contours, only that those sentences which do have it have nonfinal discourse function. There are sentence types with falling intonation contours which have nonfinal discourse function, e.g. imperatives. Even questions need not be marked for nonfinality by intonation. (In Finnish, no questions are so marked, not even polarity questions.)

It is in good agreement with markedness considerations that we have a rule of interpretation for the marked nonfinal contour but not for the final contour. In consonance with the logic of markedness, the unmarked 'final' contour marks finality only where it contrasts with the marked intonation; otherwise, it carries no inherent message.

It turns out, then, that there is a neat complementarity in the dialogue functions of our two intonational rules (D.emphasis) and (D.nonfinal). The former serves to connect a dialogue move to moves preceding it, implying that the discussion could not have started with the emphatic sentence. The latter serves to connect a dialogue move to subsequent moves, signaling in turn that the discussion is not expected to end with the nonfinally inflected sentence.

This is a simple and aesthetically pleasing theory of intonational focusing. What is best about it, it allows one to make surprisingly complicated and precise predictions about subtle but yet quite sharp intuitions. I shall try to substantiate this claim in the following subsection.

4. Applying the Dialogue Rules

Let us go through the simple example (11)–(12) in rather more detail to see how the game rules actually grind out the predictions made.

The game of dialogue connected with (11)–(12) might run as follows. Initially, the presupposition (13) is among the questioner's assumptions while the answer (12) is among those of the answerer. The first move is by the questioner, Q, who asks (11). (11) is entered on the board, the answerer A can infer that Q holds (13) and enters it in his record of Q's assumptions. A, knowing the rules of the game, put forward (12) as an answer to (11). Q, also aware of the rules, applies (D.emphasis) and construes (12) as a response to (11); applying (D.nonfinal), he knows that something else could be added.

Accepting (12), Q adds it among his assumptions as well as among his record of A's assumptions. A on his side knows to enter (12) among his record of Q's assumptions. When the presupposition (13) is deleted as redundant, all assumption lists are identical and the aim of the cooperative dialogue has been attained.

The dialogue is incomplete, however, for the suggestion of nonfinality is left hanging in the air. What is Q's interpretation of it? On the basis of earlier considerations, there are two choices: either (12) is at the same time an appeal for Q to make some complementary move, or it implies that A does not mean (12) as a completed move. There is no obvious countermove for Q to make; so presumably A intends that his answer should not be assumed to constitute a full answer to (12). And this is exactly what the nonfinal intonation 'means' in the context at hand.

Looking at (11)–(12) from a 'logical' point of view, what verbal description would best express the pragmatic inferences I just drew? The following is as close a paraphrase as I can come up with.

(15)   Someone wants tea and I want tea but maybe someone else wants tea too.

The first conjunct of (15) describes the presuppositional force of the added emphasis; the middle conjunct expresses the assertion, and the last conjunct interprets the message of the nonfinal intonation. Admittedly, the last conjunct is a rather lame attempt, as the modal logic of *maybe* is left unclear. But there is no simple extensional sentence which would express the precise force of nonfinality in (12) without wronging the facts.

Something like (15) is likely to appear in a structuralist account of (12). However, there is a crucial shortcoming in a theory which is limited to generating paraphrases to focused sentences. While a context free rule essentially deriving (15) from (12) does give a rough description of the conversational force of (12), it can at best approximate the level of observational adequacy. It describes what (12) may impart to a listener, but not how (12) does it, even less why it has exactly the meaning (15) in the context at hand. The dialogue game account seems to explain both the how and the why.

The last claim gains plausibility when the other interpretation of (12) is staged and predicted. For simplicity, let me replace (11) by (14) which makes explicit the presupposition of (11) in its rhetorical use:

(14)   – Nobody wants tea.
(12)   – I want tea.

No further assumptions need be made: player A entertains (14) and player B (12) . The first move (14) is A's, by the rule (D.say). B, whose aim is to refute A, counters by (12). Applying (D.emphasis), A can construe (12) as a response to his (14). Its function is easy to calculate. It is not a question; far from accepting (14), it directly contradicts (14) by implying (13). Hence (12) must be construed as a denial of (14) by rule (D.reply). At this stage of the game, A has entered B's claim on his record and vice versa; the stage has only been set for a resolution of the debate. And applying (D.nonfinal), *A* knows that *B* does not intend to end the debate, either.

What further moves are possible? First, (12) could implicate that *B* does not mean he is the only friend of tea; i.e., his thesis can be made stronger still. But also, and more interestingly, *B* may be inviting *A* to react to his challenge. And in this case, there will be several further moves available for *A*. One of them is to apply (D.reply) once more. And surely one characteristic though not very fruitful next move for *A* to take in a debate like (14)–(12) is to deny *B*'s reply in turn. More reasonably, *A* may try to dissuade *B* by less direct means.

Looking back, the logical force of (12) in this context is not (15) but rather something like

(16)   It is not true that nobody wants tea; I do for one, what do you say to that?

The first conjunct of (16) reflects the denial of (14); the middle conjunct is the assertion, and the last conjunct again conveys the suggestion of nonfinality. In this case, it is even harder to find an extensional paraphrase which would convey the challenge expressed in the nonfinal emphasis.

From the dialogue game approach it is obvious that (and why) each focused sentence will have a variety of natural paraphrases, depending on, and predictable from, the dialogue context. It will not help to defend (15) as the only paraphrase by pointing out that (nonfinality aside) (15) and (16) are logically equivalent even if formally distinct; for it is precisely formal distinctness that the paraphrase approach builds on. Logically, all expansions of a focussed sentence will be (and ought to be) equivalent with the sentence minus extra emphasis. To fail to represent (12) in the two contexts we have described by different paraphrases is to fail to differentiate between the implications of the two occurrences.

As a last example, let us consider a denial of a singular claim by another.

(17)   You blew it.
(18)   *You* blew it.

Player *A* opens with his assumption (17). Observe that (18)–(17) in reversed order would not form a well-formed dialogue; this is predicted by the present theory. *B* counters with (18). What if *B* had repeated (17) instead? In that case, there is no overt signal in *B*'s message which would connect it with *A*'s assertion. *B*'s contribution would sound a meaningless imitation of the literal words used by *A*.

What does the nonfinal emphasis in (18) tell A? By now routinely A connects (18) as a countermove to (17). What is the connection? (17) being a move by (D.say), (18) can only be meant as a reply to (17). It is not an expression of acknowledgement nor a question, so it must be a contradiction. But (18) is not logically incompatible with (17). Some additional assumption must be held by B which makes (17) and (18) incompatible. The minimal choice is

(19)   Not both of us blew it.

When (18) is added in the list of B's assumptions, (18) becomes a well-formed reply. This is an example of how conversational implications arise as a consequence of constraints of dialogue well-formedness.

What about the nonfinal intonation? It is hard to understand (18) as an incomplete reply; given (19), (18) is as definitive a refutation of (17) as one can hope. Hence only the challenge for further comments remains.

Summing up, the discourse value of (18) in the dialogue (17)–(18) comes to something like

(20)   Someone blew it, not both of us blew it, I did not blow it, but you did, or try to show otherwise.

The challenge to the opponent is again missed in any extensional translation of (20).

In this case, there is little hope of finding context-independent rules applying on the form of (18) which would assign (20) to it as a possible paraphrase. For the second conjunct of (20) is clearly a function of the particular assertion which preceded (18).

The context (14) to (12) teaches one important lesson. Unlike (11), (14) does not create an existential presupposition at all. The observation is important since it shows that a focused sentence like (12) does not necessarily imply any existential presuppositions. There are many types of dialogue moves to which a sentence may be addressed to by means of intonational focusing. Hence the difficulty in deciding what it really is that a focussed sentence minimally implies. In fact, *it* implies nothing more or less than it says; its use may imply very different things in different contexts. Therefore the implications of a focussed sentence should not be represented in terms of a single paraphrase associated with it, or even a set of paraphrases, but with a function from contexts to implications. The dialogue rules for focusing intonation serve to specify just this function.

More generally, in a certain sense, an attempt to translate focussed sentences into more explicit paraphrases is like putting the cart before the horse, or, to improve on the metaphor, building the stables around the horses. Starting from a possible countermove in any of an unlimited set of dialogues, one tries to recreate the dialogical environment by constructing additional sentences describing aspects of all dialogues where the move could be used. This strategy, it seems, is a consequence of not recognizing the pragmatical parameters explicitly. If no environment is provided in which a sentence is to be interpreted, this environment has to be built stone by stone within the semantic representation itself.

In contrast, the dialogue approach takes dialogues as given and devises rules for interpreting sentences in a dialogue context. These rules define the discourse function of sentences implicitly, instead of attempting an explicit definition by paraphrases. Of course, the horses end up in the stables which-ever way one proceeds; but one can reasonably claim that one of the strategies is a more sensible one.

Note the point of my criticism of the structuralist approach. It is not that the methodology of quantificational expansions would be wrong, as far as it goes: it does have certain intuitive appeal. This is in part due to the fact that natural language itself uses syntactic constructions to the same effect as intonational contrasts. Cleft sentences and "pseudo-cleft" relative clauses for example have predominantly textual function.

The point is rather that the methodology is insufficient in the absence of further principles of interpretation of the formalism. And when one starts considering what these further principles might look like, one finds that they can equally well be defined so as to be applicable directly to English, leaving out the intermediate structures.

Thus the point is closely parallel to Hintikka's point concerning the semantics of natural languages. Just as Hintikka's semantical games skip a syntactic level of logical form and interpret sentences directly in their models, game-theoretical pragmatics skips syntactic representations of focus and presupposition and interprets pragmatic means of expression directly in their contexts of use.

III. INTERACTION WITH SEMANTIC RULES

1. Focus and Negation

The fact that there is no absolute gap between rules of dialogue games and

rules of the semantic games of verification allows for the possibility of interaction between the two classes of rules.

Ambiguity of ordering with respect to discourse rules is most likely in the
case of a semantic rule with a clear discourse function. One such rule is the
game rule for negation. The difference in meaning between a negated sentence
and an equivalent positive one is clearest in discourse. A negated sentence
serves as a denial or contradiction of an antecedent — explicit or implicit —
assumption. The same contradiction could be made in terms of some positive
equivalent sentence, but it would require a more thorough semantic analysis
in order not to be missed or at least misconstrued.

A reflection of this function of negation is the often noted fact that
existential claims are usually couched in positive form. Negated sentences do
not as a rule serve to introduce new individuals in a discourse. Thus though

(21)   I did not catch all of the words.

is logically equivalent to

(22)   I missed some of the words.

only (22) is naturally continued with

(23)   They were spoken too indistinctly.

meaning specifically the words missed, not the whole bunch. These properties
of negative sentences are reflected in the semantical game rule for negation:

(G.not) When a player has put forward an assertion of form $X - not - Y$,
         his opponent undertakes to defend $X - Y$.

The discourse function of *not* is spelled out in so many words in the above
formulation: a player who makes a negative assertion in fact ascribes his
opponent the underlying positive claim.

In the semantical game connected with (21), (G.not) is applied first
so as to construe the speaker of (21) as the opponent of a universal claim
attributed to his opponent. Although a successful strategy of refuting that
universal claim involves finding counterexamples to it, presenting them is not
the dialogue aim of the speaker of (21).

For the purposes of focus interpretation, the game rule for negation acts
like another rule of dialogue games. Naturally, (G.not) can be applied only
in a competitive dialogue. Hence the appearance of a negation can serve as
a clue for the dialogue purpose of an assertive move. A negative sentence is
likely to express a denial of an antecedent claim.

2. Ordering Ambiguities

A moment's reflection shows that a simple sentence like

(24)   *Annie* does not want tea.

has a wide range of possible shades of meaning. When an appropriate context is provided, it can be understood at least in any of the following ways:

(25)   (a) It's not Annie who wants tea,   but someone else.
                                             if anybody.
        (b) Annie, for one, is not one who wants tea.

(26)   (a) It's Annie who does not want tea, not someone else.
        (b) At least Annie is one who does not want tea.

Appropriate contexts for (25)–(26) to arise are, in the same order,

(27)   (a) Annie wants tea.
        (b) Everyone wants tea.

(28)   (a) Jane does not want tea.
        (b) Who does not want tea?

These intuitions seem both clear and systematic. They also admit of a systematic explanation in terms of the rules already given.

The first point to make is that the difference between (25) and (26) is patently a matter of *scope*: the negation belongs to the main clause of the paraphrases (25), while it is in the subordinate clause in the paraphrases (26). My claim is that it is this property that explains the ambiguity of (24) in the two contexts (27) and (28).

Specifically, there are two essentially different game strategies available for the interpretation of (24), depending on the order of application of the rules (G.not) and (D.emphasis). Expansions (25) describe game strategies where (G.not) is applied before (D.emphasis), while (26) correspond to applying (D.emphasis) before interpreting the negation.

This difference in rule ordering is made explicit by syntactic dominance relations in the respective expansions (25) and (26), just as we can explicate the ambiguity of a sentence like

(29)   I have a solution for every problem

by expanding it to one or the other of

(30)   I have a solution which solves every problem

or

(31)   Every problem is such that I have a solution for it.

Theoretically, then, there is nothing new to the multiple ambiguity of (24):
it represents another case of a well-documented type of ambiguity in natural
language.

Let me substantiate this thesis by a closer look at the games connected
with (24) in the contexts (27) and (28).

Assume player *A* has asserted (27) (a) and *B* continues with (24). What
should *A* think of *B*'s contribution? Three dialogue rules apply: (G.not),
(D.emphasis) and (D.nonfinal). The task is to make the best sense of (24)
the rules allow.

Intonation gives away that (D.emphasis) has to be applied on the emphasis
on *Annie* sooner or later: hence (24) will be a countermove, not an independent assertion by (D.say). It cannot well be a move by (D.answer), for no
questions were asked. It has to be a move by (D.reply), then. What kind of
reply? It is not a question. It certainly does not accept (27) (a) either, being
the negation of it. So it is a denial. And indeed, (G.not) can be applied to it,
construing *B* as an opponent of *A*'s preceding assertion (27) (a).

After the application of (G.not), *A* has to consider the sentence

(32)   *Annie* wants tea

attributed by *B* to his opponent *A*. What does the emphasis on *Annie* convey
in (32)? Interestingly, it cannot be a simple reference to the *identical* subject
of *A*'s identical assertion (27) (a) — this would make the whole contrast
vacuous. Some *other* assumption must be implicit in *B*'s lists. There are two
likely candidates, corresponding to the two tags in the paraphrase (25) (a).
Possibly *B* has a different person in mind who he thinks does want tea. And
indeed (D.emphasis) is properly applicable in (32) if *B*'s own assumptions
include, e.g.,

(33)   Jane wants tea.

But it may be that *B* has no idea who might want tea; in fact, he may be just
reacting to the dubious assumption of *A*'s that

(34)   Someone wants tea.

And again, (D. emphasis) can be applied to (32) if (34) is found among *B*'s
record of *A*'s assumptions.

Finally, (D.nonfinal) can be applied to indicate that (24) is not intended to be the last word about who wants tea and who doesn't; for instance, B may go on to present his different view (33) or A may justify his assumption (34).

The paraphrase (25) (b) lacks the implications of uniqueness of (25) (a). This makes it appropriate for (24) in the context (27) (b). The reasoning is the same as in the previous case up to the application of (G.not) as the first rule, which construes B as the opponent of (32), an instance of A's previous universal claim (27) (b). From here on, things are simpler than in the previous example, as (D.emphasis) can now directly relate (24) to (27) (b). No hidden assumptions are needed to account for the emphasis.

Let us now look at (24) in the contexts provided by (28). Note that here the negation in (24) is repetition from the context, hence it is not likely to have been put in to express B's dialogue intent. This guess is confirmed when an attempt is made to apply (D.emphasis). In order to obtain a match, (G.not) must *not* be applied first so as to delete *not* from (24). So (D.emphasis) has to apply first.

In the context (28) (a) the reasoning repeats the steps we already went through in connection with the example (17)–(18). As in that example, a hidden assumption of uniqueness (or at least incompatibility of (24) and (28) (a)) must be interpolated. Such an assumption is apparent in the paraphrase (26) (a), too.

The question (28) (b) does not carry a uniqueness presupposition. Therefore (26) (b) is a more appropriate paraphrase to (24) in the context of (28) (b). The games connected with the dialogue (28) (b)–(24) are step by step analogous to those associated with (11)–(12). The reader who wants to check again how and why (24) comes out here as a partial answer to an honest question or as a challenge against a rhetorical one can look back to (11)–(12).

Two more general points emerge from the preceding examination. One might have thought that it is not necessary to assume a scope ambiguity in order to capture the different textual functions of a negative sentence like (24). Is it not enough to pay attention to the *aim* of a move? Perhaps what has been analyzed as use of (G.not) as a dialogue move is simply use of (24) as a correction, while the other rule order actually boils down to use of (24) as a friendly comment?

This will not work, unfortunately. For as we saw, (24) can be used as a contradiction to two quite different assumptions, namely (27) (b) and (28) (a). In order for (D.emphasis) to be able to refer back to (27) (a) it has to apply in (24) at a stage where (24) does not have a negation: otherwise the constant parts of the assumption and the rejoinder do not match.

The ordering assumption thus seems not only well motivated (it captures the distinction between the contexts (27) (a) and (28) (a) for (24)), but simply unavoidable, if (D.emphasis) is to retain the simple form it has.

Further, there is a temptation to ascribe the nuances in the interpretation of nonfinality which differentiate (26) (a) and (26) (b) to an ordering ambiguity between (G.not) and (D.nonfinal). However, this does not seem to correspond to the facts of the situation. Rather, (D.nonfinal) does not interact with (G.not) at all. The choice of the player who is likely to continue the dialogue is, if anything, a function of the character of the game, in the manner explained earlier. Even then there is only a slight preference in probabilities. An added piece of information can be elaborated by the speaker or invite comment from the listener about as easily as an objection may do the same. This is why (D.nonfinal) is formulated in the impartial way it is. This formulation yields the correct prediction that nonfinal intonation does not exhibit scope properties.[7]

3. Focus and Quantifier Scope

If the conceptual tools developed here cut any ice, they ought to provide an explanation for a classical case of scope ambiguity which is almost (but not quite) resolved intonationally. I mean the famous pair

(35)   He does not speak to *ànybody*.
(36)   He does not speak to *ánybody*.

The final emphasis on *any* suggests the meaning "He speaks to nobody", while the nonfinal intonation favors the interpretation "He won't address just any arbitrary person". These interpretations correspond to different scope resolutions. The former interpretation comes about when *any* (as a universal quantifier) takes scope over negation, the latter when *any* stays within the scope of *not*.

To see how these preferences arise, notice first that (36) has a variant in which the auxiliary is in a higher clause:

(37)   It is not true that he speaks to anybody.

This paraphrase makes it clear that the negation in (36) serves a dialogue purpose. An application of (D.not) to the negative auxiliary construes (36) as a denial of

(38)   He speaks to *ánybody*.

The emphasis on *any* at the same time locates the disagreement on the quantifier: the suggested correction therefore is a variant of (38) which contrasts with (38) in quantifier character. That is obviously something like

(39)   He only speaks to certain special people.

(39) is accordingly what (36) suggests by denying the opposite. The suggestion is conveyed by the nonfinal emphasis, which implies that there is more to say about who is spoken to — the very implication which (39) makes explicit. The final emphasis makes no such suggestion and therefore reinforces the interpretation of (36) as a universal negation.

But as can be expected from earlier considerations, the scope suggestion of nonfinal emphasis is not quite watertight. (36) can be interpreted as a universal negation too, if the context allows other interpretations for the nonfinal accent. Here is one:

(40)   — He does not speak to me.
        — Actually, he does not speak to *ánybody*.

In the context (40), (36) comes to have the favorite sense of (35). This is predictable, for now the nonfinal emphasis has another more natural interpretation: it construes the reply as a defence against the first speaker's implicit accusation of discrimination.

This shows once again that the nonfinal emphasis does not in itself have scope properties. It just suggests continuation, and an eminently natural one is forthcoming if (36) is construed as a denial of (38) so as to imply (36).

What is important in the account just given, it does not only explain why the scope preferences go as they go in (35)–(36), but also why they are indeed just preferences.[8]

APPENDIX: PHONOLOGY OF INTONATIONAL FOCUSING

The phonology of intonational focusing is not yet fully understood, partly for a lack of functional criteria of distinctness for intonation patterns. The interpretational efforts made in this paper are designed to help sharpening such criteria. So far, I have made the following assumptions about the phonology of focusing.

1. Unmarked Stress

I assume that there is for a given sentence a syntactically and lexically determined unmarked (unfocused) metrical and melodical pattern. It does not matter just how that pattern is determined. However, for definiteness, I shall develop one proposal.

In it, stress is analysed in terms of the metrical theory of stress of Liberman (1972) and Liberman and Prince (1977), with some deviations. The unmarked stress pattern of a sentence is calculated as a function of its syntactic constituent structure and the lexical category of its words. A partial order of prominence among the syntactic constituents of a sentence is determined by the rule

(1)   An immediate constituent B of a phrase C is no weaker than another immediate constituent D of C, if B follows D and contains a member of a major lexical category (N, A, V).

(1) singles out the last non-enclitic constituent of any phrase as its strongest constituent.

If the strongest constituent of a phrase C is terminal, call it the strongest terminal constituent of C. Let a terminal constituent be its own strongest terminal constituent. Then definition (1) can be extended recursively by

(2)   The strongest terminal constituent of a phrase C is the strongest terminal constituent of the strongest immediate constituent of C.

As a result, the nuclear stress of a sentence will in the unmarked case be found on the last full word of the sentence.

There are alternative proposals for defining prominence relations among terminal constituents on the basis of constituent prominence relations. The following projection principle will do here.

(3)   If a constituent B is stronger than a constituent C, then the strongest terminal constituent of B is stronger than that of C.

I assume word level stresses as given so that the rule (3) ultimately defines a partial order of prominence among individual syllables of a sentence.

That partial order of prominence is the basis of the phonological representation of stress I shall use, viz. the *metrical grid* introduced by Liberman (1972). A metrical grid is, as Liberman describes it, a *system of hierarchically ordered periodicities*: in simpler words, it articulates a sentence at once horizontally into rhythmic periods and vertically into prominence peaks and lows.

In my version of the metrical grid, a sentence is represented by the set of its individual syllables in their natural temporal (left-to-right) order. Formally a metrical grid for a sentence $S = (s_1, \ldots, s_n)$ will be a decreasing chain G of subsets of an ordered set $G_o = S \cup (e_1, \ldots, e_m)$ where the e_i are empty syllables (pauses) and the order of G_o extends that of S. The first member of G is G_o and $G_{k+1} \subseteq G_k$ for all k.[9]

The metrical grid for a sentence S is aligned with the terminal prominence order of S by the rule

(4)   If s_i is no weaker than s_j, then s_i belongs to every G_m where s_j belongs.

For instance, in *thirteen men* the syllabic prominences are *men* > *teen* > *thir*. A metrical grid properly aligned with these prominence relations is

(5)   men G_3
                          teen   men G_2
                  thirteen   men G_1
                  thirteen   men G_0 .

2. Pauses

The gird (5) involves a sequence of ascending stresses without suitable intervening lows which is experienced as a disturbing *stress clash*. I define

(6)   A sequence (s_i, s_j, s_k) of syllables adjacent in G_n ($n > 0$) is an *ascending triple* if s_k belongs to every G_m where s_j belongs, and s_j belongs to every G_m where s_i belongs.

Besides adjusting relative prominence relations, stress clashes can be avoided by interpolating suitable pauses. By holding a long enough pause between *thirteen* and *men* it is possible to mitigate the clash. This is reflected in the metrical grid: (7) has no ascending triples.

(7)   men
                          teen   men
                  thirteen e men
                  thirteen e men

The height of a pause in the metrical grid presumably shows in duration, possibly also in segmental effects.

Pauses function generally as boundary signals, marking major constituent boundaries. They also act as boundary signals in focusing. A pause is not likely within a focused constituent nor in the middle of a deaccented stretch of background material. A familiar example of this is

(8)   I *didn't* come, because you told me.

Where a pause is made between *come* and *because* if the subordinate clause acts as an independent explanation and not as background material subordinate to the emphatic denial. This contrast in pronunciation can be represented in the grid formalism by inserting pause elements.

3. Focusing and Deaccenting

In Chomsky (1971), there is a lengthy discussion of the determination of possible domains of focus given the position of the most prominent syllable. The approach to syllable prominence from the basic concept of relative constituent prominence solves Chomsky's problem by turning it around.[10]

For assume, starting from the production end, that one wants to focus a certain constituent of a sentence. This means that the relevant phrase will be promoted in the prominence hierarchy of the sentence. In terms of the metrical grid, the emphasized phrase will be raised in the hierarchy of prominence above its context.

That it is the whole emphasized phrase that is promoted in prominence seems to correspond to the phonetical facts. Intuitively, at least, when a complex constituent is focused, not only the main stress of the constituent is emphasized, but the whole stress pattern is put in relief. For instance, if the verb phrase of

(9)   The farmer *killed the duckling*.

is focused, not only the first syllable of *duckling* is emphasized, but that of *killed* as well. Thus, there is a significant contrast between the grid representation of (9) and that of (10), both contrasting with the unmarked pattern.

(10)   The farmer killed the *duckling*.

The following three grids are tentative representations:

(11)   duck
               far   duck
               far   kill   duck
         The farmer killed the duckling (unmarked);

(12)   duck
                    killed   duck
          The farmer killed the duckling = (9);

(13)   duck
          The farmer killed the duckling = (10).

The consequences of focusing a constituent for the placement of the strongest
syllable are simple to calculate using the rules (1)–(4). What can be the
domain of focus, when the emphasis is on a given syllable s? The answer is
of course, any constituent whose strongest syllable, according to the rules of
unmarked stress placement, is s. This is just Chomsky's rule.[11]

As a special case, when the emphasized syllable is the one which according
to the rules of unmarked stress placement would carry nuclear stress anyway,
the domain of focus could be any constituent including the stressed syllable,
in particular, the whole sentence, as far as Chomsky's rule can tell.

What this shows is that the placement of nuclear stress is not alone sufficient to determine the domain of focus, in view of contrasts like (11)–(13).
In general, ordinal prominence among syllables is a valuable cue for domain
of focus only where focusing upsets the unmarked relative prominence
relations defined by (1)–(4).

Where relative prominence is insufficient, domains of focus are de-
lineated by pauses and, as in (12)–(13), by *deaccenting*, or flattening of the
contour of a neighboring off-focus stretch of speech.

As is registered in (D.emphasis), I consider focusing and deaccenting just
sides of one and the same coin. In deaccenting a familiar stretch of speech,
one at the same time puts the remaining material in relief. Conversely, what is
left outside the domain of focus is designated as familiar material.[12]

Sometimes there seems at first to be a genuine contrast between the purposes of signaling familiarity by deaccenting and emphasizing a point by focusing. However, in such cases an explanation for the feeling should be sought in
properties of an implicit dialogue context. Thus for instance compare

(14)   I *thought* you'd make it (and you did).
(15)   You *thought* you'd make it (but you failed).

While the function of the intonational pattern in (14) seems primarily to be
to designate the subordinate clause as a shared presupposition, and the
emphasis on *thought* just an accidental consequence of deaccenting, (15)
seems to be expressly making a contrast between wishes and reality (a focus
on *thought* marks it as the right choice of words).   ·

Actually, the contrast is explained by closer attention to the dialogue contexts in which (14)–(15) are most naturally at home. As the parenthetical addition indicates, (14) is natural as an *addition* in a cooperative dialogue:

(16)   – I made it.
(17)   – *I thought* you'd make it.

The second move accents (and deaccents) the first speaker's claim, adding a boast for a good prediction. The deaccented subordinate clause becomes a shared presupposition, and the rest represents a new claim.

In contrast, (15) is most naturally thought of as a *correction* of the same putative claim (as indicated by the parenthetical clause in it):

(18)   – I made it.
(19)   – You *thought* you'd make it.

Being a correction, (19) denies the truth of an opponent's presupposition (marked as such by deaccenting) and adds the focal word *thought* as a rectification. Here (19) can actually be construed to emphasize *thought* alone, as *you* represents material present in the first move.

Thus the feeling of difference in the aims of focusing between (14) and (15) is explained by simple differences in dialogue context: the aims of the sentence as a dialogue move and the domain of focus.

4. Accent

I am making one distinction concerning the accentuation (pitch inflection) of a focused phrase. I claim that there is a significant opposition between what I call a *final* (emphatic) accent and a *nonfinal* (contrastive or list) accent on a focused phrase.

Unless the focused word is a short monosyllable, this accentual distinction is realized directly – and I would say primarily – on the focused phrase. Final accent is realized by a high tone on the accented syllable followed by a fall, while nonfinal accent is characterized by a low tone on the accented syllable followed by a rise.

In Finnish, where there are few monosyllables and no final rise in questions, the local contrast is the only clue for the finality-nonfinality opposition. In English, the accentual distinction is accompanied by a contrast in boundary tone in declarative sentences. Final accent has no specific after effects, while nonfinal accent assigns a terminal rise to the whole utterance. When the focused word is a short monosyllable, the latter contrast may carry the whole distinctive load of the opposition.[13] These intuitive findings are supported by the few experimental samples I have seen so far (see Figures 1–2).[14]

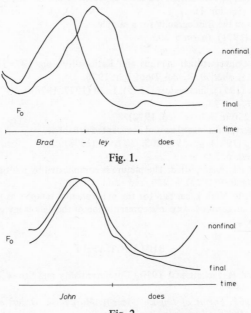

Fig. 1.

Fig. 2.

However, the final-nonfinal accent opposition can be realized in questions too, superimposed on a polar question intonation. Thus there is a clear intuitive contrast between

(20)   Does *Bràdley* live here?

with a high falling accent on *Bradley* (glossed by something like "I mean Bradley, does he live here?") and a low-rising version

(21)   Does *Brádley* live here?

suggesting one of the paraphrases "And Bradley then, does he live here?" or "Does Bradley, of all people, live here?". While (20) is a simple question, (21) sounds inquisitive or doubtful. These two shades of (21) correspond nicely to the list and corrective implications of nonfinal accent on declarative sentences.

The Academy of Finland and M.I.T.

NOTES

* This paper was completed in 1979. A revised and abbreviated version of the paper (excluding material on intonation) has since appeared in Carlson (1983).

[1] Cf. Appendix (Section 4).

[2] See references in the Bibliography for a sample.

[3] Cf. Chomsky (1971), fn. on p. 205.

[4] See Section III.

[5] See esp. his 'Conversational Maxims and Rationality', pp. 197–216 in *Language in Focus*, ed. by A. Kasher, D. Reidel, Dordrecht 1976.

[6] E.g. Chomsky (1971), Jackendoff (1972), Ladd (1977, 1978).

[7] Cf. Ladd (1977), p. 23.

[8] Cf. Daneš, p. 230 in Bolinger (ed. 1972).

[9] G_0 level is reserved for stressless and deaccented syllables.

[10] See Chomsky (1971), pp. 199–205. Cf. Ladd (1978).

[11] See esp. *op. cit.* p. 205.

[12] This account is oversimplified. The picture is complicated by multiple focusing.

[13] Cf. e.g. Jackendoff (1972), p. 259, and Ladd (1978).

[14] I am grateful to Mark Liberman for the experimental samples as well as for a lot of good advice and suggestions. Any misrepresentation of the data is my own doing.

BIBLIOGRAPHY

Akmajian, A. and R. Jackendoff: 1970, 'Coreferentiality and Stress', *Linguistic Inquiry* 1, 124–6.

Bolinger, D.: 1965, *Forms of English: Accent, Morpheme, Order*, ed. by I. Abe and T. Kanekiyo, Harvard University Press, Cambridge.

Bolinger, D. (ed.): 1972, *Intonation*, Penguin, Harmondsworth, 1972.

Carlson, L.: 1976, 'Language-Games and Speech-Acts', in *Papers from the III Scandinavian Conference of Linguistics*, ed. by F. Karlsson, Turku.

Carlson, L.: 1983, *Dialogue Games: An Approach to Discourse Analysis*, Synthese Language Library 17, D. Reidel Co., Dordrecht.

Chomsky, N.: 1971, 'Deep Structure, Surface Structure, and Semantic Interpretation', in *Semantics: An Interdisciplinary Reader in Philosophy, Linguistics and Psychology*, ed. by D. Steinberg and L. Jakobovits, Cambridge University Press, Cambridge, pp. 183–216.

Crystal, D.: 1969, *Prosodic Systems and Intonation in English*, Cambridge University Press, Cambridge.

Daneš, F.: 1960, 'Sentence Intonation from a Functional Point of View', *Word* 16, 34–54.

Daneš, F. (ed.): 1974, *Papers on Functional Sentence Perspective*, Mouton, The Hague.

Gunter, R.: 1974, *Sentences in Dialog*, Hornbeam Press, Columbia SC.

Halliday, M.A.K.: 1967, *Intonation and Grammar in British English*, Mouton, The Hague.

Hintikka, J.: 1973, *Logic Language-Games, and Information*, Oxford University Press, Oxford.

Hintikka, J.: 1976, 'On the Limitations of Generative Grammar', in the *Proceedings of the Scandinavian Seminar on Philosophy of Language*, Philosophical studies published by the Department of Philosophy, University of Uppsala, Uppsala.

Hintikka, J.: 1976a, 'Quantifiers in Logic and Quantifiers in Natural Language', in *Philosophy and Logic*, ed. by S. Körner, Basil Blackwell, Oxford.

Hintikka, J.: 1976b, *The Semantics of Questions and the Questions of Semantics*, Acta Philosophica Fennica 28, No. 4, North-Holland.

Hintikka, J.: 1977, 'Language-Games', in the *Festschrift for G.H. von Wright, Acta Philosophica Fennica* 29.

Hintikka, J. and M.: 1982, 'Sherlock Holmes Confronts Modern Logic', in E. Barth and J. Marteus (eds.) *Argumentation*, John Benjamins, Amsterdam 1982, pp. 55–76.

Hirst, D.J.: 1974, 'Intonation and Context', *Linguistics* 141, 5–16.

Hultzén, L.: 1959, 'Information Points in Intonation', *Phonetica* 4, 107–120.

Jackendoff, R.: 1972, *Semantic Interpretation in Generative Grammar*, M.I.T. Press, Cambridge, Ma.

Kuno, S.: 1972, 'Functional Sentence Perspective', *Linguistic Inquiry* 3, 269–320.

Ladd, D.R., Jr.: 1977, *The Function of the A-Rise Accent in English*, Indiana University Linguistic Club.

Ladd, D.R., Jr.: 1978, *The Structure of Intonational Meaning*, Ph.D.Diss., Cornell University.

Leben, W.: 1976, 'The Tones of English Intonation', *Linguistic Analysis* 2, 69–107.

Lee, W.R.: 1956, 'Fall-Rise Intonation in English', *English Studies* 37, p. 62–72.

Li, C.N. (ed.): 1976, *Subject and Topic*, Academic Press, New York.

Liberman, M.: 1975, *The Intonational System of English*, Ph.D.Diss., M.I.T., Cambridge, Ma.

Liberman, M. and I. Sag: 1974, 'Prosodic Form and Discourse Function', in *Papers from the 10th Regional Meeting*, Chicago Linguistic Society, pp. 416–427.

Schmerling, S.F.: 1976, *Aspects of English Sentence Stress*, University of Texas Press, Austin.

Schubiger, M.: 1956, 'Again: Fall-Rise Intonations in English', *English Studies* 37, 157–60.

Schubiger, M.: 1958, *English Intonation: Its Form and Function*, Max Niemeyer, Tübingen.

Sgall, P., E. Hajičova, E. Benešova: 1973, *Topic, Focus, and Generative Semantics*, Scriptor Verlag, Kronberg Taunus.

Sharp, A.E.: 1958, 'Falling-Rising Intonation Patterns in English', *Phonetica* 2, 127–152.

Stenius, E., 1967, 'Mood and Language-Game', *Synthese* 17, 254–274.

Wittgenstein, L.: 1953, *Philosophische Untersuchungen – Philosophical Investigations*, Basil Blackwell, Oxford.

UMBERTO ECO

INTENSIONAL MAN *VS* EXTENSIONAL MAN:
A DIFFICULT DIALOGUE

1. INTRODUCTION

Any semiotic approach (cf. Eco. 1976)[1] should distinguish between a theory of codes and a theory of sign production, that is between a theory of signification and a theory of communication. In other words it is indispensable to distinguish between the criteria of organization of the cultural encyclopedia (a merely intensional system of meaning postulates) and the various phenomena of communicational interaction (among which there is the extensional use of languages, that is, the use of languages in order to designate actual or possible states of the world).

A system of signification is a social product that can be established (and recognized as such) even though one does not design it for the purposes of communication and even though one does not resort to it in order to designate states of actual or possible worlds. For example, one can decide to correlate each finger of one's hands to the first ten Roman emperors: thus, for instance, a given finger of the left hand *means* the second Roman Emperor, whose name is Tiberius and whose properties are of having reigned from 14 to 37 A.D., whose prime minister was Sejanus and so on . . . Such a system of signification (which allows one to name Tiberius by raising a given finger) can however be described and semiotically analyzed apart from the question as to whether one has established it with the intention of naming Roman emperors or not. In principle each of the ten fingers can be correlated at the same time to an imaginary attribute of the fourth person of the Trinity as described in an unwritten novel by Jorge Luis Borges. In this case one would have two different signification systems with two different content planes and two homonymous expression planes. If, in the course of a conversational interaction, one mistakes the designation of a divine attribute with the name of an Emperor, such a misunderstanding does not affect the organization of the two systems of signification *qua* systems of signification; it rather concerns the felicity conditions of a given process of textual actualization.

The third chapter of Voltaire's Zadig, which will be examined in this paper, represents a paramount example of such a semiotic situation. As we

335

L. Vaina and J. Hintikka (eds.), Cognitive Constraints on Communication, 335–350.
This translation © 1984 *by D. Reidel Publishing Company.*

will see, Zadig is here concerned first with a complex intertwining of visual signs (imprints, clues and symptoms) and then with the linguistic expression of the contents previously expressed by these non-verbal devices. However in this story not only the functioning of two semiotic systems, but also the discrepancy between intensional and extensional approach are made blatantly evident, so that – as in a sudden epiphany – a whole web of semiotic questions is brilliantly displayed.

It must be clear that the following analysis does not represent an interpretation of Voltaire's text. Zadig's chapter 3 is taken as a "pre-text", that is, as a transparent report about three different texts, namely:

(a) the text represented by an ensemble of physical phenomena that Zadig assumes as significant devices;

(b) the text represented by the discourse by which Zadig tells the story of his interpretation of the text (a) – this second verbal text being a metalinguistic discourse dealing with the semiotic nature of the first (visual) one;

(c) the text represented by the dialogues between Zadig and the King' and Queen's officers.

The three texts must be approached from a double point of view: they deal with the semiotic rules of signification which make them potentially understandable and they are inserted in a process of communicational interaction in which they are used in order to designate states of the world. It happens that – during the dialogical interaction – the speakers are using the same expression in order to name individuals belonging to different possible worlds, which in their turn depend on the speakers' propositional attitudes. As we will see, while Zadig shows a certain embarrassment in distinguishing between intensional and extensional approach, his opponents are unable to recognize the practical (as well as the theoretical) possibility of such a discrepancy.

Fortunately the misfortune of Zadig and the communicational mish-mash he is involved in will allow us to make clear the reasons of the semiotic agony he is suffering.

2. VOLTAIRE'S TEXT[2]

Zadig found that the first moon of marriage, even as it is written in the book of Zend, is of honey, and the second of wormwood. After a time he had to get rid of Azora, who had become too difficult to live with, and he tried to find his happiness in the study of nature. "No one is happier," said he, "than a philosopher who reads in this great book that God has placed before our eyes. The truths he discovers belong to him. He nourishes and ennobles his soul. He lives in peace, fearing nothing from men, and his dear wife does not come to cut off his nose."

Filled with these ideas, he retired to a house in the country on the banks of the Euphrates. There he did not pass his time calculating how many inches of water flow in one second under the arches of a bridge, or if a cubic line more rain fell in the month of the mouse than in the month of the sheep. He did not contrive to make silk from spiders' webs, or porcelain from broken bottles; but he studied above all the characteristics of animals and plants, and soon acquired a perspicacity which showed him a thousand differences where other men see only uniformity.

While walking one day near a little wood he saw one of the queen's eunuchs hastening towards him, followed by several officers, who seemed to be greatly troubled, and ran hither and thither like distracted men seeking something very precious they have lost.

"Young men," cried the Chief Eunuch, "you haven't seen the queen's dog, have you?"

"It's not a dog," answered Zadig modestly, "it's a bitch."

"That's so," said the Chief Eunuch.

"It's a very small spaniel," added Zadig, "which has had puppies recently; her left forefoot is lame, and she has very long ears."

"You have seen her then?" said the Eunuch, quite out of breath.

"Oh, no!" answered Zadig. "I have not seen the animal, and I never knew the queen had a bitch."

Just at this moment, by one of the usual freaks of fortune, the finest horse in the king's stables escaped from a groom's hands and fled into the plains of Babylon. The Master of the King's Hounds and all the other officials rushed after it with as much anxiety as the Chief Eunuch after the bitch. The Master of the King's Hounds came up to Zadig and asked if he had not seen the king's horse pass by.

"The horse you are looking for is the best galloper in the stable," answered Zadig. "It is fifteen hands high, and has a very small hoof. Its tail is three and a half feet long. The studs on its bit are of twenty-three carat gold, and its shoes of eleven scruple silver."

"Which road did it take?" asked the Master of the King's Hounds. "Where is it?"

"I have not seen the horse," answered Zadig, "and I have never heard speak of it."

The Master of the King's Hounds and the Chief Eunuch had no doubt but that Zadig had stolen the king's horse and the queen's bitch, and they had him taken before the Grand Destur, who condemned him to the knout and afterwards to spend the rest of his days in Siberia. Hardly had judgment been pronounced than the horse and the bitch were found. The judges were in the sad necessity of having to rescind their judgment, but they condemned Zadig to pay four hundred ounces of gold for having denied seeing what he had seen. Only after the fine had been paid was Zadig allowed to plead his cause, which he did in the following terms.

"Stars of Justice," he said, "Unfathomable Wells of Knowledge, Mirrors of Truth, that have the solidity of lead, the hardness of iron, the radiance of the diamond, and much affinity with gold, since I am permitted to speak before this august assembly, I swear to you by Ormuzd that I have never seen the queen's honourable bitch or the king of kings' sacred horse. Let me tell you what happened.

"I was walking toward the little wood where I met later the venerable Chief Eunuch and the very illustrious Master of the King's Hounds. I saw an animal's tracks on the sand

and I judged without difficulty they were the tracks of a small dog. The long, shallow furrows printed on the little ridges of sand between the tracks of the paws informed me that the animal was a bitch with pendent dugs, who hence had had puppies recently. Other tracks in a different direction, which seemed all the time to have scraped the surface of the sand beside the fore-paws, gave me the idea that the bitch had very long ears; and as I remarked that the sand was always less hollowed by one paw than by the three others, I concluded that our august queen's bitch was somewhat lame, if I dare say so.

"As regards the king of kings' horse, you may know that as I walked along the road in this wood I saw the marks of horse-shoes, all equal distances apart. That horse, said I, gallops perfectly. The dust on the trees in this narrow road only seven feet wide was raised a little right and left three and a half feet from the middle of the road. This horse, said I, has a tail three and a half feet long, and its movement right and left has swept up this dust. I saw beneath the trees, which made a cradle five feet high, some leaves newly fallen from the branches, and I recognised that this horse had touched there and was hence fifteen hands high. As regards his bit, it must be of twenty-three carat gold, for he rubbed the studs against a stone which I knew to be a touchstone and tested. From the marks his hoofs made on certain pebbles I knew the horse was shod with eleven scruple silver."

All the judges admired Zadig's profound and subtle perspicacity, news of which came to the ears of the king and queen. In the ante-rooms, the throne-room, and the closet Zadig was the sole topic of conversation, and although several of the Magi thought he should be burned as a sorcerer, the king ordered the fine of four hundred ounces of gold to which he had been condemned to be returned to him. The clerk of the court, the ushers, the attorneys called on him with great pomp to bring him these four hundred ounces. They retained only three hundred and ninety-eight for judicial costs, and their lackeys demanded largess.

Zadig saw how dangerous it was sometimes to be too knowing, and promised himself, on the first occasion that offered, not to say what he had seen.

The occasion soon presented itself. A stage prisoner escaped, and passed beneath the window of Zadig's house. Zadig was questioned, and made no reply. But it was proved he had looked out of the window. For this crime he was condemned to five hundred ounces of gold, and, as is the custom in Babylon, he thanked his judges for their indulgence.

"Good God!" he said to himself. "A man who walks in a wood where the queen's bitch or the king's horse has passed is to be pitied! How dangerous it is to look out of the window! How difficult it is to be happy in this life!"

3. CODES

Disenchanted by marriage, that is by the direct contact with another individual, Zadig devotes himself to the study of nature. It is not by chance that Zadig calls Nature "the great book": he is concerned with Nature as a code, as a system of signs. In the second paragraph it is said that he does not pass his time in calculating how many inches of water flow under a bridge, and he does not try to make porcelain from broken bottles, that is, to produce new items of the furniture of the world he lives in. He studies "the characteristics of animals and plants". In other words. Zadig is interested in the properties of cultural units and in the description of these properties. He is interested in an *intensional* description of the world or in how to define, in terms of semantic properties, the classes of objects that constitute the furniture of the world. He looks for general relations of signification (any *a* stands for *b* – or any *a* can be analyzed in terms of *b*) and is not concerned with concrete acts of communication, to be submitted to an *extensional* verification. He is the Master of the Codes or of the Encyclopedia. Now, one day he walks in a little wood where something happens before he meets the officer of the queen. What he sees is told later, during the trial before the Grand Destur, but what I am trying to do now is exactly to re-establish the right sequence of events according to their temporal order. In other words, I am re-establishing the *ordo facilis* of the *propositions of the fabula* (or story) that the *plot* has mixed up according to an *ordo difficilis*. Moreover, I am also making explicit these propositons that the plot leaves as presupposed.[3]

So Zadig sees animal tracks on the sand and recognized them as the tracks of a small dog. To be able to isolate tracks as tracks and to recognize them as signifying a certain class of animals, means to share a precise competence or a *code of imprints* (cf. Eco, 1976, 3.6). Imprints constitute the most elementary case of sign-production since the expression, correlated to a given content, is not usually produced as a sign (there can also be imprints of natural events, like the traces of an avalanche – and in the case of the queen's dog, the animal had no intention of producing a sign) until the moment one recognizes it and decides to assume it is a sign. To interpret an imprint means to correlate it to a possible physical cause. The physical cause is merely possible since one can recognize an imprint even in the pages of the boy scouts handbook: a previous experience has produced a sort of cultural convention according to which a given physical shape, no matter where it is found, refers back to the class of its possible causes. One can draw the outline of a dog's imprint and tell someone else that, whenever this expression is found, the corresponding content is "dog". It is important to agree on the fact that an imprint does not necessarily refer back to an individual. One can teach a computer to recognize the imprints of a glass of red wine upon a table by giving it certain precise instructions, namely the fact that the imprint must be circular, that the diameter of the circle must be two to three inches, and that this circle is made with a liquid red substances (one can also feed the computer with more precise chemical data). Once fed with the information,

including both the description of the expression and the definition of the
correlated content, the computer ought to be in the position of recognizing
every possible imprint of this type. Notice that a code of imprints also
involves synecdochical conventions, since the imprint of a glass of wine does
not visually reproduce the form of the glass, but at most the form of its
bottom; likewise the imprint of a dog's paw reproduces the form of the paw
and is correlated to the class of dogs only by a further link. Moreover the
code can list imprints at different levels of pertinence, that is, it may give
general instructions making one able to recognize glasses or dogs in general
as revealed by different expressions of different size and shape, or may
analytically list the imprints of different kinds of glasses and of different
races of dogs. Thus an imprint can be correlated both to a genus and to a
species. In our story Zadig possessed both kinds of information and was able
to recognize not only "dog" but also "spaniel".

Let us suppose that the encyclopedia of Zadig was rich enough to allow
him to recognize also the imprints of the dogs. However, it is one thing to
recognize the traces of dogs, and yet another thing to infer that they belong
to the dog which has left the imprints of the paws and a third thing to infer
that therefore the dog was a bitch and that that bitch had puppies recently.
That's why for the moment I shall only consider Zadig's capability to recognize imprints, that is, his competence about the properties of things and about
the expressions that conventionally refer back to these properties. It must be
clear that by "things", at this point, I mean general ideas or concepts. The
encyclopedia is an intensional machinery, Zadig knows only *meaning
postulates* of the kind "if x has the property of being a dog, then x has also
the property of having four paws" and "if x has the property of being a bitch
then x has also the property of having dogs".

It goes without saying that the same happens when Zadig discovers the
marks of four horse-shoes. Both cases display the same semiotic mechanism.
The case of the horse is however more complex: it ought to be considered
more carefully. All the conclusions that one can draw from this case can also
be applied to the story of the dog.

Zadig recognizes the imprints of the horse. The fact that the marks are all
the same distance apart may also be registered by the encyclopedia as
expressing "stallion". Otherwise they constitute the starting point for an
inference not so dissimilar from the one allowing Zadig to detect that the
bitch has recently given birth to puppies.

The text does not cite another important semiotic feature that Zadig must
have detected in both cases: *vectors*. Vectors are aspects of a given expression

that physically embody a spatial or a temporal feature which conveys a spatial or temporal feature of the corresponding content. The dictionary of imprints establishes that, given the morphological description of certain imprints referring back to a class of moving imprinters, these imprints as expressions, have an apex or a top and a base, and that the imprint expresses the fact that the possible imprinter is moving from bottom to top. As for animals (crabs excepted), the apex of the imprint expresses the potential or the actual movement of the possible imprinter (Eco, 1976, 3.6.5.).

But Zadig also discovers other semiotic features, namely *symptoms* and *clues*. In symptoms the expression is a ready-made physical event that refers back to the class of its possible causes. Red spots on the face mean measles. Symptoms are different from imprints: the shape of the imprint is a projection from the pertinent features of the shape of the imprinter, whereas there is no point to point correspondence between the symptom and its possible cause. A symptom is correlated to its cause since the concept of the symptom is one of the semantic markers of the componential representation of the cause: to produce red spots on the face is one among the coded properties of measles. Zadig recognizes symptoms when he detects that the dust on the trees was raised right and left, three and half feet from the middle of the road. The position of the dust is the symptom that something caused its disposition. The same happens with the leaves fallen from the branches. According to the code, Zadig knows that both phenomena are symptoms of an external force which has acted upon a resistant matter, but the code does not provide him with any information concerning the nature of the cause.

Clues, on the other hand, are objects left by an external agent in the spot where it did something, and somehow recognized by the code as physically linked to that agent, so that from their actual or possible presence the actual or possible past presence of the agent can be detected.

The difference between symptoms and clues is due to the fact that with symptoms the encyclopedia records a *necessary* present or past contiguity between the effect and the cause, and the presence of the effect sends one back to the necessary presence of the cause; whereas with clues the encyclopedia records only a *possible* past contiguity between the owner and the owned and the presence of the owned sends one back to the possible presence of the owner. In a way clues are complex symptoms, since one must first detect the necessary presence of an indeterminate causing agent and then take this symptom as the clue referring back to a possibly more determined agent — conventionally recognized as the most usual owner of the object left on the

UMBERTO ECO

spot. That is why a criminal novel is usually more intriguing than the detection of a pneumonia.

Zadig recognizes clues when he detects, from the gold on the stone and the silver on the pebbles, that the bit of the horse was of 23 carat gold and the shoes were shod with scruple silver. However the code only tells Zadig that if gold and silver were upon the stones then it should have been some golden and silver owner which left them, but no encyclopedic information can make him sure that that owner was a horse, namely the one signified by the imprints. Therefore, at first glance, gold and silver are still acting as symptoms and not yet as clues: at most the encyclopedia tells him that even horses, among many other possible agents, may be the bearers of golden and silver paraphernalia.

So far Zadig, the master of the encyclopedia, still knows only generalities and has no means to outline any connection from the data he has accumulated.

Notice that, up to this point, what Zadig knows is exactly what he has previously known (even if he had not discovered the traces in the wood). Zadig knows, being the code master, that certain imprints, symptoms and clues signify certain entities. Having, however, discovered imprints, clues and symptoms in *that* wood and at *that* precise moment, he is in the position of knowing something more.

4. EXISTENTIAL INFERENCES

The imprint of a horse-shoe means "horse". But the imprint of a horse-shoe left in a precise place means "*A* horse was here". Once placed within a precise environment, an imprint becomes the element of a visual sentence conveying an indexical proposition. We are presently witnessing a first elementary process of communication. Nobody had the intention of communicating something to Zadig, but Zadig takes the traces as if they were communicating something to him — as if somebody used these means to communicate his presence to him. Earlier Zadig was concerned with pure meanings, with intensions of a set of individual concepts. Now, he is concerned with *individuals*, and with *bound variables*: there is at least an x which has the property of being a horse and which has passed through here. Since Zadig knows that a possible imprint refers back to the class of its possible imprinters, he can now infer that an actual occurrence of the general type provided by the encyclopedia refers back to an actual occurrence of the type-imprinter. Passing from *type* to *token*, Zadig shifts from the universe of intensions to the universe of extension. The same of course happens as far as symptoms and clues are concerned.

So far Zadig knows, however, only disconnected individual facts, namely:

— an *x* which is a horse and which has passed through there;
— a *y* (undetermined) which has broken the branches;
— a *k* (undetermined) which has rubbed something golden against a stone;
— a *j* (undetermined) which has left silver clues on certain pebbles.

Neither the encyclopedia nor the laws of empirical science — nor those of formal logic — permit him to give a unified shape to this disconnected series of data.

5. TEXT

But Zadig is not only the master of codes and of existential inferences. He is also the master of texts and intertextuality. If the traces on the sand were common names inserted into a sentence conveying an indexical proposition, the various visual sentences he is dealing with can constitute either a disconnected *series* or a coherent *sequence*, i.e., a text. One of the first requirements for a text to be coherent is a link between co-referent expressions: "Lucy was ill. Lucy recovered." is not yet a text if one does not know whether the two occurrences of the name *Lucy* are co-referential. Given two separate sentences as "Lucy wal ill" and "She recovered", they constitute a coherent text only if it is possible to definitely ascertain that the *she* of the second sentence can be referred to the *Lucy* of the first. One of the best ways to establish co-references is to find out a textual *topic* able to unify semantically the sentences of a text. To find out a topic always represents a case of abduction.

The notion of abduction (often considered as the same as hypothesis) was proposed by C.S. Peirce[4]:

Suppose I enter a room and there find a number of bags, containing different kinds of beans. On the table there is a handful of white beans; and, after some searching, I find one of the bags contains white beans only. I at once infer as a probability, or as a fair guess, that this handful was taken out of that bag ...

There is a synthetic inference "where we find some very curious circumstances, which would be explained by the supposition that it was the case of a certain general rule and thereupon adopt that supposition".

Hypothesis and/or abduction are distinguished by Peirce from deduction and induction in a way that can easily be applied to our subject. In deduction, given a general Rule and a Case, a Result is deduced. There-fore:

> *All horses move their tail so as to sweep up the dust*
> *There was a horse*
> *Therefore the dust must be swept up*

In induction given a Case and a Result, a general Rule is formulated as probable:

> *Every time I saw horses I also saw the dust swept up by their tail*
> *Therefore (probably) all horses do this.*

In hypothesis/abduction given a Rule and a Result, a Case is inferred:

> *All horses move their tails so as to sweep up the dust*
> *But there the dust is swept up*
> *So probably there was a horse*

Peirce however gives the impression of conceiving the hypothesis not only as the inference to a Case but also as the inference to a Rule, so that the above example could be rephrased as follows:

> *Here the dust is swept up* (the Result is unquestionable)
> *If I adopt the rule according to which all horses etc.,*
> *Then I can (probably) infer that there was a horse.*

A "certain" rule is presupposed (among many other possible explanations) and only on that "supposition" the "fair guess" concerning the Case is attempted. The difference between hypothesis and abduction does not consist in the difference between inference to a Case and inference to a Rule, but consists in the quantity of reasons one has before making a "fair guess". An hypothesis is *accepted* as the best explanation among conflicting hypotheses, while an abduction is simply *entertained*, before more rigorous comparisons with alternative hypotheses can be made.[5] Abduction is a first tentative movement towards hypotheses. Now, the identification of a textual topic (as the rule that defines the "aboutness" of the text and establishes a coherent relationship between different and still disconnected textual data) is an instance of abduction. The fact that one frequently does not know whether the topic one has discovered is the "real" one or not, so that the activity of textual interpretation can give birth to different and conflicting semantic actualizations, proves that every interpreter always makes abduc-tions about one among the many possible readings of a text. And so does

Zadig. Once a series of general coded intertextual conventions is supposed, according to which horses sweep the dust with their tail and bear golden bits and silver horse shoes, as well as stones retain small fragments of malleable metal bodies that violently collide with them – at this point, even though several other phenomena could have produced the same effects, Zadig is able to try his textual re-construction. A general coherent picture takes shape: a story with only *one* subject, co-referred to by different symptoms and clues, is definitely outlined.

At this point, of course, even the text concerning the bitch can be definitely organized: the bitch was lame, it recently had puppies, and the tracks beside the fore-paws indicate that the animal had long ears.

Notice that Zadig does not possess the scientific certainty that his hypothesis is true: it is however textually and intertextually verisimilar. Acting as the text master Zadig pronounces, so to speak a teleological judgement. He decides to interpret the data he has assembled as if they were harmoniously interrelated.

Zadig *knew* before that there was a horse, and that there were four other unknown agents. He *knew* that these five agents were individuals of the actual world of his experience. Now he also *believes* that there was a horse with a long tail, fifteen hand high, with a golden bit and a silver hoof. But such a horse does not necessarily belong to the actual world of Zadig's experience. It belongs to the textual world Zadig has built up, to the world of Zadig's strongly motivated beliefs, that is, to the possible world of Zadig's propositional attitudes.

Zadig knew through his existential inference that there was a horse (and a dog), one among many. This horse, still a bound variable and not yet an individual constant, has become the subject of Zadig's text. That is all. It is important to recognize the modal nature of Zadig's epistemic world to understand what will happen later, when he meets the officers of the queen and of the king.

6. AN ODD DIALOGUE

The Master of the King's Hounds and the Chief Eunuch do not have any semiotic subtlety. They are not interested in the properties of concepts, they only know individuals, their propositions concern only individual constants. In particular they know *one* given bitch and *one* given stallion. They move within a strictly referential universe and they give the individuals they know proper names. Expressions like "the queen's dog" and "the king's

horse" appear to be definite descriptions, but I would like to consider them
as *degenerate proper names*, like "the Bank of England" (they are in fact
cases of *antonomasia*; notice that "the queen's dog" as a definite description
is rather imprecise, since it refers to a bitch, but as an antonomastic degenerate proper name it works perfectly and identifies one and only one
individual).

"Have you seen the individuals whose proper name is Queen's Dog and
King's Horse?" — such is the question put forth by the officers.

To answer this question, Zadig has two alternatives. He may accept the
extensional game: dealing with people interested in singling out given individuals, he can try a second abduction, that is, he is in the position of making
a "fair guess" according to which both the horse and the dog of *his own*
textual world are the same as those known by the officers. This kind of
abduction is the one usually made by a detective: "the possible individual I
have outlined as an inhabitant of the world of *my beliefs* is the same as the
individual of *the actual world* someone is looking for". Such is the procedure
usually implemented by Sherlock Holmes. But Holmes and his equals are
just interested in what Zadig was not: Holmes wants to know how many
inches of water flow under a bridge, and how to make porcelain from broken
bottles.

Being only devoted to the study of the book of nature, Zadig should take
a second alternative. He might answer: "according to the world of *my*
hypotheses I strongly *believe* that *a* horse and *a* dog were here — I do not
know whether they are identical or not with *the* individuals *you* are referring
to".

At first glance Zadig chooses the first alternative. As a good Sherlock
Holmes he bluffs: "*your* dog is rather a bitch and *your* horse is the best
galloper in the stable . . . " Acting as doctor Watson, the officers are flabber-
gasted: "That's so!". But when the officers take for granted that Zadig knows
their own animals and — pretty reasonably — ask "where are they?", then
Zadig tries to withdraw: "I have not seen *them* and I have never heard speak
of *them*". Which means that he does not really want to play the extensional
game proposed by the officers.

In doing so Zadig behaves rather contradictorily. He plays at the same time
a double game, the extensional and the intensional one — rather unsuccess-
fully, as is proved by the unpleasant experience he has to undergo later.
Apparently Zadig has been the victim of a miscalculation. If there is a miscalculation then there is a (broken) rule. The disgrace of Zadig — as well as
the disgrace of the dialogue we are witnessing — must be explained by singling

out some semiotic rules that have been violated — or some semiotic procedures that are in themselves, and potentially, misleading.

There should be something, in the way the officers have posited their
question, which made Zadig fall into a trap. Let us call this trap a referential
one. The question of the officers has obliged Zadig to enter a referential
discourse even though he was reluctant to do so.

It is commonly assumed that when one introduces the subject of a
sentence into the discourse, the individual corresponding to this subject is
presupposed to exist in order for the proposition to be true. If one says "the
King of France is Bald" one presupposes the existence of an individual who
has the property of being King of France (if one says "the King's horse is
lost" one presupposes that there is one and one only existing King's horse).
People usually think that it is indispensable to ascertain the actual existence
of the subject of the sentence in order to make the sentence either meaningful or pragmatically felicitous (the important differences between these two
alternatives being for this moment immaterial). Thus several cases are discussed in which either one introduces the King of France and someone else
objects that there is no King of France or the same speaker oddly asserts that
the King of France is bald and that there is however no King of France. As
instances produced in a laboratory for the sake of formal reasoning, these
examples are undoubtedly interesting, but in natural discourses things go
rather differently. If I ask someone "Do you think that John will come
soon?", it is unlikely that he will object and say "but there is no John" or
"but John does not exist". Usually a normal speaker who has never heard of
John answers "I do not know" or "I do not know John": two ways of
implicitly assuming that, since the question has *posited* him, John exists.

I intentionally used the verb "to posit": every speech-act involving individuals does not "presuppose" but rather *posits* their existence, which is
automatically accepted by the addressees not only on the grounds that he
who makes an assertion commits himself to the truth of the asserted proposition, but also for the simple reason that every speech-act involving individuals
is a *world creating device*. Every speech-act posits the individuals it names
along with their world. One can escape this linguistic power, this semiotic
fascination, only when one has precise evidence of the non-existence of these
individuals. To say that speech acts are *world creating devices* instead of
considering them as *world presupposing devices*, enormously changes the
semiotic perspective. In a *presuppositional* perspective actual experience
comes first, language comes second (linguistic expressions becoming true
or false according to the experience that verifies or falsifies them). In a

positional perspective language comes first and determines our experience; it is the human mean to produce beliefs and certainties, the paramount tool of a strategy of "truification", that is, the way in which the truth is imposed upon the addressee's mind.

Zadig is the best example of such a "truifying" strategy. As soon as the King's Horse and the Queen's Dog are named, he takes them as unquestionably existing individuals. Furthermore he implicitly states that "there is one x which bears the properties So and So and which is the same x the officers name as K and for every y if y has the properties So and So then it is the same as x; therefore the y of the world of my propositional attitudes cannot be but the x of the officers". (It is true that he says "It's not a dog", but he immediately adds "It's a bitch": he does not deny the existence of the individual, his correction is simply *de dicto*, he means that the individual the officers call the "Queen's dog" has the property of being a bitch and, hence, is improperly christened).

7. ZADIG TRIES TO WITHDRAW

Zadig is so proud of the officer's astonishment that he needs time to realize that he, the master of intensions, is definitely dominated by their extensional rule. He senses the danger when the officers try to definitely involve him into their game: "Where is it?". Now Zadig understands that he has betrayed his vow: he had not wanted to be committed anymore to extension and simply wished to devote himself to the knowledge of the general book of nature. He desperately tries to withdraw: "I have not seen it and I have never heard speak of it" – which is true, of course, but the truth has been spelled out too late. It is perfectly reasonable that the officers do not believe him. Parenthetically, since the imprints also displayed vectorial features, he would have been able to tell which road the animal took. Since he had engaged himself in the extensional game, he should have given this information. Withdrawing too late, he behaves incoherently. In any case, the officers cannot accept his last assertion: for extensional people, one cannot name and describe an individual, and then assume that it does not exist *in this world*; for extensional people, one who speaks of something must have seen it; for extensional people, the idea of a speaker dealing with intensions is unacceptable. Zadig is condemned to pay "for having denied seeing what he had (undoubtedly) seen". What a splendid model for a dialogue between a man of good intensions and other men of limited extension.

However there was no justification for Zadig. Being also a text master, he should have acknowledged not only the power of proper names and definite descriptions but also the power of definite articles and pronouns as identity operators. During the conversation with the officers he constantly refers to the dog and to the horse by mean of definite shifters: "*It*'s a bitch . . . *she* has very long ears . . . *It*'s tail is . . . *The* horse . . . " Since language is a world creating device, Zadig has contributed to building up a world that he later tried to cast in doubt. He cannot demand to be taken seriously since he behaves like the *insipiens* of Anselm's ontological argument: "the one who has the necessary property of existing does not exist". Zadig has no right to take back his intensional freedom. He had reneged it at the beginning of the dialogue.

8. ZADIG GETS WORSE

Few remarks about the last adventure of the unfortunate Zadig. He has not probably understood the reasons for his failure. He promises to himself not to tell anymore what he has seen – an infelicitous promise. He should rather have promised not to assign to the actual word the individuals tentatively outlined as elements of the world of his propositional attitudes.

Thus when the prisoner escapes, Zadig does not offer the information which he has. But in this case there was no gap between actual and possible worlds, between bound variables and individual constants, between intension and extension. Zadig stubbornly refuses to understand that difference (which was so clear to him at the beginning of the story), and is really indefensible. To make him pay five hundred ounces of gold was only justice. "How difficult it is to be happy in this life!", says Zadig as a moral for his story. The moral is of course another one: how difficult it is, even for a wise man, to distinguish between intensional and extensional semantics.

One might object that the very topic of the story is Power. Living under the rule of the King, Zadig has no freedom under any circumstance. The Grand Destur determines the parameters of both truth and falsity, in any case Zadig has to pay. This moral is also true, but it is dependent on the previous (the semiotic) one. The Grand Destur establishes his power by dealing with language as if it were always transparent, and as if words were things: he who speaks of a dog knows this dog, speaking means to have seen, the world is a thick world of concrete referents. No power is attributed to imagination. Indeed. However there is no ruler who is not supported by the agreement of the ruled ones. The moment he fell into the extensional trap, the moment he said "*the* dog" and "*the* horse", Zadig accepted the game of the Power and became one of the Power's accomplices. Power is rooted in language and any quest for freedom begins with the semiotic criticism of semiotic over-determination.

University of Bologna

NOTES

[1] *A Theory of Semiotics*, Indiana University Press, 1976.
[2] Trans. by H.I. Woolf and Wilfrid S. Jackson, in Voltaire, *Zadig and Other Romances*, privately printed for Rarity Press, New York, 1931.
[3] See Eco, *The Role of the Reader*, Indiana University Press, Bloomington, 1979.
[4] *Collected Papers*, 2.623–625.
[5] As for the distinction between inference to a rule and inference to a case (as well as for the distinction hypothesis/abduction) I refer to the researches of Paul R. Thagard: "The Unity of Peirce's Theory of Hypothesis", *Transactions of the C.S. Peirce Society* **13**, 1977, and 'Semiosis and Hypothetic Inference in Ch. S. Peirce', *VS* **19–20**, 1978 (where Thagard criticizes my former views on this subject).

STEVEN CUSHING

DYNAMIC MODEL SELECTION IN THE
INTERPRETATION OF DISCOURSE

ABSTRACT. In this paper we argue that the interpretation of discourse involves primarily the *selection* of semantic models, rather than their construction, as is suggested in a number of recent proposals (e.g., Stenning, 1977; Reichman, 1978). We begin with a modified version of a logical framework developed by van Fraassen (1971) (based on Tarski (1936)) and specifically augment it to allow for relativized quantification (Cushing, 1976) and a dynamic reading of satisfaction rules (Cushing, 1977). We then argue that a selection account of discourse interpretation falls right out of the relativized rule, along with an explanation for at least some "conventional implicatures" (Karttunen and Peters, 1979).

1. MODELS AND SATISFACTION

1.1 Given a semantic representation language $\mathscr{L}$ containing predicate constants and individual constants and variables, an *interpretation* I of $\mathscr{L}$ is a triple $<D, R, \{f\}>$, where D is a set of individuals, the *domain* of I; R is a function, the *interpretation function* of I, that assigns members of D to individual constants in $\mathscr{L}$ and sets of lists of members of D to predicates in $\mathscr{L}$, the length of a list being equal to the number of arguments in the predicate to which it corresponds; and $\{f\}$ is a set of functions, the *assignment functions* of I, that assign members of D to variables in $\mathscr{L}$. A *model M* for $\mathscr{L}$ is a pair $<D, R>$, an interpretation of $\mathscr{L}$ without its assignment functions. Since "a factual situation comprises a set of individuals bearing certain relations to each other," such "a situation can be represented by a relational structure $<D, R_1, \ldots, R_i, \ldots >$, where D is the set of individuals in question and $R_1, \ldots, R_i, \ldots$ certain relations on D," i.e., sets of lists of members of D (van Fraassen, 1971, 107). Models thus serve intuitively to relate formulas in $\mathscr{L}$ to the factual situations they are intended to describe by mapping their constants into D and $\{R_1, \ldots, R_i, \ldots\}$. The "variable" character of the symbols assigned values by an f relative to those interpreted by R is reflected in the fact that a *set* of (f)s corresponds to a fixed $<D, R>$ to comprise an interpretation I.[1]

1.2 The distinction between R and f gives us two different levels on which the satisfaction of formulas can be defined, i.e., on which formulas in $\mathscr{L}$ can be

351

L. Vaina and J. Hintikka (eds.), Cognitive Constraints on Communication, 351–361.
© 1984 *by D. Reidel Publishing Company.*

said to be true or false under I. First we define satisfaction relative to an assignment of values to variables, by giving rules like (1)–(6),[2] where "$M \vDash (A) [f]$" is read as *f satisfies*

(1) $M \vDash (x_1 = x_2) [f]$ iff (i.e., if and only if) $f(x_1) = f(x_2)$;

(2) $M \vDash (P(x_1, \ldots, x_n)) [f]$ iff $(f(x_1), \ldots, f(x_n)) \in R(P)$;

(3) $M \vDash (A \& B) [f]$ iff $M \vDash (A) [f]$ and $M \vDash (B) [f]$;

(4) $M \vDash (\neg A) [f]$ iff it is not the case that $M \vDash (A) [f]$;

(5) $M \vDash ((\forall x) A) [f]$ iff $M \vDash (A) [f']$ for whatever assignments f' for M are like f except perhaps (i.e., at most) at x;

(6) $M \vDash ((\forall x) (B; A)) [f]$ iff $M \vDash (A) [f']$ for whatever assignments f' for M are like f except perhaps at x for which $M \vDash (B) [f']$.

A in M or *M satisfies A given f*. Given these rules, we can define "$A \supset B$", read *if A then B*, as "$\neg (B \& \neg A)$", and we can define "$(\exists x)$", read *there are*, as "$\neg (\forall x) \neg$". Second, we define satisfaction by a model, by saying that *M satisfies A*, written "$M \vDash (A)$", if $M \vDash (A) [f]$ for whatever assignment functions f there are for M.[3] Intuitively, this can be read as saying that A is true of the factual situation that is represented by the relational structure into which $\mathscr{L}$ is interpreted, regardless of what values are given to variables by the assignment functions of an interpretation.

2. SIMPLE AND RELATIVIZED QUANTIFICATION

Rule (5) evaluates *simple quantifications* like (7), which

(7) $(\forall x) A$

represent the meanings expressed by sentences like (8), for which

(8)   Whoever there is studies quantifiers.

$x = $ "x" and $A = $ (9), while (6) evaluates *relativized quantifications*

(9)   Study-quantifiers (x)

like (10), which represent the meanings expressed by sentences like

(10) $(\forall x) (B; A)$

(11), for which x and A are as for (8) and $B = $ (12).[4] In general,

(11)   Whoever is a linguist studies quantifiers.

(12)   Linguist (x)

B and A in (10) are lists of formulas in $\mathscr{L}$, the *relativization formulas* and the *principal formulas*, respectively, of (10); both lists for (11) are of length 1. Given (5) and (6), the relativized quantification (10) is logically equivalent to the simple quantification (13), reflecting the synonymy of (11) with (14), for example, but this

(13) $(\forall x)\,(B \supset A)$
(14)   Whoever there is, if he is a linguist, then he studies quantifiers.

fact does not generalize to quantifiers other than $\forall$, because there are quantifiers Q for which there is *no* truth-functional connective c for which (15) is logically equivalent to (16).[5] The relativized case thus

(15) $(Q\,x)\,(B; A)$
(16) $(Q\,x)\,(B\,c\,A)$

must be considered separately from the simple one, despite its apparent superfluity in the case of $\forall$, which suffices for our purposes (with $\exists$) in all other respects.

3. STATIC *VS.* DYNAMIC RULE APPLICATION

3.1 Rules like (1)–(6) are standardly viewed as applying "statically," i.e., as passively describing a state of affairs, a relationship that obtains between a formula and an interpretation, but they can also be viewed as applying "dynamically," i.e., as actively assigning to formulas the values of a feature [± satisfied].[6] On the static view, such rules are inherently bivalent, because of the "iff" that occurs in their formulation: either $M \vDash (A)\,[f]$ or not, depending on the content of the relevant rule. The dynamic view, however, allows for a third "truth value," because of the possibility that a rule gets stopped in the course of its operation, before it gets to assign an appropriate value. We can say that A is *true* (under I, M, f, and so on), if A is assigned the value [+ satisfied] by the relevant rule; *false*, if it is assigned the value [− satisfied]; and *neither* (true nor false), if the rule gets stopped for some reason before it can make an assignment. Given a rule like (4), a formula and its negation will be assigned opposite [satisfaction] values, assuming that they get assigned at all. In the event that a rule stops, neither the formula nor its negation gets assigned a value, and neither of them is true. Satisfaction simply *is not an issue* for such a formula or its negation under the given I, M, or f.

In particular, let us assume that (6) applies by testing (f)s first against B in (10) and then against A and that testings of both kinds must actually have taken place in order for the rule application to have been successfully carried through to completion. If (6) finds assignments f' that satisfy B in M and then finds that each of those satisfies A, then it assigns the feature value [+ satisfied (by f in M)] to (10). If it finds (f')s that satisfy B but then finds that some of those fail to satisfy A, then it assigns the feature value [− satisfied] to (10). If it fails to find any (f')s at all that satisfy B, and so has nothing to test against A, then it simply grinds to a halt without rendering any judgement as to the relation between (10) and [± satisfied]. In the first case, (10) is true under f in M of the factual situation whose relational structure it is interpreted into by M. In the second case, its negation is true of that factual situation: (10) itself is false. In the third case, (10) is simply irrelevant to the factual situation: neither it nor its negation is true, because satisfaction is not an issue for them for the model and assignment in question.

3.2 This condition of application for (6) is especially of interest in the case in which B in (10) contains no free occurrences of the variable of quantification and, more generally, no free variables at all. It is a mistake to regard such instances of (10) as "intuitively meaningless because they purport to be saying something about everything but do not . . . " (Keenan, 1971, 261). "We may assume that, for a predicate formula φ that is independent of x, $(\forall x)\ \varphi$ and $(\exists x)\ \varphi$ simply coincide with φ" (Stolyar, 1970, 157),[7] and we can determine what happens in the relativized case by carefully examining what (6) really says about that case. What can we say, first, about an assignment f' that is like f except perhaps at x, when B in (10) does not contain x? If B contains other free variables, then f will assign values to those variables and every f' will assign exactly the same values to those variables, since f' differs from f, and therefore from every other f', at most at x, so B is satisfied by every f' or by none according as B is satisfied or not by f. Since f' differs from f at most at x, in other words, f' *is* f, as far as B is concerned, because B does not contain x and so is *blind to the difference* between f and f'. Under our dynamic reading of (6), whether or not there is an f' that satisfies B is what determines whether or not satisfaction by f is an issue for (10), so satisfaction by f will be an issue for (10) according as f itself does or does not satisfy B. This is because f itself is an f', differing from itself at most at x, just as every other f' differs from f at most at x.

If B not only lacks the variable of quantification, but is entirely devoid of free variables, then even f itself is irrelevant to the satisfaction of (10) by f. We know from (6) that f satisfies (10) in M if and only if whatever f' satisfies B in M satisfies A in M, and we have decided to interpret this dynamically in a specific way. If B contains no free occurrences of the variable of quantification, then it is blind to the differences among the various (f')s, but, if it contains no free variables at all, then it is also blind to the differences among the various (f)s, before we even get around to sorting them into (f')s. This means that the satisfaction of B in M depends not on any assignment, but only on the model itself, and that this is the case also, therefore, for whether satisfaction is an issue for (10).

3.3 Consider (17) and (18), for example. Formula (17) is the

(17) $(\forall x) ((\exists x)$ Linguist (x), Linguist (x); Study-quantifiers $(x))$
(18) $(\forall x) ((\exists x)$ (Linguist (x); Study-quantifiers $(x))$, Study-quantifiers (x); Linguist $(x))$

$\forall$-quantification of (9) relativized to (12) and to (19), the

(19) $(\exists x)$ Linguist (x)

$\exists$-quantification of (12); (18) is the $\forall$-quantification of (12) relativized to (9) and to (20), the $\exists$-quantification of (9) relativized

(20) $(\exists x)$ (Linguist (x); Study-quantifiers $(x))$

to (12). Since (19) and (20) contain no free variables — their "x"'s being already bound by $\exists$ before the $\forall$s in (17) and (18) can get to them — they serve to determine whether satisfaction is an issue, respectively, for (17) and (18). Using (21) for (17) and (22) for (18),

(21) (a) $(\exists x)$ Linguist (x) $(= 19)$
     (b) $(\forall x)$ (Linguist (x); Study-quantifiers $(x))$
(22) (a) $(\exists x)$ (Linguist (x); Study-quantifiers $(x))$ $(= 20)$
     (b) $(\forall x)$ (Study-quantifiers (x); Linguist $(x))$

(17) or (18) gets assigned [+ satisfied] if both (a) and (b) are true, i.e., satisfied; [− satisfied] if (a) is true but (b) is not; and neither if (a) is not true. It follows that the meanings represented by (17) and (18), respectively, are those expressed, respectively, by (23) and (24),

(23)   All linguists study quantifiers
(24)   Only linguists study quantifiers

the *all*-quantification and the *only*-quantification, respectively, of (9) relativized to (12), as shown, respectively, in (25) and (26) (Cushing, 1979b).[8]

(25)   (All x) (Linguist (x); Study-quantifiers $(x))$

(26)   (Only x) (Linguist (x); Study-quantifiers (x))

In general, in fact, we can state the equivalences in (27) and (28), in

(27)   (All x) $(B; A) = (\forall x) ((\exists x) B, B; A)$
(28)   (Only x) $(B; A) = (\forall x) ((\exists x) (B; A), A; B)$

which, in each case, a formula that represents the meaning of a sentence that can have three "truth values" is reduced to one that involves only bivalent quantifiers – interpreted dynamically in a specific way – thus obviating the need for explicit satisfaction rules for the trivalent quantifiers themselves.

3.4 What we end up with, in other words, is an *explanation* for the existence of "conventional implicatures" – e.g., (a) in (21) and (22) – a goal that Karttunen and Peters (1979, 15), for example, explicitly forego "at present." Conventional implicatures follow naturally from the logic of satisfaction rules, once the details of relativization are worked out and dynamic interpretation is allowed. To rule them out would require the imposition of an otherwise ad hoc restriction on satisfaction rules[9] – the prohibition of Bs in (10) with no free variables – so it is really their absence that would have to be explained, if there were found to be none in connection with natural language.

4. SELECTION *V.S.* CONSTRUCTION IN DISCOURSE INTERPRETATION

4.1 Now suppose we are given a model M. We have seen that a quantificational formula whose relativization formula contains no free variables will have satisfaction in M as an issue according as the relativization formula is or is not satisfied in M. Another way to put this would be to say that M *selects* among such formulas according as whether or not it satisfies their relativization formulas. M selects those formulas whose relativization formulas it satisfies and rejects those formulas whose relativization formulas it does not satisfy. Once this selection is made, it then goes ahead and assigns values of [± satisfied] to those formulas it has selected, entirely ignoring those it has not.

Suppose, however, that we turn this around and look at what happens from the *formula*'s point of view. Let there be given a quantificational formula whose relativization formula contains no free variables. Satisfaction will be an issue for that formula in a model, if its relativization formula is satisfied in that model, and will not be an issue in a model, if the relativization formula is not satisfied in the model. We can just as well say, then, that it is the *formula* that is doing the selecting here, and not the model. Such a formula selects those models in which satisfaction is an issue for it and rejects those models in which it is not, and it does this by determining whether or not its relativization formula is satisfied individually in each model. Relativization formulas in which there are no free variables thus turn out to serve as *criteria for model selection* for the formulas whose relativization formulas they are.

4.2 In linguistic communication, a speaker produces a discourse – a structured sequence of sentences – with the aim of bringing a real or imagined "factual situation" to the awareness of a hearer. The situation may or may not be directly present – e.g., visible – to the hearer, but, in either case, it is *re*presented for him by the sentences in the discourse. Let there be given a discourse $\{s_i, i = 1, \ldots, n\}$. Before the discourse begins, the hearer has no idea at all (ideally) what is going to be said, so the class of models that he can take as being models of the situation the speaker will try to convey to him contains every model that there is that is consistent with the lexicon of the language that is being used. When the hearer hears s_1, he narrows that class down, considerably, to the class of models that satisfy s_1; when he hears s_2, he narrows the class of relevant models down still further, and so on for each s_i, until $i = n$ and the discourse is completed. By this time the hearer has narrowed the class of relevant models down to those in which every sentence in the discourse is satisfied, i.e., to the intersection of the sets of models that satisfy each sentence individually.

In particular, suppose that there are sentences s_j and s_k such that $j < k$ and such that the formula that represents the meaning expressed by the negation $\neg s_j$ of s_j occurs as a relativization formula – without free variables – of the formula that represents the meaning expressed by s_k. At some point in the discourse, the hearer will hear an utterance *of* s_j and thus narrow the class of models he has derived from the earlier sentences in the discourse down to the subclass of those that satisfy s_j. Satisfaction is an issue for s_k, however, only in models that do *not* satisfy s_j – since $\neg s_j$ is a relativization formula of s_k – and all of these models have been rejected by the time the hearer hears an utterance of s_k. Since satisfaction is not an issue for s_k in any of the models that the hearer has been led to believe the speaker is trying to convey, he has no choice but to conclude that the sentence s_k is inappropriate to the discourse. In the dialogue suggested in (29), for example, the

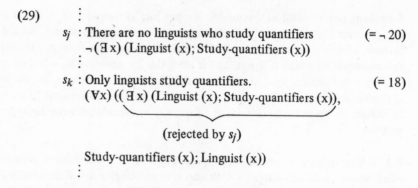

(29)

s_j : There are no linguists who study quantifiers   (= ¬ 20)
$\neg (\exists x)$ (Linguist (x); Study-quantifiers (x))

s_k : Only linguists study quantifiers.   (= 18)
$(\forall x) ((\exists x)$ (Linguist (x); Study-quantifiers (x)),

(rejected by s_j)

Study-quantifiers (x); Linguist (x))

hearer will balk at the statement that only linguists study quantifiers, because he has already been told that linguists do not study quantifiers and thus has no models left in which the *only* statement can be either true or false.

4.3 More standard accounts of discourse interpretation maintain that "as a conversation proceeds, each conversant *builds* a discourse model" (Reichman, 1978, 283, emphasis added), rather than selecting a class of models from all those that the language provides. In contrast with such *construction* accounts, our *selection* account bases itself squarely on logical form and satisfaction, thus investing those notions with psychological significance; it also makes what seems to be the correct prediction in a crucial *Gedanken* experiment. A construction account

sees the existential statements containing indefinite phrases as progressively *building up a domain of interpretation* of elements and their set relations. . . . This *construction of a domain* can continue through the course of the text as new objects are introduced.
(Stenning, 1977, emphasis added)

Such an account, taken literally, predicts that a hearer (or reader), if presented with the discourse in (30), for example, will answer a

(30)   John has a dog.
It has brown spots and likes to eat meat.

question like (31) with (32) or some equivalent. Since the hearer is

(31)   Does John have a cat?
(32)   No.

"*building up* a domain of interpretation . . . *as new objects are introduced*," the only objects that are (represented) in this domain by the time he hears

(31) are John, a dog, some spots, and (possibly) some meat. Since a cat has not been introduced in the discourse, the hearer will not have added a cat (representation) to his domain, so there will not be one there, and he will respond to (31) with (32).

According to our selection account, however, the hearer does not *build* a domain of interpretation containing the *objects* introduced in the discourse, but *selects* those models – with their domains – that are consistent with (the meanings of) the *sentences* that make up the discourse. Upon hearing the discourse (30), he rejects all models that do not contain John, all of *those* models that do not contain a dog that is owned by John, all of *those* models in which that dog does not have brown spots, and, finally, all of *those* models in which John's brown-spotted dog does not like to eat meat. By this point, quite a few models have been ruled out, but all those that remain are consistent with (30); some of these will contain a cat that John has and some of them will not, because the context has not yet enabled the hearer to select between these two classes. When confronted with (31), therefore, the hearer will reply not with (32), but with (33), (34), or some equivalent.

(33)   I don't know.
(34)   You haven't told me yet.

It seems that, in a controlled experiment in which the subject knows that he is being tested for *something* and may, therefore, be trying to second-guess or outwit the experimenter, a response of (32) to (30)–(31) would not be entirely unlikely, but that, in a natural situation in which the hearer does not suspect that something funny is going on, he would respond straight-forwardly to (30)–(31) with (33) or (34). If this is correct, then it confirms the selection account as the principal mode of discourse interpretation, though construction – of "images", perhaps (Miller, 1979a, b; Jackendoff, 1979) – may also play a secondary role.

St. Anselm College,
Manchester, New Hampshire

NOTES

[1] This framework can be refined in various ways, such as by allowing there to be more than one domain D, by replacing predicates with a functional notation, by permitting these functions to have internal structure, and so on. See Cushing (1979a) for discussion of these three options, in particular, and their implications for the study of the lexicon.

[2] Adapted from van Fraassen (1971), freely modified as needed.

[3] The ambiguity between *whatever there are* and *whatever there are in I* is deliberate. Nothing of interest here depends on it.

[4] More precisely, (10) represents the meanings expressed by sentences like (i), which is synonymous with (11) but differs from (8) exactly

(i)   Whoever there is *who is a linguist* studies quantifiers

in the presence of a *restrictive relative clause* corresponding to B in (10). The term *restricted quantification* is thus also used, e.g., by Stolyar (1970, 154) and Fodor (1975, 139). We assume, of course, for these examples, that D is the set of people and that R assigns (12) the set of linguists and (9) the set of those who study quantifiers.

[5] See Cushing (1976, 1982) for a formal proof of this important fact.

[6] We distinguish two types of semantic features, *constitutive* and *assigned*; the distinction is a conceptual one, with overlap between the two types being possible. Constitutive features are those that can be viewed as "making up" meanings, much as phonetic features like [± voiced] might be said to make up "phonemes"; for examples, see the features for *all* and *only* discussed in Cushing (1979b). Assigned features are those that get assigned to meanings in the course of some process, much as a feature [± stressed] might be said to get assigned to syllables in phonological interpretation; for an example other than [± satisfied], see the feature [± definite] proposed for embedded sentential meanings in Cushing (1972). For this usage of "meanings", see Cushing (1982).

[7] This is, in fact, the traditional view:

> Suppose x is a function, or one-many relation, which assigns an entity to each variable. In Tarski's terminology, x is said to *satisfy* a formula y of L if y comes out true for the values of its free variables which are assigned to those variables by x. Vacuously, then, if y is a statement (hence devoid of free variables), y is satisfied by every function x or by none according as y is true or false.
>
> (Quine, 1966, 142)

> If A does not contain the individual variable a as a free variable, the value of $(\forall a) A$ is the same as the value of A, for any system of values of the free variables. If A contains no free variables, and if a is any individual variable, $(\forall a) A$ has the same denotation as A.
>
> (Church, 1956, 176, n. 313)

See Cushing (1976) for more discussion.

[8] Strictly speaking, the $\exists$ in (18) must be interpreted statically, for the equivalence between (18) and (26) to hold, despite the dynamic interpretation of the $\forall$. This suggests the existence of a constitutive feature [± dynamic] for ostensibly bivalent quantifier meanings, rather than the semantic universal proposed for all quantifier meanings in Cushing (1977). See note 6.

[9] See note 7.

REFERENCES

Church, Alonzo: 1956, *Introduction to Mathematical Logic, Volume I*. Princeton, N.J.: Princeton University Press.

Cushing, Steven: 1972, 'The Semantics of Sentence Pronominalization', *Foundations of*

Language **9**, 186–208. Reprinted in Yasui, Minoru (ed.) (1975) *Kaigai Eigogaku Ronso* (Selected Articles and Theses on Linguistics), Tokyo: Eichosha.

Cushing, Steven: 1976, 'The Formal Semantics of Quantification', UCLA doctoral dissertation. Available from University Microfilms, Ann Arbor, Michigan.

Cushing, Steven: 1977, 'Discourse, Logical Form, and Contextual Model Selection: The Unity of Semantics and Pragmatics in Presupposition and Anaphora'. Discussion paper presented to MIT Workshop on Language and Cognition, May 1977.

Cushing, Steven: 1979a, 'Lexical Functions and Lexical Decomposition: An Algebraic Approach to Lexical Meaning', *Linguistic Inquiry* **10**, 327–345.

Cushing, Steven: 1979b, 'Semantic Considerations in Natural Language: Crosslinguistic Evidence and Morphological Motivation', *Studies in Language* **3**, 181–201.

Cushing, Steven: 1982, *Quantifier Meanings: A Study in the Dimensions of Semantic Competence*, Amsterdam: North-Holland.

Fodor, Jerry A.: 1975, *The Language of Thought*, New York: Thomas Y. Crowell.

van Fraassen, Bas C.: 1971, *Formal Semantics and Logic*, New York: The Macmillan Company.

Jackendoff, Ray: 1980, 'Belief-Contexts Revisited', *Linguistic Inquiry* **11**, 395–413.

Karttunen, Lauri and Stanley Peters: 1979, 'Conventional Implicature', in Choon-Kyu Oh and David A. Dineen (eds.), *Syntax and Semantics, Vol. 2, Presupposition*, New York: Academic Press.

Keenan, Edward L.: 1971, 'Quantifier Structures in English', *Foundations of Language* **7**, 255–284.

Miller, George: 1979a, 'Construction and Selection in the Mental Representation of Text', *Cahiers de l'Institut de Linguistique de Louvain* **5**, 185–197.

Miller, George: 1979b, 'Images and Models, Similes and Metaphors', in Ortony, Andrew (ed.), *Metaphor and Thought*, Cambridge: Cambridge University Press.

Quine, W. V.: 1966, 'On an Application of Tarski's Theory of Truth', Chapter XI of *Selected Logic Papers*, New York: Random House.

Reichman, Rachel: 1978, 'Conversational Coherency', *Cognitive Science* **2**, 283–327.

Stenning, Keith: 1977, 'Articles, Quantifiers, and their Encoding in Textual Comprehension', in Freedle, R. O. (ed.), *Discourse Production and Comprehension*, Hillsdale, N.J.: Lawrence Erlbaum Associates.

Stolyar, Abram A.: 1970, *Introduction to Elementary Mathematical Logic*, Cambridge, Mass.: MIT Press.

Tarski, A.: 1936, 'Der Wahrheitsbegriff in den formalisierten Sprachen', *Studia Philosophica* **1**, 261–405.

GHEORGHE PĂUN

MODELLING THE DIALOGUE BY MEANS OF
FORMAL LANGUAGE THEORY

ABSTRACT. We discuss the possibility of modelling the dialouge as a system of action
in the sense of [6], pondering on the linguistic formalization of the rules governing the
correct development of the process and their relationships with the type of the language
determined.

1. INTRODUCTION

In what follows, we shall understand the dialogue as a "conversation between
two or several persons" [2]. In fact, we shall use as synonymous the words
"dialogue" and "conversation".

We shall consider dialogue as an exchange of rejoinders (belonging to a
fixed finite set of rejoinders) rather than an exchange of information taking
place in certain space and time. In other words, we focus on the syntactic
level of the dialogue, on its formal development.

Just at this level of abstraction, the following formalism for describing a
conversation was proposed in [8]. Let X be the set of participants which a
given dialogue involves, $X = \{1, \ldots, n\}$, and let R be the finite set of rejoinders which the persons labelled by $1, 2, \ldots, n$ are uttering. The rejoinders
in R are, in fact, semantic marks associated with classes of rejoinders. For
instance, we can take the following: q = question, a = answer, aa = affirmative
answer, c = comment, etc. At each moment, exactly one participant from
X is speaking (let us denote them by s), uttering a phrase which belongs to
some semantic category whose mark is in R. We say that s is pronouncing a
rejoinder from R. Each rejoinder is uttered for a set of addresses, a subset A
of X. Let us suppose that in a given moment, a participant has a special
position in the conversation: it is the leader, the "chairman". We denote him
by c. The four items, c, s, A, r, completely describe the dialogue at this time;
the quadruple (c, s, A, r) is called a *state* of the conversation. Let St =
$X \times X \times 2^X \times R$ be the set of all states. Thus, the conversation can be
described by some string in St*. (St* is the free monoid generated by St
under the operation of concatenation and the null element λ.) Any shift in
the role of the speaker, the chairman, the addressees and the occurrence of
any new rejoinder marks the passing to a new state of the conversation.

363

L. Vaina and J. Hintikka (eds.), Cognitive Constraints on Communication, 363–371.
© 1984 *by D. Reidel Publishing Company.*

In this frame, a linguistic approach to dialogue was proposed in [4] in order to model the correct evolution of the process.

We call a *conversation grammar* the system

(1) $G = (X, R, S_0, S_\infty, \varphi)$

where X, R are as above, $S_0, S_\infty \subset$ St are the set of initial states, respectively, the set of final states, and φ: St* $\to 2^{St}$ is the next-state function. The set of all correct conversations is defined by

$$L(G) = \{ x \in St^* \mid x = s_0 s_1 \ldots s_n, n \geqslant 1, s_0 \in S_0, s_n \in S_\infty,$$
$$s_i \in \varphi(s_0 s_1 \ldots s_{i-1}) \text{ for any } i = 1, 2, \ldots, n \}.$$

In [4] examples of conversations were discussed whose associated languages are regular, context-free non-regular, and, respectively, context-sensitive non-context-free languages. (See [9] for the formal language theory terminology.) Moreover, it was proved that if the next state depends only on a bounded number of preceding states (the conversation is said to have a weak historicity), then the associated language is regular.

However, the above definition of the conversational grammars has an infinite feature: the next state mapping φ is defined on the infinite set St*. In real cases we do not deal (directly) with this mapping, but a set of *rules* are pointed out defining the correct evolutions of the conversation.

2. THE RULES OF THE DIALOGUE

Clearly, there are many rules governing the development of different types of dialogue. Our purpose is not to exhaust their formalization (this seems to be a hard task), but just to discuss a set of such rules from the point of view of their formalization in the frame of the linguistic model of action systems proposed in [6].

By examining different types of dialogue, we can set off three classes of dialogue rules:

(a) *Protocol rules*, i.e. rules defining the type of the conversation. Two subclasses can be distinguished:

(a1) *General protocol rules* acting on the dialogue as a whole.

Examples: rules about the choice/change of the chairman, the choice/change of the speaker and of addressees, the beginning and the end of a conversation, etc. Many such rules can act on the rejoinder crossing restrictions. Let us state some such rules for the case when we deal with rejoinders which are to be followed by an answer (as the questions). In this case we can

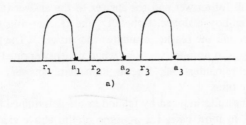

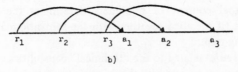

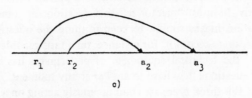

Fig. 1.

consider to be correct (i) only the "uncrossed" evolutions of the dialogue, that is, the exchanges of rejoinders of the type described in Figure 1.a. (a rejoinder is uttered only after answering all the previous rejoinders), or (ii) the "crossed" evolutions which keep the order in the sense of Figure 1.b. (if two rejoinders r_1, r_2 were uttered in this order, then they must be answered in the same order), or (iii) the "crossed" evolutions in which the pairs rejoinder-answer may be intersected (Figure 1.c.).

(a2) *Partial protocol rules*, that is, rules involving only some participants which have a privileged position in dialogue.

For example, only certain participants may play the part of the chairman/speaker (let us have in mind the position of the teacher in a classroom), certain persons may break in on a conversation without the chairman's permission, the rejoinders of certain participants must be immediately answered, and so on.

(b) *Rejoinders rules*, i.e. rules entailed by the rejoinders types.

For example, there are rejoinders which do not require answers ("I want to inform you about . . . "), but there are other rejoinders which call for an answer (the questions, the phrases beginning with "Tell me, please . . . "), or, furthermore, call for answer and for answer to the answer (Consider again a teacher – school-boy dialogue. Generally, the teacher asks a question, the student answers and the teacher evaluates the answer.). The typology can be enlarged, taking into account the time when the answer must be uttered. For instance, some rejoinders ask for an immediate answer, others may be answered at any time.

Generally, the rules induced by rejoinders are determined by the rejoinder semantics, but, in most cases (as in some of the above examples in parentheses), the verbal content of rejoinders determines the rule. Thus, the rejoinder syntax (if specified together with the semantic mark) can identify the corresponding rule.

(c) *Technical rules* related to the "technical" capabilities of participants.

To explain this, let us consider the case of a person which must answer a question. Clearly, he must "memorize" this question for some time interval. This memorization means simply to keep in mind the question or to put it down on paper, or to record it, for instance, on a tape-recorder (dictaphone). In this respect, the technical equipment of participants has implications on the number of questions they have to answer at any moment.

The rules of the three types are simultaneously acting on a given dialogue. Thus, a large set of dialogue types can be considered. Clearly, some rules are mutually contradictory, others are equivalent, etc. For example, if the protocol rule "any rejoinder (which asks for an answer) must be immediately answered" is acting, then the rejoinder rule "the rejoinder r may be answered at any time" must be cancelled. Also, if the dialogue is of the form described in Figure 1.a., then the capability of some participants to memorize a great number of rejoinders is superfluous.

Roughly speaking, since all the rules adopted in a given dialogue must be observed, in fact, only their "intersection" is actually acting.

3. THE FORMALIZATION OF DIALOGUE RULES BY MEANS OF THE LINGUISTIC MODEL OF ACTION SYSTEMS

In [6] both simple (only one actor is considered) and compound systems of actions are defined. Although the dialogue is an action of two or more persons, at any given time only one of them is active – the speaker. The others, including the chairman, may be considered to be passive, to do nothing. (See [3] for a similar treatment.) Therefore, the dialogue implies to use an intermediate kind of action systems.

However, in order to exemplify this type of linguistic approach, let us briefly present the *simple system of action specified by dependences* (shortly, d-SSA) defined in [6] as a quadruple

(2) $\Sigma = (A, A_0, A_\infty, \Gamma)$,

where A is the finite set of elementary actions, $A_0, A_\infty \subset A$ are, respectively, the set of initial and of final actions and Γ is a finite set of directed graphs without circuits, having the vertices in A.

The graphs in Γ define dependences between the actions taken as vertices. The language determined by Σ consists in those strings of actions which can be obtained by interpenetration of all linearizations of graphs in Γ. Formally, this language can be constructed in the following way.

Let $\gamma = (M, U)$ be a directed graph without circuits, $M = \{a_1, \ldots, a_n\}$. A string $a_{f(1)} \ldots a_{f(n)}$ is called a linearization of γ iff for any edge $(a_i, a_j) \in U$ we have $i = f(i'), j = f(j')$, for some $i' < j'$. Let $\Gamma = \{\gamma_1, \ldots, \gamma_t\}$ and for any γ_i let Z_i be the set of all linearizations of γ_i. For an arbitrary vocabulary V and for $x, y \in V^*$ we define

$$\text{Shuf}(x, y) = \{x_1 y_1 \ldots x_p y_p \mid p \geq 1, x_i, y_i \in V^*, x = x_1 \ldots x_p, y = y_1 \ldots y_p\}.$$

For $L_1, L_2 \subset V^*$ we put

$$\text{Shuf}(L_1, L_2) = \underset{\substack{x \in L_1 \\ y \in L_2}}{\bigsqcup} \text{Shuf}(x, y),$$

and

$$\text{Shuf}^0(L_1) = \{\lambda\},$$
$$\text{Shuf}^{i+1}(L_1) = \text{Shuf}(\text{Shuf}^i(L_1), L_1), i \geq 0,$$
$$\text{Shuf}^*(L_1) = \underset{n \geq 0}{\bigsqcup} \text{Shuf}^n(L_1).$$

Now, let us construct the languages

$$W_i = \text{Shuf}^*(Z_i), i = 1, 2, \ldots, t.$$

Then

$$L(\Sigma) = \text{Shuf}(W_1, \text{Shuf}(W_2, \ldots, \text{Shuf}(W_{n-1}, W_n)) \ldots)) \cap A_0 A^* A_\infty.$$

(Since the operation Shuf is associative, the order in the above construction is irrelevant.)

In view of the results in [5] where the operations Shuf, Shuf* were investigated, it follows that L (Σ) is a context-sensitive language for any Σ. Common actions were identified in [6] which lead to non-context-free languages L (Σ).

Let us return to the dialogue and to the rules considered in Section 2. Clearly, some of them, such as those about individual privileges in connection with the role of chairman and of speaker, or about the compatibility between the speaker and the set of addressees, can be expressed by means of the set of states: we can take as vocabulary a subset A of the set $X \times X \times 2^X \times R$, namely, the set of correct states according to these rules. Thus the set of correct states must be introduced in the model.

Many rules can be formalized by means of directed graphs in the same way as the Γ above does; such rules are those with reference to rejoinders asking for answers or for answer and answer to the answer, etc.

In order to define the interval between the rejoinders and the answers (the above model of d-SSA's does not contain such facilities), we shall introduce in the model a new component, P, consisting in mappings $\rho_i : U_i \to N \cup \{\infty\}$ associated to the graphs $\gamma_i = (M_i, U_i)$ in Γ. We interpret this component in the following way: if $(a_i, a_j) \in U_k$ then the state a_j must occur after at most ρ_k (a_i, a_j) changes of the state after the state a_i has occurred.

As the state identifies both the speaker and his rejoinder, in this way we can formalize any rejoinder rule previously discussed, as well as some protocol rules (to answer immediately the rejoinders of certain persons).

Now, let us consider the technical rules. A mapping $m : X \to N \cup \{\infty\}$ can express them. ($m(i)$ is the maximum number of rejoinders that the participant i can memorize.)

At this stage, our model looks as follows

$$\Sigma = (X, R, A, S_0, S_\infty, \Gamma, P, m),$$

with the above discussed components.

They have remained outside the rules described in Figure 1. These rules directly act on the strings of states and cannot be linked with the above components of the model. These rules and other dichotomic rules (related to conditions which have or not to be fulfilled) can be introduced in the model as positional parameters, taking, for instance, the values 0 and 1 for the two alternatives. For example, we can write

$$(3) \qquad \Sigma = (X, R, A, S_0, S_\infty, \Gamma, P, m, j_a, j_b, j_c)$$

where j_α, $\alpha \in \{a, b, c\}$ is 1 when the condition in Figure 1. α, is to be observed and $j_\alpha = 0$ otherwise.

Therefore, almost all the above discussed rules can be formalized in this way. Two problems of practical significance naturally arise: which is the place of the language L (Σ) in the Chomsky hierarchy depending on the rules incorporated in Σ and (a related problem) how the language L (Σ) can be algorithmically constructed? In fact, we look for an algorithm which starts from the system Σ and produces a grammar for the language L (Σ). These problems are of practical interest since the grammar/automaton which generates/recognizes the language L (Σ) simulates the dialogue; its development can be predicted using the grammar/automaton working. As this grammar/automaton corresponds to a higher level in the Chomsky hierarchy (is nearer to type-3 level), it is easier to handle the system Σ, its associated language.

4. THE CONSTRUCTION OF L (Σ)

It is easy to find simple usual conversations which lead to non-regular languages, or even to non-context-free languages.

On the other hand, since the model (3) considerably exceeds the model (2), the procedure used in [6] to construct the language L (Σ) cannot be used again. However, a fact is beyond all doubt: for any Σ as above, the language L (Σ) is a context-sensitive one. If Σ is given, a context-sensitive grammar G can be algorithmically constructed such that L (G) = L (Σ). The construction, although straightforward, is long and we omit it. Moreover, a set π of a context-sensitive rewriting rules can be constructed so that if we codify the system Σ in a suitable manner as a string w (Σ) on a vocabulary V, then we have L (Σ) = L (G_Σ), where G_Σ = (V, A, w (Σ), π) (V is taken as nonterminal vocabulary, A is the terminal vocabulary, w (Σ) is the start string of the grammar and π is the set of production rules).

Another way to construct L (Σ) is the following one: Let $c_1, \ldots, c_t$ be all the rules formalized by a given system Σ. If we can construct the languages L (c_i) of those strings in A^* which observe the condition c_i (and ignore the other conditions), then we obtain L (Σ) = L (c_1) $\cap \ldots \cap L$ (c_t). Thus, the problem of constructing L (Σ) is reduced to the problem of constructing the simpler languages L (c_i), $i = 1, 2, \ldots, t$.

For example, the condition imposed by S_0, S_∞ leads to the language

$$L (S_0, S_\infty) = S_0 A^* S_\infty.$$

Similarly, the rule in Figure 1.a. implies considering the language L (c_{1a}) as consisting in strings obtained by concatenating *some* linearizations of the graphs in Γ. (The operations Shuf, Shuf* cross the pairs rejoinder-answer and hence cannot be used.)

The language L (c_{1a}), and the language L (S_0, S_∞), are regular. The existence of some regular languages among L (c_i), $i = 1, 2, \ldots, t$ is important since the family of regular languages is closed under intersection, and, more-over, if L_1 is regular, then $L_1 \cap L_2$ is of the same type as L_2 for any L_2. Thus, if all languages L (c_i) would be regular, then L (Σ) would be regular too.

The conditions in Figure 1.b. and 1.c. do not lead to regular languages. In order to prove this, let us consider the following example.

$$X = \{1, 2\},$$
$$R = \{q, a, e\}, q = \text{question}, a = \text{answer}, e = \text{evaluation of the}$$
$$\text{answer},$$
$$A = \{s_1, s_2, s_3\}, s_1 = (1, 1, \{2\}, q), s_2 = (1, 2, \{1\}, a),$$
$$s_3 = (1, 1, \{2\}, e),$$
$$S_0 = \{s_1\},$$
$$S_\infty = \{s_3\},$$
$$\Gamma = \{\gamma\}, \gamma = (A, \{(s_1, s_2), (s_2, s_3)\}),$$
$$P = \{\rho\}, \rho((s_1, s_2)) = \rho((s_2, s_3)) = \infty,$$
$$m(1) = \infty, m(2) = \infty,$$
$$j_a = 0, j_b = 1, j_c = 0.$$

(The person 1 asks some questions, the person 2 answers and the person 1 evaluates each answer.)

Let the regular language be

$$L = \{s_1^i s_2^j s_3^k \mid i, j, k \geqslant 1\}.$$

Obviously, we have

$$L(\Sigma) \cap L = \{s_1^t s_2^t s_3^t \mid t \geqslant 1\}.$$

As this language is not a context-free one, it follows that L (Σ) is not context-free either.

The same language is obtained if we take $j_a = 0, j_b = 0, j_c = 1$.

Consequently, the strongest general result about the type of L (Σ) in the Chomsky hierarchy for arbitrary Σ, is that of the possibility to algorithmically construct a context-sensitive grammar for L (Σ). It remains to investigate the relationships between L (Σ) and the families of matrix languages intermediate between the family of context-free languages and that of context-sensitive languages (see [7] for the matrix languages theory).

Bucharest Institute of Mathematics

REFERENCES

[1] Marcus, S.: 1974, 'Linguistics as a pilot science,' *Current Trends in Linguistics* 12, (Th. Sebeok, ed.), Mouton, The Hague, Paris.

[2] Marcus, S.: 1978, 'A dialogue about dialogue,' Manuscript for United Nations University.

[3] Nowakowska, M.: 1976, 'Towards a formal theory of dialogues,' *Semiotica* 17, 291–307.

[4] Păun, Gh.: 1976, 'A generative model of conversation,' *Semiotica* 17, 21–33.

[5] Păun, Gh.: 1977, 'New operations with languages,' *Stud. Cerc. Matem.* 29, 521– 533, (in Roum.).

[6] Păun, Gh.: 1979, 'A formal linguistic model of action systems,' *Ars Semiotica* 2, 33–47.

[7] Păun, Gh.: 1981, 'Matrix grammars,' *Ed. Stiintifica si Enciclopedica*, Bucharest, (in Roum.).

[8] Poythress, V.: 1973, 'A formalism for describing rules of conversation,' *Semiotica* 7, 285–299.

[9] Salomaa, A.: 1973, *Formal Languages*, Academic Press, New York and London.

L. A. ZADEH*

PRECISIATION OF MEANING VIA TRANSLATION INTO PRUF

ABSTRACT. It is suggested that communication between humans – as well as between humans and machines – may be made more precise by the employment of a meaning representation language PRUF which is based on the concept of a possibility distribution. A brief exposition of PRUF is presented and its application to precisiation of meaning is illustrated by a number of examples.

1. INTRODUCTION

Of the many ways in which natural languages differ from synthetic languages, one of the most important relates to ambiguity. Thus, whereas synthetic languages are, for the most part, unambiguous, natural languages are *maximally ambiguous* in the sense that the level of ambiguity in human communication is usually near the limit of what is disambiguable through the use of an external body of knowledge which is shared by the parties in discourse.

Although vagueness and ambiguity[1] can and do serve a number of useful purposes, there are many cases in which there is a need for a precisiation of meaning not only in communication between humans but also between humans and machines. In fact, the need is even greater in the latter case because it is difficult, in general, to provide a machine with the extensive contextual knowledge base which is needed for disambiguation on the syntactic and semantic levels.

The traditional approach to the precisiation of meaning of utterances in a natural language is to translate them into an unambiguous synthetic language – which is usually a programming language, a query language or a logical language such as predicate calculus. The main limitation of this approach is that the available synthetic languages are nowhere nearly as expressive as natural languages. Thus, if the target language is the first order predicate calculus, for example, then only a small fragment of a natural language would be amenable to translation, since the expressive power of first order predicate calculus is extremely limited in relation to that of a natural language.

To overcome this limitation, what is needed is a synthetic language whose expressive power is comparable to that of natural languages. A candidate for such a language is PRUF [81] – which is a meaning representation language for natural languages based on the concept of a possibility distribution [80].

373

L. Vaina and J. Hintikka (eds.), Cognitive Constraints on Communication, 373–401.
© 1984 *by D. Reidel Publishing Company.*

In essence, a basic assumption underlying PRUF is that the imprecision which is intrinsic in natural languages is possibilistic rather than probabilistic in nature. With this assumption as the point of departure, PRUF provides a system for translating propositions or, more generally, utterances in a natural language into expressions in PRUF. Such expressions may be viewed as procedures which act on a collection of relations in a database — or, equivalently, a possible world — and return possibility distributions which represent the information conveyed by the original propositions.[2]

In what follows, we shall outline some of the main features of PRUF and exemplify its application to precisiation of meaning. As a preliminary, we shall introduce the concept of a possibility distribution and explicate its role in PRUF.[3]

2. POSSIBILITY AND MEANING

A randomly chosen sentence in a natural language is almost certain to contain one or more words whose denotations are fuzzy sets, that is, classes of objects in which the transition from membership to nonmembership is gradual rather than abrupt. For example:

> Hourya is very *charming* and *intelligent.*
>
> It is *very unlikely* that *inflation* will end *soon.*
>
> In *recognition* of his *contributions*, Mohammed is *likely* to be *promoted* to a *higher position*

in which the italics signify that a word has a fuzzy denotation in the universe of discourse.

For simplicity, we shall focus our attention for the present on canonical propositions of the form "N is F," where N is the name of an object, a variable or a proposition, and F is a fuzzy subset of a universe of discourse U. For example:

$$(2.1) \quad p \triangleq \text{John is very tall}$$
$$q \triangleq X \text{ is small}$$
$$r \triangleq (\text{John is very tall}) \text{ is not quite true}$$

where:

In p, $N \triangleq$ John, and *very tall* is a fuzzy subset of the interval $[0, 200]$ (with the height assumed to be measured in centimeters).

In q, $N \triangleq X$ and *small* is a fuzzy subset of the real line.

In r, $N \triangleq$ John is very tall, and *not quite true* is a linguistic truth-value [77] whose denotation is a fuzzy subset of the unit interval.

Now if X is a variable taking values in U, then by the *possibility distribution* of X, denoted by Π_X, is meant the fuzzy set of possible values of X, with the *possibility distribution function* $\pi_X: U \to [0, 1]$ defining the possibility that X can assume a value u. Thus,

(2.2) $\pi_X(u) \triangleq \text{Poss} \{X = u\}$

with $\pi_X(u)$ taking values in the interval $[0, 1]$.

The connection between possibility distributions and fuzzy sets is provided by the

Possibility Postulate. In the absence of any information about X other than that conveyed by the proposition

(2.3) $p \triangleq X$ is F,

the possibility distribution of X is given by the *possibility assignment equation*

(2.4) $\Pi_X = F$.

This equation implies that

(2.5) $\pi_X(u) = \mu_F(u)$

where $\mu_F(u)$ is the grade of membership of u in F, i.e., the degree to which u fits one's subjective perception of F.

As a simple illustration, consider the proposition

(2.6) $p \triangleq X$ is SMALL

where SMALL is a fuzzy set defined by[4]

(2.7)   SMALL $= 1/0 + 0.8/2 + 0.6/3 + 0.4/4 + 0.2/5$.

In this case, the possibility assignment equation corresponding to (2.5) may be expressed as

(2.8) $\Pi_X = 1/0 + 0.8/2 + 0.6/3 + 0.4/4 + 0.2/5$

with Π_X representing the possibility distribution of X. In this case — and more generally — the proposition $p \triangleq N$ is F will be said to *translate* into the possibility assignment equation

$\Pi_X = F$

where X is a variable that is explicit or implicit in N. To express this connection between p and the corresponding possibility assignment equation, we shall write

(2.10) N is $F \rightarrow \Pi_X = F$.

When X is implicit rather than explicit in N, the possibility assignment equation serves, first, to identify X and, second, to characterize its possibility distribution. For example, in the proposition

(2.11) $p \triangleq$ Clara has dark hair

X may be expressed as

X = Color (Hair (Clara))

and the possibility assignment equation reads

(2.12) $\Pi_{\text{Color (Hair (Clara))}}$ = DARK.

Before proceeding further in our discussion of the relation between possibility and meaning, it will be necessary to establish some of the basic properties of possibility distributions. A brief exposition of these properties is presented in the following.

Joint, Marginal and Conditional Possibility Distributions

In the preceding discussion, we have assumed that X is a unary variable such as color, height, age, etc. More generally, let $X \triangleq (X_1, \ldots, X_n)$ be an n-ary variable which takes values in a universe of discourse $U = U_1 \times \ldots \times U_n$, with X_i, $i = 1, \ldots, n$, taking values in U_i. Furthermore, let F be an n-ary fuzzy relation in U which is characterized by its membership function μ_F. Then, the proposition

(2.13) $p \triangleq X$ is F

induces an n-ary joint possibility distribution

(2.14) $\Pi_X \triangleq \Pi_{(X_1, \ldots, X_n)}$

which is given by

(2.15) $\Pi_{(X_1, \ldots, X_n)} = F$.

Correspondingly, the possibility distribution function of X is expressed by

$$\pi_{(X_1, \ldots, X_n)} (u_1, \ldots, u_n) = \mu_F (u_1, \ldots, u_n),$$
$$u \triangleq (u_1, \ldots, u_n) \in U$$
$$= \text{Poss} \{ X_1 = u_1, \ldots, X_n = u_n \}.$$

As in the case of probabilities, we can define marginal and conditional possibilities. Thus, let $s \triangleq (i_1, \ldots, i_k)$ be a subsequence of the index sequence $(1, \ldots, n)$ and let s' denote the complementary subsequence $s' \triangleq (j_1, \ldots, j_m)$ (e.g., for $n = 5$, $s = (1, 3, 4)$ and $s' = (2, 5)$). In terms of such sequences, a k-tuple of the form $(A_{i_1}, \ldots, A_{i_k})$ may be expressed in an abbreviated form as $A_{(s)}$. In particular, the variable $X_{(s)} = (X_{i_1}, \ldots, X_{i_k})$ will be referred to as a k-ary *subvariable of* $X \triangleq (X_1, \ldots, X_n)$, with $X_{(s')} = (X_{j_1}, \ldots, X_{j_m})$ being a subvariable complementary to $X_{(s)}$.

The *projection* of $\Pi_{(X_1, \ldots, X_n)}$ on $U_{(s)} \triangleq U_{i_1} \times \ldots \times U_{i_k}$ is a k-ary possibility distribution denoted by

$$(2.16) \quad \Pi_{X_{(s)}} \triangleq \text{Proj}_{U_{(s)}} \Pi_{(X_1, \ldots, X_n)}$$

and defined by

$$(2.17) \quad \pi_{X_{(s)}} (u_{(s)}) \triangleq \sup_{u_{(s')}} \pi_X (u_1, \ldots, u_n)$$

where $\pi_{X_{(s)}}$ is the possibility distribution function of $\Pi_{X_{(s)}}$. For example, for $n = 2$,

$$\pi_{X_1} (u_1) \triangleq \sup_{u_2} \pi_{(X_1, X_2)} (u_1, u_2)$$

is the expression for the possibility distribution function of the projection of $\Pi_{(X_1, X_2)}$ on U_1. By analogy with the concept of a marginal probability distribution, $\Pi_{X_{(s)}}$ will be referred to as a *marginal possibility distribution*. As a simple illustration, assume that $n = 3$, $U_1 = U_2 = U_3 = a + b$ or, more conventionally, $\{a, b\}$, and $\Pi_{(X_1, X_2, X_3)}$ is expressed as a linear form

$$(2.18) \quad \Pi_{(X_1, X_2, X_3)} = 0.8aaa + 1aab + 0.6baa + 0.2bab + 0.5bbb$$

in which a term of the form $0.6baa$ signifies that

$$\text{Poss} \{ X_1 = b, X_2 = a, X_3 = a \} = 0.6.$$

To derive $\Pi_{(X_1, X_2)}$ from (2.18), it is sufficient to replace the value of X_3 in each term in (2.18) by the null string Λ. This yields

$$\Pi_{(X_1, X_2)} = 0.8aa + 1aa + 0.6ba + 0.2ba + 0.5bb$$
$$= 1aa + 0.6ba + 0.5bb;$$

and similarly

$$\Pi_{X_1} = 1a + 0.6b + 0.5b$$
$$= 1a + 0.6b.$$

An *n-ary* possibility distribution is *particularized* by forming the conjunction of the propositions "X is F" and "$X_{(s)}$ is G," where $X_{(s)}$ is a subvariable of X. Thus,

(2.19) $\Pi_X [\Pi_{X_{(s)}} = G] \triangleq F \cap \bar{G}$

where the right-hand member denotes the intersection of F with the cylindrical extension of G, i.e., a cylindrical fuzzy set defined by

(2.20) $\mu_{\bar{G}} (u_1, \ldots, u_n) = \mu_G (u_{i_1}, \ldots, u_{i_k}),$
$$(u_1, \ldots, u_n) \in U_1 \times \ldots \times U_n.$$

As a simple illustration, consider the possibility distribution defined by (2.18), and assume that

$$\Pi_{(X_1, X_2)} = 0.4aa + 0.9ba + 0.1bb.$$

In this case,

$$\bar{G} = 0.4aaa + 0.4aab + 0.9baa + 0.9bab + 0.1bba + 0.1bbb$$
$$F \cap \bar{G} = 0.4aaa + 0.4aab + 0.6baa + 0.2bab + 0.1bbb;$$

and hence

$$\Pi_{(X_1, X_2, X_3)} [\Pi_{(X_1, X_2)} = G]$$
$$0.4aaa + 0.4aab + 0.6baa + 0.2bab + 0.1bbb.$$

There are many cases in which the operations of particularization and projection are combined. In such cases it is convenient to use the simplified notation

(2.21) $X_{(r)} \Pi [\Pi_{X_{(s)}} = G]$

to indicate that the particularized possibility distribution (or relation) $\Pi [\Pi_{X_{(s)}} = G]$ is projected on $U_{(r)}$, where r, like s, is a subsequence of the index sequence $(1, \ldots, n)$. For example,

$$X_1 \times X_3 \Pi [\Pi_{(X_3, X_4)} = G]$$

would represent the projection of $\Pi [\Pi_{(X_3, X_4)} = G]$ on $U_1 \times U_3$. Informally, (2.21) may be interpreted as: Constrain the $X_{(s)}$ by $\Pi_{X_{(s)}} = G$ and read out the $X_{(r)}$. In particular, if the values of $X_{(s)}$ — rather than their possibility distributions — are set equal to G, then (2.21) becomes

$$X_{(r)} \; \Pi \; [X_{(s)} = G].$$

We shall make use of (2.21) and its special cases in Section 3.

If X and Y are variables taking values in U and V, respectively, then the *conditional possibility distribution* of Y given X is induced by a proposition of the form "If X is F then Y is G" and is expressed as $\Pi_{(Y|X)}$, with the understanding that

$$(2.22) \quad \pi_{(Y|X)} \, (v|u) \triangleq \text{Poss} \, \{ Y = v | X = u \}$$

where (2.22) defines the conditional possibility distribution function of Y given X. If we know the distribution function of X and the conditional distribution function of Y given X, then we can construct the joint distribution function of X and Y by forming the conjunction ($\wedge \triangleq$ min)

$$(2.23) \quad \pi_{(X, Y)} \, (u, v) = \pi_X(u) \wedge \pi_{(Y|X)} \, (v|u).$$

Translation Rules. The translation rules in PRUF serve the purpose of facilitating the composition of the meaning of a complex proposition from the meanings of its constituents. For convenience, the rules in question are categorized into four basic types: Type I: Rules pertaining to modification; Type II: Rules pertaining to composition; Type III: Rules pertaining to quantification; and Type IV: Rules pertaining to qualification.

Remark. Translation rules as described below relate to what might be called *focused* translations, that is, translation of p into a possibility assignment equation. More generally, a translation may be *unfocused*, in which case it is expressed as a procedure which computes the possibility of a database, D, given p or, equivalently, the truth of p relative to D. A more detailed discussion of these issues will be presented at a later point in this section.

Modifier rule (Type I). Let X be a variable which takes values in a universe of discourse U and let F be a fuzzy subset of U. Consider the proposition

$$(2.24) \quad p \triangleq X \text{ is } F$$

or, more generally,

$$(2.25) \quad p = N \text{ is } F$$

where N is a variable, an object or a proposition. For example,

$$(2.26) \quad p \triangleq \text{Lucia is young}$$

which may be expressed in the form (2.24), i.e.,

$$(2.27) \quad p \triangleq \text{Age (Lucia) is young}$$

by identifying X with the variable Age (Lucia).

Now, if in a particular context the proposition X is F translates into

(2.28) X is $F \rightarrow \Pi_X = F$

then in the same context

(2.29) X is $mF \rightarrow \Pi_X = F^+$

where m is a modifier such as *not, very, more or less*, etc., and F^+ is a modification of F induced by m. More specifically: If m = not, then $F^+ = F' =$ complement of F, i.e.,

(2.30) $\mu_{F^+}(u) = 1 - \mu_F(u), \ u \in U.$

If m = very, then $F^+ = F^2$, i.e.,

(2.31) $\mu_{F^+}(u) = \mu_{F^2}(u), u \in U.$

If m = more or less, then $F^+ = \sqrt{F}$, i.e.,

(2.32) $\mu_{F^+}(u) = \sqrt{\mu_F(u)} \, , u \in U.$

As a simple illustration of (2.31), if SMALL is defined as in (2.7), then

(2.33) X is very small $\rightarrow \Pi_X = F^2$

where

$$F^2 = 1/0 + 1/1 + 0.64/2 + 0.36/3 + 0.16/4 + 0.04/5.$$

It should be noted that (2.30), (2.31) and (2.32) should be viewed as default rules which may be replaced by other translation rules in cases in which some alternative interpretations of the modifiers *not, very* and *more or less* may be more appropriate.

Conjunctive, Disjunctive and Implicational Rules (Type II).

If

(2.34) X is $F \rightarrow \Pi_X = F$ and Y is $G \rightarrow \Pi_Y = G$

where F and G are fuzzy subsets of U and V, respectively, then

(2.35) (a) X is F and Y is $G \rightarrow \Pi_{(X, Y)} = F \times G$

where

(2.36) $\mu_F \times_G (u, v) \triangleq \mu_F(u) \wedge \mu_G(v).$

(2.37) (b) X is F or Y is $G \to \Pi_{(X, Y)} = \bar{F} \cup \bar{G}$

where

(2.38) $\bar{F} \triangleq F \times V, \bar{G} \triangleq U \times G$

and

(2.39) $\mu_{\bar{F} \cup \bar{G}} (u, v) = \mu_F(u) \vee \mu_G(v).$

(2.40) (c)   If X is F then Y is $G \to \Pi_{(Y|X)} = \bar{F}' \oplus \bar{G}$

where $\Pi_{(Y|X)}$ denotes the conditional possibility distribution of Y given X, and the bounded sum $\oplus$ is defined by

(2.41) $\mu_{\bar{F}'} \oplus \bar{G}(u, v) = 1 \wedge (1 - \mu_F(u) + \mu_G(v)).$

In stating the implicational rule in the form (2.40), we have merely chosen one of several alternative ways in which the conditional possibility distribution $\Pi_{(Y|X)}$ may be defined, each of which has some advantages and disadvantages depending on the application. Among the more important of these are the following [1], [41], [62] :

(2.42) (c_2)   If X is F then Y is $G \to \Pi_{(Y|X)} = \bar{F}' \cup G;$

(2.43) (c_3)   If X is F then Y is $G \to \Pi_{(Y|X)} = F \times G \cup F' \times V;$

(2.44) (c_4)   If X is F then Y is $G \to \pi_{(Y|X)} (v|u) = 1$ if $\mu_G(v) \geqslant \mu_F(u),$
$$= \frac{\mu_G(v)}{\mu_F(u)} \text{ otherwise;}$$

(2.45) (c_5)   If X is F then Y is $G \to \pi_{(Y|X)} (v|u) = 1$ if $\mu_G(v) \geqslant \mu_F(u),$
$$= \mu_G(v) \text{ otherwise.}$$

Quantification Rule (Type III). If $U = \{u_1, \ldots, u_N\}$, Q is a quantifier such as *many, few, several, all, some, most*, etc., and

(2.46) X is $F \to \Pi_X = F$

then the proposition "QX is F" (e.g., "many X's are large") translates into

(2.47) $\Pi_{\text{Count } (F)} = Q$

where Count (F) denotes the number (or the proportion) of elements of U which are in F. By the definition of cardinality of F, if the fuzzy set F is expressed as

(2.48) $F = \mu_1/u_1 + \mu_2/u_2 + \ldots + \mu_N/u_N$

then

$$(2.49) \quad \text{Count}(F) = \sum_{i=1}^{N} \mu_i$$

where the right-hand member is understood to be rounded-off to the nearest integer. As a simple illustration of (2.47), if the quantifier *several* is defined as

$$(2.50) \quad \text{SEVERAL} \triangleq 0/1 + 0.4/2 + 0.6/3 + 1/4 + 1/5 + 1/6 + 0.6/7 + 0.2/8$$

then

$$(2.51) \quad \text{Several } X\text{'s are large} \rightarrow \Pi_N$$
$$\sum_{i=1}^{\Sigma} \mu_{\text{LARGE}}(u_i)$$
$$= 0/1 + 0.4/2 + 0.6/3 + 1/4 + 1/5 + 1/6 + 0.6/7 + 0.2/8$$

where $\mu_{\text{LARGE}}(u_i)$ is the grade of membership of the ith value of X in the fuzzy set LARGE.

Alternatively, and perhaps more appropriately, the cardinality of F may be defined as a fuzzy number, as is done in [79]. Thus, if the elements of F are sorted in descending order, so that $\mu_n \leqslant \mu_m$ if $n \geqslant m$, then the truth-value of the proposition

$$(2.52) \quad p \triangleq F \text{ has at least } n \text{ elements}$$

is defined to be equal to μ_n, while that of q,

$$(2.53) \quad q \triangleq F \text{ has at most } n \text{ elements},$$

is taken to be $1 - \mu_{n+1}$. From this, then, it follows that the truth-value of the proposition r,

$$(2.54) \quad r \triangleq F \text{ has exactly } n \text{ elements},$$

is given by $\mu_n \wedge (1 - \mu_{n+1})$.

Let $F\downarrow$ denote F sorted in descending order. Then (2.52) may be expressed compactly in the equivalent form

$$(2.55) \quad FG\text{Count}(F) = F\downarrow$$

which signifies that if the fuzzy cardinality of F is defined in terms of (2.52), with G standing for *greater than*, then the fuzzy count of elements in F is given by $F\downarrow$, with the understanding that $F\downarrow$ is regarded as a fuzzy subset of $\{0, 1, 2, \ldots\}$. In a similar fashion, (2.53) leads to the definition

(2.56) $FL\text{Count}\,(F) = (F\!\downarrow)' - 1$

where L stands for *less than* and subtraction should be interpreted as translation to the left, while (2.54) leads to

$$FE\text{Count}\,(F) = (F\!\downarrow) \cap ((F\!\downarrow)' - 1)$$

where E stands for *equal to*. For convenience, we shall refer to $FG\text{Count}$, $FL\text{Count}$ and $FE\text{Count}$ as the FG cardinality, FL cardinality and FE cardinality, respectively. The concept of FG cardinality will be illustrated in Example 9, Section 3.

Remark. There may be some cases in which it may be appropriate to normalize the definition of $FE\text{Count}$ in order to convey a correct perception of the count of elements in a fuzzy set. In such cases, we may employ the definition

(2.57) $FEN\text{Count}\,(F) = \dfrac{FE\text{Count}\,(F)}{\text{Max}_n\,(\mu_n \wedge (1 - \mu_{n+1}))}$.

Truth Qualification Rule (Type IV). Let τ be a linguistic truth-value. e.g., *very true, quite true, more or less true*, etc. Such a truth-value may be regarded as a fuzzy subset of the unit interval which is characterized by a membership function $\mu_T\colon [0, 1] \to [0, 1]$.

A truth-qualified proposition, e.g., "It is τ that X is F," is expressed as "X is F is τ." As shown in [79], the translation rule for such propositions is given by

(2.58) X is F is $\tau \to \Pi_X = F^+$

where

(2.59) $\mu_{F^+}(u) = \mu_T\,(\mu_F\,(u)).$

As an illustration, consider the truth-qualified proposition

Susana is young is very true

which by (2.58), (2.59) and 2.31) translates into

(2.60) $\pi_{\text{Age (Susana)}} = \mu_{\text{TRUE}}^2\,(\mu_{\text{YOUNG}}\,(u)).$

Now, if we assume that

(2.61) $\mu_{\text{YOUNG}}\,(u) = (1 + (\tfrac{u}{25})^2)^{-1}, u \in [0, 100]$

and

$$\mu_{\text{TRUE}}(v) = v^2, v \in [0, 1]$$

then (2.60) yields

$$\pi_{\text{Age (Susana)}} = (1 + (\frac{u}{25})^2)^{-4}$$

as the possibility distribution function of the age of Susana.

A more general type of translation process in PRUF which subsumes the translation rules given above is the following.

Let $\mathscr{D} = \{D\}$ denote a collection of databases, with D representing a generic element of $\mathscr{D}$. For the purposes of our analysis, D will be assumed to consist of a collection of possibly time-varying relations. If R is a constituent relation in D, then by the *frame* of R is meant the name of R together with the names of its columns (i.e., attributes). For example, if a constituent of D is a relation labeled POPULATION whose tableau is comprised of columns labeled Name and Height, then the frame of POPULATION is represented as *POPULATION* ‖ *Name* | *Height* | or, more simply, as POPULATION [Name; Height].

If p is a proposition in a natural language, its translation into PRUF can assume one of three — essentially equivalent — forms.[5]

(a) $p \rightarrow$ a possibility assignment equation;
(b) $p \rightarrow$ a procedure which yields for each D in $\mathscr{D}$ the possibility of D given p, i.e., Poss $\{D|p\}$;
(c) $p \rightarrow$ a procedure which yields for each D in $\mathscr{D}$ the truth-value of p relative to D, i.e., Tr $\{p|D\}$.

Remark. An important implicit assumption about the procedures involved in (b) and (c) is that they have a high degree of what might be called *explanatory effectiveness*, by which is meant a capability to convey the meaning of p to a human (or a machine) who is conversant with the meaning of the constituent terms in p but not with the meaning of p as a whole. For example, a procedure which merely tabulates the possibility of each D in $\mathscr{D}$ would, in general, have a low degree of explanatory effectiveness if it does not indicate in sufficient detail the way in which that possibility is arrived at. On the other extreme, a procedure which is excessively detailed and lacking in modularity would also have a low degree of explanatory effectiveness because the meaning of p might be obscured by the maze of unstructured steps in the body of the procedure.

The equivalence of (b) and (c) is a consequence of the way in which the concept of truth is defined in fuzzy logic [77], [2]. Thus, it can readily be shown that, under mildly restrictive assumptions on D, we have

$$\text{Tr } \{p|D\} = \text{Poss } \{D|p\},$$

which implies the equivalence of (b) and (c).

The restricted subset of PRUF which we have discussed so far is adequate for illustrating some of the simpler ways in which it may be applied to the precisiation of meaning. We shall do this in the following section.

3. PRECISIATION OF MEANING – EXAMPLES

There are two distinct and yet interrelated ways in which PRUF provides a mechanism for a precisiation of meaning of propositions. First, by expressing the meaning of a proposition as an explicitly defined procedure which acts on the fuzzy denotations of its constituents; and second, by disambiguation – especially in those cases in which what is needed is a method of differentiation between the nuances of meaning.

In what follows, we shall illustrate the techniques which may be employed for this purpose by several representative examples, of which Examples 6, 7, 8 and 9 relate to cases in which a proposition may have two or more distinct readings. Whenever appropriate, we consider both focused and unfocused translations of the given proposition.

EXAMPLE 1

(3.1) $p \triangleq$ John is very rich.

Assume that the database, D, consists of the following relations

(3.2)   POPULATION [Name; Wealth]
          RICH [Wealth; μ]

in which the first relation, POPULATION, tabulates the wealth, Wealth_i, of each individual, Name_i, while the second relation, RICH, tabulates the degree, μ_i, to which an individual whose wealth is Wealth_i is rich.

Unfocused translation: First, we find John's wealth, which is given by

(3.3)   Wealth (John) = $_{\text{Wealth}}$ POPULATION [Name = John].

Second, we intensify RICH to account for the modifier *very* by squaring

RICH,[6] and substitute Wealth (John) into $RICH^2$ to find the degree, δ, to which John is very rich. This yields

(3.4) $\delta = (_\mu RICH \, [Wealth = \,_{Wealth}POPULATION \, [Name = John]\,])^2$.

Finally, on equating δ to the possibility of the database, we obtain

(3.5)   John is very rich
            $\rightarrow \pi\,(D) = (_\mu RICH \, [Wealth = \,_{Wealth}POPULATION \, [Name = John]\,])^2$.

Focused translation: On interpreting the given proposition as a characterization of the possibility distribution of the implicit variable Wealth (John), we are led to the possibility assignment equation

(3.6)   John is very rich $\rightarrow \Pi_{Wealth(John)} = RICH^2$

which implies that

(3.7)   Poss $\{$ Wealth (John) $= \mu\} = (\mu_{RICH}(u))^2$

where μ_{RICH} is the membership function of the fuzzy set RICH, with u ranging over the domain of Wealth.

EXAMPLE 2

(3.8) $p \triangleq$ Hans is much richer than Marie.

We assume that the database, D, consists of the relations

(3.9)   POPULATION [Name; Wealth]

and

            MUCH RICHER [Wealth1; Wealth2; μ]

in which μ is the degree to which an individual who has Wealth1 is much richer than one who has Wealth2.

Unfocused translation: Proceeding as in Example 1, we arrive at

(3.10)   Hans is much richer than Marie $\rightarrow$
            $\pi(D) = {}_\mu MUCH\ RICHER\ [_{Wealth}POPULATION \, [Name = Hans]\,;$
            $_{Wealth}POPULATION \, [Name = Marie]\,]$.

Focused translation:

(3.11)   Hans is much richer than Marie $\rightarrow$
            $\Pi_{(Wealth\,(Hans),\,Wealth\,(Marie))} = $ MUCH RICHER

which implies that

(3.12) Poss { Wealth (Hans) = u_1 , Wealth (Marie) = u_2 } =
μMUCH RICHER (u_1, u_2).

EXAMPLE 3

(3.13) $p \triangleq$ Vera is very kind.

In this case, we assume that kindness is not a measurable characteristic like height, weight, age, wealth, etc. However, we also assume that it is possible to associate with each individual his/her index of kindness on the scale from 0 to 1, which is equivalent to assuming that the class of kind individuals is a fuzzy set KIND, with the index of kindness corresponding to the grade of membership in KIND.

Unfocused translation: Assume that D consists of the single relation

(3.14) KIND [Name; μ]

in which μ is the degree of kindness of Name. Then

(3.15) Vera is very kind $\rightarrow \pi(D) = (\mu$KIND [Name = Vera]$)^2$.

Focused translation: A special type of possibility distribution which we need in this case is the *unitor*, $\perp$, which is defined as

(3.16) $\pi_\perp(v) = v,\ 0 \leqslant v \leqslant 1$.

In terms of the unitor, then, we have

(3.17) Vera is very kind $\rightarrow \Pi$Kindness (Vera) $= \perp^2$

which implies that

(3.18) Poss { Kindness (Vera) = v } = v^2 , $0 \leqslant v \leqslant 1$.

This follows at once from (3.15), since

(3.19) Kindness (Vera) = μKIND [Name = Vera] .

EXAMPLE 4

(3.20) $p \triangleq$ Brian is much taller than most of his close friends.

Unfocused translation: For the purpose of representing the meaning of p, we shall assume that D is comprised of the relations

(3.21)   POPULATION [Name; Height]
          FRIENDS [Name1; Name2; μ]
          MUCH TALLER [Height1; Height2; μ]
          MOST [ρ; μ].

In the relation FRIENDS, μ represents the degree to which an individual whose name is Name2 is a friend of Name1. Similarly, in the relation MUCH TALLER, μ represents the degree to which an individual whose height is Height1 is much taller than one whose height is Height2. In MOST, μ represents the degree to which a proportion, ρ, fits the definition of MOST as a fuzzy subset of the unit interval.

To represent the meaning of p we shall express the translation of p as a procedure which computes the possibility of D given p. The sequence of computations in this procedure is as follows.

1. Obtain Brian's height from POPULATION. Thus,

$$\text{Height (Brian)} = {}_{\text{Height}}\text{POPULATION [Name = Brian]}.$$

2. Determine the fuzzy set, MT, of individuals in POPULATION in relation to whom Brian is much taller.

Let Name_i be the name of the ith individual in POPULATION. The height of Name_i is given by

$$\text{Height (Name}_i) = {}_{\text{Height}}\text{POPULATION [Name = Name}_i].$$

Now the degree to which Brian is much taller than Name_i is given by

$$\delta_i = {}_\mu\text{MUCH TALLER [Height (Brian), Height (Name}_i)]$$

and hence MT may be expressed as

$$\text{MT} = \Sigma_i \delta_i / \text{Name}_i, \text{Name}_i \in {}_{\text{Name}}\text{POPULATION}$$

where $_{\text{Name}}$POPULATION is the list of names of individuals in POPULATION, δ_i is the grade of membership of Name_i in MT, and Σ_i is the union of singletons δ_i / Name_i. ($\text{Name}_i \neq \text{Brian}$.)

3. Determine the fuzzy set, CF, of individuals in POPULATION who are close friends of Brian.

To form the relation CLOSE FRIENDS from FRIENDS we intensify FRIENDS by squaring, as in Example 1. Then, the fuzzy set of close friends of Brian is given by

$$\text{CF} = {}_\mu \times {}_{\text{Name2}}\text{FRIENDS}^2 \text{ [Name1 = Brian]}.$$

4. Form the count of elements of CF:

$$\text{Count(CF)} = \Sigma_i \mu_{CF}(\text{Name}_i)$$

where $\mu_{CF}(\text{Name}_i)$ is the grade of membership of Name$_i$ in CF and Σ_i is the arithemetic sum. More explicitly

$$\text{Count}(F) = \Sigma_i \mu_{\text{FRIENDS}}^2(\text{Brian}, \text{Name}_i).$$

5. Form the intersection of CF and MT, that is, the fuzzy set of those close friends of Brian in relation to whom he is much taller

$$H \triangleq \text{CF} \cap \text{MT}.$$

6. Form the count of elements of H

$$\text{Count}(H) = \Sigma_i \mu_H(\text{Name}_i)$$

where $\mu_H(\text{Name}_i)$ is the grade of membership of Name$_i$ in H and Σ_i is the arithmetic sum.

7. Form the ratio

$$r = \frac{\text{Count (MT} \cap \text{CF)}}{\text{Count (CF)}}$$

which represents the proportion of close friends of Brian in relation to whom he is much taller.

8. Compute the grade of membership of r in MOST

$$\delta = {}_\mu\text{MOST}\,[\rho = r].$$

The value of δ is the desired possibility of D given p. In terms of the membership functions of FRIENDS, MUCH TALLER and MOST, the value of δ is given explicitly by the expression

$$(3.22) \quad \delta = \mu_{\text{MOST}} \left[\frac{\Sigma_i \mu_{\text{MT}}(\text{Height(Brian)}, \text{Height (Name}_i)) \wedge \mu_{CF}^2(\text{Brian}, \text{Name}_i)}{\Sigma_i \mu_{CF}^2(\text{Brian}, \text{Name}_i)} \right].$$

Thus,

$(3.23) \quad$ Brian is much taller than most of his close friends $\rightarrow \pi(D) = \delta$

where δ is given by (3.22).

Focused translation: From (3.23) it follows at once that

$$(3.24) \quad p \rightarrow \pi_{\text{Height (Brian)}}(u) \triangleq \text{Poss} \{ \text{Height (Brian)} = u \}$$
$$= \mu_{\text{MOST}} \left[\frac{\Sigma_i \mu_{\text{MT}}(u, \text{Height (Name}_i)) \wedge \mu_{CF}^2(\text{Brian}, \text{Name}_i)}{\Sigma_i \mu_{CF}^2(\text{Brian}, \text{Name}_i)} \right].$$

EXAMPLE 5

(3.25) $p \triangleq$ Lane resides in a small city near Washington.

Unfocused translation: Assume that the database consists of the relations

(3.26) RESIDENCE [P.Name; C.Name; Population]
SMALL [Population; μ]
NEAR [C.Name1; C.Name2; μ] .

In RESIDENCE, P.Name stands for Person Name, C.Name for City Name, and Population for population of C.Name. In SMALL, μ is the degree to which a city whose population figure is Population is small. In NEAR, μ is the degree to which C.Name1 and C.Name2 are near one another.

The population of the city in which Lane resides is given by

(3.27) $_{\text{Population}}$ RESIDENCE [P.Name = Lane]

and hence the degree, δ, to which the city is small may be expressed as

(3.28) $\delta_1 = {}_\mu\text{SMALL} \left[{}_{\text{Population}}\text{RESIDENCE} \left[\text{P. Name = Lane} \right] \right]$.

Now the degree to which the city in which Lane resides is near Washington is given by

(3.29) $\delta_2 = {}_\mu\text{NEAR}$ [C.Name1 = Washington;
C.Name 2 = $_{\text{C.Name}}$ RESIDENCE [P.Name = Lane]] .

On forming the conjunction of (3.28) and (3.29), the possibility of D — and hence the translation of p — is found to be expressed by ($\wedge \triangleq$ min)

(3.30) Lane resides in a small city near Washington $\rightarrow \pi(D) = \delta_1 \wedge \delta_2$

where δ_1 and δ_2 are given by (3.28) and (3.29).

Focused translation: The implicit variable in this case may be expressed as

(3.31) $X \triangleq$ Location (Residence (Lane)).

Thus, the goal of the focused translation in this case is the computation of the possibility distribution of the location of residence of Lane.

To illustrate the effect of choosing different databases on the translation of p, we shall consider two cases each of which represents a particular assumption concerning the relations in D.

First, we consider the simpler case in which the constituent relations in D are assumed to be:

(3.32)   SMALL [C.Name; μ]

(3.33)   NEAR [C.Name1; C.Name2; μ] .

In SMALL, μ is the degree to which the city whose name is C.Name is small. In NEAR, μ is the degree to which cities named C.Name1 and C.Name2 are near each other.

From NEAR, the fuzzy set of cities which are near Washington is found to be given by

$$C.Name1 \times \mu \text{ NEAR [C.Name2 = Washington]} .$$

Consequently, the fuzzy set of cities which are near Washington and, in addition, are small is given by the intersection

$$SMALL \cap C.Name1 \times \mu \text{ NEAR [C.Name2 = Washington]} .$$

With this expression in hand, the focused translation of p may be expressed as

(3.34)   Lane resides in a small city near Washington $\rightarrow$

$\Pi_{\text{Location}} (\text{Residence (Lane)}) = \text{SMALL} \cap C.Name1 \times \mu$

NEAR [C.Name2 = Washington] .

In the case to be considered next, the relations in D are assumed to be less directly related to the denotations of words in p than the relations expressed by (3.32) and (3.33). More specifically, we assume that D consists of the relations

(3.35)   LIST [C.Name; Population]

DISTANCE [C.Name1; C.Name2; Distance]

SMALL [Population; μ]

NEAR [Distance; μ] .

In LIST, Population is the population of C.Name. In DISTANCE, Distance is the distance between C.Name1 and C.Name2. In NEAR, μ is the degree to which two cities whose distance from one another is Distance are near each other. As for SMALL, it has the same meaning as in (3.32).

For our purposes, we need a relation which tabulates the degree to which each city in LIST is small. To this end, we form the composition[7] of LIST and SMALL, which yields the relation

(3.36) $G \triangleq$ SMALL [C.Name; μ] $\triangleq$ LIST [C.Name; Population] $\circ$
          SMALL [POPULATION; μ]

in which μ is the degree to which C.Name is small. Actually, since LIST and SMALL are functions, we can write

(3.37) μ_G(C.Name) = μ_{SMALL}(Population (C.Name))

in which the right-hand member of (3.37) expresses the degree to which a city whose population is Population (C.Name) is small.

Now from DISTANCE we can find the distances of cities in LIST from Washington. These distances are yielded by the relation

(3.38)   DC $\triangleq$ C.Name1 $\times$ Distance DISTANCE [C.Name2 = Washington] .

Furthermore, on forming the composition of this relation with NEAR, we obtain the relation

(3.39) H [C.Name; μ] $\triangleq$ NEAR [Distance; μ] $\circ$
C.Name1 $\times$ Distance DISTANCE [C.Name2 = Washington] .

In H [C.Name; μ], μ represents the degree to which C.Name is near Washington. More explicitly:

$$\mu_H(\text{C.Name}) = \mu_{NEAR}(\text{Distance of C.Name from Washington})$$

in which the distance of C.Name from Washington is obtained from DC by expressing the distance as a function of C.Name.

At this point, we have constructed from the given database the relations which were given initially in the previous case. With these relations in hand, the translation of p may be expressed compactly as

(3.40) $\Pi_{\text{Location (Residence (Lane))}} = G \cap H$

where G and H are defined by (3.36) and (3.39), respectively.

EXAMPLE 6

(3.41) $p \triangleq$ Vivien is over thirty.

The literal reading of p may be expressed as

$p_1 \triangleq$ Age of Vivien is greater than thirty

which translates into

(3.42) $p_1 \rightarrow$ Age (Vivien) > 30.

In many cases, however, the intended meaning of p would be

$p_2 \triangleq$ Vivien is over thirty but not much over thirty.

In this case, the translation of p_2 into PRUF would be expressed as

(3.43) $\Pi_{\text{Age (Vivien)}} = (30, 100] \cap _{\text{Age1}} \times _{\mu} \text{MUCH OVER}' \, [\text{Age2} = 30]$

in which $(30, 100]$ is the age interval $30 < u \leqslant 100$; MUCH OVER [Age1; Age2; μ] is a relation in which μ is the degree to which Age1 is much over Age 2; and MUCH OVER$'$ is the complement of MUCH OVER. More explicitly, (3.43) implies that

(3.44)   Poss { Age (Vivien) = u } = 0   for $u \leqslant 30$

        $= 1 - \mu_{\text{MUCH OVER}}(u, 30)$, for $u > 30$.

EXAMPLE 7

(3.45) $p \triangleq$ John is not very smart.

Assuming that D consists of the relation

SMART [Name; μ]

in which μ is the degree to which Name is smart, the literal translation of p may be expressed as (see Example 3)

(3.46) $p \rightarrow \Pi_X = (\perp^2)'$

where

$X = _{\mu}\text{SMART [Name = John]}$

and $(\perp^2)'$ is the complement of the square of the unitor.

However, if the intended meaning of p is

(3.47) $p_1 \triangleq$ John is very (not smart).

then the translation of p into PRUF would be

(3.48) $\Pi_X = (\perp')^2$.

Note that (3.48) implies that

(3.49)   Poss $\{ X = v \} = 1 - v^2$

whereas (3.46) implies that

(3.50)   Poss $\{ X = v \} = (1 - v)^2$.

EXAMPLE 8

(3.51) $p \triangleq$ Naomi has a young daughter.

There are three distinct readings of p:

$p_1 \triangleq$ Naomi has only one daughter and her daughter is young;

$p_2 \triangleq$ Naomi has one or more daughters of whom only one is young;

$p_3 \triangleq$ Naomi has one or more daughters of whom one or more are young.

Assume that D consists of the relation

DAUGHTER [M.Name; D.Name; μ_{DY}]

in which M.Name and D.Name stand for Mother's name and Daughter's name, respectively, and μ_{DY} is the degree to which D.Name is young.

The translations of p_1, p_2 and p_3 may be expressed as follows

$$(3.52) \quad p_1 \to \pi(D) = \delta_1 \wedge \mu_1$$

where

$\delta_1 = 1$ if Naomi has only one daughter, i.e., if

Count $(_{\text{D.Name}}$DAUGHTER [M.Name = Naomi]$) = 1$

and $\delta_1 = 0$ otherwise;

and

$\mu_1 \triangleq$ the degree to which Naomi's daughter is young, i.e.,

$\mu_1 = \mu_{DY}$DAUGHTER [M.Name = Naomi].

Turning to p_2 and p_3, let the set of daughters of Naomi be sorted in descending order according to the degree of youth. For this set, then, let

$\mu_i \triangleq$ degree of youth of ith youngest daughter of Naomi.

Now applying the concept of fuzzy cardinality (see (2.52)) to the set in question, we obtain at once

$$(3.53) \quad p_2 \to \pi(D) = \mu_1 \wedge (1 - \mu_2)$$

and

$$(3.54) \quad p_3 \to \pi(D) = \mu_1.$$

EXAMPLE 9

$$(3.55) \quad p \triangleq \text{Naomi has several young daughters.}$$

In this case, we assume that D consists of the relations

DAUGHTER [M.Name; D.Name; μ_{DY}]

and

SEVERAL [N; μ]

in which the first relation has the same meaning as in Example 8, and μ in SEVERAL is the degree to which an integer N fits one's perception of *several*. Furthermore, we assume that p should be read as p_3 in Example 8.

With these assumptions, the translation of p may be expressed compactly as

$$(3.56) \quad p \to \pi(D) = \sup ((\geqslant \circ \text{SEVERAL}) \cap$$
$$FG\text{Count} (_{\text{D. Name}} \times _\mu \text{DAUGHTER [M.Name = Naomi]}))$$

where FGCount is defined by (2.55); sup F is defined by

$$(3.57) \quad \sup F \triangleq \sup_{u \in U} \mu_F(u)$$

where F is a fuzzy subset of U and μ_F is its membership function; and $\geqslant \circ$ SEVERAL is the composition of the relations $\geqslant$ and SEVERAL, i.e., (see note 7)

$$\mu_{\geqslant \circ \text{SEVERAL}}(u) = \mu_{\text{SEVERAL}}(n) \quad \text{for } n \leqslant n_{\max}$$
$$= 1 \quad \text{for } n \geqslant n_{\max}$$
$$n_{\max} \triangleq \text{smallest value of } n \text{ at which } \mu_{\text{SEVERAL}}(u) = 1.$$

Intuitively, the composition of $\geqslant$ and SEVERAL serves to precisiate the count expressed in words as "at least several." The intersection of ($\geqslant \circ$ SEVERAL) and the FGCount of the daughters of Naomi serves to define the conjunction of "at least several" with the FGCount of daughters of Naomi; and the supremum of the intersection provides a measure of the degree of consistency of "at least several" with the FGCount in question.

As a concrete illustration of (3.56), assume that the fuzzy relation SEVERAL is defined as

$$(3.59) \quad \text{SEVERAL} \triangleq 0.5/2 + 0.8/3 + 1/4 + 1/5 + 0.8/6 + 0.5/0.7.$$

Then

$$(3.60) \quad \geqslant \circ \text{SEVERAL} = 0.5/2 + 0.8/3 + 1/4 + 1/5 + 1/6 + \ldots .$$

Furthermore, assume that

$$(3.61) \quad _{\text{D.Name}} \times _\mu \text{DAUGHTER [M. Name = Naomi]} =$$
$$1/\text{Eva} + 0.8/\text{Lisa} + 0.6/\text{Ruth}$$

so that

(3.62) FGCount $(_{D.Name} \times _{\mu}$ DAUGHTER [M.Name = Naomi]$)$ =
          $1/1 + 0.8/2 + 0.6/3$.

From (3.60) and (3.62), we deduce that

(3.63) $(\geqslant \circ$ SEVERAL$) \cap FG$Count $(_{D.Name} \times _{\mu}$ DAUGHTER
          [M.Name = Naomi]$)$ = $0.5/2 + 0.6/3$

and since

          $\sup (0.5/2 + 0.6/3) = 0.6$

we arrive at

(3.64) $\pi(D) = 0.6$

which represents the possibility of the given database given the proposition p.

4. CONCLUDING REMARK

The above examples are intended to illustrate the manner in which PRUF may be employed to precisiate the meaning of propositions expressed in a natural language. Such precisiation may be of use not only in communication between humans, but also — and perhaps more importantly — in communication between humans and machines.

University of California at Berkeley

NOTES

* Computer Science Division, Department of Electrical Engineering and Computer Sciences and the Electronics Research Laboratory, University of California, Berkeley, California 94720. Research supported by the National Science Foundation Grants IST8018196 and MCS79-06543.
[1] As is pointed out in [81], ambiguity, vagueness and fuzziness are not coextensive concepts. Specifically, a proposition, p, is *fuzzy* if it contains words with fuzzy denotations, e.g., $p \triangleq$ Ruth has *dark* skin and owns a *red* Porsche. A proposition, p, is *vague* if it is both fuzzy and ambiguous in the sense of being insufficiently specific. For example, the proposition $p \triangleq$ Ruth lives *somewhere near* Berkeley is vague if it does not characterize the location of residence of Ruth with sufficient precision. Thus, a proposition may be fuzzy without being vague, and ambiguous without being fuzzy or vague.
[2] As will be seen in Section 2 and 3, PRUF is a language in a somewhat stretched sense of the term. Basically, it is a *translation system* in which only the simpler procedures

may be represented as expressions in PRUF. For the description of complex procedures, PRUF allows the use of any suitable mathematically oriented language.

3 In our exposition of the concept of a possibility distribution and the relevant parts of PRUF we shall draw on the definitions and examples in [79], [81] and [82].

4 We use uppercase symbols to differentiate between a term, e.g., small, and its denotation, SMALL. The notation

$$(2.9) \qquad F = \mu_1/u_1 + \ldots + \mu_n/u_n$$

which is employed in (2.7) signifies that F is a collection of fuzzy singletons μ_i/u_i, $i = 1$, $\ldots$, n, with μ_i representing the grade of membership of u_i in F. More generally, F may be expressed as $F = \Sigma_i \mu_i/u_i$ or $F = \int_U \mu_F(u)/u$. (See [78] for additional details.)

5 It should be noted that (b) and (c) are in the spirit of possible-world semantics and truth-conditional semantics, respectively. In their conventional form, however, these semantics have no provision for fuzzy propositions and hence do not provide a sufficiently expressive system for our purposes.

6 If the frame of RICH is RICH [Wealth; μ] then the frame of RICH^2 is RICH^2 [Wealth; μ^2], which signifies that each μ in RICH is replaced by μ^2. This representation of *very rich* is a consequence of the translation rule (2.31).

7 If the membership functions of R $[X; Y]$ and S $[Y; Z]$ are expressed as $\mu_R(x, y)$ and $\mu_S(y, z)$, respectively, then the membership function of the composition of R and S with respect to Y is given by

$$\mu_R \circ S(x, z) = \sup_y (\mu_R(x, y) \wedge \mu_S(y, z)).$$

REFERENCES

Bandler, W. and Kohout, L.: 1978, 'Fuzzy relational products and fuzzy implication operation,' *Proc. Third Workshop on Fuzzy Reasoning*, Queen Mary College, London.

Bellman, R. E. and Zadeh, L. A.: 1977, 'Local and fuzzy logics,' *Modern Uses of Multiple-Valued Logic* (G. Epstein, ed.), D. Reidel, Dordrecht, 103–165.

Black, M.: 1963, 'Reasoning with loose concepts,' *Dialogue* **2**, 1–12.

Bobrow, D. and Collins, A. (eds.): 1975, *Representation and Understanding*, Academic Press, New York.

Boyce, R. F., Chamberlin, D. D., King III, W. F., and Hammer, M. M.: 1974, 'Specifying queries as relational expressions,' *Data Base Management* (J. W. Klimbie and K. L. Koffeman, eds.), North-Holland, Amsterdam, 21–223.

Brachman, R. J.: 1977, 'What's in a concept: structural foundations for semantical networks,' *Int. J. Man-Machine Studies* **9**, 127–152.

Briabrin, V. M. and Senin, G. V.: 1977, 'Natural language processing within a restricted context,' *Proc. Int. Workshop on Natural Language for Interactions with Data Bases*, IIASA, Vienna.

Chomsky, N.: 1971, 'Deep structure, surface structure, and semantic interpretation,' *Semantics: An Interdisciplinary Reader in Philosophy, Linguistics and Psychology*, (D. D. Steinberg and L. A. Jakobovits, eds.), Cambridge University Press, Cambridge.

Cresswell, M. J.: 1973, *Logics and Languages*, Methuen, London.

10. Damerau, F. J.: 1975, 'On fuzzy adjectives,' *Memorandum RC 5340*, IBM Research Laboratory, Yorktown Heights, New York.

11. Davidson, D.: 1967, 'Truth and meaning,' *Synthese* 17, 304–323.

12. Deluca, A. and Termini, S.: 1972, 'A definition of a non-probabilistic entropy in the setting of fuzzy sets theory,' *Information and Control* 20, 301–312.

13. Fine, K.: 1975, 'Vagueness, truth and logic,' *Synthese* 30, 265–300.

14. Frederiksen, C.: 1975, 'Representing logical and semantic structure of knowledge acquired from discourse,' *Cognitive Psychology* 7, 371–458.

15. Gaines, B. R.: 1976, 'Foundations of fuzzy reasoning,' *Int. J. Man-Machine Studies* 6, 623–668.

16. Gaines, B. R., and Kohout, L. J.: 1977, 'The fuzzy decade: a bibliogrpahy of fuzzy systems and closely related topics,' *Int. J. Man-Machine Studies* 9, 1–68.

17. Goguen, J. A.: 1974, 'Concept representation in natural and artificial languages: axioms, extension and applications for fuzzy sets,' *Int. J. Man-Machine Studies* 6, 513–561.

18. Grice H. P.: 1968, 'Utterer's meaning, sentence-meaning and word-meaning,' *Foundations of Language* 4, 225–242.

19. Haack, S.: 1978, *Philosophy of Logics*, Cambridge University Press, Cambridge.

20. Harris, J. I.: 1974, 'Fuzzy sets: how to be imprecise precisely,' DOAE Research Working Paper, Ministry of Defense, Byfleet, Surrey, United Kingdom.

21. Hersh, H. M., and Caramazza, A.: 1976, 'A fuzzy approach to modifiers and vagueness in natural language,' *J. Experimental Psychology* 105, 254–276.

22. Hisdal, E.: 1978, 'Conditional possibilities: independence and non-interaction,' *Fuzzy Sets and Systems* 1, 283–297.

23. Hughes, G. E., and Cresswell, M. J.: 1968, *An Introduction to Modal Logic*, Methuen, London.

24. Jouault, J. P. and Luan, P. M.: 1975, 'Application des concepts flous à la programmation en langages quasi-naturels,' Inst. Inf. d'Entreprise, C.N.A.M., Paris.

25. Kampé de Feriet, J. and Forte, B.: 1967, 'Information et probabilité,' *Comptes Rendus*, Academy of Sciences, Paris, 265A, 152–146, 350–353.

26. Katz, J. J.: 1966, *The Philosophy of Language*, Harper & Row, New York.

27. Kaufmann, A.: 1975, 'Introduction to the Theory of Fuzzy Subsets,' *Applications to Linguistics, Logic and Semantics* 2, Masson and Co., Paris.

28. Khatchadourian, H.: 1965, 'Vagueness, meaning and absurdity,' *Amer. Phil. Quarterly* 2, 119–129.

29. Labov, W.: 1973, 'The boundaries of words and their meanings,' *New Ways of Analyzing Variation in English* 1, (C. J. N. Bailey and R. W. Shuy, eds.), Georgetown University Press, Washington.

30. Lakoff, G.: 1973, 'Hedges: a study in meaning criteria and the logic of fuzzy concepts," *J. Phil. Logic* 2, 458–508. Also in *Contemporary Research in Philosophical Logic and Linguistic Semantics*, (D. Dockney, W. Harper and B. Freed, eds.), D. Reidel, Dordrecht, 221–271.

31. Lakoff, G.: 1973, 'Fuzzy grammar and the performance/competence terminology game,' *Proc. Meeting of Chicago Linguistics Society*, 271–291.

32. Lambert, K. and van Fraassen, B. C.: 1970, 'Meaning relations, possible objects and possible worlds,' *Philosophical Problems in Logic*, 1–19.

33. Lehnert, W.: 1977, 'Human and computational question answering,' *Cognitive Science* 1, 47–73.

34. Lewis, D.: 1970, 'General semantics,' *Synthese* **22**, 18–67.
35. Linsky, L.: 1971, *Reference and Modality*, Oxford University Press, London.
36. Lyndon, R. C.: 1976, *Notes on Logic*, d. Van Nostrand, New York.
37. Machina, K. F.: 1972, 'Vague predicates,' *Amer. Phil. Quarterly* **9**, 225–233.
38. Mamdani, E. H., and Assilian, S.: 1975, 'An experiment in linguistic synthesis with a fuzzy logic controller,' *Int. J. Man-Machine Studies* **7**, 1–13.
39. McCarthy, J. and Hayes, P.: 1969, 'Some philosophical problems from the standpoint of artificial intelligence,' *Machine Intelligence* **4**, (D. Michie and B. Meltzer, eds), Edinburgh University Press, Edinburgh, 463–502.
40. Miller, G. A. and Johnson-Laird, P. N.: 1976, *Language and Perception*, Harvard University Press, Cambridge.
41. Mizumoto, M., Fukame, S., and Tanaka, K.: 1978, 'Fuzzy reasoning methods by Zadeh and Mamdani, and improved methods,' *Proc. Third Workshop on Fuzzy Reasoning*, Queen Mary College, London.
42. Mizumoto, M., Umano, M. and Tanaka, K.: 1977, 'Implementation of a fuzzy-set-theoretic data structure system,' *Third Int. Conf. on Very Large Data Bases*, Tokyo.
43. Moisil, G. C.: 1975, 'Lectures on the logic of fuzzy reasoning,' *Scientific Editions*, Bucarest.
44. Montague, R.: 1974, *Formal Philosophy* (Selected Papers), Yale University Press, New Haven.
45. Montgomery, C. A.: 1972, 'Is natural language an unnatural query language?,' *Proc. ACM National Conf.*, New York, 1075–1078.
46. Nalimov, V. V.: 1974, *Probabilistic Model of Language*, Moscow State University, Moscow.
47. Negoita, C. V., and Ralescu, D. A.: 1975, *Applications of Fuzzy Sets to Systems Analysis*, Birkhauser Verlag, Basel, Stuttgart.
48. Newell, A. and Simon, H. A.: 1972, *Human Problem Solving*, Prentice-Hall, Englewood Cliffs, N.J.
49. Nguyen, H. T.: 1978, 'On conditional possibility distributions,' *Fuzzy Sets and Systems* **1**, 299–309.
50. Noguchi, K., Umano, M., Mizumoto, M., and Tanaka, K.: 1976, 'Implementation of fuzzy artificial intelligence language FLOU,' *Technical Report on Automation and Language of IECE*.
51. Partee, B.: 1976, *Montague Grammar*, Academic Press, New York.
52. Putnam, H.: 1975, 'The meaning of 'meaning',' *Language, Mind and Knowledge* (K. Gunderson, ed.), University of Minnesota Press, Minneapolis.
53. Quine, W. V.: 1970, *Philosophy of Logic*, Prentice-Hall, Englewood Cliffs, N.J.
54. Rescher, N.: 1973, *The Coherence Theory of Truth*, Oxford University Press, Oxford.
55. Rieger, B.: 1976, 'Fuzzy structural semantics,' *Proc. Third European Meeting on Cybernetics and Systems Research*, Vienna.
56. Sanchez, E.: 1977, 'On possibility qualification in natural languages,' *Electronics Research Laboratory Memorandum M77/28*, University of California, Berkeley.
57. Sanford, D. H.: 1975, 'Borderline logic,' *Amer. Phil. Quarterly* **12**, 29–39.
58. Schank, R. C. (ed.): 1975, *Conceptual Information Processing*, North-Holland, Amsterdam.
59. Schotch, P. K.: 1975, 'Fuzzy modal logic,' *Proc. Int. Symp. on Multiple-Valued Logic*, University of Indiana, Bloomington, 176–182.

60. Schubert, L. K.: 1972, 'Extending the expressive power of semantic networks,' *Artificial Intelligence* **2**, 163–198.

61. Searle, J. (ed.): 1971, *The Philosophy of Language*, Oxford University Press, Oxford.

62. Sembi, B. S., and Mamdani, E. H.: 1979, 'On the nature of implication in fuzzy logic,' *Proc. 9th Int. Symp. on Multiple-Valued Logic*, Bath, England, 143–151.

63. Simon, H. A.: 1973, 'The structure of ill structured problems,' *Artificial Intelligence* **4**, 181–201.

64. Staal, J. F.: 1969, 'Formal logic and natural languages,' *Foundations of Language* **5**, 256–284.

65. Stitch, S. P.: 1975, 'Logical form and natural language,' *Phil. Studies* **28**, 397–418.

66. Sugeno, M.: 1974, 'Theory of fuzzy integrals and its application,' Ph.D. thesis, Tokyo Institute of Technology, Japan.

67. Suppes, P.: 1976, 'Elimination of quantifiers in the semantics of natural languages by use of extended relation algebras,' *Revue Internationale de Philosophie*, 117–118, 243–259.

68. Tarski, A.: 1956, *Logic, Semantics, Metamathematics*, Clarendon Press, Oxford.

69. Terano, T., and Sugeno, M.: 1975, 'Conditional fuzzy measures and their applications,' *Fuzzy Sets and Their Applications to Cognitive and Decision Processes*, (L. A. Zadeh, K. S. Fu, K. Tanaka and M. Shimura, eds.), Academic Press, New York, 151–170.

70. van Fraassen, B. C.: 1971, *Formal Semantics and Logic*, Macmillan, New York.

71. Wenstop, F.: 1976, 'Deductive verbal models of organizations,' *Int. J. Man-Machine Studies* **8**, 293–311.

72. Wheeler, S. C.: 1975, 'Reference and vagueness,' *Synthese* **30**, 367–380.

73. Woods, W. A.: 1975, 'What is in a link: foundations for semantic networks,' *Representation and Understanding* , (D. B. Bobrow and A. Collins, eds.), Academic Press, New York, 35–82.

74. Zadeh, L. A.: 1972, 'Fuzzy languages and their relation to human and machine intelligence,' *Proc. Int. Conf. on Man and Computer*, Bordeaux, France, S. Karger, Basel, 130–165.

75. Zadeh, L. A.: Jan. 1973, 'Outline of a new approach to the analysis of complex systems and decision processes,' *IEEE Trans. Systems, Man and Cybernetics SMC*-3, 28–44.

76. Zadeh, L. A.: 1975, 'Calculus of fuzzy restrictions,' *Fuzzy Sets and Their Applications to Cognitive and Decision Processes*, (L. A. Zadeh, K. S. Fu, K. Tanaka and M. Shimura, eds.), Academic Press, New York, 1–39.

77. Zadeh, L. A.: 1975, 'Fuzzy logic and approximate reasoning (in memory of Grigore Moisil),' *Synthese* **30**, 407–428.

78. Zadeh, L. A.: 1975, 'The concept of a linguistic variable and its application to approximate reasoning,' *Inf. Sci.* **8**, Part I, 199–249; *Inf. Sci.* **8**, Part II, 301–357; *Inf. Sci.* **9**, part III, 43–80.

79. Zadeh, L. A.: 1977, 'A theory of approximate reasoning,' *Electronics Research Laboratory Memorandum M77/58*, University of California, Berkeley. Also in *Machine Intelligence* **9**, (J. E. Hayes, D. Michie and L. I. Kulich, eds.), Wiley, New York, 149–194.

80. Zadeh, L. A.: 1978, 'Fuzzy sets as a basis for a theory of possibility,' *Fuzzy Sets and Systems* **1**, 3–28.

81. Zadeh, L. A.: 1978, 'PRUF – a meaning representation language for natural language,' *Int. J. Man-Machine Studies* **10**, 394–460.

82. Zadeh, L. A.: 1979, 'Possibility theory and soft data analysis,' *Mathematical Frontiers of the Social and Policy Sciences*, (L. Cobb and R. M. Thrall, eds.), Westview Press, Boulder, 69–129.
83. Zadeh, L. A.: 1981, 'Test-score semantics for natural languages and meaning-representation via PRUF,' *Empirical Semantics*, (B. B. Rieger, ed.), Brockmeyer, Bochum, 281–349.
84. Zadeh, L. A.: 1983, 'A computational approach to fuzzy quantifiers in natural languages,' *Computers and Mathematics* 9, 149–184.

DAVID D. McDONALD

CONVERSATIONS BETWEEN PROGRAMS[1]

It is easy to read about computers "sending messages" or "giving orders" without really knowing what this really means. One of the goals of this paper will be to remedy this by giving the reader a background in the kinds of representations that computer programs have and what they do with them. There is, however, a larger reason for looking at program "conversations": programs can give us a special window on what it means to communicate, a model against which we can compare our own communication, since, unlike people, programs can be examined as closely as we like and dissected and modified for experiments.

We do not want to say that the telephone that we use for talking with a friend is itself "communicating" with the other telephone, but what about an automatic dialer or the new telephone advertising systems? With programs, we have an opportunity to look at a smoothly graded range of "communicators", from the computational equivalent of the telephone, through programs that carry out involved negotiation without being "aware" of what they are doing, to programs that can tell you why they said what they said and what they expected to gain by it. By analyzing the spectrum of program conversations, we can begin to identify what the basic components of a conversation are and just how it is that communication takes place.

The first conversation we will take a look at is quite similar to a human conversation in its form: two programs talking directly to each other, asking questions and giving replies alternately. These programs are talking over the ARPA net.[2]

Program A on one computer wants to open a channel to program B on another over which it will later send some data. Establishing the channel requires negotiating mutually agreeable transmission speeds and signal formats, an offer-counter-offer process which can take considerably more time than this to complete.

Computer A: 1, 360
Computer B: 6, 350
**   A: 3, 1, 1, 2**
**   B: 5, 1, 1**

L. Vaina and J. Hintikka (eds.), Cognitive Constraints on Communication, 403–424.
© 1984 by D. Reidel Publishing Company.

```
A: 3, 1, 1, 3
B: 5, 1, 1
A: 3, 1, 1, 1
B: 4, 1, 1
A: 3, 2, 1, 150
B: 4, 2, 150
A: 6
A: 8
B: 6
```

Like most system programs, A and B use a compact numerical code that obscures the meaning of their messages, but (very) liberally translated, their conversation reads like this:

A: Please talk to me on lines 360/361.
B: OK. You talk to me on 350/351.
A: Can you do CVSD?
B: No, but I can do LPC.
A: Can you do RELP?
B: No, but I can do LPC.
A: How about LPC?
B: LPC is fine with me.
A: Can you use 150 microsecond sampling?
B: I can use 150 microseconds.
A: I am ready.
A: and you?
B: I am ready too.

Next is an example of another kind of "conversation" between programs. Actually it more resembles a monologue or perhaps a proclamation. The three "definitions" are excerpts from a program that writes treatments for computer-generated animated films.[3]

(Think of it as a "screen writer".) They are instructions directed at another program (the film's "director") who will use them as the basis of its decisions of what the characters should look like and how they should act.

```
(define cinderella character
     (process initial description
          (physical (and beautiful shabby))
          (personality (and good friendly hard-working shy))
          (role-in-story most-important)))
```

```
(define step-mother character
    (process initial-description
        (physical ugly)
        (personality (and mean selfish strong evil))))

(define (relationship-of step-mother cinderella) relationship
    (process initial description
        (and is-obedient-to is-tolerant-of)))
```

Unlike the first example, these definitions almost need no translation. They use ordinary English words instead of numbers, and their syntax is transparent to anyone who has ever used a Hewlett-Packard pocket calculator.[4]

At the same time, the fact that we can read them so easily should give us pause. Surely what a program understands when it reads "beautiful" or "hard-working" isn't the same as what we understand. For that matter, how is it that a program can send or understand those expressions at all? Don't computers only manipulate ones and zeros?

As we will see, the answers to both of these questions are tied up with the nature of how computers represent and manipulate the information that controls their behavior. It will turn out that what to us are the obvious differences between these two conversations — the fact that the first one used numbers and the second used English words — are actually the things that they have most in common. In their "internal format", a number like "360" and a word like "beautiful" are objects of the same sort to a program and accrue their meaning in the same way.

The significant differences are subtle. They have nothing to do with form or even content but rather with differences in convention and protocol — key aspects of what it means to hold a conversation or to intentionally communicate. The first example was a negotiation that loosely followed a predefined script; either program could take the initiative and to a certain extent change the subject. Both programs were active at the same time during the conversation, concentrating just on the negotiation process. The second example was utterly different. You could not point to any one place in the director and say that "it" specifically was listening to the screen writer; instead, the screen writer issued its proclamations broadly, posting them on a common bulletin board as it were. The screen writer did not know when or how the director would make use of its messages and it packaged them by character, which was convenient for it, rather than by trait, which could have been particularly useful to the director.

It is this kind of difference that provides us with our mirror for our own conversations. No one kind of program conversation has all of the properties which associate with our own. By looking at how the properties mix and redistribute we can begin to see what is essential and what is merely window-dressing. But before looking at some of the different forms program conversations take, we should learn something about their representation and interpretation. This will provide us with the conceptual tools for comparing the forms against each other.

1. THE MEDIUM – REPRESENTING MESSAGES

In high school algebra, we wrote equations using everyday letters and numerals. They were our medium. The same characters appeared elsewhere – as parts of words, as the names of streets, in post codes, etc. But in algebra class our special interpretation of them made them different. They became "variables" and "constants". We combined them into expressions that represented "equations", and exchanged them, crossed them out, and recombined them (all according to the rules of algebra and arithmetic), and in so doing were able to use them to solve complex problems.

Of course, it is not the intrinsic, graphic properties of, eg., the letter "X" that made it suitable to represent an algebraic variable, just as they are not what make it suitable to represent the sound of the English velar fricative when we write. It is simply a matter of convention. We say that the letters and numerals are part of a "representational system" for algebra (which also includes glifs like "=", ">", etc.). Your relationship to letters and numerals is exactly the kind of relationship that a computer program has to the representational systems of the computer. The elements of a representational system do not have any meaning as such, rather, someone (a person, a programmer, a program) can use them conventionally to mean something – to represent, or "stand for" something. Then if their convention is shared by someone (or thing) else, then the two can use the representational system to have a conversation.

In this section, we will survey the kinds of representations programs use. One thing to bear in mind is that particular representations do not exist in a vacuum. They must be supported – "implemented" – in terms of other representations, just as an "X" is implemented by crossed diagonal lines on paper. The chain of implementation moves down through "higher level languages", to "machine code" to the logic of the computer hardware. The existence of particular representational capabilities in a program implies the presence of other support facilities which may well be expensive or inefficient. Highly abstract, concept rich representations are avoided in every-day programs unless they are absolutely necessary because of the difficulty of developing them. As a consequence, very few existing programs have sufficient models of their own actions to be said to be behaving intentionally – they send messages without knowing what they are saying.

1.1 Levels of Representation

The "definitions" of the screen writer program are a good place to start in a survey of program representations because of their (initial) resemblance to English. Texts are an extremely common form of input/output representation for programs simply because programs are designed by people and people are more comfortable with representations that resemble their ordinary language than with, say, 18 digit binary numbers.

The definitions are passed from the screen writer program to the director program in essentially the same representation as they appear here in this paper: strings of characters. We understand this representation by scanning it with our eyes, moving left to right, from the top of the page to the bottom, clumping characters into words and the words into phrases according to the punctuation (here spaces and parenthesis), all on the basis of the English typographic convention that we assimilated when we learned to read.

A computer program does exactly the same thing, scanning the text and picking out words and parenthesized phrases on the basis of conventions built into them. (The process that does this is referred to as a *parser*). The difference comes with what happens after the initial scan: while a person would typically refer back to a text and reread it whenever they needed to remember what it said, a program will invariably read a text only once, converting the text into a different representation as it reads and then do its "remembering" in terms of the new "internal" representation.

The program converts its representation in order to save itself effort. Character strings are not intrinsically optimal for computers (no one represen-tation is – optimality depends on the job to be done), and their use involves no small amount of "overhead" in the form of the string parser and its rules. Consider how awkward it would be if, say, every time it wanted to know what the third word of a statement was it had to reparse it character by character. On the other hand, if the content of the text could be represented in a language that was simpler to interpret, then the program effort we save can be put to more profitable uses.

In the case of the screen writer program, character strings are converted into the representation known as "list structure". Lists have a relatively simple, uniform structure and consequently require a simpler parser to interpret than the character string representation does. Consider the screen writer's first "proclamation", repeated below. As a character string, it consists of 188 characters. We see it as representing 18 words and 7 nested parenthetical expressions, but that is only because we know the intended meaning of the space character, and the parentheses. (Imagine what it would be like to read that definition if there has been a mistake in the printer and words were separated by, say, an "x" rather than a space: the words would still be distinguishable but now we would need to work at it − to develop a new parser − in order to make them out.) The identity of the words and the structure of the parentheticals − the output of the parser − are exactly the information directly represented by the *list structure* version of the definition. (The rest, such as the spelling and the indentation, is typically not totally lost but rather shunted aside as minor properties of the objects in the list structure, as we shall see.) List structure is conceptualized in terms of "atoms", which cannot be further decomposed (these are what the English words become), and "lists", which are composed of any number of other lists or atoms. As a list structure, the definition now consists of one list of four items; the first three items are atoms and the fourth is another list, this time one of six items: three atoms and a three lists; and so on down.

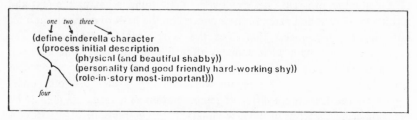

Like any other software data-structure in a computer, list structure is examined by applying (possibly sequences of) functions to it. A very elegant technique is used involving combinations of only two functions: "first" and "rest".[5]

The first element of the list **(physical (and beautiful shabby))** is the atomic element **physical**, and the rest of it is the one element list **((and beautiful shabby))**. The first element of that list is **(and beautiful shabby)** and its rest is empty. Defined in this way, there is no limit to the length or depth that a list can have and additions or modifications can readily be made.

Of course, list structure must itself be represented, otherwise what are the functions "first" and "rest" to manipulate? This next "lower" level of representation is totally invisible to the program that thinks in terms of lists. List structure requires two supporting phenomena for its representation: "pointers" and "list cells". These usually correspond directly to natural phenomena in the hardware of the computer, but for expository purposes, they are usually represented with arrows and boxes respectively. Below is a fragment of the proclamation as it would look at this level.

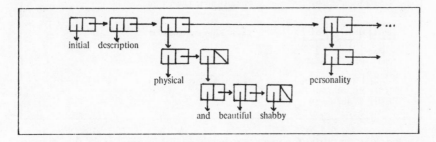

At the level of pointer and cell notation, the functional structure of a list becomes explicit. For each first-rest pair, there is a corresponding list cell (box). The cell has two halves, each containing a pointer (arrow). The left points to the first element of the list, and the right half to its rest. This "indirect" notation is used because an atom like "beautiful" or a list like "(role-in-story most-important)" can be common to many lists at once and we would like to keep only one record of their associated properties.

Let me now go down still another layer to the point where we have an explicit representation of the "pointers to atomic elements" that the list cells contain. We could, of course, continue to go much lower into the machine-level representations and then into the representations used by operators within the machine, but this is far enough for present purposes.

In the most common cases, pointers have a direct representation in terms of physical addresses in a computer's memory. Conceptually if not literally, a general purpose, stored program computer consists of a "memory" and a "processor", where the memory may be thought of as sequence of cells (called "words" or "bytes") which can be selected and accessed according to their number in the sequence – their "address". As a specific example, the Digital Equipment Corporation PDP/10, the computer most commonly used for "list processing" applications, has a memory consisting of a quarter million cells (two to the eighteenth power) and each cell is large enough to contain two addresses. Given these (physical) representational resources, a pointer is represented straightforwardly as a number, i.e. the address of some memory cell, and list-cells with their two halves are represented directly as individual memory cells. Here is a picture of part of the earlier list structure in this format. The boxes are now memory cells at the addresses indicated by the small numbers to their left. Numbers inside the boxes are to be interpreted as pointers, picking out other memory cells.

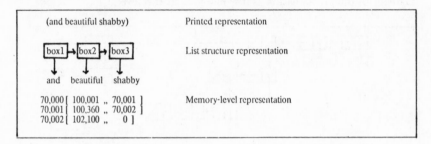

One very important convention has been made explicit in this picture. The pointers from list cells to atoms, 100,360 for "beauty" for example, pick out particular memory cells just as the pointers to other list cells do. By convention, the parser that converts the character string representation into this underlying representation for list structure sees to it that whenever the same word, e.g., "beauty" appears in the input character string, the very same pointer — memory address — is selected to stand for it in the new list cell. This technique gives us a concrete representation for symbols that is both compact and convenient for the computer, and has only the minimum baggage needed to meet the semantics of a symbol, namely reference to it (i.e. inclusion in the lists) and testing for identity (i.e. the numeric equality predicate).

Other parts of the program can check if a given item is the word "beauty" by checking that the pointer which points to that item is the same pointer as the one that they know points to "beauty". (In the common technique described here, this means comparing two numbers; with other techniques for representing symbols it might be comparing two voltage levels or the elapsed times of two signal propagations, or even comparing the spelling of two character strings.) Since the memory cell representing "beauty" can contain pointers like any other cell, these pointers can be used to associate with the cell whatever other facts the program knows about the word (for example that it is spelled "b e a u t y"). Thus, by convention, the spelling might be recovered by treating the pointer to "beauty" as if its cell (100,360) were the pointer to a list-cell (which it is syntactically!) and asking for its "first" element. The "rest" of beauty's cell could point to yet another list structure which encoded further properties according to some conventional syntax.

Clearly just because a program employs the same set of characters that we use for the word "beauty" doesn't mean that it is prepared to use them as a description of a sunset. There is nothing about the structure of a pointer or a memory location per se which carries those properties that we associate with the use of the word. Indeed, at this level of representation, it is no different for a program to refer to English words than for it to use numbers as the negotiators did. Both representations collapse into the same primitive operations of comparing addresses to tell if two symbols are the same. To the program itself it would have made no difference if the definition had been written just as lists of symbols to be compared with symbols already embedded in the program, e.g.

```
(12 34 3
    (82 31 94
        (2 (0 1234 234))
        (4 (0 789 542 653 9876))
        (5 7)))
```

It would, of course, have made a world of difference to the human programmer, who never could have written the program unless she was allowed to use symbols that were meaningful to her. But that brings us to the next section.

2. THE CONTENT

The messages that computer programs pass to each other, for all their diversity in form and representational level, have only two kinds of contents: symbols and pointers.

Symbols are atomic. The receiving program does not break them down or study their parts; it takes them uninterpreted and compares them against equally uninterpreted objects of its own. This operation is one of the fundamental building blocks of computation[6] and pervades programs at all levels of representation. Pointers may happen to be atomic, but the receiving program understands them in a special way (consider "beauty" in the last section). If the receiver shares the right conventions with the message sending program, it will be able to use a pointer to locate and investigate a possibly arbitrary amount of information. In human terms, pointers are like names. If you know the name of a certain grocery store, then you can look up its

phone number in the phone book or find out its credit worthiness by asking
the Better Business Bureau.

2.1 Levels of Interpretation

Before elaborating on this notion of message content as solely symbols and
pointers, we should first take a broad look at how program's interpret their
input. How a message is interpreted is ultimately far more important than
how it is represented, if for no other reason than because two programs with
different interpreters can react in totally different ways to the same message.

Any program is fundamentally a body of instructions to some interpreter.
The instructions, however represented, are of two basic kinds: actions and
tests. The domain of what the instructions can sense or effect depends upon
the characteristics of the interpreter. In real-time manufacturing control
programs and the like, the instructions will effect machines and processes in
the outer world, however in most programs, the effected domain is just data
structures maintained by the computer. (Note that if a suitable representation
is used, these data structures can include the program itself (!) a very powerful
technique.)

Everyday computing systems consist of level upon level of interpreters.
The programmer sits down and writes a program as a file of text in a high-
level language. When it is read into the machine, the interpreter for the high-
level language, itself a program, reacts to the text file and either creates
procedures in a lower-level language or directly performs some action(s)
according to what the programmer called for. In order to do its job, the high-
level interpreter either had been compiled earlier into a representation that
could be directly interpreted by the hardware of the computer ("machine
language") or else it was itself being interpreted by another program (which
was compiled) at the same time as it was interpreting the programmer's text.
In some "very high" applications languages, yet a third level of interpretation
is inserted into the process, and in modern computers, the machine language
itself is treated as an interpreted language and the hardware is really interpreting a "micro-code".

Throughout this sequence, what is an interpreter at one level is a data
structure at another. What a given object means, be it a voltage level, a
sequence of tokens in some representation, or a whole program, is a matter
of what the interpreter that processes it will do in reaction to it. Different
interpreters may do entirely different things to the same object, and thus,
in some sense, it means different things to them.

Consider the proclamations of the screen writer program. They each began in much the same way:

(define cinderella character (process . . .))
(define step-mother character . . .
(define (relationship step-mother cinderella) relationship . . .

The director program, which receives these proclamations, will process them with its own special interpreter. (We are now talking about processing that occurs after the parser has converted the text into a list structure.) To this interpreter, the word "define" (when it is the first item of a toplevel list) has a special meaning. "Define" is a signal to the interpreter to take those expressions and create a new set of data structures that cross-index them and generally convert the information into a representation that is more amenable to the director program proper. "Define" is a signal that the rest of each such expression has a predictable structure and can be converted to the new representation in a uniform way. Roughly speaking, the second item in a "definition list" (e.g. "cinderella") will be associated with the third item ("character") and the fourth ("(process initial description . . .)") by two special links. From the programmer's point of view, these links recorded that "cinderella is a character", and that "cinderella has specified the physical, personality, and role-in-story aspects of her initial description", but from the interpreter's own point of view it is just manipulating list structures, whose meanings exist for it only in terms of their relative positions.

2.2 Attaching Meaning to a Symbol

When programs pass information to each other, it is the interpreters that "vivify" those programs that are really understanding the messages. They understand messages ultimately in terms of matches between the literal content of the message and some token(s) in the text of the program. This will be in a "test" part of the program, typically a conditional expression prepared for several alternative symbols, and the result will be a particular action.

If an interpreter treats a token not as a symbol but as a pointer, then the matching operation is merely postponed. The token will be used indirectly to access some other data structure according to conventions built into the interpreter. That new structure could be a symbol or yet another pointer in which case the process would iterate until a direct, literal interpretation was possible and a real action taken. (Note that since the interpreter itself is just a data structure, it can be read by yet another interpreter, perhaps one that was capable of constructing English explanations of a program's operation, at which point those conventions would no longer be "built in", but would have become an explicitly modeled structure that the (larger) program could talk about.)

The third possibility for a message token besides a symbol or a pointer is that it is an expression in some language. This, however, is just a complication of the original possibilities and not something really new since the parser that deciphers the message is just an interpreter like any other, and operates on the same principles. Consider an expression like this one which, at least to the human author of the program, is an example of a conventional syntax.

(for attraction-towards-enemies (negative medium) strength high)

To the parser, the words "for" and "strength" are symbols that it understands and which it will use as it reconfigures the expression into a form that will be more tractable for the director.

The rest of the terms in the expression are part of the director's vocabulary. The director program is, of course, yet another interpreter, operating on these derived data structures to produce the specifications of character shape and movement that are to be the input to what is in effect the "cameraman" program. The word "attraction-towards-enemies", for example, is a very rich term for the director with a classification and associated procedures (i.e. it is a pointer). The rest of the terms in the expression: "negative", "medium", and "high", are symbols to the director: Its evaluative procedures are structured by the same terms and perform their tests by comparing alternatives embedded in its interpreter(s) and marked by those symbols with the symbols it finds in the expression (that is, in the expression as restructured by the parser).

The director has a vocabulary that it understands, words like "negative", "medium", "character", "relationship", "physical", or "personality", and a vocabulary that it can interpret but which it really does not comprehend at all. This second vocabulary is for us the most content-full words in the whole text, words like "cinderella", or "beautiful", or "shy". However to the director, "cinderella" is only a kind of "character" and "shy" is only a kind of "personality-character-descriptor". Both of these terms are part of its interpreter and tell it what kinds of expressions it can expect to find with "new" terms like these. Below, for example, is what the director knows about the symbol "shy".

In the last analysis, meaning often boils down to a specification of

```
(define shy personality-character-descriptor
      (process suggestions
            (for speed low strength low)
            (for attraction-towards-enemies (negative medium) strength high)
            (for attraction-towards-strangers (negative high) strength high)
            (for attraction-towards-friends (positive low) strength low)
            (for (establish ?character shy)
                  '(method:
                        type convey
                        value (bind ((other (character-that-satisfies
                                                        (stranger-of ,character nil))))
                                    (avoids ,character other)))
                  strength 'medium)))
```

conditions on usage. So it is here: At some point in the process of working out its description of the characters, the director will need to know the implications of the character "cinderella" being described as "shy" — what does that token add to the character's properties? To find out, it will interpret this description.

Suppose for example that when directing a scene that involves "cinderella" and a character described as an "enemy" of cinderella, the director needs to know how cinderella should act. What it does is to collect suggestions from the expressions associated with her, such as that she is "shy". It does this by drawing on its intrinsic knowledge of "keywords" in the definitions, knowlege that was written directly into its interpreter. In this case since the other character is described as an "enemy", it knows that the relevant kind of suggestion is signaled by the word "attraction-towards-enemies". It understands that word not in the general purpose way that the programmer does but rather in conjunction with a particular directorial activity, namely fixing the definitions — its meaning lies in the connections that it makes between associations embedded within the interpreter and the data that the interpreter interprets, or in other words in the actions that the interpreter performs because it is there.

3. THE FORM

Program conversations take a great many forms: addressed mail, bulletin boards, forced feeding, even telepathy. Taken in isolation, some of these forms appear to resemble human conversations hardly at all, but taken as a group, we find a gradual progression from trivial, unconscious "stimulus-response" behavior to complex, model-based, robust operations with multiple levels of interpretation. One feels reluctant to draw the line on proper "conversation-hood" in any one place, especially considering that fundamentally both the simplest and the most complex programs use the same means — comparison of symbols — to understand what they are told. This range of abilities is what makes a study of program conversations interesting: it provides a mirror to hold up to our own conversations where we can distinguish the essential from the inessential.

For communication to take place, it is not necessary for the receiving party to understand what the message meant to the sender, only that upon receipt of the message the receiver (somehow) do what the sender intended. The message itself is just a particular arrangement of tokens in a particular representation. It does not carry any indication of the senders intent. If the receiver were a telepath (see below), it could look and see what was intended, but otherwise, communication occurs only because both parties are obeying a common set of conventions.

3.1 Bulletin Boards

One convention which is often overlooked when considering human conventions is who the intended receiver is. In most conversations, human and computer, who the addressee is is directly indicated by name or by pointing of some sort, but this need not be the case. In some kinds of programs, one program module may uncover information that it knows will be useful to other modules without knowing which modules those would be. What it does is to post the information on a "bulletin board". The other modules will periodically scan the bulletin board to see if there is any information on it which they can use.

The "Hearsay" speech-understanding program[7] pioneered this approach to inter-program communication. The central problem in the DARPA speech projects of which this was one was the inherent uncertainty of the assignment of phonemes to the acoustic features that the programs started from. In Hearsay, this problem was dealt with by making it possible to maintain multiple hypotheses about what the correct assignments were and then evaluating the hypotheses as they each attempted to extend themselves as new information about the speech signal was acquired. Hearsay was designed as a collection of "knowledge sources" ("KS") operating at a series of abstract levels from the acoustic feature, through the phonetic segment, word, syntactic phrase, and semantic unit. Each source watched the black board for new hypotheses at particular levels, the hypotheses being labeled by, for example, their position in the speech stream and this serving as their "address" to determine which KS's should pay attention to them. This use of "pattern matching" on the features of a message in order to determine its audience dynamically (i.e. not until the message is actually sent) is characteristic of "production systems" in general.

At any given moment, dozens if not hundreds of hypotheses might be simultaneously active, raising the question of how to process them efficiently given that they are not all of equal value. In Hearsay this was done by not only having the KS's extend the hypotheses but evaluate them as well. Computational resources were then applied in proportion to a hypothesis's rating[8] and adjusted dynamically. In subsequent extensions to Hearsay[8] the elaboration and evaluation process has been applied recursively, allowing the same kind of multi-level analysis to be applied to the control structure itself. In effect, the actions of KS's have themselves become messages in a conversation – a negotiation – among higher-level knowledge sources deciding their fate.

3.2 Addressed Mail

Programmers are only human. Consequently they find it natural to use metaphors from their own experience. Possibly the most powerful metaphor available is to treat each program or program module as though it were a person and have program modules communicate by sending each other messages – just like people do. Each module, commonly called an "actor",[9] is conceptually a full computer in its own right. Ultimately, as the expense of computing hardware continues to drop, they will be implemented as literally separate computers; at the present time, actors are constructs within programs, employing interpreters to carry their messages and decode their "scripts".

An actor is described by listing the messages it can receive and the script it is to follow in each case. The example given a few pages back of the screen writer's definition of "shy" is precisely an actor, though the notation may obscure it. The director can send a message to the "shy-actor", for example:

(ask suggestions for establish cinderella shy)

This matches within the shy-actor with one specific message that the actor is prepared to receive (repeated below), in the process instantiating the variable in the message, "character", to "cinderella". Notice how the bulk of the message was just so much "syntactic sugaring" – filler words added to make the message more comprehensible to the people who deal with the program. The only real information in the message is the identification of which of

shy-actor's messages it was (which could have just as well been written "sa-5")
and the name of the specific character.

```
(define shy personality-character-descriptor
    (process suggestions
        ...
        (for (establish ?character shy)
            '(method:
                type convey
                value (bind ((other (character-that-satisfies
                                            (stranger-of ,character nil))))
                            (avoids ,character other)))
                strength 'medium)))
```

The shy-actor's reply is itself a message (every expression is in these programs)
to the effect that shyness can be conveyed by showing "cinderella" avoiding
strangers.

   Actors are an example of the use of symbols and pointers in a very pure
form. As an actor, "shy" is a pointer leading off to its list of messages
accepted and their (schematic) replies. The messages are uninterpreted
symbols that the actor matches against its own list. The variables within
messages (such as "character") are expressions, manipulated by the trivial
actor message parser, and interpreted as establishing a link between two
symbols — the "value" of the variable as included in the specific message and
the symbol within the expression that is instantiated as the actor's reply.

3.3 Forced-feeding

Human conversations are usually mixed-initiative. That is, all the parties to
the conversation will typically have subjects that they want to bring up,
questions to ask, observations to make, etc. Only a very few program
"conversations" meet these criteria. Almost always, one of the programs will
completely control the other, "demanding" that it answer certain questions
or perform certain actions. Even the negotiation example that began this
paper is not truly a case of mixed initiative. The two programs were following
a fully specified script which dictated what the legitimate responses to any of
the other programs remarks could be. If either had deviated from that script
it would not have been understood; the only real initiative option they had
was to totally break off communications.

   The reasons for this lack of flexibility are clear: it is not needed. Except
for "real world" applications such as controlling assembly lines, programs
operate in totally artificial environments. The full range of interactions that

might be needed can be anticipated in advance and accommodated in the programs with a minimum of overhead. If an ordinary program is given an input it is not prepared for, there will be an error. At some expense, one can construct a "robust" program that will not break down, even over a very wide range of inputs. Computer operating systems, text editors, and compilers must be like this. The price one pays for introducing flexibility into a program is high, both in programmer time invested and in the increased size and running time of the program. Flexibility requires anticipating the entire range of stimuli that may arise and explicitly providing for them or else selecting judicious defaults for the unknown cases. Success comes by having sufficiently adequate models of what "correct" inputs will look like so that they can recognize nonsense inputs as such.

At the very opposite end of the scale from the interactions of complex operating systems with their abundant (if usually tacit) models of possible conversations is the very simplest of program conversations, the request and reply protocol of the *subroutine call*. One is reluctant to call this a conversation both because its pattern is absolutely rigid and because the programs, being bereft of any models of what they are doing, operate entirely unconsciously. Yet the potential is there. Information is conveyed, and naming operations occur that in another guise in another, more substantial program, we could call part of a proper conversation. In any case, they provide a convenient "ground floor" for present purposes.

Consider these two simple programs, expressed in the LOGO programming language.

```
To stick-person (height)
    set unit height/5
    set head-size unit
    set body-size 2*unit
    ...
    rotate north
    draw-body body-size
    draw-head head-size
    ...
    end
```

What is interesting here is how the variable information is passed between the two programs. The calling program, "stick-person", has computed a number of quantities and stored them as the value of variables that are defined only within the stick-person program. We can imagine how, in a much expanded version of this program that had models of the data structures it

```
To draw-head (diameter)
    set radius diameter/2
    forward radius
    circle radius
    draw-eyes diameter
    ...
    end
```

used, there would be some commentary available to describe the role these variables played and what sorts of things their values were.

Consider what happens as the value of one of these variables, i.e. "head-size" is passed to "draw-head". Draw-head knows nothing about the internal structure of stick-person. In particular, it knows nothing about what stick-person's variables represent. Nor for that matter does stick-person; but there is nothing standing in the way of our giving it a model that it could use e.g., to tell us where the variable was used and what actions were contingent on its value. Draw-head on the other hand does not even know that those variables exist, or even that stick-person exists. It only knows that it has been called with a certain value for its parameter. At best it might know that it had been passed a number (as opposed to a character string), but it knows nothing more about what that number represents because there is a total block between the internal world of stick-figure and the world of draw-head.

This "black-out" between calling program and subroutine can be the source of interesting bugs. Notice that the orientation of the head is determined by stick-person alone. Draw-head will start up with whatever orientation the pointer has when it is called. There is no independent check within draw-head to insure that the head that it draws is correctly oriented on the body, and further more it could not have such a check (as written) since the necessary information is only represented in the internal computational state of stick-person. If the draw-body subroutine neglects to properly reset the orientation before it returns,[10] then the head may end up dangling from the side of the shoulder since the misorientation cannot be communicated to draw-head.

3.4 Telepathy

The information blackout between two programs is of course true of human beings as well. Two simple programs passing information via parameters know as little about each others computational states as two people know about the neurological states of each other's minds. However, for programs, this situation is not a necessary one. Programmers can, and often do design programs that are effectively telepaths. If one program is given information about another program's structural conventions — what names it uses for its variables, what these variables represent, etc. — and if it is technically possible for the program to have access to the state of the other program, then it can read its mind.

Programs with this capability are common place in large operating systems. One simple instance is the program that keeps the log of the systems activities: what jobs are run, what resources they consume, what people own them, etc. The parts of the operating system that are actively engaged in executing the jobs and managing the resources operate unconsciously. But the logging program (usually just one more job) is equipped with special knowledge. It knows the locations within the system of the tables that describe the active jobs and resources and it knows their format. It can read the system tables and copy out what it needs, unbeknownst to the operating system proper.

4. WHY DON'T THEY JUST USE ENGLISH?

One final question to consider is "why don't programs have their conversations in English?" This has been asked quite seriously. English (or Russian or Hebrew etc.) is a universal language apparently capable of expressing any thoughts we can have. Computer programs, on the other hand, are notoriously idiosyncratic in their representations. Every programmer has a different style, uses different conventions, and modularizes her programs in a different way. Consequently when programs are to be combined, a tremendous effort must be expended to determine and compensate for their differences. If there were some universal interface protocol (i.e. "English") available, the savings that would be made would make its development worth while almost regardless of cost. An English speaking program would be very large — certainly in the hundreds of thousands of machine words — but the applications that have been considered for an "English-interface" are larger still, i.e. multi-million item data-bases such as military spare-parts inventories. Currently every time a new applications program needs to be "wired-into" such a data-base, a separate effort is required to translate the representational conventions of the data-base into the terms the applications program uses. If instead both programs spoke English as their interface language, no extra effort would be required — the applications program would formulate its request ("How many number 6 bolts are in stock in New Jersey?") and the data-base would formulate its answer ("11,326") in a language that both programs already understood and that would be that. So at least the story goes.

Unfortunately, it is not at all that simple. When people suggest the use of English as an interface, they imagine what it would be like to put themselves in the position of the two communicating programs and get a rosy picture. What they neglect is that as human beings and speakers of English, they share not only a language but a vast amount of experience. Should one person use a word that the other doesn't know, or use a word in a new way, the other person is quite capable of deducing what the word must mean by making an extrapolation from the rest of the message context and from an *a priori* notion of what kinds of meanings would make sense conceptually.

To a program however, English is just another conventional syntax. Once the intervening levels of parsers is past, any communication initially couched in English will still be understood only in terms of symbols and pointers. Unless conventions are developed that will make those symbols and pointers sensible to the particular program in question, no communication will happen.

If we really did want to develop an English language interface between two programs, then we would have to give the programs a conceptual structure to match. Given two programs constructed entirely independently by teams of programmers with different styles, the first thing that would happen across an English interface between them would be a slow groping negotiation in search of common terminology. The point of using English would have been to avoid needing to know the code level details of, e.g., accessing an item in the data base in favor of giving requests in general terms such as "*tell me how many C-130's there are in Kansas*". Here is where the problem arises however. The two camps of programmers will probably agree on the semantics of *tell me* but they may well not have had the same ideas about *in Kansas*. To one group that might have meant "physically present", while to the other it meant "assigned to Kansas" (even though currently being serviced in California).

Like people, two robust programs will be bound to eventually realize that they mean different things by the same words, but when this happens the programs may be severely handicapped unless their conceptual structures are rich enough to allow them to move to a level of description (still expressed in English of course) where the differerence in their definitions can be compared. This could well only be the level of the literal machine code structures inside them, and if that were the case, the programs would have to have extensive knowledge about programming in general and their own internal architectures in particular — something that is miles beyond the current state of the art in representation.

All this, and they would continue to suffer the overhead of translation into and out of English for every transaction. However, it is probably true that a program with sufficient knowledge of the domain it worked in and of its own structure to be able to converse in English with another program would be able to reprogram itself. What the two programs would then do in the course of their initial negotiations over definitions would be to establish a common set of conventions — conversations between programs are supported by common conventions or they do not work at all, regardless of the level at which their messages are represented. Having once established what their conventions were to be, the programs could reasonably be expected to shift the conventions over to some other, more expedient message representation. In other words, once two programs had learned to communicate to each other in English, they would immediately reprogram themselves to use a simpler language, unencumbered by linearity and structural ambiguities imposed on human beings by the physics of speech which we have continually to live with.

University of Massachusetts at Amherst

NOTES

[1] This paper was written while the author was a graduate student at the Artificial Intelligence Laboratory of the Massachusetts Institute of Technology. Support for the laboratory's artificial intelligence research is provided in part by the Advanced Research Projects Agency of the Department of Defence under Office of Naval Research contract N00014–75–C–0643.

[2] The "ARPANET" was developed by the Defense Advanced Research Projects Agency, and is maintained by the Defense Communications Agency for the use of DOD funded researchers. It presently links over a hundred computer installations and dialup sites from London to Honolulu with electronic mail and shared computer resources. The ARPANET pioneered the large-scale application of dynamic routing and packet switching.

[3] These examples and the details that follow are taken from the Doctoral Thesis of Kenneth Kahn, Technical report 540, MIT Artificial Intelligence Lab, Cambridge MA.

[4] It is called "reverse-Polish notation": Every expression is enclosed within matching parentheses. The first word after each left-parenthesis is the name of a function or relation and all of the subsequent expressions up to the matching right-parenthesis are the function's arguments.

[5] This technique and the other basic ideas of list processing are due to the work of Newell, Simon, and Shaw in the mid-fifties on the language IPL–1.

[6] Indeed, a universal Turing machine can be constructed using a compare and transfer operation plus just the successor function and a representation of zero. See the discussion in 'Computation, Finite and Infinite Machines' by Marvin Minsky, Prentice-Hall.

[7] Erman, Hayes-Roth, Lesser, and Reddy, 'The Hearsay-II Speech-Understanding System: Integrating Knowledge to Resolve Uncertainty', *Computing Surveys* **12**, No. 2, 1980.

[8] For example, Stefik, M., 'Planning with Constraints', Ph.D. Thesis, Stanford University, 1980 or Balzer, Erman, and Williams 'Hearsay-III: a domain-independent base for knowledge-based problem solving', Tech. Rep. USC/Information Sciences Institute, Santa Monica, California, June 1977.

[9] See Hewitt and Smith 'Towards a Programming Apprentice', *IEEE Transactions on Software Engineering* **SE-1**, No. 1, 1975, for an elaboration on this and related notions.

[10] Goldstein has made a study of the kinds of bugs that crop up in stick figure programs like these. This one would be called an "interface" bug (Goldstein 'Understanding Simple Picture Programs' AI-TR-294, Artificial Intelligence Laboratory, MIT, 1974).

INDEX OF NAMES